The Buddha Within

Tathagatagarbha Doctrine According to the Shentong
Interpretation of the Ratnagotravibhaga

S. K. Hookham

State University of New York Press

Published by
State University of New York Press, Albany

©1991 State University of New York

For information, address State University of New York Press,
194 Washington Avenue, Suite 305, Albany, NY 12210-2384

Production by Christine M. Lynch
Marketing by Bernadette LaManna

Library of Congress Cataloguing-in-Publication Data

Hookham, S. K., 1946–
    The Buddha within: Tathagatagarbha doctrine [sic] according to
the Shentong interpretation of the Ratnagotravibhaga / S. K. Hookham.
        p.   cm. — (SUNY series in Buddhist studies)
    Includes bibliographical references.
    ISBN 0-7914-0357-2. — ISBN 0-7914-0358-0 (pbk.)
    1. Tathāgatagarbha (Buddhism) 2. Sunyata. I. Title.
  II. Series.
    BQ4450.H66 1991
  294.3'422—dc20   89-49755
                                                                    CIP

10 9 8 7 6 5 4 3

This work is dedicated to my parents, my husband,
all my Dharma friends,
and in particular to Michael Lear.

CONTENTS

Acknowledgments

For the initial and sustaining inspiration for this work I thank first my Guru, Khenpo Tsultrim Gyamtso and then Michael Hookham, my husband. Both of them, over the years, have contributed to my understanding of Buddhadharma at such a profound level that anything I write reflects their influence.

The original work was accepted in 1986 for a D. Phil degree at Oxford University. In this present work, the original has been substantially reorganized and rewritten in order to make it more accessible to the informed general reader on religious philosophy and the serious Buddhist practitioner.

This work concerns how the *Ratnagotravibhaga* and the *Ratnagotravibhagavyakhya* can be interpreted from the Shentong point of view. For this I am indebted initially to Tenpa Gyaltsen Negi for his help in translating the root text and the introduction to Kongtrul's commentary, and second to Shentong informants, Khenpo Tsultrim Gyamtso, Thrangu Rimpoche, Tenga Rimpoche, Lama Thubden, Khenpo Palden Sherab, and Khenpo Katar. I would also like to take the opportunity to thank Karma Thinley Rimpoche, Kalu Rimpoche, Gendun Rimpoche, and above all Bokar Rimpoche for their instruction and empowerments over the years, which have established me in the "view" of the Kagyu lineage.

For their explanations and comments on the Rangtong point of view, I thank Geshe Wangchen and Geshe Tekchok.

I am grateful to the members of the Sanskrit department of Oxford Oriental Institute for their support and interest. My years in Oxford have greatly deepened my knowledge of, and respect for, the Western academic tradition. In this connection, I would also like to mention my supervisor Dr. Paul Williams, my examiner Professor D. Seyfort Ruegg, Dr. M. Broido, and Simon Baugh for their stimulating and encouraging discussions and comments.

For financial support while completing this work, I thank the Northern Ireland Education Authority, the Boden Fund, and the Spalding Trust. I am grateful to Wolfson College for use of its facilities and financial assistance for expenses incurred in visiting my Lama informants and supervisor. I thank all my friends who have helped me in various ways with proofreading and so on, especially Angela Skrimshire for her tireless and invaluable help in preparing this thesis on the word processor, seemingly endless proofreading, and her advice and suggestions on layout. Also I thank Tenpa Gyaltsen and Chryssoula Zerbini for checking my translation of and footnotes on Kongtrul's RGV commentary, and Roger Keyes and Katie Goguen for final proof-reading and indexing.

Finally, I thank my mother for her encouragement towards the production of this book from the thesis. As an informed general reader on religious philosophy, she tackled the daunting task of rereading the original more than once, making copious notes in order to assist me in the rewrite.

Yogin Khenpo Tsultrim Gyamtso's Spontaneous Verses On The Subject Of Rangtong And Shentong

When meditating on the profound emptiness, all one's difficulty is self-empty. In the sky-like self-emptiness, make no effort to stop or to accomplish anything.

If one knows how to rest within the Clear Light, all the virtues are spontaneously existent. In the spontaneous primordial purity, undo conceptual effort.

Because apparent existence is self-empty, there are no illusions to stop. Because the ultimate emptiness-of-other exists, there is no spontaneous existence to accomplish. Beyond stopping and accomplishing, a la la!

The manifest world of samsara and nirvana, all such appearances occur,
Yet they occur in the open expanse of the Clear Light.
Although they proliferate, they proliferate in the expanse of openness,
So if one does not cling, their dissolution is exposed.

If one knows the mind's true condition to be the Clear Light Nature and the manner of the adventitious stains to be empty,
Then, effortlessly, equal love for self and others arises.

By the power of the Clear Light, sun shining in the heart,
May the darkness of conceptual thought fade into the expanse of openness.

Khenpo Tsultrim spontaneously composed these verses in reply to questions put to him in Oxford in March 1989.

Chapter 1

General Introduction

At various times and places within the Buddhist tradition, intellectual understanding has gained ascendancy over the more intuitive or mystical understanding of the yogin meditator. Although the scriptures abound with statements reaffirming the vital role of the faculty of "faith" *(sraddha)* in the process of realization and enlightenment, a strong body of thought within Buddhism places the intellectual faculty as supreme over faith, and actively denies even the existence of intuitive wisdom beyond the dualism of knower and known. This present work aims, through scriptural reference and argument, to pose a challenge to those westerners who are in danger of adopting such a one-sided view of the Buddhist tradition.

It is hoped that this present work will prove useful to both the general reader as well as the specialist in the field of religious studies and particularly Buddhism. The subject matter raises issues of profound religious, philosophical, and practical importance to the whole field of Buddhist studies. Accordingly, I have devoted the first section to clarifying these issues so that the reader may approach the next two sections with them fully in mind.

These issues include the Buddhist doctrine of emptiness, the Buddha's wisdom mind, Buddha qualities, faith and insight as means of apprehending absolute reality, the meaning of non-conceptuality, the meaning of Buddha nature and so on.

All these issues are discussed in the light of the fact that from earliest times the Buddha's doctrine of ultimate reality has been presented both in positive as well as in negative terms. On the positive side, the Buddha is described as eternal, non-conditioned, compassionate, all-knowing and so forth, having realized nirvana, which is eternal, non-conditioned, bliss and so on. On the negative side, the Buddha is described as having realized nirvana, which is the cessation of all that is conditioned, impermanent, suffering and so on. He realizes this through ceasing to cling to conceptual creations, either positive or negative.

The fourteenth century Tibetan master, Dolpopa, of the Jonangpa school promulgated a teaching that emphasized that what is conditioned, impermanent, suffering and so on is illusory and hence self-empty (rangtong); what is non-conditioned, permanent, bliss and so on is Reality.* This Ultimate Reality is empty in the sense that the ignorant mind that clings to conceptual creations can find nothing to grasp onto or understand. Since conceptual creations are illusory and unreal, Ultimate Reality can be described as empty of them. In other words, it is empty of what is other than itself. In Tibetan the term for this is "Shentong" (literally emptiness-of-other).

The second section gives some of the history and context of the various traditions that develop the implications of this "Shentong" nature of reality. Of prime importance here is the Tathagatagarbha doctrine of Buddha-nature, which arose in India around the third century A.D. at almost the same time as the Prajnaparamita sutras. The relationship between Prajnaparamita and Tathagatagarbha (Buddha-nature) doctrine has been a central issue for the original Indian commentators and for Tibetan and other Mahayana commentators ever since. It is central to the *Ratnagotravibhaga* [RGV] and its commentary *Ratnagotravibhagavyakhya* [RGVV], which seem to have been written primarily in response to this very question.

The third section of this present work shows how the issues and background introduced in the previous two sections relate to the study and interpretation of a key Sanskrit commentarial work. This work consists of the RGV and RGVV, which are known in the Tibetan tradition as the "*Mahayanottaratantrasastra*" *(Theg pa chen po rgyud bla ma'i bstan bcos)* and its auto-commentary *(rang'grel)*. Although the Tibetan tradition counts the RGV as one of the five works of Maitreya and the RGVV as a work of Asanga—fifth century A.D.—it is more likely that both are a composition by the third century Indian writer Saramati.[1]

In this third section, the RGV and RGVV are briefly paraphrased with a view to bringing out the particular features of a Shentong interpretation of Tathagatagarbha doctrine, following such Tibetan commentators as Dolpopa—thirteenth-fourteenth centuries—the Kagyu Lamas Rangjung Dorje—thirteenth-fourteenth centuries—Mikyo Dorje—fifteenth century, and Jamgon Kongtrul—nineteenth-twentieth centuries—and contemporary Kagyu-Nyingma Lamas such as Khenpo Tsultrim Gyamtso Rimpoche, Gendun Rimpoche, and Thrangu Rimpoche. The essential feature of a Shentong interpretation of Tathagatagarbha doctrine is that the Buddha is literally within all beings as their unchanging, permanent, non-conditioned nature. Shentongpas explain scriptural statements that the Buddha is present as a seed to be figurative only, because Buddha is by all accounts considered

---

* See "Conventions Used" p. 367 of this work.

to be non-conditioned, eternal, unchanging, bliss, compassion, wisdom, power, and so on. For Shentongpas the fact that Buddha is non-conditioned means the essence of Buddha is complete with all the Buddha Qualities in a timeless sense. There is no question of them arising from a seed.

By way of contrast, reference is made to the parallel "Rangtong" interpretation stemming from Ngog—thirteenth-fourteenth centuries— through Rongton—1367–1449—a Sakya Lama. Both the Rangtong and the Shentong traditions of interpretation of Tathagatagarbha doctrine are thought to stem from Sajjana in Kashmir in the eleventh century. Comparison also is sometimes made in this present work with the RGV commentary by Gyaltsab—fifteenth century—a Gelugpa Lama; the commentary is known as the *Dartik*. Professor D. Seyfort Ruegg, who has written more on the subject of Tathagatagarbha and related subjects than any other Western academic, bases his explanations of the RGV for the most part on the *Dartik*, as does E. Obermiller who produced the only existing complete translation of the RGV and RGVV in any Western language. The RGV on its own is also available in translation under the title *The Changeless Nature* by Katia and Ken Holmes.[2]

The third section of the present work also provides a footnoted translation of Kongtrul's introduction to his commentary on the RGV.

Further Comments

The distinction between self-emptiness (rangtong) and Emptiness-of-other (Shentong) is not merely, nor indeed primarily, of academic interest. It has implications of profound proportions for the Buddhist practitioner, touching on his whole attitude to himself, the world, the Guru and others, the path, and above all meditation practice. The controversy within the Tibetan tradition of when, if at all, the rangtong-Shentong distinction should be introduced to the disciple is a live issue today and will, I am sure, be a live issue among Western Buddhists for a long time to come. The reason it is and should always be a live issue is that by all accounts the realization of Enlightenment lies beyond concepts, positive, negative, gross, or subtle. Until that point is reached, subtle unacknowledged concepts lurk in the background of the mind. The rangtong-Shentong controversy brings them into the foreground where they can be properly examined and addressed.

The problem lies in the practical need to express what is by definition precise and yet inexpressible. Negations, pinpointing what it is not, help remove imprecision, but there is the danger that what was to be expressed through negation is itself negated by this process. Shentong type statements and arguments are to remedy this fault by appealing to a faculty which understands through direct experience, untainted by conceptual creation. Shentong reasoning is based on the assumption that there is such a faculty and the proof of it lies in the experience of the meditator. For this reason it can be argued that it is unsuitable as a subject of intellectual investigation and should only be introduced to the experienced meditator when he/she is ready. Others argue that since even ordinary beings have the faculty to respond with ''faith'' to inspired utterances, much as we respond intuitively to poetry, there is good reason to introduce it early on.

It would take more than a single work of this kind to examine the whole range of traditions based on the Tathagatagarbha sutras, (for example, Cittamatra, Hua Yen, Rangtong Madhyamaka and others), so this present work presents primarily the Shentong Yogacara Madhyamaka interpretation of Tathagatagarbha doctrine as expressed in the *Ratnagotravibhaga* and the *Vyakhya*. The importance of these texts is that they are the only texts on Tathagatagarbha preserved in Sanskrit.

The present study is of particular relevance because the RGV and the Tathagatagarbha doctrine on which it is commenting, form the all-important link between the Sutra-Madhyamaka traditions and the Tantra-Siddha traditions that were introduced from India into Tibet in the eleventh century. These two traditions were originally quite distinct, and although the task of linking them began in India just before Buddhism died out there towards the end of twelfth century, the Tibetans continued this process in finer detail. Dolpopa's Shentong doctrine brings out the connection particularly well by making explicit the distinction between self-emptiness and Emptiness-of-other found implicitly in the Sutras and Tantras.

Perhaps a warning is in order here for the reader who thinks self-emptiness is a translation of the term *svabhavasunyata* (emptiness of self-nature) of the Prajnaparamita Sutras and associated commentarial traditions. It is not. Self-emptiness is an expression promulgated by Shentong commentators such as Dolpopa and Kongtrul expressly for distinguishing the empty nature of illusion *(rangtong)* from the Empty nature of Reality (Shentong). *Svabhavasunyata* and *prakrtisunyata* can be understood in two different ways, depending on whether one understands them to be referring to rangtong or to Shentong.[3]

Because Rangtong Madhyamikas (such as the followers of Gyaltsab and Ketrub of the Gelugpa school) take the ultimate truth taught by the Buddha to be the self-emptiness of illusion, they do not accept that there is any Ultimate Reality to discover beyond this. For this reason, these followers rightly do not use the convention of a capital *R* for reality or *A* for absolute in their translations. For Shentong Madhyamikas, the whole point of establishing the empty nature of illusion (rangtong) is to discover the Reality of the Absolute Buddha Wisdom Mind (Paramarthabuddhajnana) beyond the reaches of the conceptual mind that can only function in terms of grasping its own creations. I have pondered for a long time over the question of the appropriateness of using capitals for such a "Reality" since it might imply it was conceptually graspable. Finally, I have come to the conclusion that since this "Reality" refers to the living presence of the Buddha within all beings and the sacred nature of all our experience when seen unobscured by ignorance, it should, out of respect, be referred to with capitals.

The present work is the first book in a Western language to discuss at length the views of Tibetan Shentong writers on the basis of their own works. Previously, Western scholars have tended to make comments concerning Dolpopa and the Jonangpa Shentong doctrine based on the views of their largely Gelugpa informants. Because of the disquietingly different use of familiar terminology by writers commentating from a Shentong point of view, Gelugpa and also Sakya scholars often dismiss the Jonangpa formulation of the Buddha's doctrine out of hand as being non-Buddhist. To do so is to dismiss a recurrent theme of the Buddhist tradition found throughout its textual heritage. Even though, like the Gelugpa followers of Gyaltsab and Ketrub, the scholarly Theravadin traditions choose to ignore or explain away passages in their scriptures that are suggestive of a Shentong view, it cannot be denied that they have been so integral to the earliest collections of texts that even their opponents could not justify their removal on the grounds of inauthenticity.

The Omniscient Dolpopa's Prayer That Unties the Vajra Word Knots[4]

OM: May it be Accomplished!

I pray to all the Conquerors and their sons in the ten directions to bestow their blessing.

May they have pity on those stuck in impoverished *(ngan)* views and hold them in their compassion.

May they have pity on those who hold that the whole of the Buddha's teaching on emptiness concerned self-emptiness alone and hold them in their compassion.

May they have pity on those who hold that the whole of the Buddha's teaching on emptiness concerned a non-affirming negation alone and hold them in their compassion.

May they have pity on those who hold that the whole of the Buddha's teaching on emptiness concerned mere nothingness alone and hold them in their compassion.

May they have pity on those who hold that the whole of the Buddha's teaching on emptiness concerned non-appearance alone and hold them in their compassion.

May they have pity on those who hold that the whole of the Buddha's teaching on emptiness concerned total nothingness alone and hold them in their compassion.

May they have pity on those who hold that non-elaboration (*nisprapanca*) is always self-emptiness alone . . . a non-affirming negation alone . . . mere nothingness alone . . . non-appearance alone . . . total nothingness alone and hold them in their compassion.

May they have pity on those who hold that the whole of the Buddha's teaching on freedom from extreme philosophical positions concerned self emptiness alone . . . a non-affirming negation alone . . . mere nothingness alone . . . non-appearance alone . . . total nothingness alone and hold them in their compassion.

May they have pity on those who hold that the whole of the Buddha's teaching on absence concerned self-emptiness alone . . . a non-affirming negation alone . . . mere nothingness alone . . . non-appearance alone . . . total nothingness alone and hold them in their compassion.

May they have pity on those who hold that the whole of the Buddha's teaching on openness concerned self-emptiness alone . . . a non-affirming negation alone . . . non-appearance alone . . . total nothingness alone and hold them in their compassion.

The intended meaning of the whole of the Buddha's teaching on emptiness always being the most profound true nature is the Place of Emptiness *(stong pa'i gzhi)*.

The intended meaning of the whole of the Buddha's teaching on freedom is the Place of Freedom *(bral ba'i gzhi)*.

The intended meaning of the whole of the Buddha's teaching on absence is the Place of Absence *(med pa'i gzhi)*.

The intended meaning of the whole of the Buddha's teaching on openness is the Open Place *(dben pa'i gzhi)*.

Those who understand correctly in this way are more learned than the most learned, brighter than the brightest, profounder than the profoundest, more solid than the solidest, wider than the widest, Guru of the highest Guru, the highest of the highest.

Therefore this is the Ultimate True Nature that is the Prajnaparamita, the Madhyamaka, and the Mahamudra.[5]

Section One
The Issues

Chapter 2

Introduction to the Rangtong-Shentong Distinction

2.1 The Origin and Significance of Buddhist
Commentarial Traditions

Buddhist commentarial traditions relate to meditation experience; scriptural sources are used literally as backup material (*rgyab rten*, back support). Professor Robert Thurman made this point in his paper at the Oxford Conference of the International Association of Buddhist Studies (IABS) in 1982 concerning the works of Tsongkapa. Meditation experience is called "realization Dharma" (*rtogs pa'i chos*),[1] in contrast to scripture which is called "transmission Dharma" (*lung gi chos* or *bstan pa'i chos*). Realization Dharma means the teacher's own Enlightenment that he transmits to the disciple through the disciple's own meditation experience. This kind of transmission is the essence of what is called "a practice lineage" (*grub rgyud*). Practice lineages believe they are transmitting the original Enlightened experience of the Buddha through meditation practice in contrast to a Teaching or Exposition lineage (*bshad rgyud*), which is the oral transmission of the Buddha word and explanations based on it—Sutras and Sastras (commentaries). Although the canons of the Buddha word were not written down until at least 380 years after His lifetime, previous to that it was transmitted through the oral tradition of memorized recitation.

Because of the fundamental importance of the realization Dharma to the Buddhist spiritual tradition, scriptures are supposed to be commented on only by Enlightened teachers who thereby transmit, by means of their commentaries, a part of their own realization. Therefore, from the academic point of view, there are two possible lines of enquiry. One is to pursue what the text is as a historical document, that is, the history of the fragments that comprise it and so on, and the other is how different traditions have interpreted the text and what this might tell us about the Buddhist experience from the practitioner's point of view.

In the Tibetan tradition, it is important—in principle at least—to receive the transmission (*lung*) which, although technically can take the form of oral permission, more commonly consists of a ritual reading of a scripture in question. This is to connect the reader with the blessing of the realization lineage. The example often given is that of an electric current being passed down a wire. Once broken, the current is gone. Thus, the written word without the blessing of the lineage is regarded as impotent. However, a transmission lineage that has been broken, for example, the RGV when Maitripa rediscovered it,[2] can be "brought back to life" by a "direct" transmission from the Sambhogakaya or Dharmakaya. Maitripa had such a transmission from Maitreya.

Even more important than the transmission of the text however, is the personal instruction of a living realized teacher, that is, someone who has inner experience or realization of Enlightenment. For example, Dolpopa [*Ri Chos* (RC) 288] explains that yogins do not worry about names but rely on special instruction. The special instruction Dolpopa is referring to is the instruction by means of which the teacher introduces the student to the true nature of his own experience.

This cannot be transmitted through texts alone. Over the centuries new texts and commentaries have appeared reflecting the social, political and even more importantly, spiritual problems of their day. For example, the sophisticated philosophical climate in India in the early centuries of this era caused Buddhist doctrine to become increasingly philosophical in its formulation. This does not necessarily mean that the realization Dharma encoded in it was changing. Although it is conceivable, we have no way of telling. What we can discover, however, is what living masters are saying and transmitting today and exactly what they mean by their realization—to the extent that one is able to understand it.

Someone from the Tibetan Buddhist tradition, for example, wishing to study a text such as the RGV seeks first a transmission for the root text and one or more commentaries on it. He/she regards a multiplicity of commentarial transmissions on the same text an asset. It allows for flexibility in meeting the demands of different levels of understanding.

There is a fundamental difference, therefore, in the approach of a modern Western academic and a traditional practicing Buddhist. The tendency of the former is to present a supposedly objective account of the text, treating it as a historical document, and trying to place its message in relation to the history of ideas. The traditional Buddhist scholar is looking at the text as a means of supporting what he has already experienced in meditation.

My own approach is to try to give, as a Western academic, an objective account of how a particular realization tradition explains a particular doctrine in a particular historical document. It is hoped that by relating different interpretations to their practical implications in terms of meditation, a reasonable explanation for their diversity will emerge.

I have used explanations obtained through oral transmission from mainly Kagyu-Nyingma Lamas to construct a generalized model from which to gain an overview of a particular tradition. One could proceed from there to examine the texts in detail to see what evidence, if any, there is for supposing that the model fits the texts. Where, for example, a commentator has obviously misunderstood a Sanskrit term or relies heavily on a passage that is of doubtful authenticity and so on, his model obviously becomes questionable in historical terms. In this way it should be possible at some point to work back from present day interpretations, using them as models for understanding earlier texts. Obviously, in contrast to the process of following a living tradition, such work is highly speculative.

In this present work, we shall see how different commentators have used ambiguities in the original Sanskrit and Tibetan to support their own particular doctrinal message.

2.2   The Rangtong-Shentong Distinction

Exact equivalents of the terms self-emptiness, rangtong *(rang stong)*—not to be confused with *svabhavasunyata* [appendix 2]—and emptiness-of-other, Shentong *(gZhan stong)* are not found in any known Indian source. As terms they seem to be an innovation of the Tibetan commentators and particularly of the Jonangpa School, which uses them in contradistinction to each other. This is not to say that the Indian sources do not recognize a rangtong-Shentong distinction, as such. Indeed, if Shentongpas are right, this is where it originates, albeit implicitly rather than explicitly. To those who accept that the rangtong-Shentong distinction exists in the Sutras and their commentaries, Shentong is the doctrine of the "Third Dharmacakra," which includes the Sutras that teach the truly existing Dharmata *(chos nyid don dam bden grub tu ston pa)*[3] and the Tathagatagarbha. Thus, it is the Buddha's final and most profound (ie., Nitartha) teaching, the correct understanding of which is fundamental to all higher meditation practices including the Tantras, Mahamudra, and Dzogchen.

A powerful body of opinion in the Tibetan tradition, however, denies that a rangtong-Shentong distinction is made in the Sutras. The Gelugpa school, in particular, denies the existence of a level of doctrine that supersedes the essentially rangtong message of the Second Dharmacakra. For them the third Dharmacakra does not give a whole new dimension to the Buddha's teaching as it does for Shentongpas. Furthermore, they make strenuous efforts to refute Shentong interpretations of Sutras and important commentarial traditions because, far from considering it essential to the understanding of higher meditation practices (the Tantras, Mahamudra, or Dzogchen), it is believed by some that it is a misleading or even a non-Buddhist doctrine. Those who accept rangtong but totally deny the validity of Shentong are what one might call "exclusive Rangtongpas."

However, of those who accept the rangtong-Shentong distinction as valid and in accordance with the Sutras and their commentaries, some choose to concentrate on rangtong teachings and may call themselves "Rangtongpa," while others concentrate on Shentong teachings and call themselves "Shentongpas." Furthermore, some teachers choose to expound a certain scripture from a rangtong point of view for some pupils and the same scripture from the Shentong point for others—apparently this was done by Sajjana.[4] Other teachers dismiss the rangtong-Shentong distinction saying a deep understanding of the one is indistinguishable from the other. Finally, there are those who, although their teachings reveal a recognition of the rangtong-Shentong distinction in principle, do not express it in those terms; indeed the Sutras themselves belong to this category—if Shentong-pas are to be believed. [See also remarks in introduction and appendix 2.]

2.3   The Meaning of Rangtong

Literally rangtong translates as "self-emptiness." The full expression is "each empty of its own essence" *(rang rang gi ngo bos stong pa)*. Take, for example, a scriptural statement like "all phenomena (dharmas) are empty." If this "empty" is taken to mean self-empty, then the statement clearly states that all phenomena are without an essential nature of their own. In the Buddhist tradition this observation arises through logical analysis. Since every phenomenon is totally interrelated with other phenomena there is no possibility of an entity existing independently, that is, in its own right. One could say that modern man has discovered the self-emptiness of phenomena by scientific experimentation and analysis. Even atoms or the particles that comprise them are no longer thought of as discrete entities in themselves. Their nature is proving most mysterious and difficult to grasp conceptually. The safe, common sense, solid material world around us has been intellectually analyzed away. Whatever else a chair or table is, it is certainly not a solid entity. Yet emotionally it still comes as a shock when our material world starts to fall apart around us. Buddhism's message to us is that this emptiness has soteriological as well as intellectual and practical significance; the first emerges through the integration of intellect and emotions in meditation.

The phenomena (dharmas) that are self-empty in this way are what constitute the things we take as real in our everyday experience. That is to say all ordinary things are illusory phenomena that we are deceived into thinking are real entities when they are not. They are empty in a negative sense like when we talk of empty dreams, promises, and lies; their emptiness is their exposure as sham.

Buddhism, however, does not only use "emptiness" in a negative way. Walter Liebenthal in his appendix to the *Chao Lun* [138] makes the following remark concerning a certain view of emptiness:

The term sunyata [emptiness] therefore has two meanings, "appreciating" if applied to Truth, and "depreciating" if applied to illusion. This is difficult to grasp.

A positive or "appreciative" use of the term is typical of the Shentong view, but since Rangtongpas also speak of emptiness in this way, caution is needed.

Seeing the self-empty nature of phenomena has two facets, the shocking, somewhat negative experience of seeing phenomena as "unreal" and the positive experience of spaciousness, limitlessness, changelessness, and unobstructedness.[5] When asked, Thrangu Rimpoche felt the term 'self-emptiness' implied both these aspects, the negative as well as the positive.

This spacious nature of emptiness is synonymous with Dhatu, the Element, which like the element space[6] pervades everything and allows everything to occur, while remaining unaffected. Like space it is what makes it possible for the six sense faculties to function. Everything occurs in it just as the whole world exists in space [RGV 2:27].

Nevertheless, Dolpopa [RC 386] warns us that when the image of space is used, there is a difference in the way it applies to apparent reality (samvrtisatya) and Ultimate Reality. On reflection one has to concede that to say apparent reality is empty, absent, nothing—like space—is quite other than to say the ineffable Absolute Reality, Buddha Wisdom Mind (Buddhajnana) is empty, changeless, limitless, unobstructed, and unobstructable—like space. The distinction Dolpopa draws our attention to is subtle, yet far-reaching, as we shall see.

2.4   The Meaning of Shentong

Emptiness of Other (Shentong) refers to Ultimate Reality, which is said to truly Exist because it is empty of existence, non-existence both and neither. It is none other than the Buddha Wisdom Mind (Buddhajnana), ineffable, mysterious, and beyond the reach of the ordinary conceptual consciousness *(vijnana)*. It is what truly exists behind all the sham. It is what we aspire to experience or realize when our veils, that is, mental obscurations, are gone.

One might legitimately ask why this Wisdom Mind (jnana) should be referred to as empty at all? Did we not say above that emptiness meant exposure as sham? When phenomena are described as empty does it not mean they are illusory? How could the Buddha's Wisdom Mind be an empty absence of anything if it is all that truly is?

The answer is that the Emptiness of the Buddha Wisdom Mind is not self-emptiness but Emptiness-of-other. Its Emptiness is its glory like a sky empty of clouds. It is unspoilt, untainted, unobstructed, and free. Here

Emptiness suggests an absence of faults or limiting factors, not of Reality. The Buddha Wisdom Mind is empty of faults or limiting factors, which in this case means conceptual ideas of existence, non-existence, both or neither—in other words it means it is empty of any conceptually created phenomenon whatever. The conceptual process grasps at conceptually created phenomena which are imperfect in the sense that they are sham, that is, they deceive beings by seeming to exist when in fact they do not; they are limiting in that they obstruct or obscure the true nature of Ultimate Reality.

Whereas rangtong is accessible both through logical analysis and meditation experience Shentong is only accessible through meditation experience.[7] It is Reality as revealed to the Yogi and, at a verbal level, can only be taught through intimation, imagery, symbols and so forth. When meditating on the Emptiness of that Reality, one is focusing on a Ground, a Base or a Place that is empty of that which might have spoiled it.[8] Thus, here the Empty Base *(stong gzhi)* is the Buddhajnana and the "other" of which it is empty is all that is unreal—apparent reality (samvrtisatya).

2.5   The Importance of the
Rangtong-Shentong Distinction

Much of the writing on Buddhism in the West makes statements about both the ordinary self-emptiness of things (rangtong) and the Emptiness that is the extraordinary True Nature of Ultimate Reality (Shentong), but rarely are these two ways of talking about emptiness clearly distinguished. Sometimes this is because the writers or the translators do not recognize the distinction; sometimes they intuit a Shentong-type view but present it in such a way that arguments establishing ordinary emptiness *(rangtong)* become confused with those establishing Shentong. Another layer of confusion is produced by not realizing that typical Shentong-type teachings such as Mahamudra and Dzogchen are sometimes given a rangtong gloss, especially by Gelugpa scholars. This, in part, springs from an attempt, certainly on the side of the present Dalai Lama,[9] to abate the long standing hostility stemming from remarks made by the Sakya Pandita in the thirteenth century and perpetuated in certain sections of the Gelugpa establishment today towards Dzogchen. As in the case of Shentong, there always seems to have been those who doubted the validity of Dzogchen as a genuine Buddhist tradition. Laundering it with a rangtong gloss protects it from the ravages of the "exclusive Rangtongpa." However, for the serious student of Buddhism an important element of the Buddhist tradition is thereby distorted.

From the time of Tsongkapa's chief disciples, Gyaltsab and Ketrub, the orthodox Gelugpa approach has been to actively explain away any passages in the Buddhist scriptures suggestive of the Shentong view. Often, as in the case of the *Ratnagotravibhaga*, this involves long, elaborate and somewhat convoluted argument—as in Gyaltsab's commentary on the RGV known as the "*Dartik*." Other Rangtong commentators explain the RGV from a rangtong point of view without at the same time attempting to exclude the possibility of a Shentong interpretation.[10] It can be argued, as in this present work, that the most natural reading of the RGV and the Tathagatagarbha Sutras on which it comments is a Shentong one. Indeed, the Shentong master Dolpopa's commentary on the RGV and RGVV is little more than a summary of the latter text arranged under a structure of headings.

Unfortunately for those who intuit a Shentong meaning somewhere behind the Buddha's words, it is possible to listen to Gelugpa teachings for a long time before realizing that it is precisely this intuition that is being denied. The definitions and the "difficult points" of the Gelugpa school are designed specifically to exclude a Shentong view; they take a long time to master. Once they have been mastered it is sometimes very difficult to step back and question them afresh. A famous Lama of this century, Gendun Chopel, did just that and wrote a very powerful and illuminating refutation of his own Gelugpa position.[11] Although regarded by the Gelugpa establishment as an example of a person led astray by much study, he is generally recognized as a great scholar even by his critics.

My intention is not to be sectarian here but to redress a balance. Because of their penchant for scholarship, Gelugpas have already produced far more published works in Western languages on Buddhism and Madhyamaka than any of the other Tibetan traditions. It is important that readers in the field be alerted to this and that it become common knowledge that, although an initial impression might suggest the Gelugpa is the most orthodox of the Tibetan traditions, in fact the reverse is true. The Nyingma, Kagyu, and Sakya traditions are older and have stronger links with their Indian forbears than the relatively late Gelugpa. Whereas the founders of the first three schools were Sanskritists working directly with Indian Gurus, the Gelugpa school was founded by a non-Sanskritist who had only Tibetan Gurus; its doctrine is therefore based on the translations of others when the knowledge of Sanskrit was on the wane in Tibet. Therefore, the fact that among Tibetan scholars it is almost invariably the Gelugpas themselves who recognize their particular version of Prasangika Madhyamaka to be the most orthodox should cast serious doubt upon this claim.

Thus, the importance of the rangtong-Shentong distinction in Buddhist Sutras and commentarial works can only be properly understood and evaluated in the light of a far deeper knowledge than we have at present concerning the full range of the older commentarial traditions.

Let us leave aside for the moment the views of the Gelugpa Madhyamikas and other exclusive Rangtongpas and consider why others, Rangtong and Shentong alike, regard Prasangika Madhyamaka as the highest school of Buddhist tenets. In their view, it pushes conceptual analysis to its limits because it shows the self-emptiness of all conceptualizable phenomena without itself conceptually establishing anything. It leaves the conceptual mind suspended without support or reference point since it sees that what is ultimately the case (paramarthasatya) is conceptually ungraspable.

The problem for meditators is how to relate to this realization. What can they rely on to discover reality or truth if the conceptual mind cannot be trusted? They are still in need of instruction and clarification and this is where the importance of the rangtong-Shentong distinction becomes evident. Since it is of its essence that language be conceptually graspable, there exists inevitably a tension between what is to be expressed and the means of expressing it. In common discourse, we refer to things expressed in language as if they were discrete entities with a reality of their own. Madhyamaka analysis removes this false impression but this does not mean ordinary language cannot be used to talk about what is Ultimately Real (paramarthasatya). However, at this stage—that is, at the stage where it is understood that there are no conceptual entities to be grasped—Madhyamaka arguments no longer apply. Not to understand this and to apply the rigors of Prasangika Madhyamaka reasoning to language at the post Prasangika Madhyamaka stage is to deny oneself a level of discourse beyond the commonplace.

> Thus, through one understanding arising from focusing outwards and one arising from focusing inwards, a division between the subject of intellectual analysis and that of meditation has arisen.[12]

The discussion among Tibetan scholars and practitioners concerning the rangtong-Shentong distinction is important not so much for establishing who is right as for refining one's understanding. Since any formulation of the nature of Absolute Reality (paramarthasatya) falls short of perfection, because of the inevitable tension mentioned above, every system has its own strengths and weaknesses. In considering these, the aspirant to truth refines his/her capacity to recognize subtle distinctions and is alerted to conceptual pitfalls that for a meditator must be avoided. An image that is commonly used is that intellectual investigation sharpens the intelligence (prajna) like a knife. Meditation is like using that knife to remove delusion.

Chapter 3

Emptiness from the Shentong Point of View

3.1 Progressive Stages of Meditation on Emptiness

The term "emptiness" (sunyata, *stong pa nyid*) is central to Buddhism and is found in the Pali tradition as one of the three "Liberations." Though scholarly commentators no doubt understand it to mean self-emptiness, it would require great care to determine which, if any, Pali traditions have understood or do understand it in a more Shentong way. Generally speaking, however, it is Mahayana Buddhism that investigates emptiness in depth.

Khenpo Tsultrim in his book *Progressive Stages of Meditation on Emptiness* gives a very useful introduction to the subject from a Shentong point of view, that is, from the point of view of those who accept that the Buddhist scriptures do make a rangtong-Shentong distinction. In this short text, Khenpo Tsultrim outlines how, as one's understanding of emptiness deepens, the focus of one's meditation shifts. He gives five main stages to the process; each is named after the Buddhist tradition that it represents most typically.

He calls the first stage the "Sravaka meditation on non-self." Here the focus of the meditation is the skandhas,[1] which are seen to be empty of a personal self as a single, lasting independent entity. The base *(pratisedhyavastu, dgag gzhi)** is the skandhas and the thing refuted *(pratisedhya, dgag bya)*† is the self of the person.

The second stage is called the "Cittamatra Approach."[2] Here the focus of the meditation is the mind-stream, each moment of which consists of a perceiving consciousness and a perceived object-of-consciousness. This stream is the dependent nature (paratantra, *gzhan dbang*) because it arises dependent on previous causes. It is the base *(pratisedhyavastu,* gagshi) that is empty of duality. Duality is what is to be refuted *(pratisedhya,* gagcha). "Duality" here means a duality of a difference in substance between the outer perceived object-of-consciousness and that which perceives it, the inner perceiving consciousness. As in a dream, the object is simply a manifestation of the same mind that is aware of it. Thus, whereas in the Sravaka

---

*pronounced gagshi
†pronounced gagcha

meditation the subjective belief in a personal self is refuted, in Cittamatra the objective belief in an outer world is refuted.

Furthermore, the Cittamatra Approach distinguishes three uses of the term emptiness. The self of the person and the objective world as a different substance to the observing mind are described as imaginary (parikalpita, *kun rtags*); they are empty in the sense that they do not exist at all. The mind-stream of perceiving consciousnesses and their objects is described as "dependent-in-nature" (paratantra, *gzhan dbang*); it is empty in the sense that it is the base (gagshi) empty of the imaginary nature (i.e. gagcha). The true nature (parinispanna, *yongs grub*) of phenomena is the emptiness of the dependent nature (the gagshi) of the imaginary nature (the gagcha). It is empty or emptiness in the sense of the truth or true nature that has to be seen in order for realization to arise. So the focus of the meditation is the mind-stream and what is to be seen is its emptiness (parinispanna). Thus, the imaginary nature is empty because it is what is to be refuted. The dependent nature is empty because it is what remains as empty when the imaginary nature is refuted and the true nature (parinispanna) is empty (or emptiness) because it is the true nature of phenomena that must be realized.

The third stage of the progression according to Khenpo Tsultrim is the Svatantrika Madhyamaka Approach. Here the focus of the meditation is all dharmas—both outer and inner. They are the base (gagshi) and they are empty of self-nature *(svabhava, rang bzhin)*. This removes the impression that there is any "substance" in either the inner perceiving mind or the outer perceived object. Since the consciousness and its object both arise in dependence on each other, neither has independent existence and therefore neither can be a substance. Thus, the base (gagshi) cannot be the mind-stream as a substance in which there is no duality of subjects and objects (the Cittamatra view). The base (gagshi) has to be apparent phenomena (i.e. samvrtisatya) and that which is to be refuted (gagcha) is self-nature *(svabhava)*. Apparent phenomena (i.e. samvrtisatya) are empty of self-nature because they are dependently arising *(pratityasamutpada)*. This means they do not exist in themselves; they are self-empty. The Svatantrikas do not distinguish three natures and three modes of emptiness. For them, there are just apparent phenomena, which are dependently arising (i.e. samvrtisatya), and their emptiness (rangtong). This emptiness is the ultimate or absolute reality about phenomena and also what must be seen in order for realization to arise. Apparent reality or apparent phenomena (i.e. samvrtisatya) is (or are) not empty in the sense of not being there at all, but empty in the sense that it is (or they are) the base (gagshi) empty of something else *(svabhava)*. The important point the Svatantrikas are making is that the whole idea of an underlying substratum to reality is conceptually incoherent. One would have to read their arguments in detail to understand how they do this.

The fourth stage in the meditation on emptiness is the Prasangika Madhyamaka Approach. Here the focus for the meditation is the non-conceptual (nisprapanca) nature of both the appearance of phenomena and their self-emptiness. That which is to be refuted (gagcha) is all conceptual creations (prapanca). This is where an attempt is made to remove all concepts of bases and things to be refuted (gagshi and gagcha).

All the stages preceding the Shentong are very analytical in approach. Furthermore, each stage analyzes more deeply on the basis of having understood the previous stages; it attempts to remedy the shortcomings of its predecessors. In this way, it parallels the progressive understanding of an individual as well as of successive Buddhist thinkers. Although the Prasangika Approach is deeply analytical in the way it refutes all positions that assert or refute anything about ultimate reality, this approach also shows how, in meditation practice, to rest the mind in that reality without any conceptual analysis or contrivance. In fact, right from the Sravaka stage the meditator is enjoined to rest in the emptiness without conceptual artifice. However, as each succeeding stage of the meditation shows, the former stage still contained within it conceptual limits. One may have rested one's mind somewhat without artifice but not completely. As the stages are traversed, the conceptual content becomes increasingly subtle until at the Prasangika stage it is hard to see that any conceptual content remains at all. In fact, Khenpo Tsultrim admits that theoretically there should be none and so the Clear Light Nature of Mind (the non-dual Buddhajnana) should become manifest as a matter of course. However, in practice this often does not happen because it is so difficult to overcome the subtle conceptual tendency to ''cut'' or analyze phenomena—accentuated by the process of following the path itself. For overcoming this, Khenpo Tsultrim states that one must develop faith in Shentong, the last stage of the process.

Before proceeding further, let it be said that Rangtongpas include all Svatantrika and Prasangika Madhyamikas who do not accept that Paramarthasatya (Absolute Reality [chapter 5.3]) is non-dual Buddhajnana [chapter 2.4]. Because Candrakirti—seventh century A.D.—is regarded by many as the greatest exponent of Prasangika Madhyamaka, there is a tendency to associate that school primarily with his system. However, Shentongpas often criticize Candrakirti[3] arguing that although he claims to be a true Prasangika Madhyamaka holding no position, in fact, his system implies he holds a position both in regard to paramartha and samvrtisatya [chapter 5]. Thus, the question of what the true Prasangika Madhyamaka is and who represents it is not a clear-cut issue. Nevertheless, in order to clarify the points made by Shentongpas, I have referred in a generalized way to the

Prasangika Madhyamaka view, sometimes supporting it as intrinsic to the understanding of Shentong and sometimes criticising it as having failed to reveal the true non-conceptual nature of Reality. In the first case, the reader should understand it to be Nagarjuna's Madhyamaka defended by Prasangika-type arguments, that is, arguments that refute all conceptual positions without positing any of their own. In the latter case, it should be understood to be a version of Prasangika Madhyamaka that, in the opinion of Shentongpas, still contains (either overtly or covertly) a conceptual residue. The key issue for Shentongpas is whether the Madhyamaka system in question refutes mind-stream theory or whether it continues to assume that Buddhajnana is a dependently arising self-empty stream of dualistic consciousnesses [chapters 2 and 4].

3.2   The Final Stage—Shentong (Yogacara Madhyamaka)

Since the Buddha's Wisdom Mind (Buddhajnana) is beyond concepts, one might be surprised to see it presented in such positive terms as "truly Existing" and "having Qualities" and so forth. Dolpopa [RC 391.4] replies that it is necessary to present Buddhajnana as a truly Existing Absolute Reality. Otherwise it is likely to be mistakenly included in the category of "all dharmas," the reality of which is negated when one establishes emptiness through Rangtong reasoning. Then, since the concept would be wrong, the attitude would be wrong and therefore, the view would be wrong. Since the view is the basis for the meditation practice, this also would be wrong, therefore, it is vital that one have the correct conceptual framework at the outset. This view is in harmony with the five reasons for teaching the Tathagatagarbha presented in the RGV [1.156–166] and the doctrine of the *Srimaladevisutra* and the other Tathagatagarbha Sutras.

Indeed, since it is beyond all concepts, it is valid to say that the final stage is beyond both rangtong and Shentong. However, for the meditator Shentong doctrine helps to overcome certain residual subtle concepts. Although Prasangika Madhyamaka is supposed to focus on the non-conceptual (nisprapanca) nature of phenomena, in practice before this is realized the meditator focuses first on apparent reality (samvrtisatya) to negate the tendency to grasp conceptually at self-entities and then on Ultimate Reality (paramarthasatya) in order to negate the tendency to grasp conceptually at emptiness. If he/she is successful, at a certain point the false notion of self-entities ceases to arise and there is no longer anything to focus on or negate. Nonetheless, the meditator might still have the subtle conceptual belief in the negating process and start to misapply it. Dolpopa [RC 482] remarks that if all were self-empty, since self-empty is nothing (mengag), that which was to be established (sgrub chos) would have been negated.

This problem is referred to in RGV [1.36]:

> *di dag 'bras ni mdor bsdu na. chos kyi sku la phyin ci log. rnam*
> *pa bzhi las bzlog pa yi. gnyen pos rab tu phye ba nyid.*
> These fruits are in short the (four) remedies that counteract the
> four mistakes about the Dharmakaya.

The RGVV explains that the four mistakes about the Dharmakaya arise from misapplying the four remedies that counteract the four mistakes about the skandhas. Beings cling to the skandhas as if they were permanent, happiness, self, and pure when in truth they are quite the reverse. To remedy their mistake they are taught to meditate on the impermanence, suffering, non-self, and impurity of the skandhas. They then make the mistake of seeing these negative qualities everywhere, thereby overlooking the true nature of the Dharmakaya, which is permanent, bliss, self, and purity.[4]

Thus, Shentong, the final stage, is taught to remedy the meditator's tendency to cling to the habit—fostered on the earlier stages of the path— of negating whatever experience arises in his/her mind. This habit leads to the tendency to try to negate the Reality of Buddhajnana by making the same mistake as those mentioned in the RGV above.

Although it is true that to call the Dharmakaya "True Permanence" and so forth, or to say true Emptiness is really the non-dual Buddhajnana can easily be misunderstood, such teachings do have the important function of remedying the former fault. Thus, Shentong is the remedy for a certain kind of misunderstanding of Prasangika Madhyamaka, notwithstanding Prasangika Madhyamaka is in turn the remedy for a certain kind of misunderstanding of Shentong.

If Shentong is taught in order to remedy the misapplication of teachings directed at destroying false concepts, it is also to alert the practitioner to the presence of a dynamic, positive Reality that is to be experienced once the conceptual mind is defeated.

Thus, Khenpo Tsultrim presents the final stage of the progressive stages of meditation on emptiness as Shentong. Whereas in Svatantrika and Prasangika Madhyamaka the absence of self-nature in apparent reality is emphasized, Shentongpas introduce a further subtlety by means of the *Sandhinirmocanasutra* (SNS) doctrine of the three natures, the three absences of essence and three modes of emptiness. In Shentong terms, the emptiness of apparent phenomena (the gagshi) of self-nature (the gagcha) is equivalent to the dependent nature's (i.e. paratantra, the gagshi's) emptiness of the imaginary nature (parikalpita, the gagcha). Thus, the paramarthasatya of Rangtong Madhyamaka is equivalent to the parinispanna of Cittamatra in the sense that it is the emptiness of the dependent nature (paratantra, the gag-shi) of the imaginary nature (parikalpita, the gagcha). The difference is, of course, that for Cittamatrins parikalpita (the gagcha) is a duality of substance between mind and its objects, not self-nature *(svabhava)* in the Madhyamaka sense. The Shentong view is that for one's understanding of emptiness to be complete one must rest in the Parinispanna (the gagshi) empty of imaginary nature (parikalpita, the gagcha) and dependent nature (paratantra, the gagcha,[5] that is, one simply rests in non-dual Jnana abandoning all effort to see absence of imaginary nature (parikalpita) in the dependent nature (paratantra).

All Buddhist systems teach that all apparent (samvrti) phenomena apparently exist, that is, exist in a samvrti way. Shentong thinkers understand this as their seeming to exist as seeming or apparent realities, which means in effect that they never actually exist at all. Gelugpa and Svatantrika Rangtongpas stress that some phenomena never truly exist *(bden grub)* or never exist with self-nature, while continuing to imply that it is possible to exist falsely or to exist without self-nature. Shentong thinkers reject such a position as totally incoherent. When Shentongpas use expressions such as ''apparent phenomena do not truly exist'' or ''do not exist with self-nature,'' they mean ''apparent phenomena do not exist.''

Rangtongpas try to refute the Shentongpas at this stage by saying that they are falling into the nihilistic extreme of denying existence to what exists. For Buddhists it is vital to avoid the extreme nihilistic position of denying the truth of karma cause and effect *(las rgyu 'bras)* on the one hand and the spiritual path and goal on the other. The Shentongpa defends himself/herself against the accusation of nihilism by saying he/she does not deny apparent reality anymore than Nagarjuna did. Nagarjuna and the Prasangikas accept seeming or apparent reality (samvrtisatya) insofar as that is how ordinary deluded beings experience the world. In other words, they would not deny to an ordinary being that he/she must suffer the consequences of his/her karma and so forth. As for the Buddha and the Buddha Qualities, these are not apparent reality. They have apparent (samvrti) counterparts that beings apprehend, but the real Buddha Qualities are Ultimate Reality, non-conditioned, non-arising, non-ceasing, ineffable, and beyond the conceptual mind. The question of the Absolute (paramartha) nature of the Buddha Qualities is subtle and difficult to understand. Since it is a central theme of Tathagatagarbha doctrine, we shall be returning to it frequently in this work.

Shentong thinkers have often been taken for Cittamatrins because they emphasize in this way the importance of distinguishing the three natures and the three modes of emptiness. Shentongpas argue that, since Cittama-trins treat the dependent nature (paratantra) as the base (the gagshi) and the parikalpita as what is to be refuted (the gagcha), they do not recognize the Parinispanna itself as the base (the gagshi). According to Shentongpas the true base (the gagshi) is What Is, variously referred to in the scriptures as the Absolute Dharmata, the Mind's True Nature, the Clear Light Nature of Mind, the Mind Itself (*sems nyid*), or the Tathagatagarbha.[6] Therefore, there is a huge difference between Cittamatra and Shentong—unless one is thinking of what Dolpopa calls Absolute Cittamatra.[7]

At this point, Rangtongpas accuse Shentongpas of falling into the po-sition of asserting as existing what does not exist. Rangtongpas point out that Prajnaparamita teachings of the second Dharmacakra say: "All dhar-mas are empty of self-nature" and the list of "all dharmas" includes abso-lute as well as samvrti dharmas. Shentongpas do not deny that the Prajnaparamita teachings of the second Dharmacakra say this, but add that if this were ultimately the case, since self-empty (or emptiness-of-self-nature) means not to exist, then absolute dharmas such as Buddha, the Buddha Qualities, Nirvana, Paramarthasatya and so forth, would all be nonexistent. To them this is nonsense. We will be returning to this argu-ment again since it has far-reaching implications. It is because the second Dharmacakra gives the impression that Absolute dharmas are ultimately empty of self-nature (rangtong) that Shentongpas such as Dolpopa class it as a provisional (Neyartha) and not the final or ultimate teaching (Nitartha) of the Buddha. They have excellent scriptural grounds for saying this be-cause the only Sutra that explicitly states which of the Dharmacakras is Nitartha and which Neyartha is the SNS. According to this Sutra, the second Dharmacakra is Neyartha and the third Nitartha. Other Shentongpas (e.g. Kongtrul) call the second Dharmacakra Nitartha and the third Dharmacakra ultimate Nitartha.

How then do Shentongpas understand the teachings of the second Dharmacakra? How is it that the Prajnaparamita Sutras can say that abso-lute dharmas are as empty of self-nature as apparent dharmas are? The Shentong reply is that the second Dharmacakra is for removing the fault of thinking ultimate reality can be grasped by the ordinary conceptualizing mind or consciousness (vijnana). Since ideas such as Buddha or the Abso-lute can be shown by logical argument to be merely conceptually created constructs, they are self-empty. However, argues the Shentongpa, when the third Dharmacakra Sutras say that the Absolute Dharmata or the Tathagat-agarbha exists, they are careful to specify that it does not exist as a concep-tually graspable entity; rather it has to be approached through "faith." When the Buddha is said to have qualities as countless as the sands of the

Ganges, it is important to notice that the Sutras lay great emphasis on these qualities being inseparable from the nature of the Buddha. They are not qualities divisible from the entity qualified (such as are refuted by Madhyamaka reasoning of the second Dharmacakra). Since Shentong thinkers accept Nagarjuna's Madhyamaka arguments, which refute all conceptually created constructs about ultimate reality, they consider themselves Madhyamakas. Furthermore, since they do not mistake the true import of the Prajnaparamita—as their opponents surely do—they consider themselves to be the great or true Madhyamikas. On the other hand, because Shentongpas take Absolute Reality to be the Clear Light Nature of Mind, the non-dual Jnana that can only be experienced or realized through meditation experience, they consider themselves the true Yogacarins. Hence, they call themselves "Yogacara-Madhyamikas." For example, Kongtrul [SKK hum 32] refers to the Shentong view as Yogacara, including it under the general heading of Madhyamaka [SKK hum 31b]. According to contemporary Shentongpas such as Kalu Rimpoche and Khenpo Tsultrim, Shentong is just another name for Yogacara Madhyamaka: simply the term "Shentong" has become more current among Tibetans these days. Khenpo Tsultrim explains that confusion sometimes arises because, for Gelugpas and Sakyapas, Yogacara-Madhyamaka means Cittamatra. Shentongpas these days do not accept that their system is Cittamatra—at least in the ordinary sense.

Although one could say that the Yogacara Madhyamaka or Shentong view comes from the Nitartha Sutras of the Third Dharmacakra as commented on in the RGV, other commentarial traditions would not accept this as the true interpretation of those teachings. In the present work, I shall be describing the contents of the RGV and its *Vyakhya* (which comments on the Tathagatagarbha Sutras of the third Dharmacakra) for the reader to judge for himself how well the Shentong interpretation fits these texts. By way of contrast, I shall also from time to time draw the reader's attention to how Rangtong commentators interpret the same passages. The message of the RGV has been heralded for centuries as the great key to the Sutras and the Tantras. It is therefore important what we understand that message to be.

3.3   No Shentong Without A Proper Understanding
of Rangtong

It is not always appreciated by either supporters of Shentong or its opponents that a proper understanding of rangtong is essential to the understanding of Shentong. Shentong supporters sometimes find rangtong reasoning too dry and intellectual for their taste and want to hurry on to the sweeping vistas of a Shentong view. This may account for some teachers refusing to acknowledge the Shentong view in order to remedy this kind of impatience.

Its opponents insist that since Shentongpas hypostatize Absolute Reality, this proves they have not correctly understood the self-emptiness of all dharmas, both absolute and apparent (samvrti) that is the teaching of the second Dharmacakra. As has just been explained, however, Shentongpas insist they do not hypostatize. Before one can even begin to understand Shentong one has to understand that the nature of all apparent (samvrti) and absolute dharmas is self-emptiness *insofar as they can be conceptualized and made objects of the ordinary dualistic consciousness (vijnana)*. Dolpopa explains [RC p. 383] that the two teachings are for different occasions *(skabs)*. The investigative time *(so so rtog pa'i skabs)* is when one examines the dharmas and finds them empty. The meditative time *(mnyam bzhag skabs)* is when one rests the Mind in its own Nature without concepts.

Kongtrul (a Shentongpa) explains rangtong as follows [SKK hum 31.4]:

dgag gzhir bzung ba'i chos gang yin pa thams cad rang rang gi ngo bos stong pas. dper na gzugs ni gzugs gyis stong pa bzhin de nyid de nyid kyis stong pa yin te. don dam dpyod byed kyi rigs pas dpyad pa gang gi tse de nyid de nyid du grub pa'i phyir.

Since concerning the base of the refutation [gagshi, i.e. any dharma] all perceived dharmas whatever are each empty of their own essence as, for example, form is empty of form, that very thing is empty of that very thing, because when one examines with the mind that distinguishes the absolute, that very thing does not exist in that very thing.

And quoting from *Madhyamakavatara* [MA] [SKK hum 31a.7]:

gang gyir de yi rang bzhin de yin phyir mig ni mig gis stong. de bzhin rna ba sna dang lce. lus dang yid kyang bsnyad par bya

Because that is its nature, the eye is empty of eye and the same is said concerning the ear, tongue, body and mind.

In other words, Kongtrul is saying that "eye is empty of eye" means there is no eye. This leaves us with a paradox. The importance of the statement from the Shentong point of view is that it forces us to focus on the paradoxical nature of experience. Conceptual analysis reveals no eye, so what is this experience we call "eye"?

There is a need to emphasize this point because Gelugpa scholars argue against it. They say that "eye is empty of eye" means the eye is empty not literally of eye, but of the self-nature of eye. For them self-nature (or inherent existence) of eye is the eye-entity that we mistakenly imagine to exist as an independent thing in itself. However, we never really see such an eye because it does not exist. Gelugpas call this the "eye-entity" that is not an object of knowledge *(shes bya)* as distinct from the samvrti—translated by

Gelugpa-orientated scholars as "conventionally existent"—eye, which is the dependently arising eye that is the actual object of knowledge *(shes bya)* of an ordinary being's consciousness.

Thus, the Gelugpa view is not particularly mysterious or paradoxical. It conforms to the standard Buddhist practice of meditation on impermanence. Everything arises and passes away in dependence on causes and conditions and there are no lasting permanent entities anywhere to cling to. Prasangika Madhyamikas and Shentongpas go further than this, however. They question the nature of those dependently arising impermanent phenomena and find nothing at all. Hence the mystery.

Mikyo Dorje in the introduction to his commentary on the MA [681] dismisses the Gelugpa interpretation of "eye is empty of eye" stating that if Candrakirti had meant the eye was merely empty of a non-existent eye but not empty of the apparent (samvrti, conventional) eye he would surely have mentioned it.

Konchog Jigme Wangpo (a Gelugpa Lama) in his *"Precious Garland of tenets"* makes the following retort:

> Nowadays, some who are vain about having high views say that phenomena are only mistaken appearances and take them to be utterly non-existent, like the son of a barren woman; then they hold that non-attention to anything is the superior practice. They do not even have the scent of Prasangika in them.
>
> (Translated by Zopa & Hopkins under the title '*Practice & Theory of Tibetan Buddhism*')

Although he does not say so, Konchog Jigme Wangpo is almost certainly alluding to the majority view among Tibetan Prasangika Madhyamikas (i.e. the other followers of Candrakirti) that "eye is empty of eye and so forth," means that the eye cannot exist even conventionally (as samvrti) because not only the emptiness but also the appearance/manifestation of eye is beyond conceptual grasping (i.e. it is nisprapanca). The appearance-manifestation of eye (or any other phenomenon) does not exist in any sense either as an existent or a nonexistent thing, or both or neither; neither does it exist as samvrtisatya or as paramarthasatya. Kongtrul defines what is self-empty as all of apparent reality (samvrtisatya), which includes all things knowable (knowable in the sense that they can be mental objects). Therefore, both existent and nonexistent (*bhava* and *abhava*, *dngos* and *dngos med*) apparent and ultimate dharmas are included.[8] Kongtrul explains [SKK hum 31b.]

> *stong pa'i gzhi ni chos can te shes bya la gang ji snyed cig srid pa'i chos thams cad do.*

That which is empty (the empty base) is the *dharmin* which is all the knowable things that there are—all the dharmas of existence (i.e. samsara).

Here "*dharmin*" means "holding the quality" of emptiness. The whole statement means that every dharma that appears to be an object of the conceptual mind (i.e. all samvrti dharmas—"all the knowable things that there are") is empty of itself. Again:

mdo na blo'i yul du byar mi rung ba rnams lta zhog. der rung ba'i
chos ji snyed pa thams cad rang rang gi ngo bos stong par.
In short, let alone what is not able to be the object of the mind, all dharmas whatsoever (that are the object of the mind) are each empty of their own nature *(svabhava)*.

Others as well as Shentong commentators object to the Gelugpa insertion of the "eye that is not an object of knowledge." In fact, in the commentary mentioned above where Mikyo Dorje criticizes it, he is defending rangtong and attacking Shentong. Needless to say, it is the version of Rangtong Madhyamaka that Mikyo Dorje and Kongtrul are defending that is the proper basis for understanding Shentong, not the Gelugpa version.

It cannot be stressed too highly that other Tibetan Madhyamaka scholars do not accept the standard Gelugpa view as Prasangika Madhyamaka and have difficulty placing it exactly among the Indian commentarial traditions. As mentioned in the last chapter, Western scholars need to exercise great caution since much of what is presented as Tibetan Buddhism these days is actually a minority view among the major Tibetan scholarly traditions. In this present work, I shall not be examining Gelugpa Madhyamaka as such and from now on any reference to the Prasangika Madhyamaka view should be understood to be the Prasangika Madhyamaka view that is broadly accepted by both my Rangtong and Shentong informants (based chiefly on Jamgon Kongtrul's *Shes bya mdzod*). The situation is, however, very complicated and it is no easy matter to make categorical statements that would apply to all Rangtong systems. Many subtle points and fine distinctions are made by different commentators and each has to be examined in his own terms in order to do him justice.

3.4   Problems of Definitions of Terms

I have made much of these points of difference between the Gelugpas and the rest because of the inevitable bias that creeps in where the reader is primarily familiar with Gelugpa works. The problem is that one finds oneself unwittingly understanding terms according to the Gelugpa gloss and thus losing the thread of the arguments put forward in other works.

For example, throughout this present work samvrtisatya has normally been translated as "apparent reality" even though here and there I have used more common translations such as "relative truth" or "conventional existence" and so forth. "Samvrti" according to Franklin Edgerton in the *Buddhist Hybrid Sanskrit* (BHS) means "convention, general acceptance, conditioned and so forth", but in Tibetan it is translated as "*kundzob*" *(kun rdzob)* which Candra Das (CD) gives as "vain, empty, spurious, void." Traditionally the examples are used of a sheep disguised as a wolf or a heap of froth giving the impression of a great mass indicating a sense of something that is disguised or blown up to appear to be what it is not. Monier Williams (MW Skt. Dictionary) has "to wrap up, envelop" as one of the meanings for samvrti. Nevertheless, Franklin Edgerton is doubtful about the etymology of taking "*kundzob*" to mean "covering" and finds something like "common sense knowledge" or "truth" to be a more standard translation for samvrti. I have chosen "apparent reality" hoping it conveys both the sense of what appears to be the case to common sense and of something that is merely apparently real.

As we saw in the last two chapters, when the scriptures say all apparent reality (samvrtisatya) is empty of self-nature, Shentongpas take this to means it does not exist at all. It merely seems to, that is, it is what is to be refuted (the gagcha). However, possibly for a Cittamatrin, and certainly for a Svatantrika or Gelugpa, samvrtisatya has a certain existent status albeit not ultimate or absolute. For them samvrtisatya is always the base (the gagshi) empty of true existence and it can never be the thing refuted (the gagcha). The very way samvrtisatva is understood by them would not permit it.

Other problems of interpretation are more far-reaching. For example, as we have seen, there is a subtle shift or play occurring in the Sutras and commentaries between treating emptiness simply as a truthful statement about apparent phenomena and treating it as the nature of Reality itself. Thus, on the one hand it can be interpreted as an eternal absolute or ultimate truth about phenomena, for example, the parinispanna in Cittamatra is the truth of the emptiness of the paratantra of the parikalpita. It is called "truly existent" (parinispanna) because it exists as the truth that brings liberation from delusion. On the other hand it can be the eternal Absolute Reality that is the mysterious True Nature of phenomena—the ineffable Emptiness. This latter interpretation is very suggestive of Shentong but not exclusive to Shentongpas. When a rangtong commentator treats Emptiness in this way, it is not hard to see why it is sometimes said that a true understanding of rangtong emptiness is none other than Shentong.

The interpretation of emptiness as a truth leads naturally into the discussion of *prasajyapratisedha* (med dgag)[‡] and *paryudasapratisedha (ma yin dgag)*.[§] Professors David Seyfort Ruegg and J. Hopkins follow the Rangtong commentators who treat these terms as negative truth statements. They understand the statement, "All dharmas are empty of self-nature" to be (to use Ruegg's terms) a non-presuppositional, non-implicative, non-affirming absolute negation (*prasajyapratisedha*, mengag). Ruegg [LM 37] discusses the use of this term at length in his section on Bhavaviveka and Candrakirti. He explains it as a negation that does not imply adherence to the opposite position, for example, to deny dharmas exist as entities by *prasajya* negation does not imply they exist as nonentities, which would have been the case had "All dharmas are empty of self-nature" been a presuppositional, implicative, affirming relative negation (*paryudasapratisedha*, mayingag). He comments that these two kinds of negation in some respects parallel the weak and strong negations of modern logic [LM 38 fn. 94].

In this way, Rangtong commentators argue that absolute or ultimate truth (paramarthasatya), that is, emptiness, is a *prasajyapratisedha* (mengag).

Shentong commentators treat the terms *prasajyapratisedha* (mengag) and *paryudasapratisedha* (mayingag) not as negative truth statements but as states of negation. Thus, *prasajyapratisedha* (mengag) in effect means "nothingness" and *paryudasapratisedha* (mayingag) means an Existent Reality. This is the way Lokesh Candra defines *paryudasapratisedha* (mayingag), that is, "something which is not nothing, but something in which something else is absent."[9]

Dolpopa, for example, [RC 86–89] explains that in terms of the Tantras a mayingag is something experienced. He explains [RC 53] that in RGVV [1.154], where emptiness is defined "as the remainder that is primordially present," it is the same as the difference between mengag and mayingag, between mere nonexistence and the base of that nonexistence *(med pa'i gzhi)*, between partial analysis *(rnam dpyod)* and complete analysis *(yongs dpyod)*, between emptiness in the sense of isolation in which there is mere freedom from prapanca and the basis of these *(stong zhing bden la spros pa dang bral ba tsam dang de rnams kyi gzhi)* and so on.

Dolpopa adds that one must realize properly and precisely this important, subtle and hard to realize manner of being *(tshul)* that is very profound

---

‡pronounced mengag
§pronounced mayingag

and dependent on special instruction *(man ngag)* that relies on the point *(artha)* arrived at through resting in that point *(artha)*.

Kongtrul [RGV commentary 11b] explains that most commentators consider the doctrine of the Second Dharmacakra to be a *prasajyapratisedha*— a non-affirming nothingness *(med par dgag pa nyid)* and he explains how Ngog's followers explain Tathagatagarbha as a non-affirming nothingness *(med par dgag pa'i mtshan myid can)* [RGV commentary 14b]. In Shentong terms, the statement—"All dharmas are empty of self-nature"—is a *prasajyapratisedha* because it means dharmas are nothing *(gang yang med pa)* [RC 53ff]. They are simply nonexistent *(med tsam)* and there is no implication that they are a base *(pratisedhyavastu,* gagshi) empty of something to be negated *(pratisedhya,* gagcha). On the other hand, Tathagatagarbha or Absolute Emptiness (Paramarthasatyasunyata) is a base empty of something to be negated (literally a base of emptiness, *med pa'i gzhi)* and so is a *paryudasapratisedha* (mayingag). Obviously, when Rangtongpas hear Shentongpas state that Emptiness is a *paryudasapratisedha* (mayingag), it is easy for them to misunderstand, for it sounds to them as if Shentongpas believe Emptiness implies the existence of conceptually created nonentities. Nothing could be further from the truth. Critics and supporters of Shentong alike must take care that definitions of terms within other systems are not misapplied when trying to understand Shentong.

In Shentong terms, if Absolute Reality (Paramarthasatya) were a nothing or a nonexistence *(prasajyapratisedha,* mengag), it would have to be subtly conceptual, because one would always be focusing on apparently existent phenomena and negating their existence. In Kongtrul's commentary [RGV 14b], he quotes Shonupal's remark about Chapa's view:

> Absolute Reality which is a non-implicative negation *(med dgag)* is things *(dngos po)* being empty of reality *(bden pas stong)*. It is also held to be an object able to be grasped by words and concepts *(sgra rtog gi zhen pa'i yul)*.

To overcome this subtle conceptual tendency the Shentong method is to recognize Absolute Reality as Buddhajnana empty of all conceptual creation (prapanca) and accessible only through faith and not through the conceptual mind.

Faith here is meant in a very special sense and cannot be explained without first discussing the Shentong view of the nature of Buddhajnana.

Chapter 4

The Shentong View of Absolute Reality

4.1 Buddhajnana

In some ways this is the main subject matter of this book since the Shentong interpretation of the Tathagatagarbha doctrine identifies Tathagatagarbha as Buddhajnana.

At this point of the discussion, however, we are looking at the identity of Emptiness (Shentong) and Buddhajnana. As was mentioned in "The Meaning of Rangtong" [chapter 2], emptiness in the sense of spaciousness is called the "absolute dhatu" *(Paramarthadhatu, don dam dbyings)*. A recurrent question that arises not only in the Tibetan, but the Chinese tradition (and no doubt others) as well, is whether the absolute dhatu is primarily emptiness (i.e. a *prasajapratisedha*, mengag) or Mind (i.e. a *paryudasapratisedha*, mayingag). In other words is the absolute dhatu self-empty or empty-of-other?

One of the reasons why both Rangtong and Shentong interpretations of the absolute dhatu are possible is that it is sometimes referred to as "emptiness" and sometimes as the "nature-of-mind." Nature-of-mind could mean either the self-empty characteristic of the moments-of-consciousness that form the samvrti mind-stream, or the clear and knowing awareness characteristic of mind. Rangtongpas do not teach that the clear, knowing awareness characteristic of mind is anything other than the mind-stream of moments-of-consciousness. Therefore, since this is clearly samvrti (because it is dependently arising) it cannot be the absolute dhatu referred to in the Sutras as changeless, limitless, non-compounded and so forth. Thus, the explanation of the absolute dhatu as the nature-of-mind can only be that it is the self-empty characteristic of mind (a *prasajyapratisedha*, mengag).

Mind as we know it always involves a perceiver and a perceived aspect, but it is taught that in the true nature of mind this duality is absent [eg. *Bodhisattvacaryavatara* BCA 9.2]. Therefore, the question arises whether this absence of duality in the nature-of-mind means both perceiver and perceived partake of the characteristic of awareness as Shentongpas say, or of the characteristic of emptiness as Rangtongpas say.[1] Paul Williams in his article "Silence and Truth" points out that what Gelugpas mean by non-dual awareness is not what is understood by Shentongpas.

In Rangtong terms, when the nature of mind is described as non-dual it simply means that the awareness characteristic of mind is a dependently arising (i.e. self empty) phenomenon. The argument is that if there were no object of awareness there would no awareness, and vice versa, so neither object nor awareness arise independently and therefore they are both self-empty. Thus, although the perceiving and perceived aspects of mind arise and are present with each moment of awareness, since they are empty of independent existence, there is no duality of truly existent objects and awarenesses in the true nature of mind. This is the case as much for vijnana as for Jnana. The difference between the two is that in a vijnana (a moment of ordinary consciousness) there is no awareness of this lack of duality whereas in Jnana there is. For this reason, the stream of apparently dualistic vijnanas is said to be impure while the stream of moments of Jnana is said to be pure. It is pure because the object of awareness is always non-duality, that is, emptiness.

Buddhajnana is taught everywhere to be a unique kind of jnana. In Rangtongpa terms, its mysteriousness is its ability to be aware of sense objects at the same time as perceiving emptiness. In other words, even when the Buddha is not in meditation his mind is pure. Rangtongpas accept that for everyone except Buddhas, awareness of emptiness excludes the awareness of sense objects, so for them pure non-dual jnana can only occur in meditative equipose.[2]

Thus, although Rangtong commentators such as Gyaltsab pride themselves on their reasonableness, there is a hiatus in their thinking. They have explained Buddhajnana as if it were a stream-of-consciousness like that of an ordinary being. Yet, they claim it functions quite differently.

It is important to understand here that all Buddhist systems of reasoning start from the assumption made in the *Abhidharma* concerning the nature of the mind-stream. It arises from the common sense notion that our experience consists of a stream of awareness that exists in time. The shortest possible moment of time that awareness lasts is a ''mind-moment'' and longer periods of awareness are made up of streams of these moments. For a moment to be a moment of awareness there must be some content that might correspond to the object of the moment before or to a new object. The object of the awareness must be as momentary as the awareness of it. Abhidharmists investigated and categorized these moments in great detail, producing long lists of all the possible kinds of consciousness, each of which was defined by its object. For example, the eye-consciousness is consciousness of form and so forth. Rangtong thinkers use what is essentially the same basic mind-stream model as the Abhidharmists. It is the model of mind that Nagarjuna finally refuted as conceptually incoherent. Although his Madhyamaka, together with the Madhyamaka systems of reasoning that arose in response to his work, is a whole vast topic in its own right, the essence of it in terms of the present discussion is that if a consciousness and its object cannot exist independently of each other, then neither can ever arise. Thus, a simplistic theory of dependent origination collapses. Nothing can arise dependent on something else if that something else cannot arise in its absence. Dependent origination cannot mean that phenomena arise dependent on each other, because there are no fundamental building blocks such as mind moments, atoms, causes, effects and so forth. Therefore, the teaching that phenomena are dependently arising means that because they are self-empty, their nature is not conceptually graspable.

How can it be, then, that in a system where Buddhajnana is a stream of moments of awareness, a moment of the Buddha's awareness can have two objects, that is a sense object and an emptiness, at the same time?

Whereas Rangtongpas find it sufficient to say dependently arising phenomena constitute a stream of consciousnesses and their objects, which are samvrtisatya, the true nature of which is self emptiness, Shentongpas find this totally inadequate as an explanation of experience. Since samvrtisatya by definition means apparent reality (i.e. what is not truly existent), it is a truism to say the true nature of samvrtisatya is self emptiness.

In fact, self-emptiness (rangtong) only describes what we mistakenly think we experience, not the true nature of experience. Shentongpas and Prasangika Madhyamikas alike freely admit that our present experience is reduced to total mystery as far as conceptual thinking is concerned and the common sense notion of a stream of moments of consciousness and its objects has been totally demolished. At this point, Shentong thinkers link the mystery of our present experience with the mystery of the Buddha's non-dual Jnana.

Our experience is present, vivid, and alive yet not graspable even in terms of concepts such as time and space. Everything collapses under the rigorous analysis of Madhyamaka reasoning. According to Thrangu Rimpoche[3] the Prasangika explanation of Prajnaparamita is that form and so forth being empty of form and so forth means that on analysis form and so forth cannot be found at all. Emptiness being none other than form and so forth means that emptiness is not one thing and form another. In other words, form itself is emptiness. This is inconceivable to the analytical mind. Both the form and its emptiness defy reason. We see form so experience tells us it is there. Reason tells us it does not exist because when we analyze it rationally and minutely there is nothing there. Thus, we are left with the direct experience of form and no conceptual explanation. Even to say it is mere appearance is to suggest that we can somehow analyze and find appearance. When we do analyze appearance, however, it also disappears. Thrangu Rimpoche demonstrated to me, quite graphically, that a sense of paradox and astonishment is essential when putting across the message of the Prajnaparamita.

This should be compared with Dolpopa's Shentong analysis of the Prajnaparamita. According to him, when form and so forth are described as empty of form and so forth, this is the self-emptiness of apparent (samvrti) form as described by Kongtrul in "No Shentong Without A Proper Understanding of Rangtong" [chapter 3.3 above]. However, the Emptiness that is described as none other than Form is Shentong. He uses the expression "Absolute Form" for that direct experience of Form stripped of all the dualistic tendencies that constitute an ordinary being's perception of form. Absolute Form and the Absolute equivalent of all other dharmas are not objects-of-consciousness, because consciousnesses and objects-of-consciousness are completely illusory phenomena with no real existence. In Absolute Form and so forth, there is no division into see-er and seen, experience and experiencer, quality and qualified and so forth. By definition the ordinary analytical mind cannot apprehend it. The interesting question is what the Absolute nature of the obscuring process is. Dolpopa quotes the *Mahaparinirvanasutra* on how every link in the twelve link chain of conditioned arising has an Absolute counterpart including ignorance *(avidya)* itself.

If it were easy for non-conceptual Awareness of the True Nature of experience to arise once one had convinced oneself that the apparent dualism of awareness was false, then there would be no need to explain the non-dual nature of Buddhajnana in more detail. Since it is not easy, Shentong is taught. It is the non-dual nature of Buddhajnana that makes it possible for Buddhas to perceive sense objects at the same time as realizing Emptiness. There is no duality of mind and what appears in the mind (i.e. what it focuses on), between Mind and its Emptiness, and between one moment and the next. In the absence of concepts, Buddhajnana is timeless and boundless. Our apparently divided consciousnesses are the timeless, boundless Buddhajnana obscured by ignorant, dualistic, conceptual thinking. The only difference between vijnana, the Jnana of Bodhisattvas and Buddhajnana is that they are completely obscured, partially obscured, and completely unobscured respectively. In essence they are all the same nondual Awareness.

Thus, unlike a Rangtong explanation of Buddhajnana, in a Shentong explanation there is no essential discontinuity between the nature of a being's awareness and that of a Buddha. This has implications in terms of meditation practice: in Mahamudra and Dzogchen practices for instance there is no attempt to suppress sensory input by closing the eyes and finally there is no distinction between meditation sessions and after session practice. This all relates to the absence of subject-object dichotomy in true Awareness and there being no necessity (even for non-Buddhas) to meditate on appearance and emptiness as two distinct objects of awareness.

Since all our ordinary experience is included in the subject-object dichotomy and since this dichotomy has no real existence, everything we experience must actually be an expression of non-dual Jnana. It must be Ultimate Reality (Paramarthasatya). Thus, Ultimate Reality must constitute a non-dual experience, *(myong bya).*[4] This experience is called the "Clear Light Nature of Mind" by Shentongpas and is introduced to the aspirant by an experienced Guru by means of special instruction and empowerment *(abhiseka, dbang).* Although further explanation of this will be given, it should be said here that in Tibetan Buddhism *abhiseka* and all that it implies is the sphere of Vajrayana, which rests on understanding that Paramarthasatya is non-dual Buddhajnana.

Exclusive Rangtongpas dispute this and this raises some fundamental and far-reaching questions about the nature of Vajrayana. Shentongpas claim that to try to practice Vajrayana with an exclusive Rangtong view that rejects non-dual experience in the Shentong sense, is little more than to go through the motions. One can make merit and build up auspicious connections, but one can never enter into the practice properly.

The Chinese Tathagatagarbha schools describe Buddhajnana as the totality of all that is, which pervades every part of all that is in its totality.[5]

The RGV quotes from the verses of the *Jnanalokalamkarasutra* [JAAS] about how klesa, karma, and the skandhas arise in the nature of Mind as worlds arise in space in a way that is very suggestive of the Chinese Hua yen doctrine and, indeed, the RGVV even quotes the *Avatamsaka* where Buddhajnana in beings is compared to a whole universe enfolded in an atom. However, Tibetan commentators do not develop the theme, preferring to reserve it for their Vajrayana Tantric commentaries where Buddhajnana is finally described not only as the essence of beings but also of all things.

Generally speaking, however, the Shentong interpretation of RGV Tathagatagarbha doctrine treats Buddhajnana simply as the non-dual nature of Mind completely unobscured and endowed with its countless Buddha Qualities (*Buddhagunas*). What these Qualities are exactly is not clearly defined and the RGV and RGVV content themselves with a general discussion of their being inseparable even from the mind of an ordinary being, and of their being the basis for Buddha activity.

4.2   Inseparable Qualities

It is often said by Rangtongpas and Shentongpas alike that the RGV and Tathagatagarbha Sutras are difficult to understand. For Rangtongpas they are hard to understand because they make statements that seem to imply that all beings have inseparable Buddha Qualities (*Buddhaguna*) and that the inseparable Qualities are the Dharmakaya. It is, to them, obvious that ordinary beings do not have Buddha qualities and the Dharmakaya having countless Absolute uncompounded Buddha Qualities has no meaning within their frame of reference. So the question they ask themselves is, how these statements should be interpreted.

For Shentongpas on the other hand, the texts are difficult to understand because they discuss profound non-conceptual experience. In Shentong, the Buddha Qualities are taught to be inseparably present, not only in the Buddha Dharmakaya, but also in ordinary beings (albeit obscured). Difficult statements are taken literally, so that "all beings have inseparable Buddha Qualities," becomes even more astonishing than the shocking (albeit reasonable) revelations of the Prajnaparamita.

Hence, "inseparable" is a concept vital to the understanding of Shentong.

i. Inseparable Qualities and the Dharmakaya

That the *gunas* are inseparable dharmas is one of the four great paradoxes taught in the *Srimaladevisutra* [SMS] and discussed in RGV and RGVV [1.24]. The RGVV [1.25 phi 13] expands:

> Concerning the stainless Buddha Qualities, they are in beings even when they are at the stage of being definitely defiled. They are their inseparable Dharmata that is present as much before as after. This is why it is inconceivable.

Further in RGV [1.154–155]:

> Here there is nothing to remove and nothing to add. See Reality perfectly and from seeing Reality, liberation occurs.
> The Element is empty of the accidental which has the characteristic of being separable. It is not empty of the supreme dharmas which have the characteristic of being inseparable.

Besides the occurrence of these two verses in the RGV, Takasaki lists nine other occurrences of them.[6] For Rangtongpas these lines are obviously quite difficult to interpret: not so for Shentongpas who quote them frequently as encapsulating the essence of their view. Clearly, for them, "Reality," the "Element," and the "supreme inseparable Dharmas" refer to the Real (Paramarthasatya) and "the accidental" (stains) to the apparent (samvrti). Dolpopa explains that the Clear Light Nature of the Mind together with all its inherently existing, inseparable, spontaneous Qualities[7] is the Dharmata, the truly Existing Essence of all the Dharmas. It is non-compounded, primordial Peace, and Nirvana.

As we have seen, Thrangu Rimpoche's Rangtong explanation of Prajnaparamita maximizes its shock effect by introducing no Shentong element for the conceptual mind to latch on to, while Dolpopa goes a step further, following the Tathagatagarbha Sutras, by calling the direct experience of form and so forth that remains beyond all concepts, Absolute Form and so forth. He links the doctrine of the inseparable *Buddhagunas* to that of Absolute Form and so forth, so that according to him it is found in Prajnaparamita literature though, of course, it finds its fullest expression in the Tathagatagarbha Sutras and the Tantras. Dolpopa quotes [RC 330.2] the *Vimalaprabha (Dri ma med pa'i 'od)* and the *Sriprajnaparamita* to support this point and then expands on it [RC 347] quoting from the *Mahaparinirvanasutra* at length. He also quotes from the *Vajra Songs (Doha)* the Tantric doctrine of every samvrti phenomenon having its Absolute counterpart.

The important question of the exact connection between these Absolute Dharmas and the *Buddhagunas* is a subject that will eventually have to be pursued beyond the confines of this present work and into Tantric Shentong doctrine. It has to be admitted that although the Shentong understanding of the inseparable dharmas in the above quotation [RGV 1.154–155] is the Absolute Dharmas, the RGVV refers to them only as the inseparable *Buddhagunas* more countless than the countless sands of the Ganges. The connection between these qualities and the nature of the dharmata is, in fact, a central issue in the RGV.[8]

Since dharmata means the true or essential nature of Dharma or dharmas, Rangtongpas take it to be self-emptiness, and Shentongpas, non-dual Jnana [SKK a'280na]. The way the Buddha qualities are viewed depends on whether the dharmata is understood to be rangtong or Shentong. In the former case, the Buddha qualities are understood to mean the self-empty Buddha qualities, appearing dependent on causes and conditions in the samvrti world of beings. In the latter case, they are understood to be the Shentong Absolute Qualities that are not dependently-arising, not known by the conceptualizing veiled mind of ordinary beings, and that are inseparably of the nature of the Absolute (paramartha) Dharmata, the Buddhajnana itself. In other words, they are changeless, non-compounded, eternal, and primordially Existent.

The Shentong view accords with the Tathagatagarbha Sutras, which abound in statements reading far less ambiguously than those in the RGV.[9] Let us, however, compare how Rangtongpas and Shentongpas explain the quotation [RGV 1.154–155] given above and see how closely it reflects their differing approaches to Prajnaparamita discussed above and in previous chapters.

The Shentong explanation is that there is nothing to remove because the klesas do not exist (i.e. they are rangtong). There is nothing to add because the Buddha Qualities have been there inseparably from the beginning (i.e. they are Shentong).

The Rangtong explanation is that "nothing to remove" is the fact that since the self-nature of both persons and dharmas never existed they do not have to be removed. "Nothing to add" means that since all dharmas are self-empty by nature to realize this only requires a change in the way one looks at them: emptiness (i.e. the not-self of the person of the dharmas) is not a quality that has to be, as it were, added to them[10]. Rongton's commentary [p. 94] states:

> There is no object (dmigs pa) whatever [associated with the] stains, the two selves, that formerly existed and then has to be removed.
> Also in the Element there is not the slightest object [associated with] purification i.e. the two not-selves, that has to be newly added.

In the following verse the supreme dharmas of which the Element is not empty is commented on as follows:

> The Supreme Dharma object (dmigs pa) is not empty of the two not-selves, because the two not-selves have primordially been its dharma. Therefore, the Element is taught free from false denial.

Rongton continues [p. 95] as follows:

> It is taught that someone, who in this manner does not see the object with the sign (rgyu mtshan) of non-existence, and does see the properly revealed perfect truth (ji lta ba bzhin du gyur pa yang dag pa'i bden pa) by his jnana of equalness in which these two are not to be removed or added, is completely Enlightened into the equalness of all dharmas. Concerning this, others do not agree that the meaning of "the element is empty of the adventitious" (glo bur dag) means that it is empty of the object of the adventitious stains, i.e. the self (glo bur gyi dri ma'i dmigs pa bdag gis stong pa) but that it is literally empty of adventitious stains. This is not justifiable however, because it contradicts how, in the nine examples, the element dwells in the klesa sheaths. Also it does not agree with the lay-out of the stained Tathata.

The message here is that the element—the self-emptiness of the two selves—is not falsely denied because it is taught to have been primordially true. If my understanding is correct this is but a trivial point. It seems to be saying that the famous verse [RGV 1.155] means no more than that emptiness is not empty of the truth of its being empty of that of which it is empty. Not only is this an unnatural reading of the original verse but it is also not in accord with the RGVV. The RGVV explains the supreme dharmas by citing the SMS on the limitless Buddha Qualities. Then, without mentioning the two not-selves, it discusses instead the "remainder" implied by the term "Emptiness":

> Therefore, the Tathagatagarbha is empty of all the klesa sheaths that are separable and removable. It is not empty of the inseparable and irremovable inconceivable Buddha Dharmas beyond [i.e. more countless than] the [countless] sands of the Ganges.

and then:

> Something in which something else is absent is empty of that. If one proceeds then to look properly, what remains is ever present and known perfectly.

In Shentong terms "what remains" is obviously Buddhajnana and, indeed, the RGVV continues with:

> . . . Concerning this, without the Jnana of Absolute Emptiness it would not be possible to realize or to think of *('du bya)* the non-conceptual pure Dhatu.

Then the SMS is quoted to illustrate this point:

> The Tathagatagarbha's Jnana is the Tathagata's Emptiness Jnana . . .

This section is commented on again in section three, but suffice it to say that here the RGVV links the Buddhajnana with the non-conceptual Dhatu and Absolute Emptiness in a section that explains the knowledge of emptiness as looking at a remainder empty of something else. Furthermore, this Buddhajnana is identified as the Tathagatagarbha Jnana in beings. Even if one does not accept the Shentong explanation of this section of the RGVV one must admit that it is at least reasonable.

Professor Ruegg [*La Théorie* 347] comments on the difficulties of the Rangtong interpretation as follows:

> Nous venons de voir dans la section précédente que c'est parce que le Tathāgatadhātu a toujours par nature des dharma purs et inséparables qu'un vyavadānanimitta n'est pas à lui surajouter [RGVV 1,

154–155]; en outre, dans plusieurs passages du RGV et de son com-
mentaire cités plus haut nous avons rencontré des allusions à une
connexion entre le Dharmakāya et ses qualités. Cette théorie est
assez remarquable car même si une connexion du rūpakāya avec
des attributs est aisément compréhensible, une connexion du
Dharmakāya absolu et impensable avec des qualités est sans doute
plus insolite.

His point here is that *Buddhagunas* are universally associated with the
manifest form-kayas of the Buddha, which arise dependent on the vision
and karma of beings. However, it is not quite as unusual as Professor Ruegg
implies for the *Buddhagunas* to be associated with the Dharmakaya, for
example, it is common in the Tathagatagarbha Sutras. Nonetheless, there is
weighty opposition to such a view and its opponents have to find an alternative explanation for RGV [1.154–155].

Gyaltsab in his *Dartik* [p. 152] gives a very similar explanation to
Rongton with an added emphasis on the necessity for not clinging to the
two not-selves, which would cause one to fall into the extreme of denying
the relative (samvrti). He then adds the following criticism of the Shentong
interpretation:

> . . . to accept the teaching of the vase being empty of vase
> etc. as samvrti self-emptiness and absolute reality to be the truly
> existing Absolute that is empty of other is the worst of all expla-
> nations including the non-Buddhist false assertions, and false deni-
> als.

When Gyaltsab says "non-Buddhist false denial" he means that to
deny the existence of samvrti is to deny the causes and effects of karma.
This reflects his belief that Shentongpas deny karma—the foundation of the
whole of the Buddha's teaching. When he says his "non-Buddhist false assertion" this reflects his belief that Shentongpas are hypostasizing an
Absolute.[11]

We have seen how Rangtongpas interpret RGV [1.154–55], but how do
they interpret the RGVV explanations and other references to the inseparable
qualities more countless than the countless sands of the Ganges? Gyaltsab
makes only the following comment:

> The inconceivable Buddha qualities beyond [i.e. more countless
> than] the [countless] sands of the Ganges, not empty of (or by) self
> nature, are inseparable and will not see separation.

According to Gyaltsab's view "inseparable" means that the Buddha
qualities are inseparable from the fruit, that is, they arise at Enlightenment.
It is not clear what he means here by "not empty of (or by) self nature" but

normally his view is that, although they are empty of inherent existence, they are not empty of their conventional nature (hence the famous maxim, a vase is empty of self-nature but not empty of vase).

Rongton [p. 96] explains as follows:

> The meaning of "not empty of the supreme dharmas" is that it is not empty of the supreme dharmas of the not-selves of the dharmas and the person. It is not justifiable to say it means not empty of the powers etc.

And:

> The supreme dharmas of the powers etc. that are pure by nature *(rang bzhin rnam dag)* and pervade all beings is intended because "Beings are the perfect Buddha's dharmata like a hidden trea-sure . . ." [RGV 4.2] and "Enlightenment holds all beings . . ." [RGV 2]. Why is the dharmata called the supreme Dharma? See the small commentary[?]:
>
> There is no dharma superior to the dharmata. Here the perfect dharmata is its nature and its qualities which are pure by nature. By meditation, taking the perfect dharmata as one's object, the qualities of the powers etc. arise so the dharmata is called pure by nature and the supreme Dharma.

Although Rongton's view is not entirely clear here—especially as to what "pure by nature" means—elsewhere he explains that the Buddhajnana and *gunas* are present in some sense in beings as a potential *(nus pa)* or latent faculty and that this reaches full development at Buddhahood. Thus, the dharmata or the true nature of beings has two aspects *(a)* the self-emptiness and *(b)* the jnana *gunas*. Although Gyaltsab's view is similar, he does not express it in quite the same way. Therefore, the exact degree to which Rongton's and Gyaltsab's view are in accord has yet to be established. Since we learn from elsewhere that Rongton understands, as Gyalt-sab does, that the *Buddhagunas* are compounded, dependently arising (i.e. self-empty) phenomena, one assumes that he accepts that Buddhajnana is also self-empty. This point needs further research.

Shentongpas oppose this view with powerful arguments backed up by the scriptures. For example, it is taught in the Mahayana and even in the Hinayana Buddhist[12] traditions that the Buddha is eternal and non-compounded and yet compassionately acting in the world.[13] How could compassion and the power to act in the world be eternal and non-compounded if they were not of the very nature of Absolute Reality? If one argues (as many Buddhists have done over the centuries) that the Buddha's mind and qualities are momentary and dependently arising (i.e. are compounded phenomena), and that He is said to be eternal merely because the continuity is never broken,[14] there is no difference between the use of the term "eternal" for the nature of the Buddha and the use of the term "impermanent" for the nature of samsara, which is also an unbroken continuity.[15] Thus, one has reduced the doctrine, which is presented as profound and difficult to understand, to nothing but a shift in the usage of the term "permanent."

On the other hand, if the qualities of the Buddha are non-compounded and eternal, then there is no question of potential and development. They are either present in beings already or they never will be. Hence, the Tathagatagarbha doctrine states that in fact beings do have these Qualities, and that they are intrinsic to a being's Nature.

The Shentong view that Buddhajnana and *Gunas* are non-compounded seems (in their view at least) to be confirmed in SNS [III 3]:

If one is not free from the mark *(mtshan ma, laksana)* of compoundedness one does not become free from the bondage of marks when seeing reality. Not being free from the bondage of marks, one is also not free from the bondage of inferior births *(gnas ngan)*. If one is not free from those two bondages, one does not succeed in seeing reality and attaining the nirvana of supreme bliss.

ii. The Concept of Uncompoundedness

In Shentong terms, the Dharmakaya is uncompounded because it does not arise from causes and conditions. Therefore it is not subject to arising, remaining, and passing away. Furthermore, to have the qualities of wisdom, compassion, and power [RGV 1.5] does not contradict uncompoundedness. Thus, the Dharmakaya can be both uncompounded and have Qualities. This is a difficult point to understand and has to be carefully explained. The key is that true uncompoundedness is beyond the conceptual duality of compoundedness and uncompoundedness. Khenpo Tsultrim makes this point[16] when explaining SKK [hum 43b]:

snang bcas snang med dam dngos po dang dngos med gnyis car las grol bas 'dus ma byas dngos don dam bden pa'i 'dus ma byas zhes bya zhing
Since it is freedom from both appearance and non-appearance, existence and non-existence, the real *(dngos)* uncompoundedness is called the Absolute Reality (Paramarthasatya) uncompoundedness.

The *Sandhinirmocana* Sutra states that the inexpressible Dharmata is called "uncompounded" *('dus ma byas)* in order to enlighten others, but in fact neither compoundedness nor uncompoundedness exist; they are merely concepts [SNS 1.3]

Rangtongpas argue that it is the self-emptiness of persons and dharmas that is uncompounded, not the jnana and *gunas*. In their view uncompounded, non-dependently arising qualities such as knowledge, love, and power and so forth, are not merely inconceivable, that is, not conceptually understandable, but also impossibilities. Furthermore, they insist that even the Buddha's Dharmakaya arises as a result of causes and conditions. Therefore, it is not uncompounded in every sense of the term. For these reasons references to the Buddha's uncompoundedness in the scriptures have to be carefully interpreted. Kongtrul discusses this problem in his commentary [32b], quoting as follows from Rongton's commentary [6a.1 on RGV 1.5]:

> *spyir 'dus ma byas kyi sgras bstan pa la bzhi ste. rgyu rkyen gyis skye 'gag yod med dang. las nyon gyi skye 'gag yod med dang. yid kyi lus kyi skye ba dang. bsam gyis mi khyab pa'i 'chi ba'i 'gag pa yod med dang. gdul bya la skye 'gag du snang ba yod med la 'dus ma byas su byas pa'o. de las skabs 'dir sangs rgyas chos sku gdul bya la skye 'gag tu snang ba med pa'i 'dus ma byas yin pa rong ston bzhed do. des na 'dus ma byas pa'i yon tan dang ldan par go dgos kyi 'dus ma byas su khas blang na mkhyen brtse nus ldan dang 'gal ba'ang shes par bya'o.*

> In general, four [uses of the term] "uncompoundedness" are taught: whether or not [a thing] arises and ceases from causes and conditions, whether or not [it] arises and ceases from karma and klesa, whether or not [it] arises as a mental body and ceases by the inconceivable death transfer, and whether or not [it] arises and ceases in the vision of beings to be trained.

Rongton argues that, although, according to RGV [1.5, 1.6], the Buddha has the quality of uncompoundedness, one should understand that, to accept that Buddha is uncompounded in the first sense, contradicts "having knowledge, love, and power." Thus, we see that Rongton takes it as given that knowledge, love, and power are compounded. In other words, for him, if the Buddha were uncompounded in the first sense (i.e. non-arisen from causes and conditions), He would not have these qualities. Since He does have them [RGV 1.4–8], the sense in which He is uncompounded in this context has to be specified. Rongton explains that the Buddha's uncompoundedness refers only to the non-arising of the Buddha's Dharmakaya in the vision of beings.

Thus, for him, neither the Dharmakaya nor the form-kayas are uncompounded in the first sense, for both arise from causes and conditions, and both are uncompounded in the second and the third sense, because neither arise from karma and klesa or suffer the inconceivable death transfer. Therefore, in this particular context, the fourth sense—not arising and ceasing in the vision of beings—is singled out as a special quality of the Dharmakaya [RGV 1.6].

RGVV [1.6] can be read in such a way as to support this view; it explains that since compounded means that which arises, remains and passes away, and since the Buddha does not have these characteristics, He is uncompounded and this should be seen to be referring to His Dharmakaya *(chos kyi skus rab tu phye ba blta bar bya'o)*. Nonetheless, it is standard Buddhist doctrine that all compounded phenomena are impermanent and the RGVV does not specify that a particular sense of uncompounded is meant here. Thus, a Shentong reading is also quite natural, that is, the Buddha together with His Qualities is uncompounded. The Shentong argument is a powerful one. How can the Buddha be a refuge for beings if He and/or His Qualities are compounded and subject to destruction?

Although it is true that RGV [1.74] adduces as one of the reasons for the Buddha's permanence, causes engendered on the path, which implies that the Buddha is compounded from causes—Shentongpas maintain that this refers merely to the apparent (samvrti) aspect of the form-kayas. Thus, Shentongpas do not say that there are no apparent, dependently-arising Buddha qualities or that the form-kayas, for example, do not occur in the vision of beings in a dependently-arising way. Indeed, they are caused and conditioned by, among other things, the acts of the Bodhisattvas on their path to Enlightenment and the karma and klesa of beings. These apparent form-kayas manifest because of or based on the Dharmakaya's Absolute inseparable Qualities, but this is not to say the Dharmakaya and the Absolute Qualities are caused. In Shentong terms the essence of those apparent form-kayas is the Absolute Form-Kayas that are the inseparable, causeless, spontaneous Qualities of the Buddha.[17]

Thus, Shentongpas do not say that beings have the Buddha qualities in the apparent sense, that is, in the eyes of ordinary beings. No Buddhist would accept that, since that would be to deny the Four Noble Truths. Rather they say they have the Absolute Buddha Qualities in the Absolute (Paramartha) sense, that is, it is what is Ultimately Real or True behind all the sham and is what the Buddhas and Bodhisattvas see [RGV 1.13]. It is in this sense that Kongtrul [SKK hum 325ba] explains that the *Bodhipaksikadharmas* are not merely partially or vaguely present in ordinary beings; they are completely present and included in the non-defiled Dhatu *(zag med dbyings)*.

iii. Inseparability and the Spontaneous Existence of the Buddha Qualities

The Shentong view that all beings primordially have all the inseparable Buddha Qualities raises a number of interesting points, not least among which is: in what sense are the Absolute Buddha Qualities inseparable and in what sense do they exist?

As previous chapters stipulated, inseparability is a key concept for Shentongpas. It should be understood in connection with the Madhyamaka dialectic. The Madhyamaka dialectic destroys the notion that qualities and the things they qualify are separate entities. In conventional terms, without qualities nothing exists; qualities that do not belong to a thing that is qualified do not exist. As is explained in the *Madhyamakakarikas* [chapter 5 verse 1, Inada's translation]:

> *nākāśam vidyate kiṃ citpūrvamākāśalakṣaṇāt/alakṣaṇaṃ prasa-jyeta syātpūrvaṃ yadilakṣaṇāt.*
> Prior to any spatial characteristic space cannot exist, if it can exist prior to any characteristics then, necessarily, it falls into the error of (imputing) a space without characteristics.

The same applies for all other qualities. Thus, quality and the thing qualified arise in mutual dependence on each other and each is empty in itself. This seems to contradict the notion of the Buddha truly Existing and having inseparable Qualities. However, to say the Buddha truly Exists and is inseparable from His Qualities, in fact, can only be understood in the light of the Madhyamaka doctrine; therefore, Shentong claims to be the Great Madhyamaka.

Before one can say the Buddha exists, one must examine the whole concept of existing, which is what the Madhyamaka does. Having established that anything that is conceivable does not truly exist, one is left with only the inconceivable.[18] Nagarjuna explains [MKK chap. 5 v.8]:

> *astitvaṃ ye tu paśyanti nāstitvaṃ cālpabuddhayaḥ/bhāvānāṃ te na paśyanti draṣṭavyopaśamaṃ śivam.*
> Those of low intelligence (i.e. inferior insight) who see only existence and non-existence of things cannot perceive the wonderful quiescence of things.

If the inconceivable "wonderful quiescence of things" were nothing at all (mengag) it would be conceivable. Therefore, it is not nothing at all (mengag). If it were something that could be qualified in any way as having any quality, it would again be conceivable as that which had this or that quality.[19] It would arise in dependence on that quality and would perish with the separation from the quality. However, the Buddha is said to be inseparable from His Qualities. There is no Buddha apart from His Qualities and those Qualities are Buddha. Since the very presence of those Qualities is evidence of the presence of the Buddha, Buddha means those Qualities. One might argue that if many qualities are attributed to the Buddha, then they are separable from each other as distinct qualities and, like the heat and light of a flame, they are conceptually divisible even if not actually divisible. There is no objection to this in Shentong terms. All the divisions into quality and qualified that we conceptually make all the time are merely conventions. They are always merely conceptual divisions and the same applies to the Qualities of the Buddha. Fire has the qualities of heat and burning. Where there is heat and burning there is fire. There is no fire separate from the qualities of heat and burning. Such notions are merely conceptual, conventional divisions. In reality fire is the inseparable qualities of heat and burning and nothing more or less. Heat cannot in fact be divided from burning. Heat is burning and burning is heat. According to the Shentongpas, the Madhyamaka refutes separable but not inseparable qualities. Therefore, although in terms of the world the Buddha has numberless, measureless, and inexhaustable qualities, in fact all these qualities are none other than the changeless, uncompounded Dharmata, or the nondual Jnana, which is the true Nature of all things. Thus, to speak of the numberless, inseparable Qualities of the Buddha is to speak of the true Nature (Dharmata) of everything.

This leads on directly to the ideas of the Chinese Cha'an schools that the Buddha is the here and now. He is the Essence or the true Nature of every experience, when it is purified of the conceptual tendency to divide the quality and the thing qualified. In other words, the vividness of experience is the Buddha, but as soon as there is the conceptual tendency to divide quality and qualified, see-er and seen and so forth (*dharma/dharmin, chos/chos can*, literally, quality and quality-haver, or *yul dang yul can*, object and object-haver), the experience loses its directness and vividness and becomes completely obscured by concepts.

If the inseparable Qualities are uncompounded and they do not exist in the ordinary sense, even for a moment, what is their manner of existing? It is called "spontaneous" *(lhun gyis grub pa)*.[20] Dolpopa [RC 193] explains the Parinispanna as existing in a spontaneous manner *(lhun grub)* and that *lhun grub* means free from momentariness *(skad cig dang bral ba)* [RC 127].[21] Then he explains [RC 176.5] that the third Dharmacakra distinguishes what is spontaneous *(lhun grub)* and what is adventitious *(glo bur ba)*.

"Adventitious" here is a translation of the Sanskrit word *"agantuka"* meaning [MW] anything added or adhering, incidental, accidental, adventitious (such as pleasure, pain or ornament), arriving of its own accord, stray (as cattle). The Tibetan word *"glo bur ba"* has the same range of meanings. In colloquial Tibetan, however, it generally means suddenness as of accidents or chance events; in Dharma terms, it means the opposite of what is of the essence of something—like stray clouds in the sky that come and go by chance, not being of the essence of the sky. In Shentong terms, whereas the essence of beings is the spontaneously existing inseparable Buddha Qualities, their stains or veils are adventitious [RGV 1.63]:

> The Mind's Nature, Clear Light, is changeless like space. The adventious stains of desire and so on that arise from wrong conceptions never trouble it.

Dolpopa [RC 321.3] explains in more detail that the thirty-seven Parinispanna *Bodhipaksikadharmas* are pure of paratantra and parikalpita (the *Bodhipaksikadharmas* being the *Jnanadevi*(s)), while the thirty-seven *Bodhipaksikadharmas* of the path are samvrti, compounded, and adventitious *(glo bur ba)*. They are removed and the spontaneous *(lhun grub)* ones are revealed. They are the Clear Light Nature *(rang bzhin 'od gsal)* and spontaneous *(lhun grub)*. In a list of alternative names for the Paramarthasatya, Dolpopa [RC 380] includes spontaneous Nature *(rang bzhin lhun grub)* and naturally present gotra *(rang bzhin gnas rigs)*.

Kongtrul [SKK hum 43b] gives the following explanation:

> *snying po de nyid glo bur gyi skyon nam dri ma thams cad kyis stong zhing bla med yon tan gyi chos rnams kyis mi stong par lhun grub tu ldan pa'i phyir*
> That *Garbha* itself is empty of all contingent faults or stains but not empty of all the supreme Quality Dharmas because it has them spontaneously.

Khenpo Tsultrim[22] gives the example of gold ore having the qualities of gold spontaneously *(lhun grub tu yod)*. In some ways "spontaneous" is a misleading translation since it normally has the connotation of action or process that occurs without external stimuli. *"Lhun grub"* in colloquial Tibetan normally implies automatic, self-caused, or spontaneous actions or processes. However, in this context "spontaneous" is not meant to suggest any action, process, or cause, but simply—to take the Shorter Oxford English Dictionary [SOED] definition—"the having [of] a self-contained . . . origin." In this context, it means without origin in the special sense of being primordially Existent. Perhaps "primordially existent" gives a better "feel" to the meaning of the term, but there are other words in Tibetan that are more literally translated as primordially Existent, as there are also for "Self-arisen." Another possible translation is "naturally" in the loose sense of effortlessly, without contrivance or artifice. This is very close to the meaning of *"lhun grub,"* but unfortunately there are already many words in Tibetan that translate as "naturally." Thus, I have decided to use "spontaneous" in order to distinguish *"lhun grub"* from these other terms. It is sometimes translated as "Self-existent" which is, perhaps, a rather free translation though capturing a certain feel of the term.

Generally speaking, because the Rangtongpas do not accept the true Existence of inseparable Qualities, their explanations of the RGV Tathagatagarbha doctrine are more complex than the Shentong. Shentongpas center all aspects of the Buddha's doctrine on one crucial point—the changeless, primordially existent Nitartha Absolute Reality with all the inseparable Qualities. The Rangtongpas, on the other hand, are ever careful to maintain many distinctions between the samvrti and paramartha factors in the base, path, and fruit of Enlightenment. Thus, from the Shentong point of view, the essential message of the RGV is the need for reliance on the power of the Enlightened Mind complete with all its inseparable Qualities in order that it emerge. Whereas from the Rangtong point of view, it is the need to develop the Enlightened mind so that through the right conditions, such as meditation on emptiness and the accumulation of merit, the qualities associated with Enlightenment might arise.

In a way, the Shentong use of the term "Exist" in the context of the Buddha Qualities, is returning to the everyday, nonanalytical use of the term. Although it affirms the Buddha Qualities as truly Existing, it does not do so in a conceptually analyzable way.[23] *Sandhinirmocanasutra* [SNS chapter 2:3] explains that a man who has never tasted sweetness can not deduce or appreciate sweetness and that in the same way the Absolute is the sphere only of the signless, intuitive awareness *(so so rang rig mtshan med spyod yul,* SKT. *pratyatmavedya-animittagocara).*

In practical terms, to affirm the Absolute Buddha Qualities has the function of inspiring faith and confidence [RGV 5.8–9]. In intimating or suggesting something, it is more akin to poetry than philosophy.

It seems that this is the fundamental point of a Shentong as opposed to a Rangtong interpretation of Tathagatagarbha doctrine and the RGV. The Rangtong approach is logically analytical; the Shentong is poetic and intuitive. The language of art and poetry suggests something to the reader through linking in with his/her personal experience and intuition. In the same way, the language of the Tathagatagarbha Sutras makes sense to the meditator who has some experience or intuition of that to which it refers.

4.3 Buddha Activity

Not only are the inseparable Buddha Qualities described as "spontaneous" *(anabhoga, lhun gyis grub)*, but Buddha Activity is also [RGVV 1.7]:

> *de ltar de bzhin gshegs pa de nyid kyi phyir 'dus ma byas shing 'jug pa med pa'i mtshan nyid las kyang lhun gyis grub par sangs rgyas kyi mdzad pa thams cad 'khor ba ji srid kyi mthar thug par thog pa med cing rgyun mi 'chad par rab tu 'jug go.*
>
> In this way the Tathagata for this very [reason] though characteristically uncompounded and non-engaging, spontaneously engages in all the deeds of a Buddha until the ultimate end of existence (i.e. the world) completely, continuously and without interruption.

Then a little further on it quotes the *Tathagatagunajnanacintyavisayavataranirdesa:*

> Manjusri, the Tathagata does not conceptualize or think, but engages spontaneously *(anabhogena, lhun gyis grub par)* and conceptionlessly in natural deeds in each place as appropriate.

Here "spontaneous" is used chiefly to indicate action without premeditation or concept. Non-conceptual action is defined [RGV 5.14] as action in which the subtle "knowledge veils" are absent:

> *'khor gsum rnam par rtog pa gang. de ni shes bya'i sgrib par 'dod*
> The knowledge veils are held to be the concepts *(vikalpa)* of the three circles *(trimandala).*

The *trimandala* is a standard term for the subtle conceptual distinctions of actor, action, and acted upon. Ordinary beings can only conceive of action as an agent acting on or through something and yet true knowledge of the Buddha's spontaneous Activity is veiled by this apparent (samvrti) knowledge of ordinary beings.

The RGV [chapter 4] expands at length on how the Buddha does not stir and yet the apparent (samvrti) kayas manifest for the benefit of beings based on the inseparable Qualities and spontaneous Activity of the Buddha's Body—like space—Speech—like an echo—and Mind—like a Wishfulfilling Jewel. The RGVV [1.7] then expands from the *Jnanalokalankarasutra:*

> Manjusri, the Unborn and Unceasing is a synonym for the Tathagata, the Arhat, the Perfectly Enlightened Buddha.

The RGVV explains that this teaches, first of all, that the Tathagata is uncompounded. Immediately after this, nine examples are given, beginning with the one of Indra's image reflected in the spotless lapis lazuli *(vaid-urya)* ground. These examples all make the same point [RGVV 1.7]:

> Manjusri, likewise the Tathagata, the Arhat, the Perfectly Enlight-ened Buddha does not stir, does not think, does not contrive, does not conceptualize, does not conceive in a dualistic manner, is con-ceptionless, is without dualistic conceptions, without thought, without mental constructions. He is cooled, without birth, without ceasing. He is invisible, inaudible, unsmellable, untastable, intan-gible, without characteristics, indiscernable, and not a discernable object.

The RGVV explains that this passage means that the Buddha's activity is free from thought and so forth, and since He is peace—one in whom all con-ceptual contrivance has ceased—it is taught that He is "spontaneous." The rest of the text teaches, by presenting examples, that through the Tathata of all dharmas being Perfect Enlightenment, it is not realized by other condi-tions. Having taught the sixteen aspects of the Tathagata's Enlightenment, finally it teaches:

> Manjusri, all dharmas are like that by nature; all dharmas are Per-fect Enlightenment. Also seeing that in beings, impure, not free from stain, faulted, there is the Dharmadhatu, He has love for be-ings and this is known as "engaging in the Tathagata's Great Com-passion."

There is an implied connection between the spontaneous Activity and the inseparable Qualities but the RGV and RGVV do not elaborate on this. In RGV [chapter 3] where the sixty-four qualities of liberation and maturation are described in some detail, they are found to be the apparent (samvrti) qualities of the Body, Speech, and Mind of the Buddha's Nirmanakaya and, unlike in the *Mahaparinirvanasutra* [MPNS], no real attempt is made in the RGV to link these qualities to the Absolute inseparable Qualities. For the development of this doctrine, one must look to the Tantras, where there are Absolute equivalents for all the samvrti signs and marks of a Buddha.

In Shentong terms, the apparent (samvrti) qualities of the Buddha ap-pear in the distorted vision of ordinary beings to whom it looks as if the Buddha is thinking, talking, and acting in a dualistic way. The *Ratna-gotravibhaga* [RGV 2.52] gives the example of a jewel on a colored cloth, arguing that just as the colored light, emanating from the jewel on account of the cloth is nothing to do with the jewel, so the apparent acting, talking, and thinking of the Buddha are not the real Buddha. He appears that way due to the coming together of three principal conditions.[24] Khenpo Tsultrim explains that the main condition is the presence of the Buddha's Dharmakaya, which is the power behind everything like the substance of the jewel. The other conditions are the formulation of powerful intentions *(pranidhana, smon lam)* by the Bodhisattvas on the path to Enlightenment. An example of such a formulation is Amitabha's vow to create a pure land into which beings may be born by remembering his name on death. Khenpo Tsultrim compares such an intention to the shape of the jewel. The third main condition is the faith and wholesome mental tendencies of beings, which he compares to the colors on the cloth. When these three main conditions are present, the Dharmakaya manifests as the samvrti form-kayas, which are not the real Buddha. Likewise the colored light reflected from the jewel, is not the jewel and not of the jewel's true nature. In Shentong terms, however, the primary concern of Tathagatagarbha doctrine is not with this kind of dualistic manifestation of Buddha activity, but with the power of the Dharmakaya itself, which is the underlying Reality behind it. In some ways, one might argue that Buddha activity is not action or activity at all, since the very words "action" and "activity" suggest an agent performing an action with or on something or somebody else. Since the Buddha's spontaneous Action, which is discussed here, is not like that, it is inconceivable. Even so, it acts on beings with complete accuracy, according to their level of understanding, and perfectly in accord with their characters.

The important point about the Buddha's Qualities and Activity being uncompounded and "spontaneous" from the Shentong point of view is that the Dharmata is not inert. It is active and functions to bring about effects.

This concept of Absolute Reality being a knowing, feeling, dynamic force that is the very essence of our being and our universe is vehemently rejected by many sections of the traditional Buddhist community. The reason no doubt is that it is too suggestive of a theistic principle; Buddhism has traditionally held itself aloof from theistic formulations of religious doctrine. Nevertheless, as Khenpo Tsultrim aptly points out, if Buddhism is fundamentally about discovering truth, the mere fact that a certain doctrine sounds like someone else's is no rationale for rejecting it out of hand. However, a major preoccupation of Buddhist scholars over the centuries has been to maintain a clear distinction between themselves and theistic religions. Interestingly, this tendency continues as Buddhism spreads to the West.

Buddhism attracts two quite different types of person in the West. There are those who are attracted by it as a religion; often such people feel that the major world religions are at heart about the same ineffable Reality, which is and has been recognized intuitively, though expressed differently, by humankind through the ages. Then there are those who are attracted to Buddhism because it appeals to their analytical mind, either in scientific or moral terms, without offending their deep suspicion of the intuitive and mystical side of religion. For this latter group the hallmark of Buddhism is its down-to-earth rationalism and absence of mysticism, which distinguish it from theism. The former group might be more cautious about how theism is defined, rejecting certain formulations of it but prepared to consider others. As well as these two groups, there are yet others who are attracted to Buddhism because, for them, it marries the intuitive with the rational in a way they feel does justice to both. As we shall see in the next section, this division of interest in Buddhism in the West is reflected in the rangtong-Shentong controversy in the Tibetan tradition.

Before moving on to discuss how the relationship of faith to analytical investigation is conceived in the different Tibetan traditions, there is one important point to consider. If the Buddha's inseparable Qualities are present in beings as their True Nature (Dharmata) and if the action of that Dharmata is spontaneous and in no way separable from the action of the Enlightened Buddha, there is a dynamic aspect to the continuity between the nature of beings and of Buddhas. The wisdom and compassion and so forth, that start to emerge on the Path are actually the manifestation of the activity of the Enlightened Buddha. Faith, the urge to renounce, aspiration, and so on acquire a special meaning since they are as much the activity of the Buddha Dharmakaya as the awakening of awareness in an ordinary being. The teachings of the Buddha awaken an Awareness that is somehow inherent within beings. It is because that Awareness is their nature that they recognize truth when they hear it. It is why they develop an aversion to their mundane, conceptual world so fraught with suffering. If they did not have that inner Awareness with which to compare their present state, neither aversion nor aspiration to freedom from it could arise. According to the Shentong interpretation, the Ratnagotravibhaga makes this point when it explains that without the Buddha Element (Dhatu)[25] there would be no aversion to samsara and aspiration for nirvana. The RGVV expands on this by identifying the Dhatu as the Tathagatagarbha and RGV [1.41] identifies it as the "Gotra" (see section on Gotra in this present work).

Mikyo Dorje explains this in his *dBu ma gzhan stong sgron me* [2a–2b], which is a treatise about the Shentong that draws on the RGV as its main textual source. He distinguishes two aspects of Buddhajnana (referred to as "ever-present Jnana of realization"). One aspect is the ever present Buddha Nature and the other is a quality of mind that is undifferentiable from this, which influences the deluded mind in such a way as to make it give up its delusions.

There are two thrusts to this giving up. There is the conceptual effort on the part of beings and the non-conceptual influence of the Buddhajnana. Maybe this is what we call "intuition"—those flashes of insight or understanding that come to us when the mind is totally relaxed.

Mikyo Dorje explains *("dBu ma gzhan stong")* [13b ff]:

'dus ma byas de bzhin gshegs snying dang. chos dbyings rang bzhin rnam par dag pa'i bden pa dang byin rlabs kyis thog med kyi tshe na rgyu rkyen med kyang. med bzhin pa'i 'dus byas glo bur gyi dri ma nyid kyis sdug bsngal la skyo ba dang. myang 'das la phyogs pa dang smon par byed do.

Although the uncompounded Tathagatagarbha and the Reality *(satya)* and influence of the pure-by-nature Dharmadhatu are primordially without causes and conditions, by means of the non-existent (literally, nothing-like) compounded adventitious stains themselves, weariness with suffering and aspiration in the direction of nirvana are produced.

Mikyo Dorje makes a subtle point here. Aversion to suffering and longing for nirvana are, generally speaking, conceptual processes. Nevertheless, such processes can only be set in motion by the uncompounded Tathagatagarbha, which is inseparable from the purity (i.e. unspoiled nature) of Reality—here referred to as the "Dharmadhatu"—and the "influence" or active presence *(adhistana)* of the inseparable Qualities.

Khenpo Tsultrim compares it to waking from a dream. There is a haunting awareness of an awakened state that makes one realize that one is dreaming. It is this haunting awareness that sets the conceptual process of waking-up in motion. One starts to think thoughts like: "This is a dream, I'd better wake-up." Without an awareness of the awakened state, however, such thoughts would be impossible. Incidentally, although concepts such as, "This is a dream. I must wake-up," are useful, they actually have nothing to do with the awakened state itself. Once one is awake one does not need such thoughts at all. In other words one stays awake conceptionlessly.

Thus, in Shentong terms, our own Buddha-nature, the haunting awareness that impels us towards Enlightenment and the spontaneous activity of the Buddhas which is intent on waking us, are not three things but one and the same Buddhajnana.

This accords with the *Avatamsaka* doctrine in which it is said that Enlightenment occurs at the very beginning of the path. Zen schools that are based on the *Avatamsaka* emphasize this initial awakening to Enlightenment and orientate their whole practice to intensifying this initial experience and then to stabilizing it.[26] Tibetan schools emphasize oral instructions by the Guru, which give the disciple a direct experience of the Nature of the Mind. The disciple's main task from then on is to learn to let his/her Mind rest in its own Nature. These doctrines and techniques are all directly related to the doctrine in the RGV, SMS and other Tathagatagarbha Sutras, that the very urge to Enlightenment is a function of Enlightenment itself.

Chapter 5

Means of Apprehending Absolute Reality

5.1   Faith

Generally, in Buddhism, faith means the faculty to appreciate, aspire to, and realize the good and wholesome. It is not blind faith *(mig med pa'i dad pa)*—a term used for blind clinging to superstition and dogma; this is never advocated as a proper means to liberation. The problem is that for those weak in both faith and reason, the terms "faith" and "intuition" become debased. They are often clung to as a means of dismissing reason; thus, they obstruct the understanding of either rangtong or Shentong.

i. Faith and Buddhajnana

The exact meaning and significance of faith (Skt. *sraddha*)[1] in Buddhism must be approached with caution. In the Pali canon (the *Anguttara-nikaya, Samyutta-nikaya* etc.) it is often mentioned as one of the five "*indriya*" and so forth. In the *Visuddhimagga* [767 fn. 31] it is mentioned in association with impermanence (*anicca*), which is the means of entry to the signless liberation (*animitta-vimokka*)—one of the three gateways to liberation. In other words, true faith is the faculty of trust that allows one to let go into one's experience. Hence it leads to the signless liberation in which there is nothing to hold on to. In Shentong terms, complete signlessness means "Buddhajnana." Therefore, a clear connection between faith and Jnana is indicated here.

The RGVV [1.1] explains the fourth Vajra-Base, Element (Dhatu), from the *Anunatvapurnatvanirdesa:*

> Sariputra, this subject matter (*artha, don*), the sphere of the Tathagata, is the sphere of experience/activity of the Tathagata. Sariputra, not even one of the Sravakas and Pratyeka Buddhas can know, see or examine this subject matter by means of their own (special) wisdom (prajna, *shes rab*), so no need to mention ordinary immature beings unless they realize it through faith in the Tathagata. Sariputra, Absolute Reality (Paramartha, *don dam par*) is to be realized through faith. Sariputra, that which is called Absolute Reality is a synonym for the Element (Dhatu, *khams*) of beings. Sariputra, the Element of Beings is a synonym for Tathagatagarbha. Sariputra, Tathagatagarbha is a synonym for Dharmakaya.

Thus, the "sphere" that Buddhas realize, that is, the Dharmakaya, although not accessible through the wisdom (prajna) of Sravakas and Pratyeka Buddhas, is accessible to ordinary beings through "faith." Indeed, it seems to be the only means. However, concerning the Dharmakaya RGV [1.7] says:

> Because it is what is to be realized through self-originated wisdom (*svayambhujnana, rang byung ye shes*), it is not something to be realized through other conditions.

RGVV [1.8] explains:

> Thus this Buddha that is the wondrous and inconceivable (*bsam du med pa*) sphere (*yul*) perfectly awakens to its inexpressible/undemonstrable nature by self-originated wisdom (*svayambhujnana, rang byung ye shes*), and this it does itself, without a teacher (*slob dbon med pa*) or hearing through others.

Since it is taught that the Dharmakaya is realized both through faith and self-originated Wisdom (*svayambhujnana*), the question is, what exactly they are, and how they relate to each other. Also, when the RGV and RGVV say that other conditions, such as teaching by others, do not bring about realization, what does this mean? Buddha, Dharma, and Sangha are integral to Buddhism; there is no question of there being no need for a teacher. RGV [5.1–15] places the value of learning from others, second only to Wisdom (prajna), which alone can remove veils. Furthermore, the Buddha's power is explained as His power to destroy the suffering and klesa of others through His wisdom and compassion. It cannot, therefore, be the case that teachers are not necessary. Therefore, what is meant when realization is said to not depend on conditions? There must be, from the above quotations, a connection between faith, self-originated wisdom, and unconditioned realization.

Another term for self-originated wisdom (*rang byung ye shes*) in the RGV and RGVV is "self-awareness" (*pratyatmavedya, so so rang gis rig*). Self-awareness (*pratyatmavedya*) is a controversial term in Mahayana Buddhism. Shentongpas understand it to be Buddhajnana, the nondual, uncompounded, Clear Light Nature-of-Mind, which is not dualistic consciousness (vijnana), but awareness without perceiving and perceived aspects. Unfortunately the term "self-awareness" and its Sanskrit and Tibetan equivalents contain an ambiguity, causing them to sound dualistic.

Since ordinary beings function conceptually within the confines of dualistic consciousness (vijnana), one might wonder how self-aware, nondual Buddhajnana could in any way be accessible to them. Although any attempt to understand it conceptually is doomed to failure by definition, according to the quotation above, it is more accessible to the faith of an ordinary being than to the wisdom (prajna) of a Sravaka or Pratyeka Buddha.

Writers, such as Dolpopa, and contemporary Lamas, such as Khenpo Tsultrim, who comment on the Tantras continually, link faith, special oral instructions that point to the direct experience of the Nature of Mind, and Tantric empowerment, as constituting the key to all "extra-ordinary" instructions.

The connection is explained as follows: Buddhajnana and its Inseparable Qualities are the Nature of the Mind. Once disciples have faith that this is the case, they can have confidence that the "Mind" which their Guru introduces them to in a very direct way through oral instruction is not only their own mind, but also the Guru's Mind inseparable from the Buddha's Mind. With this kind of confidence, there is the possibility of eventually letting go of dualistic, conceptual processes, thereby allowing the Mind to rest quite naturally in its primordial Nature. Because of the essential inseparability of the Guru's and the disciples' Mind, when disciples rest as naturally and as confidently as possible, the Guru can actually give his/her disciples some very direct experience of the non-difference between the Guru's Mind and their own. This kind of transmission is called "empowerment" (*abhiseka, dbang*); it is the basis for all Tantric practice.

Mikyo Dorje makes the point in his *dBu ma gzhan stong sgron me* [5a], that empowerment is mentioned even in the Sutras because all the Bodhisattvas are empowered by the Buddha before entering final Enlightenment. He then makes it clear that, since the Bodhisattva's Mind has always been Buddhajnana, the empowerment is merely a "means." In other words, since the Bodhisattva is primordially Buddha, his Enlightenment does not really come from the empowerment of others, even though this might, so to speak, "spark it off." In fact it is spontaneous; its Qualities are inseparable, and it is realized through "faith." Elsewhere Mikyo Dorje says:

> As it is said in the final cycle of the certain meaning (Nitartha) of the Mahayana by the Unconquerable Lord (Maitreya) concerning the meaning condensed in the nine examples [from the *Tathagatagarbhasutra* and RGV]: the Tathagatagarbha heritage of the mind in an ordinary being with great desire who has never met a Tathagata before is not even a little in evidence (resting as it does in the sheath of the klesa) because of all the klesa veils. Even so, after he has accumulated a small amount of roots of merit, and generated the aspiration to Enlightenment, since that ordinary being has partially destroyed what was veiling his mental continuum, he has

partly actualized the Tathagatagarbha. The Aryan Teacher in the *Dharmadhatustotra* teaches this at length by means of the examples of the lamp in the pot, and the waxing moon. In the *Kalacakra* it is taught that in the body, speech, mind, channels, bindu and air of the continuum of ordinary beings is a Jnana aspect that appears in a coarse form and in part only. This profound point is the instruction of the lineage stemming from the Arya Asanga. Others without this have not got it.

Notice that Buddhajnana is called "Tathagatagarbha" when veiled in ordinary beings. The ordinary being first must accumulate "roots" of merit (*punya*) through good deeds and accumulate wisdom (prajna) by listening to, reflecting on and meditating on the Dharma. Merit and wisdom cause cracks to appear in the conceptual prison that holds him/her and, just as the lamp beams out when the pot that contains it breaks, so the Buddhajnana starts to shine in the mind of the Bodhisattva when the conceptual mind relaxes. Just as the light in the pot was present in its full intensity from the beginning, so Buddhajnana is not changed by whether it is obscured or not. Thus, it is in its very nature "realized" and external conditions do not affect it. "Realized" here has to be understood as nondual realization—an inseparable Quality of the nondual Mind. The greatest mystery, as Queen Srimaladevi points out, is how it could ever become obscured. Her response is that it is inconceivable, that is, unable to be grasped by the conceptual mind.

Perhaps this sounds like the weakest point of the whole system. On the other hand, it can be seen as further confirmation that the essential point in a Shentong system is "experience." That which is experienced (*myong bya*)* is mentioned by Sakya Chogden as the Jnana empty of duality, which is experienced through meditation (*bsgom pas nyam su myong bya*).[2]

ii. Faith and Direct Experience

We have come now to the cornerstone of the Shentong system. Their main argument against Rangtongpas is as follows: if Ultimate Reality is self-empty, then there is nothing to experience (i.e. no *nyongcha*).[3] How, therefore, can it be described as bliss, wisdom, compassion and so forth? How can it be "known" in any sense at all?

Obviously, from what has been said already, we expect the Shentong "experience" (*nyongcha*) to be experience beyond the duality of experience

---

* pronounced nyongcha

and experiencer. Khenpo Tsultrim believes that it is what the Cittamatrins experienced in meditation when they managed to let go of all concepts. In his opinion, their mistake was to misinterpret the experience when they came to formulate the explanation of their view. They thought it must be an aspect of a moment of consciousness, the self-aware, self-illuminator, (*rang rig rang gsal*) that remained once the mind no longer perceived a duality in substance between perceiver and perceived. Madhyamika opponents dismissed this self-aware, self-illuminating aspect of a moment-of-consciousness with the argument that a moment-of-consciousness cannot be its own object any more than a knife can cut itself. Because Shentongpas do not explain their self-aware, self-illuminating awareness as an aspect of a moment-of-consciousness, their view is not refuted by the Madhyamaka. This is usually misunderstood by opponents to Shentong who, as we saw earlier, think the arguments that refute ordinary Cittamatra apply equally to Shentong.

In Shentong terms, the "experience" of Buddhajnana is the essence of the Path. At the end of the last chapter, it was emphasized that recognizing it is merely the beginning; the difficult part is to stabilize the experience. Complete stability is called "realization" (*rtogs pa*). The problem is that a strong wish to grasp the "experience" arises together with the fear of losing it. Subtle hopes and fears such as these obstruct it and the only recourse is, again, faith.

Kongtrul explains (*Nges don sgron me*) [p.110]:

> The mere experience (*nyams kyi myong ba tsam*) [does not give] the actual (*dngos*) realization of seeing one's own face (*rang ngo*). At that time, the sure knowledge (*nges shes*) of seen and see-er (*lta bya, lta byed*) being not two (*gnyis su med pa*) having arisen, the thought arises, "This is it! This is what I was taught to rest in without artifice (*ma bcos pa*)."

He continues by giving more detail on how subtle experiences, problems, and distractions may arise and how to deal with them.

Khenpo Tsultrim explains that, when one is resting the mind in naked awareness, a definite experience of the Clear Light Nature of Mind arises. In fact, it arises as a "flash" in one's consciousness in every moment of perception, but normally one is not aware of it. It occurs just as a moment of perception forms, in the first moment of awareness before the dualistic process sets in.[4] It can only be experienced in a nondualistic way; when the mind rests like that, it is said to be "resting nakedly in its own nature." Since, in Shentong terms, this is the essence of true meditation, those Rangtongpas who deny the existence of this which is to be "experienced" (*nyongcha*) have completely missed the point. In Shentong terms, the meditator who denies this experience (*nyongcha*) either still has subtle concepts (*spros pa*, prapanca) so does not experience it, or while experiencing it denies the reality of the experience. In this case that denial is itself a concept (prapanca).

As has been explained, it is the Guru's special instruction that introduces (*ngo 'phrod*)[5] the disciple to the Nature of the Mind (*cittaprakrti*).[6] Typically the ground is laid for the introduction (*ngo 'phrod*) by oral mind instruction (*sems khrid*), which normally involves giving the disciple questions concerning how he/she experiences his/her own mind. He/she may be asked, for example, to ponder for a week about where thoughts come from. Rather in the style of a Zen master using the Koan method, the Guru judges the understanding of his disciple from his/her responses. This is the way a Kagyupa lama, for example, tries to focus the disciple on his/her own direct experience before introducing him/her to much doctrinal content.[7] In the Tathagatagarbha Sutras and commentaries, such as the RGV, there are no actual details on how to experience the Nature of the Mind directly and yet without that experience it is not possible to understand the Shentong interpretation. Nonetheless, it is as characteristic of Tathagatagarbha as of Tantric and Mahamudra literature that it emphasizes the need to abandon concepts and to rely on faith.

Faith is essential for the actual introduction (*ngo 'phrod*) to work. It is the essence of the empowerment itself. According to Khenpo Tsultrim, the simplest and, perhaps, the most profound form of empowerment is not given in a formal ritual, but can occur in any situation created by the Guru in which the student is open enough to receive it. It can occur simply while sitting in the presence of the Guru, or through a single utterance; it cannot be insignificant that stories of realization arising in this way in human and nonhuman disciples occur in both the Pali and the Mahayana Sutras. Normally, however, empowerments are given in the course of an empowerment ritual, part of which consists of the "Word Empowerment." At this point, a phrase, word or symbol is shown with the intention of "sparking-off" the experience of direct realization. It is a ritualized form of special instruction (*man ngag*).

There is an intimate interplay between Buddhajnana and the conceptual process. One influences the other. Hence, the SMS[8] explains how even to have the concept that the Dharmakaya is Permanence, Self, Bliss, and Purity is preferable to the position of Sravakas and Pratyeka Buddhas, who do not see the sphere of the Tathagata even with their pure vision which is arrived at through meditation on emptiness.

This is a very significant statement. Dolpopa [RC 374.1] remarks that just to believe this removes many veils. Thus, he emphasizes the power of faith even in the ordinary sense of conceptual belief. In this way, the Tathagatagarbha Sutras convey a message that is full of faith in the goodness of humans and their ability to attain supreme Buddhahood. They say that merely to have a positive and open attitude towards oneself and the Buddha is better than to be well advanced on the path without it. This contrasts with the negative sounding message of the Sravaka and Pratyekabuddha vehicles (yana), which emphasize that humans, like all other beings, are born of ignorance, driven by negative passions, and doomed, but for the grace of the Buddhadharma, to suffering and death.

iii. Direct Experience as Valid Cognition

It is important not to misunderstand the Shentong emphasis on the necessity to rely on faith and non-conceptual Jnana as advocating a lack of precision. As in all Mahayana systems, valid cognition (*pramana*) is a key subject hotly discussed. Generally speaking, knowledge comes through the senses, through inference, such as the knowledge of logic, and through direct experience, such as in meditation. The study of valid cognition (*pramana*) involves the examination of the nature of these means of knowledge (*pramana*), classifying them according to (*a*) the object known, (*b*) the accuracy with which they know, and (*c*) the reliability of their knowledge. Reason, which uses inferential logic, is one form of *pramana*, and it can know conceptualizable things. However, it cannot know what cannot be conceptualized, therefore, it cannot know the Dharmata.[9] The *pramana* for knowing the Dharmata is the yogi's non-conceptual Awareness. Thus, Dharmata *pramana* is, in fact, another name for the self-originated Jnana. Such knowledge or awareness is not open to normal logical analysis, for it starts from a different premise. Normal "common sense" logic is built on the premise that there is a dualism of knower and known, quality and thing qualified and so forth. When the Madhyamikas pushed the system of logic based on these premises to their logical conclusion, it became self-contradictory and incoherent. At this point, all the basic categories that had been taken as premises were seen to be empty. This vision is called "Absolute (paramartha) *pramana*."

Dharmata *pramana* is not based on the common sense premises of ordinary beings, but on what is known or experienced by the yogin in his meditation. Therefore, once again the emphasis is on direct experience. Since this is not knowable by the dualistic thinking of ordinary beings, it is not refutable by them. Taking his nondual experience as the premise, the yogi can argue that only the non-conceptual, non-dependently arising, non-dual Jnana, with its inseparable Qualities, is ultimately Real: Dharmata *pramana* (valid cognition) sees this in a non-conceptual, nondual manner.

From the point of view of Dharmata *pramana*, which is another way of saying from the Shentong point of view, rangtong introduces the student to Reality (Paramarthasatya) indirectly. Absolute *pramana*, which sees self-emptiness, uses reason rather than faith. By this means veils of delusion are removed, and the mind becomes sufficiently purified for faith (in the Shentong sense) to arise. From the Shentong point of view, rangtong is the basis for Shentong but, used in isolation, rangtong methods are slow. Shentong-pas argue that one cannot rely on the dualistic deluded mind to undo its own delusions; finally, it is the non-deluded, noncompounded, nondual ultimate Nature of Reality itself that has the real power to remove delusion.

Since a Rangtongpa such as Gyaltsab does not accept that faith is actually the functioning of nondual Absolute Jnana, for him it can only be a conceptual faculty inferior to reason. Gyaltsab [*Dartik* 10] explains that when RGV and RGVV [1.153] state that Sravakas and Pratyeka Buddhas must rely on faith to realize absolute truth, it is because they do not have the full collection of reasons (*rigs pa'i tshogs*) as Mahayanists have; therefore, they must supplement their practice with faith in the Buddha, for as a person of valid cognition (*pramana*), His word can be relied upon. Ruegg[10] gives Gyaltsab's view on the role of reason and the meaning of faith and intuitive knowledge and explains the Gelugpa point of view in general, saying that faith (*sraddha*) is seen as a means of purifying the mind (*citta*) and not, properly speaking, a characteristic component of the understanding of emptiness. Incidentally, none of this is supported in the RGVV comments on the verses in question.

Gyaltsab [*Dartik* 8b] argues against those who say absolute truth (paramarthasatya) is not an object of knowledge (*shes bya*). Indeed, the main thrust of Tsongkapa's Rangtong system is to stress the role of reason by commenting that what is discovered in meditation in no way goes beyond that which is reached by analysis. Superficially this looks as if it is completely at odds with the Shentong approach; it requires extremely careful research both in the commentarial, and oral traditions of the Gelugpas in order to see how exactly terms, such as "reasoning," "meditation," and "analysis," are used.

Although we have said that Rangtongpas rely on reason more than faith, this is not to say they do not ultimately rely on meditation experience. Non-exclusive Rangtongpas first ascertain the self-emptiness of apparent phenomena (samvrti) through reasoning, with the intention that the conceptionless meditation experience should arise out of that. A Shentong teacher might try the reverse approach, since the Absolute which is "known" directly can be "glimpsed" right from the start through wisdom (prajna) arising from meditation (*sgom byung gi shes rab or so so rang gi rig pa*).[11] Once the disciple has learnt to rest in the nondual Buddhajnana, the self-emptiness of all apparent (samvrti) phenomena will be self-evident. Gendun Rinpoche—an eminent Kagyu Yogi highly regarded for his meditation experience and realization—has often remarked to me that when the essential point of meditation is known intimately, even without much study, all the different Buddhist philosophical positions are easy to understand. On the other hand, if the essential point is not known one could study for years and simply become increasingly confused. Gendun Rinpoche is by no means alone in this view. It is the typical Kagyu approach. Not only do Kagyupas argue that too much study is simply confusing for the less intellectually gifted, but also that, since death may strike at any moment, it is better to experience the essential point of meditation through reliance on the direct instruction of the Guru, than to waste time approaching it from the analytical side. To support this view the example of Milarepa, the great Kagyu Yogi and poet, is used. He never studied much but gave a pithy exposition of Madhyamaka famous for its brilliance and much loved by present day Kagyupas.

Kagyu and Nyingma Lamas, with whom I have discussed the roles of faith and reason, have felt their relative importance depended on the individual and that in fact an approach suitable for one person could harm another and vice versa. Gelugpa Lamas have made similar comments though for somewhat different reasons.

The Tathagatagarbha doctrine of the RGV is taught from the two points of view—rangtong and Shentong—as will be demonstrated to some extent in the course of this present work. Rangtong is useful for individuals approaching Reality through philosophy, because it introduces no concepts outside of their experience. Shentong is useful for the individual approaching Reality through personal meditation experience and reliance on the teacher's realization plus his/her personal connection with that teacher. Both have advantages and disadvantages; both should eventually culminate at the same point which, being beyond all concepts, is neither rangtong nor Shentong.

5.2 Non-conceptuality (nisprapanca)

i. Nisprapanca as Awareness Experienced in Meditation

As we have seen, "faith," "self-originated Jnana," and "self-awareness" are the means of apprehending Ultimate Reality. The means is also described as non-contrived or non-conceptual (nisprapanca, *spros bral*). Although non-conceptuality (nisprapanca) has been central to the whole discussion so far, it is necessary at this point to recapitulate and augment what has been said.

The relationship between faith and non-conceptuality from the Shentong point of view should by now be obvious to the reader. The deepest prayer of the Mahamudra or Dzogchen practitioner is for non-contrived or non-conceptual devotion (*bcos min mos gus*) which, as the means of ultimate realization, is none other than self-originated Jnana.

The Tibetan translation of prapanca is "*spros pa*," which means "proliferation" or "elaboration." Therefore in colloquial Tibetan, it is used to mean "to elaborate on a point." The Candra Das Tibetan English dictionary [CD] has defined *spros pa* as busy-ness, employment, and activity. The Monier Williams Sanskrit English dictionary [MW] defines prapanca as expansion, development, manifestation, amplification, and diversity. Then there is the related term "*prapancaka*" meaning amplifying, and explaining in detail. "*Nis*" is added to create the negative of the term. Therefore nisprapanca means "absence of elaboration." Since this translation is clumsy and unclear, throughout this present work the translation "non-conceptual" has normally been used because it seems to be flexible enough to fit most contexts without distorting the meaning. "Concept" implies both a certain mental effort to think something and what is created by that effort. Thus, it conforms somewhat to Nanananda's observations below.

As well as nisprapanca there are, in fact, a number of expressions in Buddhist technical vocabulary that could be translated as non-conceptual, for example, *nirvikalpa, acintya, atarkatvagocara, aparikalpita,* and *asamjna*. It is not possible in this present work to investigate the differences implied by these terms and the contexts in which they are used, but such research needs to be done. Bhikkhu Nanananda has made a good beginning in his *Concept and Reality in Early Buddhist Thought, An essay on Papanca, Sanna and Sankha*. In this work he explains [p. 4–5, 6ff] how the term "prapanca" is not just the process or action of conceptual proliferation, but includes the product of that activity—the conceptual world itself:

> apparently . . . it is an inexorable subjection to an objective order
> of things.

Thus, nisprapanca *(spros bral)* means both freedom from artifice as well as freedom from subjection to an artificially created world.

In Buddhism in general, as soon as awareness moves from basic, direct, simple awareness (called "naked awareness" (*rig pa rjen bu*)[12] in Mahamudra and other meditation texts), it is said to be "proliferating" or "elaborating" (prapanca) even where this elaboration is too subtle to be called a concept in the ordinary sense. It is used both in texts and in speaking in order to refer to even the most subtle "efforts" of the mind in meditation to hold on to "good" or "true," and reject "bad" or "false" states of mind instead of letting the mind rest completely naturally in naked awareness. Thus, it is appropriate to translate "nisprapanca" as complete naturalness without artifice. This has normally been translated in this present work as "freedom from conceptual contrivance."

Kongtrul [SKK hum 67b] explains this method of meditation as follows:

> *sgom tshul bdag med don la shes rab kyis. dpyad de spros dang*
> *bral la mnyam par 'jog. dpyad gzhi rnam par mi rtog gzugs brnyan*
> *ni. khyad gzhi bzung nas khyad chos sgro 'dogs gcod. bdag med*
> *kyi lta ba ma rnyed na sgom lugs gang byas kyang de kho na nyid*
> *kyi don la gol bas de nyid rnyed dgos la. lta ba'i go ba yod kyang*
> *de'i steng du bzhag nas ma bsgoms na de kho na nyid bsgom par*
> *mi 'gyur bas. bdag med pa'i don la shes rab kyis so sor dpyad nas*
> *spros pa thams cad dang bral ba'i dbyings su mnyam pa 'jog go.*
>
> The method of meditation is, having investigated the matter/meaning (*artha*) of non-self with prajna, to rest evenly in non-conceptuality (nisprapanca). That which is investigated (literally the base investigated) is the non-conceptual image/mirror reflection. Having grasped (perceived) this special "base," cut all doubts of false denial or false assertion concerning the special Dharma. Since if one does not find the non-self view, whatever meditation method one adopts misses the Thatness, one has to find it. However, even though one has the understanding of the view, if one does not meditate resting in that, it will not become "Thatness" meditation, so, having separately investigated the matter/meaning (*artha*) of non-self, rest evenly in the nonconceptual/effortless/non-contrived (nisprapanca) Expanse (Dhatu).

Dolpopa [RC p. 399], having pointed out all the different uses of terminology for talking about false appearance (samvrti) that must be given up and the Absolute that is to be sustained, explains that, having analyzed all the scriptures like this and established one's view in deep meditation, one must let the mind rest in evenness and without concepts in naturalness (nisprapanca, *rtog med spros bral mnyam pa nyid la 'jog dgos*).

Another term used for this kind of non-conceptual meditation is "*avikalpabhavana*" (*rnam par mi rtog pa'i sgom pa*). Vikalpa (*rnam rtog*) is close to what we usually mean by concept or idea. It carries the connotation of a fixed idea or the way one habitually conceives of the world. Therefore, in colloquial Tibetan, it is used as a general word to refer to superstitions, pretensions, prejudices, suspicions, and inhibitions. Both *avikalpa* and nisprapanca express the idea of not letting the mind "fix" on anything, but to rest in naked awareness.

In fact, various words for "rest," "naked awareness," and "clarity" are used in meditation texts. They are technical terms for advanced stages of meditation experience marking distinct moments of change in awareness. Such words are used by Gurus to disciples when giving oral instruction. For example, when studying Kongtrul's *Nges don sgron me* with Bokar Tulku, he told me that the last section on meditation instruction was not worth studying until I had more meditation experience, since otherwise, all the words would simply sound the same and somewhat mundane.[13] Kongtrul explains [p. 56]:

> *bla ma dam pa grub thob rnams kyi man ngag mthar thugs.*
> This is the Siddha holy Gurus' final instruction.

Kongtrul [skk a'280na] explains that both Shentong and Rangtong Madhyamakas accept that meditation (*mnyam bzhag*) should be nisprapanca. As we know, they disagree only on the final analysis of the dharmata, that is, whether it is mere emptiness or the nondual Jnana. He adds [skk a'283ba] that Mantrayana Madhyamaka corresponds on the whole with Shentong Madhyamaka (referred to here as "Yogacara-Madhyamaka"), teaching that the Dharmata is true Self-Awareness (*rang rig*), primordially the nature of all the dharmas. He explains that the Tantric meditation-deity (*istadevata, yi dam*) appears based on Clarity-Emptiness and in a non-contrived (nisprapanca) manner (*spros med du 'char ba'i tshul*).

In all Buddhist systems (both Rangtong and Shentong) not only is the means of apprehension non-conceptual (nisprapanca) but what is apprehended, that is, Ultimate Reality, is also held to be non-conceptual (nisprapanca). However, it is only in Shentong systems that both the means of apprehending and the apprehended are Buddhajnana. Thus, although Rangtong systems regard the manner in which Buddhajnana sees as non-conceptual (nisprapanca) and what it sees as non-conceptual (*spros med yul*), the latter is not Buddhajnana.

Kongtrul [skk 13b hum] explains the difference between rangtong and Shentong as follows:

> *snga ma de la spros bral tsam las ma gsungs shing. phyi ma ni spros bral gyi ye shes de so so rang rig gi ye shes kyis myong bya'i khyad par du bshad pas so.*
> The former teaches no more than mere nisprapanca. The latter gives the special explanation of the nisprapanca Jnana which is experienced by self-aware-Jnana.

One may wonder what the nisprapanca object (*yul*) of nisprapanca awareness in a Rangtong system is. If it were merely nothing (mengag) in what sense could it be known in a nisprapanca manner? In other words, how does a moment of awareness know it without having a subtle concept (prapanca) of it? The Gelugpa system, for example, argues that there is no way of knowing that does not involve a perceiving and perceived aspect (*yul dang yul can*). Therefore, nisprapanca cannot mean for them—as it does for Shentongpas—the total loss of that distinction. For them it seems that an object (*yul*) of a moment-of-consciousness can be "other" than the consciousness that knows it (*yul can*) without necessarily being prapanca. Exactly how this point is explained within the various Rangtong systems is not the subject matter of our present discussion. Shentongpas, however, argue that the non-conceptual, non-conceptualizable (nisprapanca), Reality that is known in a non-conceptual (nisprapanca) way, is experienced and therefore cannot be nothing. In other words, it is a non-conceptual "something" and this "something" is Buddhajnana. The danger in saying it is "something" is that this can be misunderstood to mean it is a conceptually graspable entity. To avoid this mistake, Prasangika Madhyamikas prefer to say it is simply non-conceptual (mere nisprapanca)—a negation that implies neither a conceptual affirmation nor negation of Reality.

The problem for both Rangtongpas and Shentongpas is how finally to relinquish their habitual way of perceiving things or their usual "mode of apprehension" (*'dzin stangs*). The point in one's meditation practice where the transition must be made from the conceptual to the non-conceptual (nisprapanca) seems to be the hardest transition of the Path.

Although all Buddhist schools advocate the necessity for it, they each criticize the other on the grounds that they have not really achieved their goal. For example, Prasangika Madhyamikas and Shentongpas criticize the Svatantrika system for making Emptiness itself into a concept (prapanca). Again, Shentongpas criticize the Prasangika Madhyamaka system for its subtle negative concept of "mere nisprapanca." Shentongpas, in turn, are accused of having the coarsest prapanca of all. They defend themselves by saying they are the only ones who teach the Absolute nisprapanca Jnana. They add that resting in this is, in fact, the only possible alternative to prapanca.

Not everyone accepts this. Geshe Lhundup Sopa and Prof. Jeffrey Hopkins[14] present the layout of the different Buddhist schools from the Gelugpa point of view in their translation of a work by Konchog Jigme Wangpo.[15] This work [143–144] explains that the highest system of tenets is the Prasangika Madhyamaka, which teaches, according to this account, that "all nirvanas . . . are ultimate truths (paramarthasatya)," and that "a nirvana is an emptiness of the mind in the continuum of one who has completely and forever abandoned afflictions''. In effect it is saying the emptinesses in the mind-stream of a Buddha are the ''objects'' (*yul*) that are nisprapanca but, again according to this account, nisprapanca emptiness is not known simply by letting go of all concepts.

> . . . fixation with non-reflection on reality. This is our position, so it is necessary to have non-reflection as the preliminary to right discrimination, but it does not suffice to have just non-reflection.
>
> Quote from Hopkins *Meditation on Emptiness* [p. 408]

The Gelugpa theory is quite complex and the way the term nisprapanca is understood is subtly different from the Shentong. It seems that in the Gelugpa view there must be a ''subjective'' awareness (*yul can*) of ''something'' (*yul*) even in Buddhas. For Shentongpas this constitutes prapanca or conceptual contrivance; the only way out of which is to give up reflective meditation and rely on nisprapanca Buddhajnana. Shonupal states [BA 841; DN 984]:

> *shes bya'i sgrib pa spang ba'i phyir chos kyi bdag tu lta ba spang dgos par gzigs nas. lta ba de spang ba'i phyir 'bad dgos la. de yang stong pa nyid rtogs pa'i lta bas chos su lta ba spong ste. de yang 'dzin stangs 'gal ba'i sgo nas spong ba yin no. stong pa nyid kyi lta ba bskyed pa'i phyir yang lung dang rigs pa'i rgya mtshor 'jug par byed do. phyag rgya chen po'i ye shes ni 'dzin stangs 'gal bas spang bar bya ba'i gnyen po rigs pa'i stobs kyis rnyed pa'i rjes su dpag pa'i tshad ma yin na. rjes su dpag pa ni rnam par rtog pa kho na yin la. rnam par rtog pa yin phan chad ma rig pa yin par dpal chos kyi grags pa bzhed de. de spong ba la ni 'dzin stangs 'gal ba'i gnyen po med de rjes su dpag pa'i tshad ma dang 'dzin stangs 'gal na phyin ci log kho nar 'gyur ba'i phyir ro. des na lta bar ma gyur pa 'di'i gnyen po ni phyag rgya chen po'i ye shes yin la. de ni bla ma dam pa'i byin rlabs nyid las 'byung ba yin no. zhes bya ba ni bstan pa spyi'i rim pa'o.*

> Having seen that in order to relinquish the knowledge veils, it is necessary to relinquish the view of the self of the dharmas, in order to give up that view, effort is necessary, so the view of the dharmas is to be given up by the view realizing emptiness. Furthermore, it is to be given up through countering the mode of apprehension. Thus, in order to develop the view of emptiness one enters the ocean of scripture and reasoning. The Mahamudrajnana is the remedy which, by countering the mode of apprehension,

causes it to be relinquished. If it were inferential valid cognition found through the power of reasoning, since inference is merely concept (*vikalpa*), inasfar as it were concept it would be ignorance. This is what Dharmakirti maintained. To relinquish it [the mode of apprehension?], if one does not have the remedy for countering the mode of apprehension one can only go wrong in countering the inferential *pramana* and mode of apprehension. Therefore, the remedy for the non-changing [rigid?] view is Mahamudrajnana and it arises from the blessing (*adhistana*) of the True Guru. Such is the general progression of the doctrine.

Thus, one establishes non-conceptuality (nisprapanca) as one's "view" first through reasoning, and second through deep meditation. Then one can "let go" into it, abandoning one's previous "mode of apprehension."

Kongtrul [SKK 12b–13b] sets out the tenets of the different Buddhist schools as they move progressively nearer complete and perfect non-conceptuality (nisprapanca) which is, in his system, Buddhajnana. This is the system used by Khenpo Tsultrim in the progressive stages described in chapter 2 of this present work.

ii. Nisprapanca as Freedom from Extremes

The traditional test for detecting a conceptual position is the *catuskoti*, the "four-edges" (Tibetan, *mu bzhi*). The "four-edges" are to exist, not exist, both exist and not exist or to neither exist or not exist. In other words, a thing either exists or does not exist. The only other possibilities are to both exist and not exist or neither exist or not exist. Though the last two options are highly questionable they might at least be considered. Nanananda[16] explains that the *catuskoti* represented a standard device used at the time of the Buddha for challenging religious teachers. An enquirer might ask for example if the Buddha exists after *paranirvana*, or not (or both or neither). One of the ways the Buddha answered such questions was silence. It is said that in this way he did not fall over any of the "edges." Had he fallen and taken up one of the extreme positions (*anta, mtha'*) concerning existence or non-existence, he would have been open to refutation from the Madhyamaka point of view.

Dolpopa [RC 196] argues that although it is taught that Absolute Reality (Paramarthasatya) is free from extreme positions (*atyanta, mtha' las 'das pa*), this means that it is necessary to avoid extreme positions; it does not mean that Absolute Reality is itself free from Existence. In other words "extreme positions" means a conceptually established and apprehended view of existence, nonexistence, both or neither. Absolute Reality exists in an Absolute way free from such extreme positions. Rangtong commentators

argue that by such assertions the Shentong view falls into the extreme po
sition of asserting existence. In other words, they do not accept that true
Existence can be asserted without this being an extreme position.

For the Prasangika Madhyamika Rangtongpas, freedom from extreme
positions (mtha' las 'das pa) means that samvrti phenomena and paramartha self-emptiness cannot be understood conceptually because appearance
and emptiness seem to contradict each other; yet, it is incoherent to say
anything both exists and does not exist or that it neither exists nor does
not exist.

Some Prasangika Madhyamikas, for example Thrangu Rimpoche, argue
that the extreme position of "samvrti phenomena do not exist" is avoided
by saying "because they appear." Thinking about it, for that argument to
hold, samvrti phenomena must exist in some sense—the existence extreme.
On the other hand, if one does not accept that they exist in some sense,
how is the nonexistence extreme avoided? This question bears much pon-
dering.

Gelugpas argue that samvrti can be expressed as existing conventionally; in this manner the extreme position that samvrti does not exist is
avoided. To avoid the extreme position of samvrti existing, they argue that
it does not exist absolutely (paramartha). Other Prasangika Madhyamikas,
for example Thrangu Rimpoche, reject this view because in their opinion it
falls into both the extreme position of existing and that of not existing.

Most Prasangika Madhyamikas following Candrakirti, in order to avoid
all extreme positions, adopt no conceptual view at all concerning samvrti
phenomena or their emptiness. Mikyo Dorje (gZhan stong sgron me) criticizes these followers of Candrakirti for their dishonesty. His argument is
that they simply leave all the difficult questions open, pretending this lack
of explanation is supreme because it cannot be refuted by its opponents.
Like Dolpopa, in the text mentioned above, Mikyo Dorje accepts here that
Buddhajnana is all that truly exists and that apparent (samvrti) phenomena
are simply seeming realities, that is, they never did exist.

Thus, both Prasangika Madhyamikas and Shentongpas refute the existence of apparent phenomena (samvrtisatya); the former on the grounds that
appearance (samvrtisatya) is nisprapanca; the latter on the grounds that apparent phenomena (samvrtisatya) do not exist at all. In the former case,
samvrtisatya means manifest appearance and, in the latter, it means what
falsely appears (see Chapter 5.3 on the Two Realities). Gelugpas and Svatantrikas, however, regard both these as nihilistic views; they always qualify
their refutation of the existence of apparent phenomena (samvrtisatya) with
the words "they are empty of true existence" (bden pas stong), thereby
implying that they are not totally non-existent. As has already been indi-

cated, Shentongpas and other Prasangika Madhyamikas regard this as falling into the position of "both existing and not existing" which is self-
contradictory.

In the above discussion concerning the avoidance of the "four-edges"
of "extreme views," we see how Buddhist systems try to formulate their
tenets in such a way as to avoid conceptually unacceptable positions. The
two main coarse concepts that must be avoided are the extreme positions of
permanence and anihilation. The permanence extreme (*rtag pa'i mtha'*) is
to cling to what is not permanent as permanent and means chiefly to cling
to the idea that oneself or one's soul has lasting existence. This is known as
a false assertion (*samaropita, sgro brtags*), that is, ascribing reality or truth
to something that is not real or true. The nihilistic extreme is to cling to a
denial of existence to what does exist; this means chiefly to deny the causes
and effects of karma. This is known as "false denial" (*abhyakhyana, skur
'debs*), that is, denying reality or truth to what is real or true. To cling to
the impermanent as permanent is to deny absolute reality (paramarthasatya), that is, emptiness; to cling to a denial of karma is to deny apparent
reality (samvrtisatya).

In Shentong terms, the first concepts to be given up are coarse misconceptions about the self as existent and karma as nonexistent. The concept of
an existent self is replaced by the concept of a stream of moments of consciousness and smallest indivisible particles. The relatively coarse concept
of their existence is given up by the very subtle concept of emptiness,
which in turn, can only be abandoned by giving up all concepts, coarse and
subtle. Although Prasangika Madhyamaka establishes this as necessary, it is
only the Shentong Tathagatagarbha doctrine that explains that this can only
be given up by faith in the Tathagata (meaning Buddhajnana). This is because conceptual contrivance (prapanca) can become so subtle that it is
hard to detect or define. True freedom from conceptual contrivance (nisprapanca) is experienceable by meditators at an advanced level and only
proved by the emergence of the inseparable Qualities.[17]

iii. Nisprapanca as Non-conceptuality in RGV [1.9]

In RGV [1.9] the *catuskoti* is presented in a slightly unusual manner:

> *gang zhig med min yod min yod med ma yin yod med las gzhan du
> 'ang. brtag par mi nus nge tshig dang bral so so rang gis rig zhi
> ba . . .*
>
> That which is not non-existent, not existent, not existent and non-
> existent, [not] other than existent and non-existent and non-
> examinable, beyond definition, known by self awareness [is]
> peace.

This is expanded in RGV [1.10]:

> *bsam med gnyis med rtog med pa . . .*
> Unthinkable, nondual, non-conceptual . . .

and explained in RGV [1.12]:

> *brtag min phyir dang brjod min phyir. 'phags pas mkhyen phyir*
> *bsam med nyid. zhi nyid gnyis med rtog med de . . .*
> Because it is non-examinable, because it is unutterable and be-
> cause it is known by the Aryas, it is unthinkable. It is peace [be-
> cause] it is non-dual and non-conceptual . . .

RGVV [1.12] explains that "peace" here refers to the truth of Cessation
(i.e. Nirvana) and it quotes the *Jnanalokalamkarasutra* [JAAS] and then the SMS
[RGVV 1.12 phi 7b] as follows:

> *bcom ldan 'das chos 'jig pa ni sdug bsngal 'gog pa ma lags so.*
> Bhagavan, the destruction of dharmas (or a dharma) is not the
> Cessation of Suffering.

It then explains that it is the non-born, non-compounded, permanent Dharmakaya with all its inseparable Qualities, which is called the "Tathagatagarbha" when not free from the klesa.

What is interesting here is that although RGV [1.9] seems to be a presentation of the classic *catuskoti*, it is not, because it begins with "not
non-existent" instead of "not existent."[18] Both Rongton and Gyaltsab follow the RGVV in giving no significance to this change in order.

Rongton[19] explains that RGV [1.9] means that the four extreme positions
are avoided because the truth of Cessation is not something the conceptual
mind can know (*rtog ge'i blos brtag bya min*). It is only known by the
Arya's Jnana (*phags pa'i ye shes kyis so so mkhyen bya yin*). In other
words, the *catuskoti* formula is used to show that Enlightenment jnana is
non-conceptual (nisprapanca). Judging from his general view, he must mean
by this that jnana knows in a non-conceptual way (nisprapanca)—not that
the non-conceptual (nisprapanca) is jnana (in the Shentong sense). Although
Gyaltsab uses terms differently from Rongton, Thrangu Rimpoche thinks
they are fundamentally in agreement, since both accept that Buddhajnana
develops from a pure aspect of the samvrti mind-stream, which continues in
the Buddha's Enlightenment. In this they are not unlike ordinary Cittamatrins.

Gyaltsab's view is that RGV [1.9] means samvrti is not nonexistent because it exists conventionally (*tha snyad du*) and is not existent because it

does not exist in ultimate truth (paramarthasatya). This explanation is not supported by the RGVV.

Dolpopa, however, says RGV [1.9] means Cessation is Absolute Buddhajnana with the inseparable Qualities. This view is supported by RGVV [1.12]. He explains that, since it is "spontaneously" existent, it is not nonexistent—which explains why the verse begins with this. The next phrase, Dolpopa [RC p.195ff] insists, cannot refer again to Cessation or the RGV would have fallen into the position of crediting a single subject with "both existing and not-existing." From the discussion in the previous section, we know that, according to Dolpopa, the RGV [1.9] would have had to add "position" (*koti, mtha'* or *mu*) to "not non-existent" if it had simply meant Cessation was freedom from positions. Since, in his view, "not nonexistent" means Cessation exists, "not existent" must refer to apparent (samvrti) phenomena.

He reminds us of the difference between paramartha and Dharmata pramana: the former establishes what is nonexistent, the latter what is existent. He argues that if we do not observe this difference, we might misunderstand scriptural statements that would be self-contradictory if applied to the same referent. The above passage [RGV 1.9] is an example of this.

The RGVV, however, gives no indication that "not non-existent" and "not existent" in RGV [1.9] should be read as referring to different subjects and, superficially, it does not seem to be a particularly natural reading. However, as we saw above, the *Vyakhya* [RGVV 1.12] is explicit about Cessation being the Dharmakaya endowed with all the inseparable Qualities as countless as the sands of the Ganges. The SMS quotation supporting this is preceeded in the RGVV by the following quotation from the JAAS:

> *'jam dpal skye ba med cing 'gag pa med pa ni. sems dang yid dang rnam par shes pa mi 'jug go. gang la sems dang yid dang rnam par shes pa mi 'jug pa de la ni kun du rtog pa gang gis tshul bzhin ma yin pa yid la byed par 'gyur ba kun du rtog pa 'ga' yang med do. tshul bzhin yid la byed pa la rab tu sbyor ba de ni ma rig pa kun nas slong bar mi byed do. ma rig pa kun las ldang ba med pa gang yin pa de ni srid pa'i yan lag bcu gnyis kun nas ldang bar mi byed do. de ni mi skye zhes bya ba la sogs pa rgyas par gsungs pa yin no.*

Manjusri, non-born and non-ceasing cannot be applied to mind (*citta, sems*), mental faculty (*manas, yid*) or consciousness (*vijnana, rnam shes*). In that to which "mind," "mental faculty" or "consciousness" cannot be applied, there is no imagination (parikalpita, *kun du rtog pa*) whatsoever that is the imagination (parikalpita, *kun du rtog pa*) which creates the wrong way of thinking (*ayonisomanasikara, tshul bzhin ma yin pa yid la byed pa*). When the proper way of thinking (*yonisomanasikara*) is acquired, there is no arising of ignorance. Where there is no arising of ignorance the twelve limbs of worldly existence do not arise. That is non-born etc. explained at length.

The *Vyakhya* [RGVV 1.12] introduces this passage by saying that the wrong way of thinking is the cause for the arising of karma and klesa and this is the meaning of duality here. Since this is naturally ceased (*prakrti-niroda, rang bzhin gyis 'gag par*) and known by self-awareness (*prativedat, so sor rang rig*) the suffering associated with concepts (*vikalpa*) and dualism is ever non-arisen and this is what "Cessation of Suffering" means.

Given their overall view, it would be natural for Dolpopa and other Shentongpas to interpret this passage as meaning that Cessation is the cessation of karma, klesa, and the wrong way of thinking because they never existed. Cessation is the Absolute Jnana, the Dharmakaya, in which the wrong way of thinking and imagining never existed. Thus, Cessation is not the cessation of something that once existed and then ceased but that which is non-born and non-ceasing and in which ignorance and so forth never arose. Since in this way the *Vyakhya* says that Cessation Exists (albeit in a way that is unthinkable etc.) and that ignorance, the wrong way of thinking, imagination, klesa, karma and so forth never existed in it, it is justifiable to argue that the following statement [RGV 1.9] "That which is not non-existent and not existent" means Cessation is that which exists and ignorance and so forth is what does not exist. But how convincing is this? The next phrase is "not both existent and non-existent," and Dolpopa explains this means neither the Ultimate nor apparent phenomena (*samvrti*) are both existent and non-existent (which would be a self contradictory position). The next line "other than existence and non-existence" is not negated in RGV [1.9] except to say that this is not examinable or definable but only known by self-awareness. To me, this line reads naturally as "what is other than existence and non-existence is not examinable etc." Thus, (to me) RGV [1.9] reads as a mere rejection of the four positions as regards Cessation and not as an affirmation of the Shentong view. Nonetheless, Kongtrul in his RGV commentary follows Dolpopa, so he, at least, must have found his arguments convincing.

Dolpopa [RC 316.4] explains that the Buddha taught Existence because some people might think the Buddha did not exist in the Absolute and non-existence because they might think apparent reality (*samvrtisatya*) was not not existent, that is, they might think He was samvrti (as Rangtongpas do, indeed, think). However, argues Dolpopa, He is the limit of perfection (*yang dag pa'i mtha'*) and Absolute Existence (*don dam yod pa*).

Perhaps Dolpopa's view is paralleled by Seng-chao in the *Chao Lun* [p. 112ff] and Walter Liebenthal [p. 138] where they present the Absolute as not non-existing (in the ordinary sense), but existing (in a special almost symbolical sense), though in fact it is beyond existence and nonexistence (in their usual sense).

iv. Nisprapanca in the Tantras

M. M. Broido [*Journal of the International Association of Buddhist Studies*, JIABS vol. 8:35ff] provides an important discussion of nisprapanca; he gives [p. 43] a very useful note from Padma Karpo, which shows nisprapanca to be a bridge between Madhyamaka and Vajrayana (Tantra). He says that at the stage of realization of Mahamudra called "nisprapanca" (*spros bral*) one may not realize all appearance to be mind-as-such; this is realized at the stage called "one taste" (*ro gcig*). The stage called "nisprapanca" (*spros bral*) seems—by the analysis followed in this present work—to correspond to Madhyamaka, which is either Shentong or Rangtong, depending on whether appearance is recognized as nondual Absolute Jnana or not.

The significance of the rangtong-Shentong distinction in Tantric theory and practice is paramount. For example, concerning the Tantras Kongtrul [SKK hum 44b] explains:

sngags su yul can bde ba'i thabs kyis khyad. spros bral yul la khyad med rang stong lugs. gzhan stong yul yang spros bral tsam po min. rnam kun mchog ldan pra phab lta bur bzhed.
Concerning Mantra[yana], the Rangtong system is that the "object-haver" [i.e. the awareness focused on the object of awareness] is special because of the bliss-method, but the "object," nisprapanca, is not special [to Mantrayana].

The Shentong system is that the "object" also is not merely nisprapanca, but is held to be all-supremely aspected like the magical appearance in a divination mirror (*pra phab*).

Kongtrul [SKK hum 45 na] explains that the object (*yul*) nisprapanca is the same in the Paramitas and the Tantras, and he agrees with Sakya Pandit in the *sDom gsum rab dbye*, where he says that if Mantrayana had a view beyond nisprapanca it would become prapanca. Shentongpas consider it possible to approach the realization of the nondual Jnana through realizing either the object or object-haver (*yul* or the *yul can*) aspect by analytical reasoning, or by direct experience, respectively. Finally, however, the two must merge like water mixing into water.

Thus, the point about the awareness (object-haver, *yul can*) and its object (*yul*) is all-important. Rangtongpas explain Tantric method as a means of transforming awareness (*yul can*) by subtle methods such as developing "bliss" and so forth so that nisprapanca can be realized more quickly. The object (*yul*) nisprapanca is none other than the "mere nisprapanca" of their Madhyamaka view or even of Sravakas and Pratyeka Buddhas. The difference only concerns how the realization of it is brought about.

Shentongpas, however, regard Tantric method as a means of directly working with the Absolute inseparable Qualities of awareness and its objects (*yul can dang yul*) right from the beginning of the path. Shentonpas talk about awareness and its object, that is, the object-haver (*yul can*) and object (*yul*), because for ordinary beings there is apparent (samvrti) subjective experience of an objective world in which awareness and objects of awareness seem to be separate. However, since in their view this apparent duality never existed, Nisprapanca, which is nondual Reality, can be approached from either or both points of view. In other words, by resting in the non-conceptual (nisprapanca), nondual Jnana with its inseparable Qualities of Bliss, and so forth, the awareness (*yul can*) is special; thinking of the objective world or objects of awareness as expressions of the nisprapanca, nondual Jnana with inseparable Qualities, the "object" (*yul*) is also special. By meditating like this the subtle concepts (prapanca) that create divided consciousnesses are gradually dissolved and the inseparable Qualities are experienced increasingly vividly. Gradually the sense of object and object-haver (*yul dang yul can*) disappears, but this only happens completely at Buddhahood. Until then some subtle conceptual effort is required to maintain "pure vision" (*dag snang*)—the key to the Tantric Path.

Pure vision means having the confidence that all one's subjective and objective experience is Buddhajnana (even though to the ordinary consciousness it does not appear to be). Having this confidence allows the mind to relax in openness and simplicity so the ground is prepared for rapid realization. As one progresses along the path less and less conceptual contrivance is needed because the inseparable Qualities start to "shine through," as it were. Special Tantric techniques for purifying the subtle channels, breath, and drops (*nadi, prana,* and *bindu*) may also be employed. These have the effect of increasing the intensity with which the inseparable Qualities of the Buddhajnana are experienced either inwardly or outwardly as, for example, bliss, light, and the deities of the mandala. Whatever the experience, it is Shentong (empty of other) in the sense that it is a non-conceptual (nisprapanca) experience empty of conceptual dharmas. Thus, in Tantric expositions (including Mahamudra and Dzogchen) terms such as Appearance-Emptiness, Bliss-Emptiness, Clarity-Emptiness, Awareness-Emptiness both-at-once (*yuganaddha*) are used to refer to the Ultimate (*Paramartha*) Nature-of-Mind. "Emptiness" in these combinations means non-conceptual (nisprapanca) space or openness. In other words, though there is nothing to grasp (conceptually), Appearance, Bliss, Clarity or Awareness is still vividly present and is the Non-conceptual (Nisprapanca) Reality.

Thus, the difference between the Rangtong and Shentong understanding of Tantric method is radical and far-reaching. This is reflected in their use of Tantric terminology although this is often not appreciated by workers in this field nor by many would-be Tantric practitioners.

5.3   The Two Realities—Truths and the Two Visions

More needs to be said here concerning the two realities (*satya*) and the terms *yathavadbhavikata* and *yavadbhavikata* [*Study* 173]—precisely what is and the extent of what is.

i. Satya

Broido comments [JIABS vol. 8, no. 2:20, 34] that a great deal of work still needs to be done, tracing the traditions concerning not only the terms "paramartha" and "samvrti," but also the term "satya" itself.

Rangtongpas, as we have seen, say that paramarthasatya (ultimate reality) is simply the self-emptiness of the dharmas. Shentongpas say it is nondual Jnana.

Dolpopa argues that, since self-emptiness is a nothingness (mengag, a non-implicative negation), it is not reality (satya). Therefore, for him, to say that paramarthasatya is self-emptiness is to say that apparent reality is the only reality (satya). From this we gather that he, like Kongtrul, takes satya to mean something that is real in itself and not, as Rangtongpas claim, a truth about something else. This point is pivotal to his whole argument.[20]

ii. Paramarthasatya

"*Parama*" means supreme and "*artha*" here means either subject matter or meaning. Ruegg's *Literature of the Madhyamaka School of Philosophy in India*[21] refers to the *Tarkajvala* [fol 63a] by Bhavaviveka, founder of Svatantrika Madhyamaka, who analyzes the term paramartha as:

1. a compound of *artha* (that which is cognized) and *parama* (the supreme),

2. a *tatpurusa* meaning "*artha* of the supreme," namely, non-conceptual *gnosis*, and

3. that which conforms to the supreme *artha*, namely, prajna

In other words, it is either the supreme object of contemplation leading to liberation, the supreme Buddhajnana itself, or the mind that contemplates the supreme subject matter.

Dolpopa accepts all these senses of Paramartha.[22] Candrakirti, on the other hand, only accepts the first sense because, for him, paramartha means the supreme truth of emptiness known by the non-defiled mind; it is not the mind (jnana or prajna) that knows it.

Shentong commentators criticize Candrakirti from a number of points of view. For example, Mikyo Dorje objects to his definition and use of the term paramartha (*gZhan stong sgron me*):

zla grags dang seng bzang la sogs pas ni so skye'i shes pas chos kyi khams la yod med skye 'gog rigs pas brtags pas ma rnyed pa de ni don dam pa'i gnas lugs yin par 'dod do.

Candrakirti and Haribhadra etc. accept that the non-finding by an ordinary being's mind through reasoned examination, of the existence, non-existence, arising or ceasing of the dharma element is the paramartha true state . . .

and further on he says:

zla grags la sogs pas ni. don dam chos nyid kyis chos nyid ma mthong ba la don dam pa'i bden pa mthong zhes ngos 'dzin kyang de ni don dam par smos ci dgos. kun rdzobs tshig la'ang 'gal ba du ma rang lugs la khas len dgos par 'gyur bas. de'i skyon sel du nged dbu ma pas khas len ci yang med ces smra bar byed do.

Although Candrakirti etc. recognize the non-seeing of the true nature (*chos nyid, dharmata*) by the paramartha true nature (*chos nyid*) as "seeing the paramartha," why should this be called "paramartha?" Even in terms of samvrti there are many contradictions that have to be upheld by their own system, and in order to remove this fault they say, "We Madhyamikas do not maintain anything."

Here Mikyo Dorje objects to Candrakirti's definition of paramartha because Candrakirti does not explain how a non-seeing can be ultimate reality. This criticism goes hand in hand with Mikyo Dorje's general criticism of Candrakirti, which is that he tried to avoid refutation by claiming not to be asserting anything. Although the nature of *prasangika* arguments is to not assert anything, Mikyo Dorje accuses Candrakirti of asserting things, through implication, about both paramartha and samvrtisatya. In other words, he is saying that Candrakirti is not adhering to the true principles of Prasangika Madhyamaka. Incidentally, the fact that Ratnakarasanti— an influential eleventh century Vijnapti Madhyamaka master—is recorded as saying that Candrakirti abandoned his nihilism in his Tantric commentary[23] shows that criticism of Candrakirti's Madhyamaka is not restricted to Shentongpas.

Dolpopa explains, quoting extensively from Sutra, Tantra, and commentarial sources, that Paramarthasatya is what Exists because:

1. It does not have the qualities of something non-existent, that is, it is not impermanent or dependently-arising.

2. It is not the object of a confused or conceptual mind, being free from signs and concepts.

3. It is what is realized by the Aryas, being the sphere of experience (*spyod yul*) of self-aware Jnana.

iii. Samvrtisatya

Dolpopa, explains [RC 56] that apparent phenomena (samvrtisatya) have the qualities of what is not truly existent:

1. They are dependently-arising and impermanent.

2. They are the object of the confused conceptual mind—so are conceptual creations (prapanca) and the sphere of experience of ordinary beings.

Dolpopa explains that whereas Ultimate Reality (Paramarthasatya) is the essence or true nature of all dharmas, apparent reality (samvrtisatya) is merely a distorted vision of that. Thus, when one realizes Paramarthasatya, one realizes that the former apparent reality does not exist, never did exist, and never will exist. Since Nirvana is Paramarthasatya, in realizing Nirvana the aspirant realizes there is no samsara (samvrtisatya), and there never was nor ever will be. (See chapter 3 "Problems of Definitions of Terms" of this present work).

Nevertheless, Dolpopa does not dismiss samvrtisatya as unimportant. He refutes [RC 384] the limited or biased emptiness (*pradesikasunyata, nyi tshe ba'i stong pa nyid*) of the Tirthikas (*Mu stegs*), in which even karma is negated as not true. He explains [RC 371] that the klesa are purified by realizing the nature of apparent reality (samvrtisatya) and apparent reality is purified by realizing the nature of Paramarthasatya. First one should know the klesa are self-empty and then, by means of correct meditative absorption (*samadhi*), Paramarthasatya is realized. Thus, false appearance (*samvrti*) is removed by means of the non-conceptual Jnana.

iv. Ultimate Reality is not Dependent Arising

Dolpopa further explains [RC 378] that, because the scriptures say that all dharmas are empty and that emptiness means apparent phenomena are dependently arising through linked conditions (*rten 'brel*, Skt. *nidana*), some people mistakenly think that emptiness necessarily means linked conditions and so Paramarthasatya means linked conditions, that is, the dependently arising nature of apparent phenomena. This would mean that the Dharmata was dependently arising, implying it was false, nonexistent, non-dependable and so forth. He explains that the "all" in "all dharmas are empty" does not include the Dharmata, because it is not empty in the same sense.

Kongtrul makes this point by distinguishing between the ultimate object (*paramartha*) and ultimate Reality (Paramarthasatya). He explains that first the ultimate object (in the sense of object of contemplation) is established as the eternal, unchanging self-emptiness of the dharmas, but then, at the next stage, there is no true object of contemplation, there is simply Reality itself (Paramarthasatya), in which there is no contemplator, contemplated, or contemplation. Thus, Paramarthasatya means the Reality (satya) of the supreme object of contemplation (paramartha). He calls this the "Tantric masters" view on the nature of Reality [SKK tsa 46a]:

> snags su khyad chos lhag po dag gis brgyan. khyad par kun rd-
> zobs gzung 'dzin snang ba ste. bden pa med snang chu zla lta bur
> brjod. don dam ngo bo stong nyid bcu brgyad de. de yi bden pa
> gnyis med ye shes so.
> Mantra is adorned with extra special qualities (dharmas). In par-
> ticular the manifestation of apparent (samvrti) perceiver and per-
> ceived aspects is described as an unreal (*bden med*) manifestation
> like the moon in water. The ultimate essence is the eighteen emp-
> tinesses and its Reality (*bden pa*, satya) is the nondual Jnana.

Thus, according to Kongtrul, Mantrayana Reality (satya, *bden pa*) is nondual Jnana.

v. Own Nature and Other Nature (*Svabhava* and *Parabhava*)

Kongtrul puts the same point a slightly different way when he explains [SKK 31ba] that the ultimate (paramartha) nature (*rang bzhin*, svabhava) of a dharma has two inseparable aspects, own nature (*rang dngos*, svabhava) and other nature (*gzhan dngos parabhava*). Own nature (*svabhava*) is self-emptiness and other nature (*parabhava*) is Jnana. He calls both these nature "ultimate" because he defines ultimate (paramartha) as:

1. That which is permanent—both the self-emptiness and the Jnana nature of a dharma is non-compounded and non-conditioned.
2. That which is not the object of words and the mind that knows samvrti.
3. That which is the object (*yul*) of true realization.
4. That which is beyond samsara.

Thus, Kongtrul accepts that both self-emptiness and Emptiness-of-other are ultimate (paramartha). (See Appendix 2 of this present work for more detail).

vi. The Two Realities Inseparable

a. *Dolpopa's View.* Thus, Dolpopa, Kongtrul (and the Mantrayana commentators to whom he refers) explain that Ultimate Reality is what is ultimately present; it is what must be stripped of ignorant concepts, which make it appear in a false way (samvrtisatya). In Shentong terms, Ultimate Reality can be called the true nature of (or behind) apparent reality. However, this is where great caution is needed in order not to confuse Rangtong and Shentong terminology, for in Rangtong terms ultimate reality is also called the true nature of apparent reality, but in a completely different sense.

In Rangtong terms, one says that, because the true nature of all dharmas is self-emptiness (parmarthasatya), samvrti and paramarthasatya are inseparable. In Candrakirti's Madhyamakavatara (chapter 6) samvrti and paramarthasatya are explained as two aspects of one reality, meaning the dependently arising world of experience and its emptiness. He uses the expression "samsara and nirvana inseparable" in the same sense.

As far as Dolpopa is concerned, expressions like "samsara and nirvana inseparable (*dbyer med*)," "samvrti and paramarthasatya inseparable" and "dharma and Dharmata inseparable" make no sense in Shentong terms.

Dolpopa is concerned that if one is not careful the terminologies of rangtong and Shentong coincide and become indistinguishable. For example, in Rangtong terms, samvrtisatya is paramarthasatya in the sense that what is ultimately real (paramarthasatya) is the emptiness (that is, paramarthasatya) of dependently arising phenomena (samvrtisatya), that is, samvrtisatya is (or are) emptiness or emptinesses (paramarthasatya). This can also be expressed as the self-nature or essence of apparently real phenomena being self-emptiness or emptiness of self-nature (paramarthasatya) and also as paramarthasatya and samvrtisatya being inseparable—as are a quality and what it qualifies. In Shentong terms, what appears falsely as real (samvrtisatya) is actually a distorted appearance of something Real (Para-marthasatya). Therefore, one can say that the essence or true nature of ap-parent phenomena (samvrtisatya) is ultimate Reality (Paramarthasatya in the Shentong sense), but not that apparent (false) phenomena, as such, are ultimately real or that apparent (false) phenomena, as such, and ultimate Reality are inseparable. In other words, it is nonsense to say that what does not exist is (or is inseparable from) the ultimately Real.

b. *Padma Karpo's View.* The great Drukpa Kagyu scholar Pema Karpo (1526–1592) in his *dBu ma'i gzhung lugs gsum gsal bas 'byed pa nges don grub pa'i shing rta* criticizes Dolpopa's system for dividing the two realities (satya) in this way.[24] This does not seem to be because he takes emptiness to be merely a nothingness (mengag), but because, in his view, the *Heart Sutra* and other Prajnaparamita literature emphasize the inseparability of the two realities when they say that form is no other than emptiness and emptiness is no other than form and so forth. The disagreement with Dol-popa seems to be on the use of terminology rather than on meaning. Since Dolpopa uses "samvrtisatya" only for what is not reality, it clearly cannot be regarded as inseparable from the Real. Pema Karpo, on the other hand, uses "samvrtisatya" and "form" and so forth as synonyms. Therefore, for him to deny that samvrti and paramarthasatya are inseparable is to deny that form is none other than emptiness and emptiness is none other than form and so forth.[25]

c. *Tantric Terminology.* Padma Karpo is defending a use of terminology that seems to be standard in many Tantric traditions because such expressions as "samvrti and Paramartha inseparable," and "samsara and nirvana insepa-rable" constitute key Tantric terminology. They are in standard employ-ment by Kagyu and Nyingma Lamas who, unlike Dolpopa, do not restrict them to a rangtong sense. As I understand it, these Lamas use samsara and samvrti to mean the manifest world of one's experience, which is insepara-ble from Paramartha nondual Jnana. Mikyo Dorje, for example, uses the expression "samsara and nirvana inseparable" (*gZhan stong sgron me* [12bf]), having first, like Dolpopa [RC 384], identified the Dharmata of all dharmas as Shentong Sugatagarbha. This custom stems from the Tantric Siddha tradition.[26]

Unlike Dolpopa, these Tantric commentators (for example Padma Karpo, and Rangjung Dorje *Zab no nang gi don* [ZND 1]) equate expres-sions such as "manifestation and emptiness inseparable" with "samvrti-satya and parmarthasatya inseparable." It has an obvious shock effect, for the whole Buddhist tradition is built-up around the duality of samsara and nirvana, samvrti and paramartha and so on. To speak of the inseparability or equalness (*mnyam pa nyid*) of these categories is to undermine certain subtle concepts that are built-up and reinforced through the very process of following the path to Enlightenment. Dolpopa, however, was obviously afraid that such shock effect use of terminology would confuse the fundamental doctrines of the Sutras and Tantras.

vii. The Two Senses of Manifestation and Emptiness Inseparable

Dolpopa thought that by confusing the terminology of self-emptiness and Emptiness-of-other in this way, the significance of Tantric expressions like Manifestation and Emptiness inseparable and so forth would become lost. Although apparent reality is manifestation and emptiness in one sense, when ultimate Reality is described as Manifestation and Emptiness it means something quite different. Whereas apparent reality is manifestation in the sense that it appears, and emptiness in the sense that it lacks ultimate reality or self-nature, Ultimate Reality is manifestation—in the sense that it is the vivid, countless, nondual, spontaneous, inseparable Qualities, and Emptiness in the sense that it is empty of all conceptually graspable phenomena, that is, apparent reality. Apparent reality here includes the imaginary and dependent characteristics.

In this way, Dolpopa clearly distinguished between (1) the doctrine that every apparent phenomenon has two aspects: the way it falsely appears and its emptiness and (2) the doctrine that Ultimate Reality is Manifestation and Emptiness. Modern Shentongpas do not seem to lay such emphasis on this distinction—maybe because they take it as given.

viii. The Importance of this Distinction

Dolpopa [RC 231.1] explains that, by not holding the above distinction clearly in mind, some people take the emptiness of the veils and so forth to be the Dharmadhatu but deny that their manifestation, that is, their power to manifest, is also the Dharmadhatu. Thus, they aspire to realize the emptiness of the klesa and so forth and praise this emptiness as Dharmadhatu, but denigrate the power of the mind that produces them because, for them, manifestation is always samvrtisatya.

Dolpopa argues that in Rangtong terms, since the way things manifest is always self-empty, whether it is the way things manifest to ignorant beings, or the way they manifest to Enlightened beings, then (again in Rangtong terms) even the apparent world as it manifests to ordinary beings is the Dharmadhatu. Of course, in Shentong terms, this is self-evidently ridiculous. Perhaps this is what Seng Chao meant when he asked: How, if Prajnaparamita is empty in Herself, is She different from illusion? [*Chao Lun*, 71 in translation]

Dolpopa warns that we must be careful of the image of a magical apparition or illusion, because it can be used in several different ways. It can be used as an example of how illusory phenomena are self-empty and yet still appear, dependent on causes and conditions. It can also be used as an example of how the mind can, like a mirror, enable manifold images to appear in it, without itself being changed or affected by them.

Dolpopa, elsewhere [RC 368], puts the same objection slightly differently. He argues that if samvrtisatya means all that appears as existent (*bhava, dngos po*) to the vijnana and Paramarthasatya means this being empty, then even the veils, since they are self-empty, are Paramarthasatya, or at least inseparable from Paramarthasatya [RC 230.1]. As far as he is concerned this is an unacceptable position, because, for him, the self-empty nature of the veils is their nonexistence (not the Dharmadhatu); the Dharmadhatu is the alive aware quality of mind that is revealed when the emptiness of the veils is recognized. It is the ultimate Manifestation and Emptiness inseparable. In other words the veils are unreal, being merely the distorted appearance of the Dharmadhatu.

In the higher Tantric teachings of Dzogchen and Mahamudra, it is important that the meditator use the manifest world of experience, including his/her emotions and delusion as part of his/her practice. The effort to cut through delusion in order to "see" emptiness has to be relinquished. Therefore, at this stage Shentongpas regard emptiness as given and requiring no further comment. This means the focus of the practice is to see directly the manifest world as Paramarthasatya. In a sense there is not, and never was, any apparent reality, as such, to remove or "cut." What is needed is the confidence that the manifest world of one's experience is actually Paramarthasatya. Hence, the identification of samvrtisatya with Parmarthasatya made in Tantric traditions. In this way, apparent reality ceases to mean what is false, and begins to mean what appears, in the sense of the manifest world of experience that is actually Paramarthasatya. This explains the Tantric use of the expression "samvrti and Paramartha inseparable" for Manifestation and Emptiness inseparable. Dolpopa, however, sees a danger in this use of terminology since by definition the false appearance of things (samvrtisatya) cannot be ultimately real (Paramarthasatya). He emphasizes that, although for an Enlightened being the manifest world of experience is indeed Paramarthasatya, what the practitioner thinks he experiences is mostly false (samvrti). His/her task is to gain confidence in the true essence of his/her experience, which is Paramarthasatya, so that samvrti (false) appearances fall away.

Dolpopa's point is not trivial. In my experience, many Western Kagyupas (and presumably Tibetans too) think that Tantric practice and Mahamudra mean to meditate on the dependently arising world of experience (samvrti) as self-empty, because this is what they take the teachings on manifestation and emptiness inseparable (*dbyer med*) or both-at-once (*zung 'jug*) to mean.

ix. The Relationship Between the Two Realities

Khenpo Katar, an erudite Kagyupa scholar, gave the following explanation concerning the relationship between the two satyas. The relationship between the two realities is paradoxical to the conceptual reasoning mind. He says that in order for disciples to reach the understanding that goes beyond concepts (nisprapanca), they must first understand each satya separately. That is why some teachers teach them separately, for example, Tsongkapa who emphasized samvrti and Dolpopa who emphasized the Paramartha. Mikyo Dorje criticized them both because he emphasized simultaneous arising (*lhan gcig skyed pa*). The Kadampas, for example, Chapa (Phywa pa), Ngog, and Patsab (Pa tshab), in their commentaries on the MA, emphasized the both-at-once (*zung 'jug*) Nature. Khenpo Katar then explained that both-at-once is always one Reality (i.e. emptiness none other than form and form none other than emptiness etc.). According to him, this is the final view of all traditions whatever terms they may use. For example, Nagarjuna taught self-emptiness of samvrti in the *sDom tshogs* (i.e. Svatantrika), nisprapanca in the *Rigs tshogs* (i.e. Prasangika), and the Paramartha in the *bsTod tshogs* (i.e. Shentong Yogacara Madhyamaka). Likewise Asanga taught Svatantrika in the *Sravakabhumi* and *Bodhisattvabhumi*, Prasangika in the two *Vibhaga* and Shentong Yogacara Madhyamaka in the RGV. Again, Tsongkapa taught Svatantrika in the *dBu ma dgongs pa rab gsal*, Prasangika in the *Shes phyin mngon rtog rgyan*, and Shentong Yogacara Madhyamaka in the *rTen 'brel bstod pa*.

x. The Two Visions—Precisely What Is and the Extent of What Is (*Yathavadbhavikata* and *Yavadbhavikata*)

These two visions describe what the Buddha knows. He is aware of both the true nature of things as well as the extension of this to cover all there is to be known. The exact meaning of these terms has been a great source of controversy among the various Mahayana schools and various definitions of their meanings exist.[27]

Takasaki [*Study* 173] gives the SNS definition of the two terms:

1. Precisely what is (*Yathavadbhavikata, ji lta ba bzhin du yod pa nyid*) is the Tathata (*de bzhin nyid*) of all the dharmas impure (*kun nas nyon mongs, upaklesa*) and pure (*rnam par byang ba*)

2. The extent of what is (*Yavadbhavikata, ji snyed yod pa nyid*) is the ultimate (*mthar thug pa*) analysis (*rnam pa rab tu dbye ba*) of all the dharmas impure (*kun nas nyon mongs*) and pure (*rnam par byang ba*).

Takasaki [*Study* 173 fn. 8] explains that, although it is traditional in Tibet to interpret precisely what is (*yathavad bhutata, ji lta ba yod pa*) as paramarthasatya and the extent of what is (*yavad bhutata, ji snyed pa yod pa*) as samvrtisatya, this is not the original use of these terms, which both should refer to the supra-mundane (*lokottara*) jnana or supra-mundane (*lokottara*) prajna. Dolpopa's use of the terms accords with Takasaki's view, which is also the way they are used in the RGV and RGVV. The special feature of the way RGV and RGVV use the terms is that the extent of what is (*yavad bhutata*) relates to the perception that Tathagatagarbha is in all living beings. Takasaki criticizes Obermiller who adopts the "traditional" Tibetan interpretation of the term.

Rongton explains [20ff]: "precisely what is" is what is known in meditation and the "extent of what is" is what is known between sessions; that is, concerning the former, the Bodhisattvas realize the dharmata of the two selves of all beings are primordially exhausted, and concerning the latter, that the pure by nature aspect of the Omniscient One's Dharmata is in all beings.[28]

Rangjung Dorje [ZND 1] uses "the extent of what is" for samvrti and "precisely what is" for Paramartha. He clearly uses "samvrti" for Manifestation, as the expression of the Qualities of Buddhajnana, in spite of Dolpopa's objection to this kind of looseness of terminology.

Gyaltsab [*Dartik* 35.2] explains jnana of the extent of what is (*ji snyed mkhyen pa'i ye shes*) as included in "Good of Others" and as the cause of engaging in compassion (*thugs rje 'jug pa'i rgyu*) but this should not be understood to mean that compassion and "knowing the extent" are inseparable Qualities of Buddhajnana in the Shentong sense. Gyaltsab [*Dartik* 45b] explains that although Buddhas have vision of the extent (*ji snyed gzigs pa*) because they have vision of precisely what is (*ji lta gzigs pa*) and vice versa, Bodhisattvas do not. They only have vision of precisely what is when in meditation session. Since in the RGV Bodhisattvas are said to have knowledge of the extent (*ji snyed mkhyen pa*), this must be explained as not having the actual realization of it, but merely a direct realization of the dharmata of beings.

It seems Gyaltsab defines genuine "knowledge of the extent" as "knowledge of all samvrti dharmas" (in the traditional way noticed by Takasaki in his comments above). Gyaltsab [*Dartik* 42b] explains that vision of precisely what is arises from the realization that the mind's essence is self-empty and the klesa are self-empty (*rang bzhin grub pa'i ngo bo med*), and that this is the meaning of "the mind nature clear light" (*sems de rang bzhin gyis 'od gsal ba*) in RGV [1.13].[29] Gyaltsab defines "knowledge of the extent of what is" as the "knowledge that the Buddha's dharmata, self-emptiness (*rang bzhin gyis stong pa*) is in all beings."

Chapter 6

The Nature of Beings

6.1 Base, Path and Fruit

It is essential that the reader understand that the real importance of Shentong lies in how it affects the practitioner's attitude to his meditation. In fact when Gendun Rimpoche remarked that Great Madhyamaka was not a system of tenets (*grub mtha, siddhanta*) because it was not established, (that is, proved through reasoning), he was emphasizing that it was the "view" (*lta ba*) necessary for profound meditation (*sgom pa*) and intuitive spontaneous action (*spyod pa*). The view occurs in flashes, like momentary gaps through the clouds, and this is the base. "Meditation" is the path that consists essentially of stabilizing this "experience" until the fruit stage, which is characterized as complete stability (*brtan po thob pa*) and "action" untainted by effort.

In terms of the base, path, and fruit, Shentong nondual Jnana is the essence of all three. Thus, the whole concept of Dharma practice is revolutionalized [RGV 1.156–166]. No longer is the base—the original state before the path begins—the nature of an inferior, tainted individual that needs to be developed or transformed into an Enlightened being; it is Buddhajnana itself that is already accessible to an individual's experience (albeit in brief flashes of insight). The path is no longer to be thought of as a long upward pull to perfection through self-effort and self-development; it is learning to trust and let go of preconceived egotistical and dualistic notions, and allowing the naturally present Buddhajnana to emerge without obstruction. The fruit is no longer a great feat that sets the Enlightened individual above and beyond ordinary beings whom it is, nevertheless, his/her duty to help; it is the recognition of the Buddhajnana in all beings and the release of its spontaneous activity to help them. Thus, Tathagatagarbha Buddhajnana is the "base, path, and fruit inseparable." Beings (the base), Bodhisattvas (on the path) and Buddhas (the fruit) are three names for the same thing [RGV 1.48].

Rangjung Dorje [ZND 1] writes that the nondual Jnana is at the base, path, and fruit time. The base is Clear Light, which is Emptiness and Manifestation inseparable, the path is Means and Wisdom inseparable, and the fruit is the Dharmakaya and Form-Kayas inseparable. This is the Tantric division into (a) the "base"—explained as Manifestation and Emptiness inseparable being the nature of the Mind as pointed out by the Guru to his/her disciple by means of special Mind instruction: (b) the "path"— explained as meditation on the Means and Wisdom inseparable which is the meditation Deity (*Istadevata, yi dam*): (c) the "fruit"—explained as Dharmakaya and Form-Kayas inseparable, which are the spontaneous manifestions of the purified Absolute Buddhajnana.

From the Shentong point of view, for both Rangtongpas and Shentongpas, Tathagatagarbha is the focus or field of the view (*lta ba'i yul*) at the path time [Kontrul's RGV commentary 13b]. From the Shentong point of view this means that the practitioner learns to rest the mind in the Clear Light Nature of Mind. Though it cannot be focused on in a dualistic sense or be a "field" of a view outside of itself, at the path stage the individual inevitably has the tendency to divide see-er and seen (*yul* and *yul can*), hence the expression "focus" or "field" of the view. The base that is being purified on the path is the Buddhajnana. In other words, something is present that is being cleaned as well as being focused on in order for purification to take place. The fruit is the Buddhajnana free from adventitious (*glo bur ba*) stains, that is, the Dharmakaya. Dolpopa [RC 166] explains that the thing that is to be purified, that is, to be left clean (*sbyang gzhi*) in beings, is that which is left clean, the fruit of purification (*sbyang 'bras*) in Buddhas; therefore, the Tathagatagarbha is both the base and the fruit.

For exclusive Rangtongpas there is nothing present ultimately and so there is not really anything to clean. Presumably they take the image of purification figuratively. The base (or support) is emptiness; the path is the purification of the mind-stream. It is purified in the sense that it is transformed from a tainted, inferior kind of consciousness into one that is perfectly pure, clear, and superior. In fact, technically, it is a different consciousness but, presumably, just as one speaks of purifying a river, one could speak of purifying a stream of consciousness. The fruit is the pure mind-stream as the samvrti fruit and the Dharmakaya as the ultimate (paramartha) fruit.

Thus, for Rangtongpas the base, path, and fruit are not inseparable in the Shentong sense. Ruegg gives a great deal of space [*La Théorie* 142fn, 283, 290fn., 291, 295] to the discussion among Tibetan Rangtong commentators as to whether Tathagatagarbha refers to the cause or the fruit of the path. In a Rangtong system the "base" of purification (*sbyang gzhi*) is the emptiness of the mind-stream, which is obscured. The mind-stream itself must be purified of the veils that hide from it its own emptiness. Geshe Wangchen and Geshe Thegchog explain that the mind-stream is purified by focusing not only on the emptiness of the dharmas in general, but also of the mind-stream in particular (*La Théorie* 8:328, 329). So emptiness is the base in the sense that it acts as the support (*alambana*) or focus for the mind in order that it may purify itself.

Ruegg [*La Théorie* 290fn., 291] explains how Gyaltsab makes a big issue out of Tathagatagarbha being only at the level of beings (*sems can gyi gnas skabs*) when it is a cause (*rgyu'i gnas skabs*) and that the tathata that is inseparable (RGV 1.27–28] is the veiled (*samala*) tathata in the mind-stream of beings; the lineage (*gotra*) being present means that there is the capacity, within the mind-stream of beings, to transform into the three kayas.

He sums up [*La Théorie* 295] the point of view of Gyaltsab's *Dartik* by saying Tathagatagarbha (the *samala* tathata) is not strictly speaking the cause of Enlightenment, but the support (*alambana*) of the *samahitajnana* of the Arya Bodhisattvas, which is the "*cause productrice principale du Buddhajnana.*"

Gyaltsab [*Dartik* 7b] remarks that in the RGVV it states clearly that Tathagatagarbha is the name of the dhatu when obscured, and Dharmakaya is its name when it is unobscured. The conclusion he draws from this is that Tathagatagarbha refers only to the stained element. He does not accept that, just as a person receives at different stages of his life three names (i.e. child, youth, and adult) and yet retains the same identity throughout, the dhatu is identical whether called Tathagatagarbha or Dharmakaya in beings, Bodhisattvas, and Buddhas [RGV 1.48].

In Gyaltsab's and other Rangtong systems in which Tathagatagarbha is simply self-emptiness when it is obscured, the term "base of purification" (*sbyang gzhi*) does not mean "that which is made clean" as it does in a Shentong system, but "that by which purification takes place." Rongton explains that the "base" emptiness is inseparable from the fruit. He [RGV commentary 29–34] discusses the concepts of cause and fruit in connection with the concept of lineage (*gotra*). He defines the cause (*rgyu*) of the three Jewels as the object (*yul*) of the vision of the Omniscient Buddha, that is, emptiness. However, he explains the cause and fruit inseparable as the fruit being the realization of emptiness and the cause being the lineage (*gotra*) or power (*nus pa*) of a being's mind-stream—the causal aspect of Buddha wisdom. In other words, for him, Tathagatagarbha has two aspects, the gotra and emptiness. Emptiness is the non-compounded aspect of Tathagatagarbha and is changeless; wisdom is the compounded gotra aspect [*La Théorie* 142 fn.7]. Rongton, like all Rangtong systems of explanation of Tathagatagarbha doctrine, claims to be following Ngog; he (Rongton) draws distinctions between gotra, dhatu, tathata, and Tathagatagarbha, and divides some or all of these items into absolute and samvrti aspects. Nevertheless, the details of how he does this and how he squares his analysis with the various statements in the RGV differs quite considerably from, for example, the *Dartik*.

In the first chapter of the RC, Dolpopa quotes from the RGV and RGVV at length about Buddha always being present in the base.[1] Then Dolpopa [RC 398] comments that some explanations of Sutra and Tantra say cause and fruit are different in various ways, and some say they are the same. He explains that each time one meets with such explanations one must distinguish whether samvrti or Paramartha is meant, because there are two gotras, the existent and the nonexistent, and two paths, the non-conceptual and the conceptual and so on.

Dolpopa criticizes those who treat the Tathagatagarbha as something newly arisen, either as a seed or a fruit. In other words, although when Tathagatagarbha is referred to as the gotra it is often glossed as meaning seed, one should not misunderstand this to mean the seed Tathagatagarbha is other than the fruit Dharmakaya. Nothing new arises. Although it is true that RGV [1.26] refers to the Element as the cause (*rgyu*), and Enlightenment, Qualities, and Activity as conditions (*rkyen*) for the purification of the Element, this explains why the Element is described in four aspects, not that it is a cause different from its fruit. For Gyaltsab RGV 1.26 is a key verse, however, because it clearly states that the dhatu (Tathagatagarbha) is the cause of Buddhahood, which proves to him that it cannot be the Dharmakaya. From this he concludes that the whole purpose of the RGV is to show the Tathagatagarbha is not the Dharmakaya. Shentongpas on the other hand say the exact opposite, that is, the purpose of the RGV is to show that the Tathagatagarbha is the Dharmakaya.

6.2   Tathagatagarbha

i. The Shentong and Rangtong Approaches Compared

Wherever it occurs, the term Tathagatagarbha refers to the power within beings that enables them to become Buddha. The Tathagatagarbha Sutras develop the idea by saying that it is a power had by all beings, (that is, not just by Bodhisattvas), thereby implying it is an innate aspect of a being's mind. Predictably, from what has gone before, Rangtongpas understand this to mean the self-emptiness aspect and Shentongpas the nondual Jnana.

Kongtrul [RGV commentary 11a ff.] points out that, in fact, there is scriptural authority for defining Tathagatagarbha as:

1. nisprapanca
2. the clear light nature of mind (*prabhasvaracittaprkrt*)
3. the alayavijnana
4. Bodhisattvas and beings

From the Shentong point of view the statement that:

1. "Tathagatagarbha is nisprapanca" means it is the nisprapanca Jnana (i.e. an affirming negation, *paryudasapratisedha*, mayingag). Kongtrul remarks that even though reputable scholars such as Bhaviveka, Vimuktasena, Haribhadra, Candrakirti, and Jnanagarbha accept nisprapanca as a *prasajyapratisedha* (mengag), in his opinion this view falls into the trap of clinging to emptiness.

2. "Tathagatagarbha is the Clear Light Nature of Mind" again means it is the nisprapanca Jnana. The RGV describes the nature of Mind as the "Clear Light" but the practice lineage explanation of this is that, although it is experienced as clear light, one should not think it is experienced in a dualistic way as light is usually experienced.

3. "Tathagatagarbha is *alayavijnana*" again means it is nisprapanca Jnana. However, Kongtrul admits such scriptural statements reflect a certain looseness of terminology.[2] For example, the *Lankavatarasutra* (LAS) and the *Vajradohas* of the Siddhas on occasion refer to Tathagatagarbha as *alayavijnana*.[3] The *Lankavatarasutra* describes the Tathagatagarbha as the *alayavijnana* with positive and negative seeds and that when there is no transformation (*gnas 'gyur*)[4] in the *alayavijnana*, known as Tathagatagarbha, there is no cessation of the vijnanas.[5] However, in the *Lankavatarasutra*[6] the *alayavijnana* itself is said to be nirvana. Shentong commentators explain that this apparent contradiction arises because the LAS does not clearly distinguish the *alayavijnana*, which is an aspect of the ordinary dualistic mind-stream, and the essence of the *alayavijnana*, which is Nirvana. They call the latter simply the "*Alaya*" because it has nothing to do with ordinary dualistic consciousness. Kongtrul explains in his commentary on the *rNam shes ye shes 'byed pa* [38a]:

> *gzung 'dzin tu snang ba'i sems dang nyon mongs pa can gyi yid dang rnam par shes pa'i tshogs drug dri ma dang ldan pa'i kun gzhi gang yin pa de ni 'khrul pa'i rtsa ba dri ma dang bcas kun gzhi'am kun gzhi'i rnam par shes pa zhes bya ba yin la. tshogs brgyad po de dag gi dri ma dang ldan bzhin tu rang gi ngo bo dri ma med pa'i rab [rang?] bzhin tu bzhugs pa la ni rgyal ba ste. sangs rgyas kyi snying por brjod cing de nyid gzhi lam 'bras bu'i gnas skabs kun tu 'gyur ba med par bzhugs pa ste.*

Although the stained *alaya* that is "the mind manifesting perceiver and perceived, the klesa-mind (*klistamanas*) and the six vijnanas" is called the stained *alaya* or the "*alayavijnana* that is the root of error," even as the eight consciousnesses (literally, accumulations) are with stain, their own essence dwells naturally without stain and, since this is the Victor, it is called the *Buddhagarbha* and this very one dwells changelessly in the base, path and fruit stages.

Although the LAS itself does not always clearly distinguish between *Alaya* as the Absolute Mind and *alayavijnana*, in general where Suzuki adopts the convention of a capitalized *M* for Mind this corresponds to what Shentongpas mean by Absolute *Alaya*.[7]

The LAS is clearly referring to such a "Mind"[8] because like the SMS and other Tathagatagarbha Sutras, it is not shy of the "self" doctrine.[9]

Nevertheless, it discusses Tathagatagarbha[10] in relation to the self doctrine of the non-Buddhists. The Buddha explains that Tathagatagarbha is a way of teaching not-self (*anatman*). In Shentong terms this means the doctrine of Tathagatagarbha teaches the True Self, which implies the *anatman* doctrine of the absence of a self in or outside of the samvrti skandhas. RGVV [1.36] discusses the same point about not-self being called "self."

4. Bodhisattvas and beings are Tathagatagarbha— Kongtrul[11] gives the Shentong explanation of this scriptural statement. He quotes RGV [1.28] and explains that beings, Bodhisattvas, and Buddhas are all essentially the Buddhajnana, which is hidden in all but the Buddhas. It is called different things at different times. The fact that it is not called Tathagatagarbha in Buddhas is only a question of terminology. In fact, since Tathagatagarbha is Buddhajnana, it has to be in Buddhas too. His explanation could perhaps be developed a little further by saying since finally Reality is revealed to be see-er and seen, the whole of what is must also be Buddhajnana and so logically it could all be called Tathagatagarbha. Thus samsara itself could be called Tathagatagarbha. In fact, RGVV [1.152] quotes from the SMS as follows:

> *de bzhin gshegs pa'i snying po mchis na de la 'khor ba zhes tshig gis btags pa lags.*[*]
> Tathagatagarbha exists and it is labeled with the name "samsara."

This is reminiscent of Hua Yen doctrine of Tathagatagarbha. Khenpo Tsultrim explained that, although logically one might think that because appearances are, in Tantric terms, Buddhajnana, they could also be called Tathagatagarbha, in fact the term "Tathagatagarbha" is never applied in this way in any Tibetan tradition. He suggested that the above line might mean that samsara arises because beings do not recognize the Tathagatagarbha.

---

[*]N.B. SMS has "*tshig de rigs pa lags so.*"

From the Rangtong point of view:

1. "Tathagatagarbha is nisprapanca" means that it is the emptiness of the dharmas which, when apprehended directly in a non-conceptual way, is nisprapanca.[12]

2. Concerning "Tathagatagarbha is the clear light nature of mind," there seems to be some disagreement among Rangtong commentators. When asked, Thrangu Rimpoche explained that "clear light" is used by Rangtongpas to denote the illuminating and knowing quality of mind that is never stained in essence (*sems gzhi la dri ma ma las*); this seems to agree with explanations given by Geshe Wangchen and other Gelugpa Lamas. However, Geshe Champa Thegchog and Geshe Wangchen also told me it was the purity of mind that is its essential emptiness of self-nature.[13] Geshe Wangchen explained that "clear light" describes the truth of emptiness of the knowing quality of mind, which is called "clear light," because even though they do not see it, it is actually clearly evident in beings. For him, as for Gyaltsab, it does not denote the Dharmakaya or a quality of the Buddha's mind. This contrasts with Rongton's explanation that clear light nature means the samvrti Tathagatagarbha, which is the aspect of the mindstream that (when purified) is the Buddhajnana.

Rongton [RGV commentary 19] explains clear light mind, natural purity and so forth, as the nature of the mind that is obstructed in ordinary beings but called "clear light" because of its nature when purified. Although the Dalai Lama addresses the question in *Tantra in Tibet—Essence of Tantra* [p.45] by arguing in favor of the Nyingma view that Buddhahood primordially exists as the subtle mind of clear light, he does not use the terms "primordially existent" and "permanent" in the Shentong sense. Rather he explains the clear light mind as an endless, ceaseless stream.[14] Rongton seems to hold a similar view and explains [p.19] that when the klesa are seen to not exist by nature in one's mind (because one sees their true nature), one sees that one's mind has natural purity, and so it is called "clear light nature." In this connection it is interesting to consider RGV [1.13]:

Because the mind's nature is clear light they see the klesa are essenceless.

From the Shentong point of view the fact that the RGV mentions the Clear Light Nature before the klesa confirms their view that it is by seeing the true nature of Mind that the klesa are seen not to exist. According to Rongton's explanation, it should have read "because they see the klesa are essenceless, they see the mind's nature is clear light."

3. "Tathagatagarbha is alayavijnana" is simply an indirect provisional (neyartha) teaching for those who are frightened of the idea that Tathagatagarbha is simply Emptiness.

4. "Tathagatagarbha is Bodhisattvas and beings" means Buddhas are not and do not have Tathagatagarbha. For example, in Gyaltsab's system, Tathagatagarbha is emptiness-of-mind when obscured by ignorance. When emptiness is no longer obscured there is no more Tathagatagarbha. Thus, Gyaltsab emphasizes that the Tathagatagarbha, as the naturally present gotra (*prakrtisthagotra*), is the stained true Nature (Tathata) and not the stainless Tathata (see Chapter 6.4 "Gotra" in this present work).

The Shentong answer to this emerges in the *Angulimalasutra* where Angulimala asks the Buddha how it is that if all beings have Tathagatagarbha, they are not already Enlightened. The Buddha replies that Tathagatagarbha is like a lamp in a pot (see Chapter 5.1 "Faith" in this present work.) The point is that the lamp is the same lamp from the beginning and the stains are all that makes the difference between Buddhas and beings.

The RGVV [1.124] clearly states that the stained Tathata, which is like the lamp in the pot, has one name (i.e. Tathagatagarbha) and the unstained Tathata, which is like the lamp out of the pot has another (i.e. Dharmakaya). Nevertheless, the lamp is still the same lamp.

The *Dartik* argues that Tathagatagarbha is only the name for the stained Tathata, in order to avoid implying that the unstained Tathata, that is, the Dharmakaya, is already in beings.[15] This establishes that the Dharmakaya is not immediately accessible to the experience of ordinary beings and also counters Buton's argument that the RGV must be non-literal (neyartha) because it says the perfect Dharmakaya is in beings (see Chapter 7.2 ii. "The Terms Neyartha and Nitartha" in this present work.)

For Shentongpas this is an outrageous distortion of the RGV's message. For them, whatever it is called, the lamp in the pot and out of the pot is always the same lamp, that is, the Tathata. It is as if the Gelugpas are arguing that the lamp is only a lamp when it is in the pot and not when it is out. This trivializes Tathagatagarbha doctrine by emphasizing that beings have an inferior or stained nature which must undergo transformation in order to become Buddha. The whole point of Tathagatagarbha doctrine, as far as Shentongpas are concerned, is that beings are never really inferior and stained in essence, because they are perfect Buddhas from the beginning.

Both Rangtongpas and Shentongpas agree that the true Nature (tathata) is the same in both beings and in Buddhas; no one maintains that beings have unstained tathata in the sense that they are not obscured. Ketrub's argument—which is, according to Ruegg, also that of Vasubandhu—is that, if beings already were the Dharmakaya, there would be no need for beings to become Enlightened.[16] This raises the same question that Angulimala asked and is answered by Shentongpas in just the same way as the Buddha answered him. There is a difference between being pure in the sense of unspoiled (as in the lamp in the pot example), and being pure in the sense of unobscured (like the lamp when it emerges from the pot). Hence the need for the path.

The Shentong interpretation of Tathagatagarbha doctrine does not imply there is no need for the path. However, according to Khenpo Tsultrim, it does try to counter an ambitious, goal orientated approach to it. If Buddha were something newly produced by following the path, it would be a conditioned phenomenon, the product of self-effort; it would not arise simply through complete relaxation of conceptual contrivance.

Nevertheless, one can defend Buton, Gyaltsab, and Ketrub's interpretation of Tathagatagarbha doctrine by arguing that it corrects the misunderstanding of those who think Tathagatagarbha doctrine means that, since one is already Buddha, there is no need to practise the path. Such a misunderstanding would justify their insistence that Tathagatagarbha did not mean one was already Buddha. Indeed, it is possible to become overconfident, favoring "high" views based on the Shentong Tathagatagarbha doctrine (such as Mahamudra and Dzogchen) without really understanding or practising them. If at the same time one despises and refuses to practise the graduated (*lam rim*) teachings that emphasize the need to purify the mind and accumulate merit, one is left destitute with no means to Enlightenment.

However, one can also argue that opponents of the Shentong view, by misrepresenting it and trivializing Tathagatagarbha doctrine, actually distort the original intention of the Sutras. Hence the warnings at end of RGV 5.

ii. The Term "Tathagatagarbha"

The Sanskrit term "*garbha*" has many meanings, one of which is womb or matrix. Takasaki uses this translation throughout his *Study*. It can also mean embryo or treasure in a mine. In other words, it can mean both something valuable or potentially valuable as well as its container or bearer. Ruegg mentions [*La Théorie* 511 fn.4] that *garbha* can mean "born from" and indeed there are contexts in which Buddha appears as father and beings as his sons. Ruegg particularly associates this doctrine with the *Sadharmapundarika* Hobogirin Chinese texts.

From the grammatical point of view, in Sanskrit, there are a number of possibilities for how Tathagatagarbha and *Buddhagarbha* should be interpreted. If it is treated as a *tatpurusa* compound, it means the *garbha* that is the Tathagata. The statement that all beings are Tathagatagarbha could then mean that *Buddhagarbha* is identical to beings, or beings are identical to the *garbha* that is the Buddha or that belongs to Buddha, or beings are identical to the *garbha* that arises from or gives rise to Buddha—like the mustard plant is identical to the seed that arises from or gives rise to the mustard plant. Thus, the terms Tathagatagarbha and *Buddhagarbha* are grammatically rather flexible and this has enabled all these alternative interpretations to arise.

In Tibetan the options are narrowed by the way "*garbha*" in the compound Tathagatagarbha and *Buddhagarbha* is translated as "*snying po*," meaning heart essence, that is, the valuable part of something that needs to be retrieved, for example, the butter from milk, sesame oil from seeds, and gold from gold ore. In addition the Tibetans add the particle "*can*" meaning "haver" or "having" to heart essence, making it a possessive compound (*bahuvrhi*). Thus, Tathagatagarbha is translated in such a way that it means "having the essence of Buddha." This means that statements in the RGV and elsewhere that in Sanskrit say, "All beings are Tathagatagarbha," in Tibetan say, "All beings are havers of the heart-essence of the Tathagata." Ruegg[17] discusses the term "Tathagatagarbha," "*Buddhagarbha*," and similar expressions in which the particle "*can*" is used in Tibetan; in Sanskrit these terms are not necessarily possessive compounds (*bahuvrhi*).[18] Although a *bahuvrhi* in Tibetan, it is still not clear whether "All beings have Tathagatagarbha" (*sangs rgyas gyi snying po can*) means that sentient beings have Buddha as their *garbha*, have the *garbha* of the Buddha, that is, have the essence that Buddha has (or is), or have the essence that becomes Buddha like the mustard seed example.

From the Shentong point of view, since any reading accords with their overall view, there is a poetic richness in all this linguistic ambiguity. For Rangtongpas the situation is different because there are certain readings they wish to exclude. Ruegg suggests that the particle "*can*" is used by the Tibetan translators in order to avoid the ambiguity that suggests beings are identical to the Buddha or *Buddhagarbha* or Tathagatagarbha, thereby keeping the quality and the qualified nicely distinct [*La Théorie* 511].

6.3   Self

One of the most characteristic and probably the most controversial aspects of Tathagatagarbha doctrine is the many references in Tathagatagarbha Sutras to the True Self or Self Paramita.

The word "self" used in this context embarasses many Buddhists, Eastern and Western, ancient and modern. This has led to tortuous transla-

tions of the simple word "*atman*" in order to avoid the taboo word "self."
For example, Jikido Takasaki [*Study* 207] translates it as "unity" and else-
where as "ego"; K. Holmes [*The Changeless Nature*] and Ming Wood
[JIABS vol. 5 no.2:82] translate it as "identity"; Mahathera Nyanatiloka
[*Path to Deliverance*] translates it as "personal" and "personality."

In spite of all this, the most obvious and accurate translation is "self"
as defined in the SOED: "That which in a person is really and intrinsically
he (in contradistinction to what is adventitious)." This is acceptable pro-
vided that the pronoun "he" here is understood to mean what a person
intrinsically is, and not what a person is in contradistinction to anyone else.

In general, beings' behavior is consistent with their believing that they
are lasting, independent self-entities with bodies and minds. However, when
one investigates the nature of the body and mind no self-entity of a lasting,
independent nature can be found. In this way, the "self" around which a
being orientates his/her life is called into question. Thus, the three characteristics of existence[19] are shown to be impermanence, suffering, and not
self. This means that none of the components of existence (i.e. the skandhas) are the self because they are impermanent; what is impermanent is
unpleasant and not the "self" and does not even belong to the self. Since
the skandhas constitute the whole of a being's existence, the self cannot be
outside them either.

In the *Annattalakkhanasutta*,[20] Buddha points out that none of the
skandhas can be the self because, if they were, they would not lead to
duhkha.[21] In Steve Collin's words: "One would have the power to change
them." In everyday terms, if I cannot control something, I say it is not me.
If suffering were what we essentially were, we would not seek to remove it.
Furthermore, when we look for our true self we are looking for what we
essentially are, discarding all that is changing and dependent on conditions
as incidental. If we were to find only changing processes and conditions,
we would conclude there was no self.

In the *Pali Canon*, the Buddha takes as given that self has the characteristics of permanence, independence, and freedom from suffering. He
then proceeds to establish that these qualities are not to be found in any
conditioned phenomena (*sabbe dhamma anatta*). He does not go so far as
to say that there is no self at all, nor does he say there is one. However, he
does say that Nirvana is permanence, non-conditioned (i.e. independent),
and freedom from suffering; the characteristics of the very self that all the
dharmas do not have.

Steve Collins remarks [*Selfless Persons* p.83]:

   . . . the denial of self in whatever can be experienced or conceptualized . . . serves to direct the attribution of value away from

that sphere. Instead of supplying a verbalized notion of what is the
sphere of ultimate value, Buddhism simply leaves a direction ar-
row, while resolutely refusing to predicate anything of the destina-
tion, to discuss its relationship with the phenomenal person or
indeed to say anything more about it.

Collins is, of course, arguing from the point of view of what is, perhaps,
the most influential section of the Theravadin tradition; Collin's comments
could equally be applied to Rangtong Prasangika Madhyamaka.

Arguably, they do not apply to the early Canons (including the *Pali
Canon*), to Shentong Yogacara Madhyamaka, nor to the Tathagatagarbhra
Sutras and the other sources of Shentong as understood by adherents to that
view. Similarly, they do not apply to the Chinese and related traditions that
stem from the Tathagatagarbha Sutras including, especially, the Hua Yen
doctrine of Fa Tsang and others. Since, taking the Shentong position here,
the Tathagatagarbha is "experience" beyond the normal implications of
that term, that is, it is not tainted by the conceptual divisions into experience and experiencer, Tathagatagarbha doctrine has much to say about the
"sphere of ultimate value" and the statement "all sentient beings have
Tathagatagarbha" does introduce the question of its relationship with the
phenomenal world.

The Self that is taught in the Tathagatagarbha Sutras is not dualistic
consciousness (vijnana), which is one of the skandhas and so by definition
adventitious. That is why it is best to avoid the term "ego" as a translation
for "*atman*" in spite of the fact that many westerners favor its use. The
reason "ego" is confusing is that it is defined [SOED] as "conscious thinking subject as opposed to the not-ego or object." Thus, it definitely implies
a dualistic frame of mind. Furthermore, "ego" has become quite a technical psychological term. "Ego" in psychological terms is the whole process
of establishing a healthy sense of identity and is entirely a conditioned phenomenon. It has nothing to do with what one truly is in essence. It might
be the process by which one clings to a sense of an abiding self within the
stream of the skandhas, but it is not that self as such. The ego-process
cannot be denied, but the abiding self within the stream of the skandhas can
and is denied by Buddhists.

It is the clinging to this nonexistent self that has to be abandoned, not
a healthy sense of identity. Therefore, it is confusing to translate not-self
(*anatman*) as not-ego. Furthermore, the Self of the Tathagatagarbha Sutras
is the truly existent self in the SOED sense. It has the characteristics of
Ultimate Reality and it would be a great mistake to translate this as "ego."

Looking closely at the ancient canonical sources (Pali and others), one
finds numerous references to what one might call the "sphere of ultimate

value," though its relationship with the phenomenal person is indeed hardly discussed at all. For example, where Nirvana itself seems to be expressed entirely in terms of extinction, like a fire going out and going nowhere, the Buddha does not stop there. He adds that it is vast and deep like an ocean—profound and difficult to comprehend. One could argue that there is nothing vast and deep about simple extinction; on the contrary, it is nothing at all.

The teaching that Nirvana is vast and deep implies it is something, but what it is has to be different from anything in samsara. Everything in samsara is shown to be dependently arising as a result of the conceptual process. Nirvana is not dependently arising and is free from conceptual processes. But in the Madhyamaka "nirvana" also is shown to not exist because the very concept "existent" arises in dependence on the concept "non-existent." When reality is seen as it is, both nonexistence and existence are seen to be mere concepts. That is why the RGV says it is Supreme Self because it is free from both self and non-self. However, it is useful to say Nirvana exists, because it remedies the idea that it is the mere extinction of something else.

It is interesting in this connection to consider the position of the Pudgalavadins. According to Fa Hsien, there were, at one time, more monks of this school than of any other. They were a tradition at least as ancient as the Theravadin and they accepted that the mind (*citta*) was not in the skandhas, outside them or both in and out, or neither in nor out and so forth. Edward Conze suggested that this is the kind of view that gave rise to the Tathagatagarbha and Cittamatrin doctrines. It is interesting that according to Conze the Pudgalavadins were virtually condemned by all other schools. One wonders to what extent their doctrine was or ever will be understood.[22]

Dolpopa [RC 89] mentions Asanga's non-self Self of the *Mahayanasutralamkara* (MSA), and he quotes [RC 78.5] at length from the *Mahaberi* and *Mahaparinirvanasutra*, which are far more explicit than the RGV concerning the nature of the Supreme Self. He explains [RC 70] how Tirthikas (*Mu stegs pa*)[*] might prefer the Great Self to Emptiness as a name for Absolute Reality. Then Dolpopa [RC 76.4] answers accusations that his view is like that of the Tirthikas. He explains that it is not the self dhatu of the Tirthikas even though it sounds like it, because it is the empty ground of the two selves (*bdag gnyis stong pa'i gzhi*)—the self of the person and the self of

---

[*]pronounced Mutegpa. This is a general term for Indian Non-Buddhist Schools of philosophy.

the dharmas, the Tathata Self, or the Pure Self (*de bzhin nyid kyi bdag dang dag pa'i bdag*).

Dolpopa then quotes terms such as the Pure Self (*dag pa'i bdag*), Tathata Self, Vajra Self, the single solid Vajra Self, and similar terms such as the Supreme Master of the Knower and Known (*shes dang shes bya'i bdag po mchog*) and the Supreme Master of All the Buddhas (*sangs rgyas kun bdag po mchog*), saying that there are many instances in the Sutras and Tantras and commentaries of the term "self" being used in Buddhist scriptures.

It is important to appreciate the psychological effect of the play on words occurring here. Some commentators[23] have tried to maintain that this doctrine of the Supreme Self introduced by the Tathagatagarbha Sutras reflects a regression back to the old Hindu notions of the Supreme Self. However, the Self posited here does not conform to the self refuted by the Buddha (i.e. a single, permanent, independent entity residing inside or outside the skandhas). In scriptural terms, there can be no real objection to referring to Buddha, Buddhajnana, Nirvana and so forth as the True Self, unless the concept of Buddha and so forth being propounded can be shown to be impermanent, suffering, compounded, or imperfect in some way.

Nevertheless, there is something a little outrageous in calling the Buddha or Buddhajnana the "*Paramatman*." This is Hindu terminology and it has always been a preoccupation (not to say obsession) of Indian Buddhism to keep itself distinct from Hinduism. The Tibetans have inherited this tendency and so, even though they accept the RGV and Tathagatagarbha doctrine, the expression "*Paramatman*" still embarasses them.

6.4   Gotra

The word "gotra" and its Tibetan counterpart "*rigs*" mean lineage in the sense of a family or species that has the power to give rise to mature individuals who can reproduce true to kind. It not only refers to the members of the lineage as a whole extending through space and time, but it also refers to the power of the lineage that enables it to continue the species true to kind. Therefore, members of a lineage both possess it as well as being it. This is a fundamental concept behind much Buddhist terminology and imagery; it is psychologically very powerful. Traditionally the family or clan lineage is at the heart of one's world view both socially and personally. It gives one a sense of identity and determines one's values. One derives from it self-confidence and dignity. Although such a way of thinking has been largely lost in modern western society, it is preserved in the institution of the royal family with its claim to royal blood.

This explanation, which is from Khenpo Tsultrim Gyamtso, is borne out by literary evidence. For example, Gampopa defines gotra (*rigs*) as "seed" (*sa bon*), "element" (*khams*), and "nature" (*rang bzhin*), and the characteristic of the Mahayana gotra (both naturally present and properly adopted) as "the power or ability to give rise to Buddha Dharmas (*sang rgyas kyi chos bskyed pa'i nus pa*)." He[24] describes the awakened and non-awakened gotra and the family (gotra) of the cut-off potential (*rigs chad rigs*). McDonell's Sanskrit English Dictionary [MAC] and Monier Williams' Sanskrit English Dictionary [MW] definitions bring out the sense of family, "blood," species and so forth, and the Buddhist Hybrid Sanskrit Dictionary [BHS] brings out the sense of seed, source, cause, and kind.

Kongtrul [RGV commentary 13a] refers to the gotra as the "like aspect" ('*dra ba'i cha*) because gotra means what is similar. Rangjung Dorje [*Zab mo nang don 14a*] explains:

> *lus sems gnyis kyi dag pa'am ye shes de ni rgyu yin te. rdzogs pa'i sangs rgyas kyi rigs 'dra yin pa'i phyir. rgyud yin te sems can nas sangs rgyas kyi bar du 'gyur ba med par rgyun 'brel ba'i phyir.*
>
> That purity or Jnana of the body and mind (both) is the cause (*hetu*), because it is the lineage/family likeness (*rigs 'dra*) of the Buddha. It is the thread (*rgyud*) because from beings up to Buddha it is a changeless continuity.

Rangjung Dorje is referring here to the pure aspect to every form, feeling, perception, thought, and consciousness that are described in the *Mahaparinirvanasutra* [MPNS], the Tantras, and elsewhere. This pure aspect is Tathagatagarbha (i.e. Buddhajnana) that is not normally perceived, hidden as it is by its impure version which must be removed. Dolpopa [RC 24] also refers to this as the gotra-likeness (*rigs 'dra*).

Thus, for Shentongpas "gotra" is used as a synonym for Tathagatagarbha and refers to Buddhajnana. For example, Dolpopa [RC 380.6] gives naturally present gotra (*rang bzhin gnas rigs*) as a synonym for Paramarthasatya.[25]

For Rangtongpas the situation is not as simple as that. Ruegg[26] gives a breakdown of the different meanings of gotra found in old Indo-Aryan [OIA] and in Buddhist Sanskrit in particular. We shall return to this subject later in this section. In general there are two reasons for creating different categories of gotra. First, to explain the different gotras for the different Buddhist vehicles (*yanas*) and also the cut-off gotra; second, to explain the use of the term gotra for both the cause of Enlightenment and for emptiness.

i. The Cut-off Gotra and the Three Yanas

In the *Pali Canon* the different kinds of followers of the Buddha are described as belonging to different lineages, depending on their degree of renunciation and desirelessness.[27] Renunciation and desirelessness are like the power of the lineage by means of which a member of that lineage is able to become a mature individual of his/her kind, that is, an Enlightened Sravaka or Pratyeka Buddha.

As Ruegg shows in *La Théorie* part one, for Mahayanists the concept of the Buddha gotra becomes an important subject of discussion. What is the power of the Buddha lineage that enables a member of that lineage to become a Buddha? Early Buddhist schools assumed Buddha had special qualities that distinguished him from ordinary beings so he was assigned his own lineage, the Buddha lineage. Since ordinary beings did not belong to it, they could never hope to become Buddha.

Mahayana doctrine, however, encourages everyone to aspire to reach complete and perfect Buddhahood. To aspire merely for the peaceful nirvana of Sravakas and Pratyeka Buddhas is frowned upon. Thus, somehow, everyone must have or be able to acquire the Buddha lineage in some sense. The question is what qualities one must have or acquire in order to belong to the lineage. Obviously one must have qualities that can eventually give rise to Buddha qualities, for example, limitless wisdom, compassion, and power to help beings [RGV 1.4]. Therefore, only a being capable of developing such qualities as wisdom and compassion could possibly belong to the Buddha lineage.[28] It might seem that this excludes from the lineage those without the slightest trace of wisdom or compassion, which would suggest not all beings had the Buddha lineage. This contradicts Tathagatagarbha doctrine, however, which teaches that all beings have the power to become Buddha. How can this be squared with the earlier teachings? In them gotra described different kinds of disciples of the Buddha or followers of the three Vehicles (*yanas*) as, for example, in Prajnaparamita literature.

The difficulty was resolved by introducing a distinction between two different kinds of gotra. Gampopa[29] explains that all beings have the naturally present gotra, but the properly adopted gotra (*yang dag par bsgrub pa'i rigs*) is special to the Mahayana family (another name for the Buddha lineage), and may or may not be awakened. This properly adopted gotra is obtained through properly adopting the right roots of merit. Beings without the right merit cannot become Buddhas and so do not belong to the Mahayana gotra. Even those with the right merit may not meet with the right conditions to awaken or activate their gotra. Thus, gotra here means the right seeds or traces in one's samvrti mind-stream that have the potential to trigger off the "development" process.

Kongtrul [RGV commentary 25b] distinguishes the gotra of proper adoption from the expanding gotra, which is present in the base and is, therefore, primordially present as the "power" of the gotra to emerge. The RGV and RGVV make only one reference to the properly adopted gotra [RGV

1.149] and their explanations in no way contradict the Shentong assumption that both the naturally present gotra and the expanding gotra are nondual Jnana (*Jnanakaya*).

In this way we arrive at three divisions of gotra: (*a*) the naturally present gotra pure by nature (*rang bzhin gnas pa'i rigs*), (*b*) the properly adopted gotra or gotra of proper adoption of roots of virtue (*yang dag blang ba or yang dag sgrub pa*), and (*c*) the expanding gotra (*rgyas gyur*).

Although in this context the properly adopted and the expanding gotra are distinguished, they are not always so. Rangtongpas, for example, use both terms to describe the expanding of the Buddha qualities on the path to Enlightenment—the naturally present gotra being the emptiness of the mind-stream of self-nature.

For Shentongpas the idea of a samvrti gotra of properly adopted roots or in this case "seeds" of merit is a somewhat peripheral idea. This was highlighted by the initial puzzlement shown by Lama Thubden—a learned and experienced Kagyu-Nyingma Lama—that Kongtrul [RGV commentary 25b] should refer to the properly adopted gotra as samvrti and Lama Thubden accounted for it by explaining that a slight distinction was being made between the expanding and the properly adopted gotra. As a Shentongpa, he focused on the expanding gotra, which is the naturally present gotra, emerging on the path to Enlightenment—as in the *Angulimala* and *Dharmadhatustotra* example of the lamp in the pot. The seeds of merit that constitute the gotra of proper adoption give the illusion that Buddha qualities are newly produced by traversing the path to Buddhahood. In fact, they merely trigger the giving up of veils. They are not themselves developed or transformed into Buddhajnana. On the other hand the expanding gotra is Buddhajnana.

Before this distinction between the different kinds of gotra became widely accepted, there was a considerable amount of controversy over the question of one or three final vehicles. Those who taught one final vehicle (*Ekayana*) argued fiercely against those who thought Pratyeka Buddhas and Sravakas could never reach Buddhahood, because their gotra determined their Enlightenment for all time. It is not clear whether there is simply a confusion of language here. It is true that some Sutras say Pratyeka Buddhas and Sravakas can never reach Buddhahood, but do they mean by this that a Pratyeka Buddha or Sravaka Arhat can never awaken from that state and change gotra? The *Ekayana* Sutras are quite specific that they can and, in fact, do change *yanas* (and thus gotras) after a very long time and through the power of the Buddha's blessing.[30]

The RGV clearly finds the doctrine of the three final vehicles misleading in that it gives the impression that there is an essential difference between those who give rise to Bodhicitta and follow the Bodhisattva path, and other kinds of beings who are necessarily inferior [RGV 1.162]. The division of the gotra into the naturally present and expanding gotra means that one can say that, although on one level it is true that until one enters the Bodhisattva path one has not the full power to become Buddha, even those without the Bodhisattva aspiration have the intrinsic power to become Buddha. As Gampopa explains,[31] all beings belong to one of five gotras and members of any of these gotras are capable eventually of attaining Buddhahood. It is just a matter of time.

ii. Gotra as Both Cause and Emptiness

The next question is, what can it be within the very nature of a being that gives him/her the power to reach supreme Buddhahood? As we saw above in the "Cut-off-Gotra and the Three Yanas", this power is called "Tathagatagarbha," but what is it exactly? The answer depends on what Buddhahood itself is conceived to be. Among the earliest records, there were various references to the nature of Buddhahood.[32] The strands of these doctrines were drawn together and expanded upon by the authors of the Mahayana scriptures. In the RGV, for example, the Buddha's Enlightenment is described as not only non-born, non-compounded, and not subject to birth and death, as signless and inconceivable, conceptionless, and stable, but also as a state of knowing Reality perfectly without any delusion or confusion, and as compassionate and active in effecting the benefit of others. Although the RGV draws mainly on Tathagatagarbha Sutras, similar statements are found in all Mahayana Sutras.

As we saw in the section on the Inseparable Qualities, the knowledge, compassion, power, and action described in the RGV [1.5] all seem to imply causes, conditions, arising, and passing away. This appears to contradict the doctrine that the Buddha is without conceptual effort, non-compounded, non-arising and non-ceasing and so forth. The RGV [5.81–84] explains that the nine examples of the Buddha Activity (from the JAAS) are given to help remove the doubts of disciples on this point. Nevertheless, as we have seen, not all commentators see this as establishing that the Buddha qualities and activity are non-compounded in the Shentong sense.

The Rangtong approach is to devise a system by which Buddhahood itself is seen as having two aspects. It proposes that the actual knowledge, compassion, and power of the Buddha are dependently arising moments of an eternally unending mind-stream, so they are not non-compounded and non-arising but their emptiness of self-nature is. Therefore, scriptural statements that seem to suggest a gotra that is primordially present, non-compounded and so forth must refer to emptiness, but statements that describe the gotra as the cause of the three Kayas of Buddha can only be explained by dividing the gotra into a) those aspects that cause Buddha qualities to develop and b) the emptiness aspect, which does not cause anything directly but is a "support" for Enlightenment in the sense that it is what beings must focus on. For these reasons, there is a great deal of discussion in Rangtong commentaries on Tathagatagarbha and gotra as to what their various aspects are and in what sense they cause Buddhahood. Indeed, in Rangtong terms, emptiness cannot be a *garbha* or gotra in the most obvious sense of these terms.

Ruegg [BSOAS 1976] puts forward arguments for interpreting gotra as "mine" or "source." He explains that in the title of the RGV "*Division of the Jewel Lineage*," "lineage" means a line of descent from Buddha, who gives rise to the Dharma from which follows the Samgha, who have the lineage that enables them to become Enlightened like the Buddha, with the qualities and activity that are the Dharma, which gives rise to Samgha and so on. Shentongpas do not dispute this sense of lineage but for them the sense of Buddhajnana being the essence of the lineage is the chief meaning of "Jewel Lineage." For them, the title expresses an ambiguity that is exploited in the layout of the text.

Ruegg [*La Théorie* 283], on the other hand, emphasizes that the RGV gives two explanations of gotra—the first being the gotra (i.e. cause) of the three Jewels, which is the last four Vajra Bases, (that is, Element, Enlightenment, Qualities, and Activity). Thus, Buddhajnana is gotra in the sense that Buddha qualities are the cause of Buddha activity and hence the Enlightenment of beings. For him, therefore, gotra here is "base of the path" in the sense of cause of the path. We are being asked to take gotra in this context to simply mean "cause" and to ignore the full connotations of the term and of its translation in Tibetan. Ruegg,[33] when explaining this division of the gotra into four, finds it clear that gotra in the title of RGV refers to a fourfold mine or matrix. I cannot say I find his arguments convincing but there is no space to give details here.[34] Indeed, as RGVV [1.152] explains:

> *de bzhin gshegs pa'i khams sems can 'di dag thams cad kyi snying por bstan pa yin no. de bzhin gshegs pa nyid sangs rgyas kyi sku rnam pa gsum gyis rab tu phye ba yin te. des na de bzhin gshegs pa'i khams thob pa'i rgyu yin pas khams kyi don ni 'dir rgyu'i don to*
>
> The Tathagata's Dhatu is taught to be the heart-essence of all beings. Since the Tathagata divides into the Buddha's three Kayas and since the Tathagatagarbha Dhatu is the cause of attainment, Dhatu means cause.

The *Srimaladevisutra* [SMS] is quoted in RGVV [1.152]:

> *bcom ldan 'das de'i slad du de bzhin gshegs pa'i snying po ni 'brel*
> *ba. rnam par dbye ba med pa. bral mi shes pa. 'dus ma byas pa'i*
> *chos rnams kyi gnas dang gzhi dang rten lags la. bcom ldan 'das*
> *de bzhin gshegs pa'i snying po ni ma 'brel ba rnam par dbye ba*
> *dang bcas pa'i chos. bral shes pa. 'dus byas kyi chos rnams kyi*
> *yang gzhi dang. gnas dang. rten lags so zhes gsungs pa'o*
> Lord, for this reason, the Tathagatagarbha is the abode, base and
> support for the uncompounded Dharmas that are connected, insep-
> arable, not knowing separation, and Lord, the Tathagatagarbha is
> also the abode, the base and the support* for the compounded
> dharmas that are disconnected, separable, and know separation.

This is the doctrine of the *Srimaladevisutra* according to which the Tathagatagarbha is the support for both the inherent, inseparable Dharmas as
well as the compounded dharmas that are not of the essence (i.e. are not
connected), are separable and dissociable. This doctrine occurs in RGV
[1.50–63]. These verses are based on the *Gaganaganjapariprccha* comparing the Dhatu to space.

Tathagatagarbha as *hetu* in the context of the SMS refers to its being
the Dhatu, which is the Tathagata with the three Kayas present in beings
and, therefore, the prime cause or "stuff" of their Buddhahood. "Dhatu"
can mean an element or elementary constituent.[35] Stcherbatsky in his *Buddhist Logic*, having noted that both *hetu* and *karana* are translated by
"*rgyu*" in Tibetan, explains that whereas *karana* means making, producing, causing and so forth, which definitely implies cause and effect, *hetu*
can simply mean "nature." Therefore, in colloquial Tibetan, *rgyu* is the
normal way of expressing what something is made of. Thus, to call the
Tathagatagarbha "*rgyu*" does not necessarily mean or imply that Tathagatagarbha is a cause different from its result—as fire is different from smoke
or an embryo from a mature adult. Since it can mean nature or "stuff," it is
an appropriate term for the "Changeless Nature".[36] Indeed, Gampopa calls
the first chapter of the *Jewel Ornament* "Tathagatagarbha, the Cause"
(*rgyu de gshegs snying po*), although Guenther rather misleadingly translates *rgyu* here as "motive."

The second explanation of gotra that Ruegg describes is gotra as it is
used in RGV [1.27], which he says is not quite the same as the gotra of the

---

*N.B. "Abode" (*gnas, nisraya*), "base" (*gzhi, adhara*), "support" (*rten, prat-
istha*).

three Jewels since it does not consist of Buddhajnana at all. He explains that Buddhajnana is simply "*un facteur associé au gotra.*" Thus, according to him, whereas the first sense of gotra relates to the RGV as a whole, the second is the subject matter of the first chapter only. His explanations follow those of Gyaltsab's *Dartik*, but do not agree with Rongton. Furthermore, neither the RGV nor the RGVV make any explicit distinction between gotra as applied to the gotra of the three Jewels and gotra as the third sign that all beings have Tathagatagarbha.

Chapter 7

The Third Dharmacakra: Neyartha or Nitartha

7.1 The Third Dharmacakra

i. The Three Dharmacakras

Dharmacakra means the "Wheel of the Dharma" and the turning of this, for all Buddhists, means a literally world shattering event. A Dharmacakra heralds the coming of a Golden Age in which the Truth of the Dharma, newly arrived in the world, teaches and liberates beings. One might expect, therefore, each of the three successive Dharmacakras of Mahayana Buddhism to bring some extraordinary teaching never heard before.

Although Tibetan scholars assign the Sutras and commentaries to a place in the three cycles for pedagogic reasons, the Sutras do not assign themselves to the three cycles even though some, for example, the *Sandhinirmocana*, mention the division of the Buddha's doctrine into three cycles or stages. The Sutras and commentaries are in fact mostly composite works; their true origin is obscured by myth and tradition. Their historical date and authorship are matters of seemingly endless speculation among modern scholars and, since each Sutra carries several layers of doctrine, it is not easy to place a complete Sutra in one cycle or another. Nevertheless, Tibetan commentators try to do this in order to introduce some order into their rich scriptural heritage.

Each Tibetan commentator has his own criteria for placing a certain text in one cycle rather than another, depending primarily on what he takes as the supreme reality (i.e. rangtong or Shentong). He then uses the three Dharmacakra structure as a pedagogic device for explaining the relationship between the neyartha and Nitartha teachings. Then, depending on what he takes to be the key doctrine of each cycle and the key doctrine of any particular Sutra or commentary, he will assign it a place within the three Dharmacakra structure.

Having done this he will proceed to define terms and interpret each text according to his overall scheme. However much modern philologists may despair of such a system of textual analysis, for good or for ill this is the very essence of the Tibetan commentarial tradition.

ii. The Third Dharmacakra as Nitartha

According to Khenpo Tsultrim, the first Dharmacakra taught how things appear (*snang tshul*), that is, impermanent, suffering, non-self, and impure; the second taught how they truly are (*gnas tshul*), that is, empty of independently existing dharmas and persons (*rangtong*). The third taught how they truly are ultimately (*gnas tshul mthar thug pa*), that is, the essence of all these empty dharmas is the great Emptiness, having the inseparable, spontaneous Buddha Qualities, complete and pure from the very beginning. Dolpopa explains [RC 172]:

> The first Dharmacakra corresponds to the preliminary practices for the profound Nitartha meditation of the Mahayana. The second Dharmacakra corresponds to the practice of the special concentration for settling into meditation of the profound subject matter/ meaning (*zab mo'i don sgom pa*). The third Dharmacakra is also in accordance with the profound secret Mantra (*guhyamantra*) which "introduces" [the disciple to the true nature of his mind] (*ngo 'phrod pa*) by presenting properly what is existent and what is not existent etc. when the special *samadhi* arises. Thus, the three Dharmacakras progressively purify the Tathagatagarbha of stain.

According to Dolpopa, the first Dharmacakra starts to teach the final meaning (Nitartha) when it says the self is neither in, nor outside of the skandhas. Although it was understood to mean simply the absence of an enduring personal self associated with or identical to the skandhas, according to Dolpopa it implied the existence of the True Self. However, since the teaching concentrated on absence of self inside or outside the apparent reality of the skandhas, it was a provisional (neyartha) teaching. Incidentally, the *Sandhinirmocanasutra* [SNS vll.17] also teaches that the Nitartha—(in this case defined as absence of self-nature, *nihsvabhava*)—was taught in all neyartha Sutras.

Continuing with Dolpopa's analysis, the second Dharmacakra, a development of the first, taught the skandhas to be empty of both self-nature of the person and self-nature of phenomena. In the first cycle, the skandhas were shown to have no enduring personal self, but since one might be left with the impression that the skandhas (comprising aggregations of partless parts and streams of mind-moments) had some kind of self-nature of their own, the second Dharmacakra was taught to remove this subtle mistake. However, since, in order to establish self-emptiness of all dharmas, the Sutras of the second Dharmacakra sometimes gave the impression that even the Absolute is self-empty, Dolpopa classes this Dharmacakra as "neyartha" [RC 177].

He describes the third cycle as consisting of the teachings on the Absolute Dhatu as found in the *Sandhinirmocana* and the Paramarthasatya Tathagatagarbha, or nondual Jnana present in the base found in the Tathagatagarbha Sutras and the Tantras. RC [135] mentions that the Sutras of the third Dharmacakra and the Tantric "Mind Commentaries" (*sems 'grel*) all teach Tathagatagarbha, the Pure Self. It should be noted here that although generally speaking the three Dharmacakras refer to Sutrayana material, Shentongpas regard Mantrayana as an extension of the third Dharmacakra.

The Shentong analysis fits easily into the layout of the RGV. RGV [1.156] teaches that Tathagatagarbha doctrine is a sequel to the Prajnaparamita doctrine of the emptiness of the dharmas, which are unreal like clouds, dreams, and magical apparitions.

Kongtrul [SKK hum 11ba] describes how according to Maitreya the first teachings of the Buddha are intended to cause renunciation to arise in beings who are attached to samsara. Then, having thus been established in the path of peace, the beings are ripened by teachings on emptiness so that they enter the Mahayana. Finally, the unassailable Dharmacakra makes them enter the field (*yul*) of the Tathagatas. This accords with RGV 1.57–59. Such a scheme also accords with the *Mahakaruna* [quoted in RGVV 1.25], which describes the progressive purification of the lapis lazuli in three stages. First, there is the teaching of impermanence, non-self, impurity, and suffering in order to give rise to renunciation. Second, there is the teaching of emptiness, signlessness and desirelessness and so forth in order to bring about the realization of the way (*tshul*) the Tathagata is. Third, there is the teaching of the irreversible Dharmacakra of the complete purification, which is to cause the various kinds of beings to enter the field (*yul*) of the Tathagata.[1]

Nonetheless, Kongtrul ends his discussion by indicating that only the Tibetan *acaryas*, Rangjung Dorje, Dolpopa, Longchenpa, and the others (*sogs*) together with their followers held the third Dharmacakra as supreme, while the majority took the second as supreme. Since these three teachers lived in the fourteenth century, we deduce from Kongtrul's account that all the early Tibetan Madhyamikas held the second Dharmacakra as supreme and must, therefore, have been Rangtongpas.

Kongtrul refers to the whole controversy about which Dharmacakra is the final one as so much meaningless chatter (*cal col*). He explains [SKK hum 10na] that Nagarjuna said the Buddha first taught self, then non-self, and finally the base reversing everything. Thus, the first Dharmacakra reversed lack of merit, the second reversed self, and the final one reversed all views. He classsifies Sutras which teach mainly about apparent phenomena (samvrti) as neyartha and those teaching mainly about the Absolute as Nitartha. Kongtrul concludes that, although the second and third can both be classed as Nitartha, the third Dharmacakra is especially Nitartha (*nges don gyi khyad par du bzhed*) because the second Dharmacakra establishes only the temporary cutting off of prapanca (*gnas skabs spros pa gcod pa*) whereas the third teaches the ultimate state (*mthar thug gnas lugs*). He calls this the Yogacara tradition (*rnal 'byor spyod pa'i lugs*) based on the highest scriptural authority.

According to Kongtrul,[2] Asanga was predicted in the *Manjusrimulatantra* as the ultimate authority on distinguishing neyartha and Nitartha teachings. Kongtrul [SKK hum 12na] explains that Asanga and Vasubandhu taught that the third Dharmacakra was ultimate Nitartha (*mtha' thug gi nges don*) without denying the second also to be Nitartha. Kongtrul discusses the different presentations of the three Dharmacakras and the two satyas at some length and mentions that the Siddha Sri Virupa (*dPal ldan chos skyong*) reasoned that both the second and third Dharmacakras must be Nitartha. This suggests an overlap between the Emptiness teachings of the Prajnaparamita Sutras of the second Dharmacakra and the general teachings of the Asolute Dharmata Sutras of the third.

Although to classify the second Dharmacakra as Nitartha does not quite accord with the SNS or Dolpopa, there is no real disagreement between them, for all three agree that a correct understanding of Prajnaparamita (second Dharmacakra) is Nitartha.

Kongtrul points out [SKK hum 12ba] that the *Mahaberi* and the other Tathagatagarbha Sutras explain repeatedly and clearly that the third Dharmacakra is supreme. He adds that the example in the *Mahakarunanirdesa* (DRS) of the cleaning of the jewel can only reasonably be interpreted as saying the third Dharmacakra is supreme.

Elsewhere Kongtrul expresses the opinion that since Nagarjuna and Aryadeva certainly accepted the example of purifying the jewel in the *Mahakarunanirdesa* they must by implication have accepted the third Dharmacakra to be Nitartha.

Those who take the third Dharmacakra as supreme find the Dharmacakras present the teaching of the Buddha as a serial progression, each Dharmacakra opening up a profound new dimension and correcting previous misunderstandings as explained in the chief Sutra sources for the Dharmacakra system (i.e. the *Mahakarunanirdesa* and the *Sandhinirmocana*).

This pattern is reflected in the *Life and Liberation of Padmasambhava* by Yeshe Tsogyal, which was rediscovered by Urgyan Lingpa (fourteenth century) and translated into French by G. C. Toussaint and into English by K. Douglas and G. Bays [158–160]. Here an account is given of four Dharmacakras even though the third is refererred to as the final one (the fourth includes the exterior Tantras). The first was taught at Benares and concerns samvrtisatya such as suffering, karma, and Vinaya, the second was taught at Rajagrha on the Prajnaparamita and is Nitartha. The third was taught at Vaisali and includes Tathagatagarbha doctrine, which is also Nitartha.

Interestingly, Professor Ruegg [*La Théorie* 56] refers us to the view of the Chinese school of Fa tsang (643–712). This school divides the teachings of the Buddha into four phases, the fourth of which is the Tathagatagarbha doctrine.

iii. Kongtrul's Distinction Between the Two Kinds of Nitartha Sutra of the Third Dharmacakra

Kongtrul makes an interesting distinction [RGV commentary 5a] between two sorts of Nitartha Sutra of the third Dharmacakra. First he mentions the "four well-known Cittamatrin Sutras" that teach the Dharmata as the truly existing Absolute shown through ordinary reasoning, and then the Sutras that give the "extra-ordinary tenets that are the detailed secret teachings." The first four include the *Sandhinirmocana*, the *Lankavatara*, and the *Avatamsaka*, while under the second heading, Kongtrul includes the *Tathagatagarbha*, the *Angulimala*, the *Srimaladevi*, the *Dharanirajesvara* (*Mahakaruna*), and the *Mahaparinirvana*. A detailed study of Kongtrul's distinction is not possible at present but I have looked at the SNS as an example of the first Sutra class and the *Srimaladevisutra* (SMS) as an example of the other, in order to investigate how Kongtrul is able to come to his conclusion.

a. The *Sandhinirmocanasutra*: Example of a Sutra Teaching the Absolute Dharmata.

Concerning the *Sandhinirmocanasutra* [SNS], Ketrub, when discussing to which Dharmacakra it belongs, states that (*a*) the characteristics of the third Dharmacakra are to teach that the parikalpita characteristic is not truly existent (*bden par ma grub*); (*b*) that the paratantra and parinispanna characteristics are real (*bden pa*); and (*c*) that ultimately the vehicles are three [Fundamentals of Buddhist Tantras (F) 48].

He then states [F 50] that the SNS[3] teaches that ultimately the vehicles are three. He also states that the SNS[4] teaches that the paratantra and parinispanna are truly existent (*bden par grub par*).

From this he concludes that the SNS is a Sutra of the third Dharmacakra and as such neyartha [F 52].

Kongtrul, of course, does not agree with Ketrub, in spite of the fact that both claim to be following the tradition of Vasubandhu. Although I personally find Ketrub's position in regard to the SNS indefensible, there is a strong body of opinion that favors it. Therefore, in appendix 4 to this present work, I briefly demonstrate by means of a *résumé* of each of the chapters of the SNS, how Kongtrul arrives at his conclusions concerning the interpretation of the SNS. From this outline we learn that:

1. The SNS emphasizes and reiterates that its teaching is Nitartha.
2. It claims the Nitartha is the teaching of the third Dharmacakra.
3. It teaches the Nitartha to be the detailed understanding of all dharmas being without self-nature (*nihsvabhavata*, i.e. the absence of self-nature of the parikalpita, the paratantra and the Parinispanna).
4. It devotes a great deal of space to teaching the Paramartha [SNS I–V], which it identifies with the Parinispanna [VII.6]. SNS VI–VII teach the Parinispanna. The Paramartha is referred to as the dhatu from time to time throughout the Sutra.
5. The description of the Element without outflow in SNS [VII.24] is particularly reminiscent of the Absolute Dhatu as understood by the Shentong commentators.

Thus, Kongtrul's assertion that the SNS teaches the Nitartha of the third Dharmacakra concerning the nature of the Absolute Dhatu is easy to follow.

It is true that I wrote the *résumé* in appendix 4 with the deliberate intention of helping the reader to see how Kongtrul reaches his conclusions concerning the Sutra. Nevertheless, Ketrub's interpretation (see above), though deserving of serious consideration on account of its influence in Tibetan Buddhist scholarship both East and West, is problematical. Although it cannot be denied that SNS VII.20 stresses there are three characteristics, parikalpita, paratantra, and Parinispanna, the SNS does not say anywhere that any of the characteristics are real or truly existent (*bden pa* or *bden par grub*). SNS [VI.8–9] compares the paratantra to a crystal that is made to appear like a ruby or other colored precious stones because of its proximity to something of that color that it is reflecting. Such a statement in isolation could be construed as giving the paratantra some sort of real existence. However, SNS [VI.5] clearly states that paratantra is dependent origination (*pratityasamutpada*); VII.5 states that absence of an arising self-nature (*utpattinihsvabhava*) of all dharmas is the characteristic of the paratantra. In other words, the SNS repeatedly asserts the absence of self-nature of the paratantra in the sense that what is dependent origination (*pratityasamutpada*) is non-arising. Neither of these terms can meaningfully be construed as corresponding to the term truly existing (*bden grub*).

The evidence for claiming that the sns teaches that ultimately the ve-hicles are three is rather tenuous. In fact, the sns does not make any state-ment regarding the ultimate fate of those who follow inferior vehicles. All that is clear is that as long as a person is by nature of inferior gotra, he/she will not attain supreme Enlightenment. This is standard for all Mahayana literature. If, when or how a being can change gotras is not a question the sns addresses. Neither does it make any statement about whether all beings have the Buddha gotra in the sense of Tathagatagarbha or not. The type of inferior gotra referred to in sns [VII.15] is referred to in Mahayana commentaries[5] alongside teachings about the Buddhagotra possessed by all beings by nature. Thus, its mention in the sns is not conclusive evidence that the Sutra excludes the possibility of certain beings ever attaining su-preme Enlightenment. The evidence is at best inconclusive.

Regarding the assertion that sns is neyartha, there has been much dis-cussion among both Tibetan and Western scholars concerning the exact us-age of such terms as *abhiprayeka* and *samdhaya* and their relation to the term neyartha [see appendix 4 for more details]. It is true that the terms occur frequently throughout the sns but not in such a way as to present any problem to a straightforward reading of the text. For those commentators who wish to interpret the text as neyartha, in spite of its own frequent assertions that it teaches Nitartha, the various nuances of the terms *ab-hiprayeka* and *samdhaya* (*dgongs pa*) and their later becoming, for some commentators at least, a signal for neyartha teachings are matters of great importance. It is well-known among Tibetan scholars, for example, that the Gelugpa tradition takes the term "*dgongs pa*" (to intend, think) to indicate neyartha teachings.

b. The *Srimaladevisutra*: Example of a Sutra Teaching "Extra-ordinary Tenets"

The above section on the sns demonstrates how it teaches what Kongtrul calls the "ordinary doctrine of the Absolute Dhatu," which establishes the single Absolute Reality as the focus of meditation.

The sms Tathagatagarbha doctrine emphasizes the inseparable nature of the Buddha Qualities and the dynamic nature of the Tathagatagarbha, which is the Dharmakaya present and active in beings from the beginning, causing them to weary of the samsaric process and aspire to nirvana.[6] There is nothing new to attain. The Dhatu is not simply a pure focus for one's med-itation practice by means of which the mind will be purified; it is the pure Mind itself that is never covered (see quotation below). Since it cannot be focused on by ordinary perception it can only be known through "faith."

The SMS is explicit about Tathagatagarbha being both Emptiness-Jnana and the inseparable Buddha Qualitites:

bcom ldan 'das de bzhin gshegs pa'i chos kyi sku thog ma ma mchis pa'i dus nas mchis pa. ma bgyis pa. ma skyes pa. mi bas pa. bas pa ma mchis pa. rtag pa. brtan pa. rang bzhin gyis yongs su dag pa. nyon mongs pa thams cad kyi sbubs nas nges par grol ba. sangs rgyas kyi chos tha dad du mi gnas pa. grol bar shes pa bsam gyis mi khyab pa gang g'a'i klung gi bye ma las 'das pa snyed dang ldan pa ni sdug bsngal 'gog pa'i ming gis bstan pa'i slad du ste. bcom ldan 'das de nyid la de bzhin gshegs pa'i snying po chos kyi sku nyon mongs pa'i sbubs nas nges par grol ba zhes bgyi'o. bcom ldan 'das de bzhin gshegs pa'i snying po shes pa nyid ni de bzhin gshegs pa rnams kyi stong pa nyid kyi ye shes lags te. de bzhin gshegs pa'i snying po ni nyan thos dang. rang sangs rgyas thams cad kyis sngon ma mthong ma rtogs lags so. bcom ldan 'das kyis ni thugs su chud cing mngon sum du mdzad do. bcom idan 'das de bzhin gshegs pa'i snying po stong pa nyid shes pa ni 'di gnyis lags te. gnyis gang zhe na. 'di lta ste. bcom ldan 'das de bzhin gshegs pa'i snying po nyon mongs pa thams cad kyi sbubs dang tha dad du gnas pa ma grol bas shes pa rnams kyis stong pa dang. bcom ldan 'das de bzhin gshegs pa'i snying po'i sangs rgyas kyi chos tha dad du mi gnas shing grol bas shes pa bsam gyis mi khyab pa gang g'a'i klung gi bye ma las 'das pa snyed dag gis mi stong ba lags so.

Bhagavan, the Tathagata's Dharmakaya exists from beginningless time, it is not made, it is not arisen, it is not to be accomplished and was not accomplished, it is permanent, stable, and pure by nature, it is well free from the sheath of the klesas, it is the inseparable Buddha Dharmas. It has the extent beyond the sands of the River Ganges, it is knowledge of the liberated (*muktajna*) and beyond imagination, it is taught by the name of "Cessation of Suffering." Bhagavan, this very [thing] is what is known as the Tathagatagarbha Dharmakaya liberated from the sheath of the klesa.

Bhagavan, this which is called Tathagatagarbha is called the Tathagata's Emptiness Jnana. The Tathagatagarbha is not previously seen or realized by Sravakas or Pratyeka Buddhas. It is understood and actualized by the Bhagavan. Bhagavan, the Tathagatagarbha emptiness knowledge is two-fold. What are the two? They are these:

Bhagavan, the Tathagatagarbha dwelling apart from all the klesa sheaths is empty of the knowledge of the non-liberated (*ma grol bas shes pa rnams—amuktajna*). Bhagavan, the Tathagatagarbha's inseparable Buddha Dharmas are not empty of the knowledge (*shes pa*)* of the liberated, the extent of the sands of the River Ganges.

Wayman in his book *Lion's Roar of Queen Srimala* [p. 98 fn 83] casts doubt on Tathagatagarbha Dharmakaya being free from klesa. However, this doubt seems to be removed by subsequent passages.

The passage quoted above neatly sums up the Shentong interpretation of Tathagatagarbha doctrine, which is used as a model for the exposition of the RGV in secion 3 of this present work.

iv. Dolpopa's Analysis

Dolpopa quotes extensively from the *Mahakaruna* and *Sandhinirmocana Sutras* concerning the supremacy of the third Dharmacakra. The *Sandhinirmocana* quotation he uses to support his presentation of the three Dharmacakras [SNS VII. 30] reveals that the first Dharmacakra teaches the four Noble Truths (*aryasatya*) for those who belong to the Sravakayana. It is a provisional, surpassable, neyartha teaching that is open to question. The second Dharmacakra is presented as being for those of the Mahayana accepting emptiness. It teaches dharmas as being without essence, non-born, non-ceasing, and primordially peace and nirvana. The third Dharmacakra is for those of all vehicles (*yana*). It teaches the emptiness of dharmas as being without essence, non-born, non-ceasing, and primordially peace and nirvana. This time the doctrine makes a perfect differentiation (*legs par rnam par phye ba*) so that it is Nitartha, insurpassable, non-provisional (*skabs med pa*), and not open to question. Dolpopa [RC 71] explains that behind the Hinayana, Mahayana and Vajrayana teachings there is but one final intention (*mtha' thug pa'i don*), which is to teach Ultimate Reality. That Ultimate Reality is itself the Nitartha. Teachings about anything other than this are about what is ultimately untrue and, therefore, provisional (*neyartha*).

Nonetheless, he explains [RC 318.6] that there are two stages of teaching on the Nitartha. The first is to establish freedom from positions (*mtha'*) and the second to distinguish what exists and what does not (*yod med shan 'byed*). He quotes from the *Ratnakuta* (*dKon mchog rtsegs pa*) where it states that self and non-self are both positions (*mtha'*) and the pure essence of both is the Madhyamaka.

---

*N.B. From the Shentong point of view the ambiguity of the word *shes pa* (*jna*) in the terms *grol bar shes pa* and *grol bas shes pa* (*muktajna*) does not matter particularly, since all its senses (i.e. knowledge, knowing, knower, mind) would be applicable.

The *Mahaparinirvanasutra* is also quoted [RC 173.1] for its parallel doctrine and Dolpopa [RC 226] explains that, by means of the third Dharmacakra instruction, the second becomes clear like seeing a mountain from the sky.

The passages from the *Mahakaruna* and *Sandhinirmocana* Sutras that Dolpopa uses to support his statements differ in wording but agree with his analysis in the following ways:

1. Both the third stage of the purification process in the *Mahakaruna* and the third Dharmacakra in the *Sandhinirmocana* are presented as being for followers of all vehicles, suggesting they are indispensable; whereas other teachings are only needed for certain individuals.

2. The second stage of the purification and the second Dharmacakra are meant only for some disciples. According to the *Mahakaruna*, it is a means for "realizing the way the Tathagata is" as opposed to "entering his field." This could be interpreted as meaning the nisprapanca nature of the Buddha is realized through properly recognizing the empty nature of all dharmas. This would, from the Shentong point of view, produce the correct nisprapanca concentration necessary for practising the Nitartha Absolute Reality meditation. "Entering the sphere" could be interpreted as the direct approach through faith and yoga found in the Tantras and the special "introducing" instructions.

3. The *Mahakaruna* definitely presents a three stage purification process that removes contingent stains from an inner core of Nitartha Absolute Reality.

4. Since the last stage of the teaching is for followers of all vehicles, but the second is not, this accords with the view that, after first developing renunciation, which is the preliminary for any Dharma practice, one may proceed either by the path of reasoning to the third Dharmacakra or directly through the path of faith and direct experience as found in the Tathagatagarbha Sutras, Tantras and so forth. This is not to say it is not necessary to realize the emptiness of apparent phenomena that is taught in the second Dharmacakra, but that it is unnecessary to go through a stage of assuming that Absolute Reality is also one of the self-empty dharmas.

Although not all Shentong commentators present the difference between the second and third Dharmacakra in exactly the same way as Dolpopa does, in principle they are much the same.[7]

v. The Third Dharmacakra is Not Cittamatra

According to Kongtrul [SKK om 281na], the majority of early and late Tibetan and some Indian pandits took the Tathagatagarbha doctrine to be Cittamatrin. In the light of this, it is interesting that Thrangu Rinpoche regards

Rangtong systems of interpretation of the RGV to be very like ordinary Cittamatra.

When asked, Khenpo Tsultrim (following SKK om 150ba) explained that for those who do not accept the Sutras of the third Dharmacakra to be supreme, their special feature is the teaching on the three natures (parikalpita, paratantra, and parinispanna), which distinguishes between what does and does not exist. The three natures are often automatically associated with Cittamatra and its alayavijnana doctrine. This has led some commentators to say that the teachings of the third Dharmacakra are Cittamatra, which is, according to all Madhyamikas, neyartha.

Dolpopa argues [RC 201-11] that Sutras such as the *Lankavatarasutra* [LAS] and SNS should not automatically be classified as Cittamatra merely because they mention the three natures. He maintains that even Prajnaparamita literature refers to these subject matters. According to RC [207] the *Astasahasrika* mentions the three natures. Dolpopa explains that the distinctive view of the Cittamatrins is that mind, thought, and consciousness (*citta, manas,* and *vijnana—sems, yid* and *rnam shes*) ultimately exist (paramartha), but in the above mentioned Sutras they are apparent phenomena (samvrti). In his view, these Sutras are Yogacara and he adds [RC 222] that Yogacara texts are not necessarily Cittamatra.

Dolpopa opposes [RC 177ff] those who say SNS is neyartha, that the middle Dharmacakra is Nitartha (Rangtong Madhyamaka), and the third is Cittamatra (neyartha). In brief his arguments are: (*a*) there is no scriptural authority for saying the third Dharmacakra is Cittamatra. It is beyond Cittamatra because it is Great Madhyamaka and accords with the Vajrayana; (*b*) the SNS says the third Dharmacakra teaches all dharmas are essenceless and this shows it is not Cittamatra.

Dolpopa [RC 221.4], when summing up how people mistakenly assign texts to the Cittamatra, explains it is because they do not have direct Mind instruction (from the Guru) or realize the two levels of Cittamatra. Having said, as we have just seen, that the Yogacara texts are not necessarily Cittamatra [RC 212], he admits that there are two kinds of Cittamatra and that the LAS makes this distinction. He adds that Absolute Cittamatra is the same as Yogacara Madhyamaka, explaining that in Absolute Cittamatra [RC 211.6] there is no perceiver and perceived (*yul dang yul can*). According to him [RC 214.1], it occurs in the *Kalacakra* as the Paramartha Dhatu-Awareness inseparable (*don dam dbyings rig dbyer med*, which would translate as *Vidhyadhatusambheda* in Skt.). It is the Absolute Mind that is the basis of samsara and nirvana. When one realizes that even mind does not exist, then this is beyond Cittamatra [RC 216.4]. Thus, Dolpopa [RC 218.2] makes a clear distinction between ordinary Cittamatra, which accepts that outer apparent things are conceptually created, and Yogacara Madhyamaka in which samsara and nirvana are direct manifestations of Absolute Mind (Buddhajnana).

Concerning this same controversy, Dolpopa refers in particular to the LAS [XXVIII 69] where it says the Tathagatagarbha was taught as a device for disciples afraid of non-self. Some commentators take this to mean that the Buddha first taught Tathagatagarbha, which sounds like the self of non-Buddhists, as a provisional teaching for those afraid of the non-self doctrine [Ruegg LM 73]. However, the fact that Tathagatagarbha is taught after establishing the not-self of the person and the dharmas, and not before, suggests that Tathagatagarbha was taught for those who already accepted the not-self doctrine and not for those who were afraid of it. Furthermore, the LAS compares the teaching of not-self to a potter making various pots from the same clay: in the same way the Buddha teaches not-self in many ways including that of Tathagatagarbha doctrine.

From the Shentong point of view, there is a sense in which Tathagatagarbha is a Nitartha teaching for those afraid of not-self. Characteristically, when a deep, but only partial, realization of not-self arises, the Clear Light Nature of Mind is not properly experienced. A typical reaction to such a partial realization is great fear. In order to overcome this fear great faith is needed: one needs the confidence to open out into one's experience without drawing back into oneself away from the not-self emptiness that is experienced as a terrifying abyss or annihilation. Tathagatagarbha doctrine can have the effect of giving the practitioner the confidence to make the necessary "leap" into non-conceptual Reality.

Kongtrul [commentary to ZND 15b.6] criticizes those who say Tathagatagarbha is neyartha. His objections are that such people are saying: (a) Buddhas arise from the path and so are compounded; (b) beings do not inherently (rang chas) have Tathagatagarbha; (c) since all knowledge is compounded, it is not possible that Prajnaparamita, Omniscience, Jnana, and Pramana are non-compounded. Therefore, they deny what is true—the Absolute; (d) the ultimate Tantra (rgyud), the Mandala Deities, and Buddhas are compounded; and (e) the Svabhavikakaya is not Buddha. This kind of talk is, according to Rangjung Dorje, like a shepherd who, having kept sheep all his life, does not recognize sheep.

7.2   Neyartha and Nitartha

i. Rangtong Explanations of Neyartha and Nitartha

Kongtrul explains that Candrakirti made his division into provisional (neyartha) and supreme (Nitartha) teachings according to the *Aksayamati-*

nirdesasutra (*bLo gros mi zad pa bstan pa'i mdo*). He adds that, since this Sutra does not mention the layout into three cycles of teaching, it cannot be taken as an authority on the subject of the status of the third Dharmacakra. Nonetheless, for centuries both Indian and Tibetan commentators have taken and still do use its definition of Nitartha to establish that the second Dharmacakra is supreme and the third is neyartha. For these commentators it is difficult to present the three Dharmacakra system as a simple progressive series of teachings, without encountering anomalies.

Whereas in the Shentong view the SNS is Nitartha because it teaches the Nitartha—by distinguishing between what is neyartha and Nitartha— those who believe the third Dharmacakra is neyartha have difficulty in explaining the SNS, which is the only Sutra to clearly state which Dharmacakras are neyartha and which ones are Nitartha. Having taken the Madhyamaka Prasangika of the second Dharmacakra as supreme, how are they to explain the *Sandhinirmocana's* saying that the first and second are neyartha and only the third is Nitartha? Forced by this to concede that in some sense the third Dharmacakra is Nitartha, Gelugpa and other commentators maintain that it is Nitartha insofar as it distinguishes between what is neyartha and what is Nitartha [SNS VII.30]. Thus, it is Nitartha in spite of the fact that, in their view, it teaches the neyartha doctrine that the paratantra truly exists and that ultimately the vehicles are three and so forth.

Gyaltsab [*Dartik* 3.3] discusses what he considers the two methods of distinguishing Nitartha and neyartha; the first follows Candrakirti by referring to the *Aksayamatinirdesasutra* and also the *Samadhirajasutra* (*'Phags pa blo gros mi zad gyi mdo* and *Ting nge 'dzin rgyal po'i mod*). Both these Sutras were source materials for Nagarjuna and used as references by Candrakirti. In these texts neyartha is equated with samvrti and Nitartha with paramartha.

The second method is from the SNS, which he explains teaches that both those doctrines that teach all dharmas do exist by nature and those that teach they do not are neyartha: the Nitartha is those doctrines that correctly distinguish which phenomena do and which do not exist by nature. Since Gyaltsab does not accept Dolpopa's view that the second Dharmacakra is neyartha because it implies the Paramartha Dharmas do not exist, presumably Gyalsab is arguing that, according to the SNS, the second Dharmacakra is neyartha because it implies that samvrti dharmas do not exist. One could argue that, since the SNS gives the dependent nature (paratantra) greater existential status than the imaginary nature (parikalpita), it corrects the view that the meaning of "all dharmas are without self-nature" is that all samvrti dharmas (including the paratantra) do not exist. However, the SNS teaches that the dependent nature (paratantra) is without self-nature in the sense of non-arising and that it is the Parinispanna that truly exists, thus supporting the Shentong view.

Although Gyaltsab refers to the SNS method of determining Nitartha and neyartha, he also suggests that one should not take the words of the *Sandhinirmocana* too literally. Since it is not to be taken literally,[8] it can be thought of as neyartha. Since it only leads to the definitive meaning, it is not the definitive meaning itself. Thus, according to this system, definitive meaning (Nitartha) means either the highest doctrine that teaches about the highest truth or reality (as in the second Dharmacakra), or a definitive (Nitartha) doctrine that makes a final clarification, but is not really expressly about the highest doctrine (as in the third Dharmacakra).

Obviously if the different Tibetan commentators cannot agree on what is the Nitartha teaching of the Buddha there will be a great deal of controversy over how the scriptures are to be classified. This is not a trivial matter, for how the scripture is classified affects the way it is interpreted, including the way even the most basic terms are defined [*La Théorie* 55].

ii. The Terms "Neyartha" and "Nitartha"

Concerning the meaning and use of the terms Nitartha and neyartha, Takasaki [*Study* 285fn.137] explains that the "Profound Teaching Kaya" in RGV [1.145] is the Nitartha, because according to RGVV [1.145] it teaches the Absolute Reality; the "Various Teaching Kaya" is neyartha, because it teaches samvrtisatya. This agrees both with how Nagarjuna, Candrakirti, Kongtrul, and Dolpopa understand the terms.

However, as we saw above, in order to explain how such an important Sutra source as the SNS can be correct in its analysis of the Dharmacakras in spite of its insistence that the second is neyartha and the third supreme, commentators who hold the second to be supreme argue that neyartha does not necessarily refer to a samvrtisatya teaching. Since "neyartha" literally means "leading to," it is argued that the fact that the second Dharmacakra "leads to" the third does not necessarily mean the former is not Nitartha. This argument was already in vogue in Dolpopa's day because he goes to some length to refute it. His objection is that if "neyartha" simply meant teachings that drew or led beings to liberation, that is, the Nitartha, [RC 71] then all Nitartha teachings would qualify as neyartha.[9]

Dolpopa explains neyartha as "untrue teachings used to draw beings on." Kongtrul [SKK hum 13na] objects to this, however, stating one can hardly call the Buddha's word untrue. Though not disagreeing with Dolpopa in principle, Kongtrul prefers to say that provisional teachings (neyartha) are true in a provisional (neyartha) way, for they truly lead beings to liberation.

Kongtrul [SKK hum 10a] distinguishes neyartha and Nitartha Sutras as follows:

theg pa gsum ga'i gdul bya'i rigs la nges par legs pa'i lam rgyud la skye rung gi thabs su gyur pa kun rdzob bden pa gtso bor ston pa'i mdo ni drang don gyi mdo'i mtshan nyid. zab mo'i don la bzod pa'i gdul bya 'ga' zhig gi ngor nges par legs pa'i lam bsgom pa las mi gnas pa'i mya 'das thob pa'i don dam bden pa gtso bor ston pa'i mdo de don dam gyi mdo sde'i mtshan nyid do

The characteristic of a neyartha Sutra is to chiefly teach the samvrtisatya as a means of truly enabling the excellent path to arise in the minds (*rgyud*) of those families (*rigs*) of beings to be tamed belonging to all three vehicles. The characteristic of the Absolute Sutra class is to chiefly teach those few beings to be tamed who can withstand the Profound Meaning, the Paramarthasatya by means of which, through truly meditating on the excellent path, the non-dwelling Nirvana is attained.

"Absolute Sutra Class" here refers to Nitartha Sutras. Dolpopa [RC 177] is adhering to such a definition of Nitartha when he equates Nitartha with Tathagatagarbha, that is, the nondual Buddhajnana, which is called the "True Self" (*bdag dam pa*) in the Tathagatagarbha Sutras.

iii. The Ratnagotravibhaga—Neyartha or Nitartha?

The RGV has been chosen as the central focus of this present work because of its overwhelming importance in the Tibetan tradition since the study of the Tathagatagarbha Sutras themselves has declined.[10] Indeed, Lama Thubden, Tenga Rimpoche, and other Kagyu-Nyingma Lamas have remarked that the RGV has all that one needs to study in order to understand and practice both the Sutras and Tantras.

The Shentong interpretation of the *Ratnagotravibhaga* has to be understood as a commentary, in Shentong terms, on the Nitartha teachings of the third Dharmacakra.

A Rangtong interpretation has to be understood in Rangtong terms. A Rangtongpa may regard the RGV as a Sastra pertaining to the third Dharmacakra and yet like Gyaltsab, for example, consider it teaches the Nitartha Rangtong Prasangika Madhyamaka of the second Dharmacakra.[11] Gyaltsab argues that since the Tathagatagarbha is essentially the self-emptiness of the mind-stream, and self-emptiness is nitartha, the RGV, which teaches Tathagatagarbha, must be nitartha.

However, if as we have just seen, "nitartha" is taken to mean direct and "neyartha" indirect, the RGV would be classed as neyartha, because, according to Buton for example, the RGV is not to be taken literally. For him, Tathagatagarbha is fruit Dharmakaya, but fruit Dharmakaya is not literally in beings. Thus, although both the *Dartik* and Buton agree that the Tathagatagarbha is self-emptiness, which is the nitartha doctrine of the second Dharmacakra, they do not agree on whether to call the RGV "neyartha" or "nitartha."

Leonard Kuijp [43] cites Sakya Chogden as saying Ngog held four of the Maitreya treatises to be neyartha and the RGV to be nitartha, and that it is about Tathagatagarbha in the sense of the pure nature (*rang bzhin rnam dag, prakrtivisuddhi*) of all phenomena, which pervades all that is knowable. He also held it should also be taken as a non-implicative negation (mengag—nothingness), being something like space. Sakya Chogden contrasts this with Tsen's view that Tathagatagarbha is the naturally pure Jnana (*rang bzhin rnam dag gi ye shes*), which pervades both Buddhas and beings and is the Clear Light Nature (*rang bzhin 'od gsal ba, prakrtiprabhasvara*).[12]

Gyaltsab [*Dartik* 3b], in the main, seems to agree with Sakya Chogden here, for he explains that the Tathagatagarbha Sutras teach absolute truth, emptiness of reality (*bden pas stong*), and nisprapanca, that is, Nitartha. However, he says that all five treatises of Maitreya are nitartha, because they teach all dharmas are empty of self-characteristic (*chos thams cad rang gi mtshan nyid kyis grub pas stong pa*). From this, he concludes that they all belong to the second Dharmacakra.

Buton held a view on Tathagatagarbha that did not correspond to either that of Rongton or of Gyaltsab. He was the learned Kadampa scholar—although G. Tucci[13] mentions he was closely connected to the Sakyapas—who compiled the Tibetan canon of the *Kangyur* and *Tengyur*. He wrote a treatise called the *bDe snying gsal rgyan* (completed in 1359) that was a study of Tathagatagarbha doctrine. Although the Jonangpas are not expressly mentioned, it is taken to represent a refutation of their Shentong position. Ruegg [*Traité* 7ff] gives an account of Buton's sources, chief among which are the *Srimaladevisutra* and the *Tathagatagarbhasutra*, because the RGV is mainly based on these two Sutras. He has been criticized for not using other important sources for the RGV and RGVV such as the *Dharanirajesvarasutra*, *Avatamsakasutra*, *Ganganaganjapariprccha*, *Anunatvapurnatvanirdesa*, *Sagaramatipariprcchasutra*, and the *Jnanalokalamkara*.

Indeed, although Buton assigned the RGV and RGVV to the Yogacara section of the *Tengyur*, it is not generally considered a Yogacara work these days (in the sense of ordinary Cittamatra), and Buton's whole system of interpretation is not favored by any school extant today.

Redawa, (a teacher of Rongton), is recorded [BA 349] as having held that the RGV was a Cittamatra text. He is also recorded as having opposed the *Kalacakra* Tantra as non-Buddhist at some point in his life [BA 336].

Jetsun Redawa first of all said that the RGV was a Cittamatra sastra and wrote a *tika* that accorded with the Cittamatra. Later when in retreat he said, "Because of seeing this, one's own Mind,* which is awareness and emptiness inseparable (*rang sems rig stong dbyer med*) is present pervading all beings, [the Buddha] taught by means of the examples of treasure under the ground and the embryo in the womb etc. that all beings have Tathagatagarbha."

Rongton assigns the RGV partly to the second and partly to the third Dharmacakras because it teaches the Nitartha doctrine of the Prajna-paramita and also the Nitartha doctrine about the Buddha qualities.[14] He does not seem to mean this in a Shentong sense exactly, but his view does contrast with other Rangtongpas who, as we shall see below, argue that all third Dharmacakra teachings are neyartha, because they were taught for a purpose and so should not be taken literally. In fact Rongton seems never to have openly affirmed or denied a Rangtong or a Shentong position and, since all the evidence is that his teachers accepted a Shentong position, one concludes that his explanations, though Rangtong in flavor, do not exclude the possibility of a Shentong interpretation.

Exclusive Rangtongpas often argue that since RGV [156–161] gives five reasons for teaching Tathagatagarbha in order to give courage to those without confidence to generate Bodhicitta, it is taught for a purpose and so should not be taken to mean that beings literally have Tathagatagarbha (in the sense of having the naturally pure Dharmakaya). Mikyo Dorje [*gZhan stong sgron me* 19a] counters this argument as follows:

Concerning this, some Snow-land (i.e. Tibetan) scholars say that the statement,
    "All beings have the Tathagatagarbha,"
is neyartha. They accept this, saying that the purpose for it is to

---

*N.B. Although in general G. N. Roerich's translation is fairly accurate for the above line "one's own Mind, which is awareness and emptiness inseparable" he has, "It is impossible to differentiate between the presence or absence of this mind." Intriguing though this comment be, it is not a correct rendering of the original!

give up the five faults. But if this were so, there would be no need to give up the five faults and there would be no fault in denigrating inferior beings, because beings would not have the Tathagatagarbha and there would be no need to believe that they had the Tathagatagarbha Dharmas. Because it would be neyartha, there would be no fault in denying the Dharmakaya Tathagatagarbha. Since it had never been there, one would not have fallen into the extreme of a false denial, but rather one would be expressing the true situation and it would be fitting to lack confidence. Since the Tathagatagarbha would not be in one's own continuum, to show a confident stance would be to cling to a lack of realism.

This secton is quoted by Kongtrul in his RGV [commentary 94a]. Mikyo Dorje continues:

Furthermore, if one speaks like this, then the Arya Asanga and the others also become invalid and unreliable [teachers] because they comment on this system of True Dharma(s) taking it literally (*dgong pa can min*) and yet [according to those who speak like this] to do so would refute (*gnod*) the purpose and actual [meaning] of what was taught by the Bhagawan and Maitreya. Therefore, we follow the Arya Asanga himself, since we do not dare to follow those who walk rough-shod over the Refuge-Giver (Asanga).

Kongtrul, in similar fashion, objects to the whole idea that the RGV Tathagatagarbha doctrine is Cittamatra, saying that this would render Maitreya, Asanga, and Vasubandhu Cittamatrins. Since this would imply their inferiority to Nagarjuna, such an assignation is demeaning and tantamount to libel. Kongtrul warns that the bad karma ensuing from harboring such wicked views equals that of abandoning the Dharma. This is all rather amusing in the light of the fact that the RGV, RGVV, and *Bhrattika* were more than likely not by Maitreya, Asanga, and Vasubandhu at all (see following sections of this present work).

Thinking about it, it is certainly hard to make sense of a system that says that what is taught for a purpose is necessarily not to be taken literally. Does it mean that only teachings that have no purpose should be taken literally? Dolpopa points out that, since all the Buddha's teachings are provisional in the sense that they are expressed in words and concepts in order to fulfill a particular need or purpose, they would all be neyartha by that reckoning. Furthermore, statements about apparent reality and Absolute Reality can both be expressed more or less literally as occasion demands [RC 171–176]. Thus, it is not the literalness or provisionality of a teaching that determines whether it is neyartha or Nitartha [RC 60].

Dolpopa defines neyartha as teachings which do not give the final doctrine, that is, teachings that do not point out the ultimate Empty Ground (*stong gzhi*). Thus, for him the RGV is clearly a Nitartha work because it presents the Buddha Element as the Ground empty of the accidental stains. Thus, it distinguishes what does exist from what does not exist.

Section Two:
Historical Background

Chapter 8

The Shentong Tradition

8.1 The Jonangpas

Having discussed the issues involved in a Shentong interpretation of RGV Tathagatagarbha doctrine, let us consider the background, influence, opponents, and distinctive points of doctrine of Dolpopa and the Jonangpa school; they were the first to popularize the term Shentong.

i. The Jonangpa Lineage

The Jonangpas trace their origin to Yumo Mikyo Dorje, twelfth-thirteenth century,[1] who was a student of Candranatha, and a pandit from Kashmir. Tradition has it that Shentong Madhyamaka doctrine arose in Yumo Mikyo Dorje's mind as he was practising Kalacakra at Mount Kailash. The lineage of Yumo Mikyo Dorje—also known as the Great Guru—was passed through his family line and then through several other masters. It was after Joklay Namgyal (*Phyogs las rnam rgyal*), born 1306, had founded the monastery of Jonang that the school became known as the Jonangpas—although the Kagyu Varanasi textbook says that Kunpang Tukje Tsontu (*Kun spangs thugs rje brtson grus*) founded the first seat of the Jonangpas. It seems (from the record in the Blue Annals) that Dolpopa Sherab Gyaltsen (1292–1361) was already about the tenth holder of that lineage. It was he who formulated the written form of their special doctrine for the first time. The school flourished for about three hundred years until, in the seventeenth century, after the time of Taranatha Kunga Nyingpo (*Taranatha kun dga' snying po*; 1575–1650's), almost all the Jonangpa monasteries and institutions were forcibly closed down (and often, converted into Gelugpa monasteries).

Since that time, the Jonangpa lineage has continued to transmit its teachings through Lamas of the Nyingma, Kagyu, and Sakya schools. The late Kalu Rimpoche is a great representative of this tradition (as well as of many others) and includes the Jonangpas as a branch of the Kagyupas. He has given the Jonangpa Tantric initiation of the Kalacakra several times in the East and West.

During the 300 years or so that the Jonangpa school flourished, it enjoyed considerable prestige and influence in Tibet. It also attracted a lot of criticism from various quarters[2] and from the Gelugpa school in particular.

Gene Smith's account in his introduction to the *Shes bya kun khyab* concerning the political reasons for closing down the Jonangpa monasteries and banning their books sounds credible when one considers that it is not very characteristic of Buddhists to fight over purely doctrinal matters. Be that as it may, ever since that time the Jonangpas have become, for the Gelugpas, an epitome of those who hold wrong views. Most of the arguments leveled against Dolpopa were anticipated by him and answered in his *Ri chos nges don rgya mtsho* (RC). More often than not, however, his Gelugpa opponents do not address his arguments as such, contenting themselves with refutations based on a misunderstanding of what he was saying.

Dolpopa's *Ri chos nges don rgya mtsho* is the definitive work on his Shentong doctrine. It is through this work and his great influence among his contemporaries that the term became famous and closely associated with the Jonangpa school of Tibetan Buddhism.

ii. Some Opponents and Supporters of Shentong

Rangjung Dorje (1284–1339)[3] was a close colleague of Dolpopa and favored his Shentong interpretation of the RGV as did and do—with slight variations of their own—the Rimay teachers of the nineteenth and twentieth centuries.[4]

Longchenpa Kunkyen Drimay Ozair (*kLong chen pa kun mkhyen dri med 'od zer*; 1308–1363) was a contemporary of Dolpopa with very similar views. However, at this stage in our knowledge, it is not clear what connection, if any, they had with each other. Rangjung Dorje was closely associated with both, being one of Longchenpa's teachers. Certainly the works of all three of these teachers are very much in harmony with the Non-Partisan (Rimay) movement and are an important early source of inspiration for it. Kongtrul [SKK om151na] names these three as the first to promulgate the long tradition (*ring lugs*) of the Great Madhyamaka, expressing the Nitartha beyond Cittamatra.

Among Dolpopa's strongest opponents were Buton (1290–1364), Gyaltsab (1364–1432) and Ketrub (1385–1483), the latter two being the foremost disciples of Tsongkhapa.[5]

iii. *The Mountain Dharma—Ocean of Nitartha (Ri chos nges don rgya mtsho*, RC)

The *Ri chos* (RC) has as its main task the establishment of the third Dharmacakra as supreme and its message as the Nitartha doctrine of Tathagatagarbha Buddhajnana eternally present in beings. Confusion arises because Buddhajnana is frequently referred to in the scriptures as the Absolute Emptiness, Absolute Dhatu, Absolute Absence of Essence, Absolute Dharmata and so forth. Dolpopa warns that if one does not distinguish rangtong and

Shentong one finds these names misleading. He uses [RC 275] the expressions Absolute Emptiness (Paramarthasunyata) and the emptiness of apparent phenomena (samvrtisunyata) [RC 275]. Although these terms express the distinction as well, if not better, than Shentong and rangtong, the latter are more the vogue. The terms Shentong and rangtong occur about one quarter of the way through the book and represent one among many similar distinctions that he draws to the reader's attention. For example, RC [275.3]:

> *rang stong dang gzhan stong gi khyad par rtogs pa'i phyir dang*
> *med cing ma grub la dben zhing 'gags pa'am dag pa tsam gang*
> *yin pa dang de rnam kyi gzhi gang yin pa'i khyad pa rtogs pa'i*
> *phyir dang. med dgag ma yin dgag dang rnam gcod yongs gcod*
> *dang spangs rtogs rang bzhin pa'i khyad par rtogs pa'i phyir*
> *dang. rang gi dngos po stong pa nyid dang gzhan gyi dngos po*
> *stong pa nyid dam stong pa'i stong pa dang mi stong pa'i stong*
> *pa'am dngos po med pa stong nyid dang dngos po med pa'i ngo bo*
> *nyid stong pa nyid kyi . . .*

. . . in order to realize the distinction between self-empty and Other Empty, and in order to realize the distinction between the negation of reality in what is nothing and non-existent or mere purity and the base (*gzhi*) of these, in order to realize the distinction between a non-affirming negation and an affirming one, between analysis and complete analysis, between the nature of relinquishment and of realization, emptiness of own existence and Emptiness of other existence or empty emptiness and non-empty Emptiness or emptiness of non-existence (non-substance) and the Emptiness of the essence of non-existence (non-subtance) . . .

In fact, the first time Dolpopa uses the term Shentong is RC [184.4]:

> *de nas sor mo'i phreng bas. ril bu zhu nas med par song ba dper*
> *mdzad de nyon mongs pa dang mi dge ba'i chos rnams stong par*
> *bstan pa 'dis 'jig rten kun rdzob kyi bden par gtogs pa thams cad*
> *rang rang ngo bos stong par bstan la zhu nas med par 'gro ba ma*
> *yin pa'i nor bu baid'urya dper mdzad nas thar pa'i mthar thug*
> *sangs rgyas mi stong par bstan pa 'dis ni don dam pa 'jig rten las*
> *'das pa'i bden pa chos kyi sku rang gi ngo bos stong pa ma yin*
> *par bstan to. Khyim stong pa dang bum pa stong pa dang klung*
> *stong pa dper mdzad nas nyes pa thams cad kyi stong par ston pa*
> *'di ni mthar thugs gi thar pa gzhan stong du bstan to.*

Then Angulimala said, "The example of the pellet being destroyed by being dissolved teaches how klesa and non-virtuous dharmas

are empty. This shows everything belonging to the mundane samvrtisatya is empty of its own essence''.

The example of the lapis lazuli jewel that was not destroyed
after the dissolving [of the pellet], teaches how Liberation, which
is ultimate Buddha, is not empty. This shows the Paramarthasatya
beyond the mundane which is the Dharmakaya is not empty of its
own essence. The examples of the empty house, empty vase and
empty valley that show the emptiness of all faults teaches the ultimate Liberation which is Other Empty (Shentong).

Dolpopa then points to what he considers to be the same doctrine in the
Mahaparinirvanasutra quoting it at length [RC 187–188]. In this [RC 188.5]
the example is given of a cow being empty of horse but not of cow, and a
horse being empty of cow but not of horse. This sounds as if it might be the
inferior "empty of each other" (*itaretarasunyata*) mentioned in the *Lankavatarasutra* [LAS], but Dolpopa explains that, on the contrary, it illustrates
how the Absolute Dharmata, the Great Nirvana, is not empty of itself. It is
Empty of other (Shentong).

Dolpopa remarks that, as always, one must distinguish inferior emptiness from Absolute Emptiness and this can be done by knowing the context, rather than relying on the terminology. An emptiness that is rejected
as inferior must by definition be samvrti emptiness, because Paramartha
Emptiness could hardly be described as inferior. Dolpopa [RC 187–188]
quotes from the *Mahaparinirvana*, as follows:

Son of the family, Nirvana is not previously non-existent. It is not
(for example) like a pot when it is unworked clay. It is not like a
pot that is destroyed and becomes nothing. It is not nothing whatever, as is a turtle's hair. It is like something in which something
else is absent (*gcig la gcig med pa*).

Notice how Dolpopa takes Nirvana, Absolute Dharmata, Dharmakaya,
Ultimate Liberation, Ultimate Buddha, Paramartha-satya, and Shentong to
be different names for the same thing. Dolpopa [RC 189.2] defines Shentong
more precisely (quoting from the *Mahaparinirvana*):

*stong pa'i gzugs 'gags pa'i rkyen gyis stong pa ma yin pa'i gzugs
kyi rnam par grol ba thob bar 'gyur te. tshor ba dang du shes
dang 'du byed dang rnam par shes pa'i bar du yang de bzhin du
rgyas par rig par bya'o. zhes pa la de dag ni rim pa ltar glo
bur dri ma'i gzugs sogs dngos po med pa stong pa nyid de rang
rang ngo bos stong pa dang. bde gshegs snying po'i gzugs sogs
dngos po med pa'i ngo bo nyid stong pa nyid de don dam gzhan
stong ngo.*

By the circumstance of empty-form ceasing, the Non-Empty Form which is Liberation is attained. Likewise, from feeling, perception and mental formations up to consciousnesses are also to be known in full in this way.

Thus, these are respectively, the emptiness that is the non-existence (*abhavasunyata*) of the accidentally stained form etc., which is their each being empty of their own essence, and the Tathagatagarbha Form etc., which are the Emptiness which is the essence of [that] non-existence (*abhavasvabhavasunyata*), the Absolute Other Emptiness.

(See Appendix 2 in this present work for more details concerning *abhava* and *abhavasvabhavasunyata*). Although this is, perhaps, the most difficult part of Shentong doctrine, judging by Dolpopa's citations it is none other than the doctrine of the Tathagatagarbha Sutras themselves. Dolpopa's citations are very long and apparently accurate. For example, Dolpopa quotes from the *Mahaparinirvanasutra* at length on how each of the skandhas and each item of the apparent world has a pure non-compounded counterpart called in the Tantras "Empty Form having all the supreme aspects" [see *La Théorie* VIII. 357] that is Tathagatagarbha. They are the Inseparable Qualities with no perceived or perceiver (*yul, yul can*), no quality and thing qualified (*chos, chos can*), and so on [see RC 211.6].

He explains [RC 396] that since apparent phenomena (samvrti) must be given up and the Absolute retained, one must distinguish carefully between what is self-empty and what is the remainder. When the self, beings, life force, life and so forth, are taught as not existing, one must distinguish carefully as to what does not exist and what does. Also, in doctrines of non-born, no signs, nisprapanca and freedom from limits, one must distinguish what is non-born and separable from what base (*gzhi*), or remainder (*lhag ma*). There is a difference between the Madhyamaka with manifestation (*snang bcas*) and without, between Cittamatra Mind Only as Absolute and as what is apparent (samvrti), between nature and artifice (*bcos ma*), between natural (*gnyug ma*) and adventitious (*glo bur*), between the different kinds of nonexistence referred to as absence of self-nature (*nisvabhava, ngo bo nyid med*) and the difference in the meanings of transformation (*gnas gyur*), between emptiness that is nonexistence (*abhavasunyata, stong pa nyid dngos po med*) and Emptiness that is the essence of [that] non-existence (*abhavasvabhavasunyata, dngos po med pa'i ngo bo nyid*), between emptiness of self-nature (*svabhavasunyata*) and the emptiness of other nature (*parabhavasunyata, rang gi dngos pos dang gzhan gyi dngos pos stong pa nyid*). He continues by saying that in the doctrines using the example of dreams and magical illusions (*sgyu ma*), there is a difference in how these images apply to apparent phenomena and how they apply to Absolute phenomena.

Dolpopa [RC 435] says two nirvanas are taught. One is a result (fruit) and one is not. The first is refuted by the paramartha reasoning (*don dam pa'i rigs pas gnod*) and the second established by Dharmata reasoning (*chos nyid rigs pas grubs pa*). The first represents a change brought about by following a path and so is apparent nirvana. The other is changeless non-compounded Reality, which is always free from the limitations of compoundedness and conceptuality. This doctrine also occurs in the SMS.

Finally, Dolpopa links Sutra and Tantra by explaining [RC 290–292] that there are two kinds of natural purity: (*a*) the purity (*dag pa*) of paratantra and parikalpita; and (*b*) the purity (*dag pa*) of the pure ground (*sbyong gzhi*) which is the Absolute Jnana, Vairocana, the Other Skandhas, the pure Eyes, Nose and so forth, Absolute Jnanadeva and Consort, the Absolute Twelve Links and so on.

iv. Comparison With Later Shentongpas

Although Dolpopa considered it a mistake to take Tathagatagarbha as rangtong, later Shentongpas such as Kongtrul consider it not so much a mistake as the first step towards understanding Tathagatagarbha. Furthermore, whereas Dolpopa used the terms rangtong and Shentong to refer to the emptiness of apparent phenomena and the Paramartha respectively, it became the custom among later commentators to use the terms for schools of tenets. Thus, the Yogacara Madhyamaka came to be known as Shentong and other Madhyamikas received the slightly derogatory name of "Rangtongpas."

This was already the vogue when Mikyo Dorje (1507–1555) wrote the *dBu ma gzhan stong smra ba'i srol legs par phye ba'i sgron me* in which he defends the Great Madhyamaka Shentong doctrine against its Rangtong opponents. He is better known, however, for having attacked Shentong in favor of rangtong, as for example, in the introduction to his commentary on the *Madhyamakavatara*. It is not clear which (if either) of these texts represented his own confirmed opinion. Paul Williams [JIPII.1983] suggests that Mikyo Dorje thought that, as the Shentong cannot be found in the Prasangika, the Prasangika needed to be supplemented. Alternatively, he may have changed his opinion. It is possible, however, that like modern Shentongpas, he opposed the teaching of Shentong until a proper understanding of rangtong had been established. Ponlop Rimpoche thought that he only wrote on Shentong at the request of his teacher. (For more details on later Shentong views, see Chapter 5.3 vi–viii "The Two Realities Inseparable"—"The Importance of the Distinctions.")

v. The Essence of the Controversy

One may wonder why Shentong should have been singled out as so controversial when in essence, as well as in expression, it is no different from the Tathagatagarbha Sutras and Sutras on the Absolute Dharmata such as the SNS and the higher meditation systems such as Mahamudra and Dzogchen. The answer may be that the Sutras in question are little studied and the RGV and RGVV—the Tibetans' chief sources of Tathagatagarbha doctrine—have always been taught as much from the rangtong as the Shentong point of view. Since the time of Gampopa, there have always been two approaches to Mahamudra (Sutra and Tantra). Therefore, opposition to Tathagatagarbha doctrine and Mahamudra has been deflected by satisfying its opponents with a version that they can accept. On the other hand Dzogchen has had almost as rough a ride as Shentong with its opponents. Although not exactly banned, it has frequently been accused of non-Buddhist origins. It may transpire that further research will reveal that in Buddhism, as in other major world religions, "mystics" often become a threat to the institutional hierarchy and therefore are fair game for attack.

As we shall see in the next chapter, Kongtrul links Shentong with the Heart-Essence teachings of the Indian Siddhas, who were often very unconventional figures. Their teachings have not come under attack by the establishment, possibly because they are normally couched in poetic rather than philosophical terms. Kongtrul refers to the Heart-Essence teachings of their "songs" (*Doha*) as incorporating the superior dialectic of the Madhyamaka with the superior yogic insight of the Yogacarins, producing the "highest summit of all the Mahayana *pitakas*" [RGV commentary 2b], and in accordance with the Tantric view.[6] Like Shentong these teachings present themselves as the ultimate meaning of both Sutra and Tantra, acting as a bridge between them.

To this day the controversy continues, fueled chiefly by those who want to refute Shentong, not just as a teaching method but as a false interpretation of the Buddha's ultimate message. They dispute that the ultimate nature of Reality is an Absolute—permanent, active, and many aspected— yet non-compounded, nondual and spontaneous. As Kongtrul states [SKK hum 43b]:

> *tshul de 'phags las gzhan blor chud dka' bas. rtsod pa'i chos gyur.*
> This tradition [i.e. Tathagatagarbha] is hard to comprehend for the minds of those other than the Aryas, so it has become a controversial teaching.

Whether most of the opponents of Shentong over the centuries have been refuting the actual Reality of Shentong (i.e. the Absolute nondual

Jnana) or merely its validity as a teaching method must be considered carefully. Certainly there are good arguments for saying that individuals who are completely enmeshed in concepts will merely use this Shentong doctrine to bind themselves even more strongly to samsara. For after all, one may think, if having Tathagatagarbha means Buddha is already one's nature, what need is there to make any effort to practise Dharma? One suspects that it has always been this tendency to use this kind of doctrine as an excuse for laziness and corruption that has led to its frequently being refuted, recoded, or ignored throughout Buddhist history.[7]

Dolpopa replies [RC 56] that the nature of beings is Paramartha Buddha. However, this does not mean that they appear as Buddha to themselves and others with their limited vision, which sees only apparent phenomena (samvrti). From this point of view of false appearance (samvrti), they are ordinary obscured sentient beings, needing to practise the path to Enlightenment.

vi. Shentong is Secret Oral Instruction

Ultimately Shentong is a secret teaching that depends on secret oral instruction without which it cannot be understood. Indeed, without it there is a very great danger of misunderstanding. Therefore, as has been said before, some teachers prefer not to introduce it into philosophical dialogue at all and might even criticize those who do. Thus, although they accept Shentong, they do not call themselves Shentongpas because of their preferred teaching method [see Kuijp 41].

Dolpopa does not dispute that the key to Shentong is secret oral instruction. He frequently refers to the need to rest meditatively in that which is known from the Guru's special instruction (*man ngag*) and uses, for example, expressions like "meditate in the non-meditatory manner" (*mi sgom pa'i tshul gyi sgom*) [RC 171] and so on. In his final comments [RC 488], he explains that the text is called the *"Lamp of the Heart Essence,"* because it shows the profound Dharmata. It is a wish-fulfilling jewel, for it unites scripture, reasoning, and profound instruction. It is not suitable to be shown to those without experience of the Nitartha Dharmata meditation. Dolpopa then adds that, although he was instructed to treat it as such, he begs to reveal it because there is no danger of a broken bond (*samaya*) for those who have not had this experience. Bond (*samaya*) is the Tantric bond of Guru and disciple that is so dangerous to try to break once thoroughly entered into. It seems that Dolpopa is suggesting here that until the experience of the Heart-Essence has been triggered in the mind of the disciple, the bond is not established.

In Dolpopa's view, the Lama's special instruction relates to certain Sutra teachings. For example, he gives [RC 437] a long quote from the *Mahaparinirvanasutra* [MPNS] concerning "being freed from mind and not freed from mind . . . and so forth," and "being without past and future and not without past and future. . . . the Tathagata acts to benefit beings and does not act to benefit them . . ." and calls this kind of teaching profound instruction (*man ngag zab mo*) [RC 438.3].

8.2 Sources of Shentong

i. The Tibetan Inheritance

The Shentongpas' own account of the traditions from which they spring provides a useful guide to how they interpret the sources that they use as a basis for their doctrine. To say their tradition actually arises from them, however, is to ignore that the same sources are used by different schools of tenets for establishing their own views, which are sometimes a long way from that of the Shentong.

Nevertheless, it is worth outlining the story from a Shentong point of view. It seems clear that among the early Madhyamikas, (third or fourth century A.D.), there were those who held ideas akin to the Tathagatagarbha doctrine of the SMS concerning an existent Absolute (see chapter 9.1 i "Authorship and Rediscovery" of this present work). During that period, two kinds of Sutras teaching an existent Absolute appeared: (*a*) the general Sutras of the third Dharmacakra and (*b*) the more detailed Tathagatagarbha Sutras (see Kongtrul's RGV commentary 5a; and Chapter 7.1 iii "Kongtrul's Distinction Between the Two Kinds of Nitartha Sutra of the Third Dharmacakra" of this present work.)

The Tathagatagarbha Sutras were hardly commented on by the Indians, presumably because the use of terms such as *Paramatman* and so on threaten Buddhism's identity *vis à vis* Hinduism. They spread to Khotan and China where they were quickly adopted and commented upon.

At the Oxford Conference of the International Association of Buddhist Studies (IABS) 1982, Professor Jikido Takasaki remarked in conversation that in general the Chinese were immediately attracted to the Tathagatagarbha doctrine and especially the doctrine of the Avatamsaka[8]. For the Chinese it harmonized with their national character and culture. By contrast they found Prajnaparamita somewhat stark and the Indian Cittamatra schools too intellectually sophisticated for their taste.

The more general third Dharmacakra Sutras came to be associated with the Yogacara/Cittamatra of Asanga and Vasubandhu from the fourth century onward. As we have seen, Shentongpas claim the Yogacara of these two founding figures was Yogacara Madhyamaka, but this view did not gain widespread acceptance until the fourteenth century and even then it did not go unchallenged. At the time of the first and second spreadings of Buddhism in Tibet, it was still widely believed by Indians and Tibetans that Asanga and Vasubandhu taught the very Cittamatra view that is so soundly criticized by the Madhyamikas. Consequently, all the third Dharmacakra Sutras were regarded as inferior to the Prajnaparamita Sutras of the second Dharmacakra. Nevertheless, the Indian Siddha tradition continued to develop the early ideas of an experienceable Absolute and express it in their songs (*Stotra* and *Doha*), which are close if not identical to Shentong doctrine.

According to Ruegg [LM], when the Tibetans first came to fetch Buddhism from India in the eighth century, the Madhyamikas were in the process of synthesizing their system with Yogacara, and the debate about external objects being mind or otherwise was a key issue. However, in these early attempts to resolve Yogacara/Cittamatra with Madhyamaka, it was understood that emptiness was a non-implicative negation and not an experienceable Absolute in the Shentong sense (see discussion below). During the second spreading of Buddhism in Tibet—tenth and eleventh centuries—the main issue was Svatantrika versus Prasangika reasoning as the best means for establishing emptiness. Although there is a refined form of Svatantrika that is also highly regarded, the Prasangika Madhyamaka method eventually gained general recognition in Tibet as the highest system of tenets (*grub mtha'*). According to Kongtrul [RGV commentary 11b], this second wave of Madhyamaka was again almost entirely Rangtong.

Thus, from India the Tibetans received the Siddha *Doha* and *Stotra* traditions (which at our present stage of knowledge seem to have been Shentong), and the Mahyamaka tradition which was almost entirely Rangtong.

During both the earlier and later spreading of Buddhism in Tibet, the Tibetans had the option of drawing on Chinese commentarial sources on Tathagatagarbha doctrine. Although there is no space to discuss these in detail here, there is abundant evidence that some at least are very much in accord with the Shentong interpretation of that doctrine. The Chinese tradition dated back to at least the seventh century. Yet official Tibetan history credits China with no positive influence on Tibetan Buddhism. Whether for political or doctrinal reasons, Chinese Buddhism was fiercely opposed and driven underground. To this day even the most liberal minded Tibetan finds it hard to credit any Chinese master with the commentarial ability of Indian masters of the same period. Thus, even though they could have drawn on the Chinese commentarial traditions on the Tathagatagarbha Sutras, they refused to do so.

The tension between the Indian and Chinese traditions is classically expressed in records of the Samye debate over the "gradual" versus the "sudden" approach to Enlightenment. The Indian favored the former and stressed neyartha teachings; the Chinese favored the latter and stressed Nitartha teachings. The Chinese are recorded in Tibetan chronicles as having lost to the Indians in the critical Samye debate; from that time their influence on Tibetan Buddhism declined.

This left the Tibetans with the discontinuity already evident in India between the Madhyamaka and the Siddha traditions. Even where individuals such as Naropa left the great Indian universities in search of Siddha transmission, there seems to have been little attempt to bridge the gulf between the largely monastic centers of philosophical learning and the rather outrageous Tantric Siddha "fringe". The story of Atisa's behavior towards the Siddha Maitripa is a case in point. Maitripa was trying to carry on his Tantric practice in secret while outwardly conforming to monastic discipline. When he was caught with his consort and alcoholic liquor, Atisa threw him out of the monastery. In similar fashion, in Tibet, when Gampopa's chief disciples were caught brewing alcoholic liquor for their *Ganacakra* (Tantric feast offering), they were thrown out by the master of discipline. Happily, on this occasion, Gampopa ran after them and called them back!

Stories like these serve to highlight the tension that inevitably exists between Tantrism and monasticism—that is, monastic life concerns the renunciation of sense pleasures and Tantric practice concerns sensuality being integral to meditation practice. The scholarly institutions professed learning, discipline, wealth, and respectability; these aspects added up to considerable power of a sort. Nevertheless, if the stories are to be believed, they did not have the depth of realization that the Siddhas had. The great masters of the day, both Indian and Tibetan, sought out Tantric masters and thus combined both sources of power.

The finding of the RGV and *Dharmadharmatavibhaga* [DhDhV] by the Siddha Maitripa in the stupa [see Kongtrul's RGV commentary 8a] marks and important moment in the relationship between the two traditions. It seems Atisa eventually repented his turning against Maitripa and took the RGV transmission either directly or indirectly from him, propagating it in Tibet himself to some extent. Thus, the very Tathagatagarbha doctrine that had been unacceptable from China was introduced into Tibet from India. It is significant, though, that, right from its advent into Tibet, there were two methods of transmission. Kongtrul explains [RGV commentary 8b–9a], that one was in accordance with Rangtong Madhyamaka and the other in accordance with the Siddha practice tradition.

Furthermore, Atisa, while in Tibet, propagated the monastic, philosophical traditions, giving Tantrism low profile. Indeed, the terms of his invitation to Tibet more or less proscribed the teaching of Tantrism. By this means, Atisa was successful in helping to establish Buddhism as the state religion of Tibet and setting up its first major monastic institutions. In order to capitalize on the new respectability of Buddhism, the Tibetan Tantrics of the second spreading followed the example of their Indian forerunners such as Maitripa; they were monks outwardly, and Tantrikas in secret. To this day ethnic Tibetan Buddhists favor this style in spite of its inherent contradictions.

Having inherited from India both the Tantric Siddha and the monastic scholarly traditions, the Tibetans were faced with the work begun in India of integrating them. A link was needed between the Sutras and Tantras. The Tathagatagarbha Sutras, the most obvious link, were not studied in Tibet any more than they had been in India and the Chinese commentarial tradition on them had, as we saw above, been rejected. This left the RGV as the only acceptable source for the doctrine of those Sutras; thus it was that Gampopa in the twelfth century triumphantly announced that the Mahamudra of his Siddha lineage derived from the RGV and in this way it bridged the gap between the mainstream Sutra/Sastra tradition and that of the Tantric Siddhas. Nevertheless, it is significant that he maintained a difference between Sutra and Tantra Mahamudra [BA 459]. One assumes this reflected the fact that scholarly opposition to Shentong type explanations was still rife.

It was not until the fourteenth century that Dolpopa, taking a long look at the Sutras, especially the Tathagatagarbha Sutras, began to see connections everywhere. It was a matter of being aware of two kinds of emptiness and two kinds of *pramana* and distinguishing which scriptural statements applied to which. The link between Sutra and Tantra was clearly the third Dharmacakra which, contrary to late Indian and current Tibetan opinion, was not primarily Cittamatrin but Shentong Yogacara Madhyamaka.

Dolpopa [RC 130] gives the ultimate meaning of Mantra (i.e. Tantra) and Prajnaparamita as the one Dharmata (i.e. Shentong). He warns that those who do not understand Tathagatagarbha, Prajnaparamita and so forth as names for the same thing and take them to be different and opposed and who, having entered Mantrayana, dispute and disdain either, are guilty of a root offence; this will take them to hell. Hence, for Dolpopa there is no doubt about the sources of Shentong doctrine.

ii. Some of Dolpopa's Indian Sources of Shentong

Among both western and Tibetan scholars, Dolpopa and the Jonangpas are often presented as having a view so revolutionary in terms of the Buddhist tradition, that their views are almost non-Buddhist in flavor.[9] Although his opponents cast aspersions concerning the source of his doctrine, Dolpopa in his great work the *Ri chos nges don rgya mtsho* [RC] quotes at great length from both Sutra and Tantra sources; barely a quarter of the text is taken up by his own comments.

Dolpopa quotes at length in the RC from the Prajnaparamita Sutras in order to show that, unless one accepts that they use "emptiness" in two distinctly different senses, they are self-contradictory. It is the context that tells the reader whether "emptiness" should be understood as self-emptiness or Emptiness-of-Other, emptiness of apparent phenomena or Emptiness that is Absolute Buddhajnana, emptiness that is synonymous with dependent-arising (*pratityasamutpada*) or Emptiness that is the eternally present Dharmata with the Inseparable Qualities [RC 201ff, 226, 275].

He supports this observation by repeatedly quoting the following lines from the *Madhyantavibhaga* [MAV]. (This is one of the four works of Maitreya regarded as key sources of Shentong by Kongtrul:[10])

> *gang zag dang ni chos rnams kyi. dngos po med 'dir stong pa nyid. de dngos med pa'i dngos yod pa. de ni de las stong nyid gzhan.*
> Here the non-existence (*abhava*) of person and dharmas is emptiness. The existence (*bhava*) associated with that non-existence (*abhava*)—that is another emptiness to that.

Dolpopa argues that if "non-existence" and "existence associated with that non-existence" were established by the same *pramana* the statement would have contradicted itself. Therefore, we have to conclude that "non-existence" is established by Paramartha *pramana* and the "other"* Emptiness is the nondual Jnana established by Dharmata *pramana*.

Dolpopa finds a parallel to Maitreya's distinction in the MPNS, which he quotes [RC 188]:

> . . . *rang gis mi stong pa'i gzhan stong.*
> . . . the other emptiness not empty of itself.

---

*N.B. 'Other' (*gzhan*), in the expression *stong nyid gzhan*, refers to the Absolute Reality being 'another' kind of emptiness (see also RC p. 356 & 363 for other examples of this usage). Shentongpas usually use "other" in the term "Emptiness of other" (Shentong) in order to refer to the unreal that the Absolute is empty of.

Again, he quotes from the MPNS [RC 386] the passage referring to Absolute Emptiness as Buddha and Jnana; it also states that, if one does not see the Non-Empty one does not see Emptiness etc. and therefore Madhyamaka is Buddha Nature. The *Ri chos* [RC 388] gives five pages of quotation from the MPNS about how Sravakas and so forth do not see the Non-Empty and yet that Emptiness must be understood to be neither empty nor non-empty, neither permanent nor impermanent and so forth.

The same idea is found in the *Abhidharmasamuccaya* that is quoted in the RGVV [1.155 81.3]:

> *de ltar na gang zhig gang na med pa de ni des stong ngo zhes yang dag par rjes su mthong la. gang zhig lhag par gyur pa de la rtag par yod do zhes yang dag pa ji lta ba bzhin du shes so.*
>
> *Yad yatra nâsti tat tena śūnyam iti samanupaśyati/yat punar atrâvaśiṣṭaṃ bhavati tat sad ihâstîti yathābhūtam prajānāti.*
>
> That in which something is absent is empty of that. Keeping the attention properly on that, what remains is said to be what exists, and this is perfectly known, properly and precisely.

Takasaki [*Study* 301 fn.59] gives the Chinese and also the Pali equivalent from the *Sunnata-vagga, Culasunnatasutta*:

> *yaṃ hi kho tattha na hoti, tena taṃ suññaṃ samanupassati:yaṃ pana tattha avasiṭṭhaṃ hoti, taṃ santam idam atthêti pajānāti.*[11]

Dolpopa quotes this [RC 191] with one or two slight differences in wording, suggesting he was either quoting from memory or from a different version of the translation. It is possible he was translating himself directly from the Sanskrit. Dolpopa adds the following comments:

> *de ltar rang stong dang gzhan stong du phye nas stong pa nyid legs par gtan la 'babs pa'i tshul 'di ni dbu ma chen po 'phags pa thogs med kyi zhal sna nas kyang gsungs te. Ji skad du. mthar thug gi dbu ma'i chos mngon par. stong pa'i mtshan nyid gang zhe na gang la gang med pa de ni des stong par yang dag par rjes su 'thong ste 'di lhag ma gang yin pa de ni 'di yod pa'o zhes yang dag pa ji lta ba bzhin du rab tu shes so.*
>
> By distinguishing between rangtong and Shentong in this way Emptiness is properly taught. This method is the Great Madhyamaka. It is said by the Arya Asanga in the *Abhidharma* [*samuccaya*] of the Ultimate Madhyamaka: "What is the characteristic of Emptiness? That in which something is absent is empty of that. Keeping the attention properly on that, what remains is said to exist (or be present) and this is perfectly known, properly and precisely.''

These lines, quoted from the *Abhidharmasamuccaya* [40], occur in the RGVV following the much quoted key verses of the RGV [1.154–155].[12]

Since there are such clear Sutra and Sastra hints at a Shentong-type interpretation of Emptiness and Jnana, not only in Mahayana but also in Pali and other early canons—too extensive to even begin to mention here— there seems little cause to seek the source of Shentong anywhere other than within the mainstream Buddhist traditions. Nevertheless, Ruegg [*La Théorie* 8, 9], aligning himself with the views of his Gelugpa sources, calls Dolpopa's interpretation quasi Vedantic, monist, and substantialist. He later admits [*La Théorie* 337], however, that in view of our present knowledge of the different systems, their origins and their development, it is premature to call the Jonangpa system Vedantic. Personally, I also consider his use of the term "substantialist" inaccurate and misleading. Certainly, therefore, at this stage of our knowledge, it is more interesting to follow the Shentong-pa's own analysis and treatment of the sources as they stand, rather than to seek to attribute their ideas to alternative sources.

iii. Other Views on the Indian Sources of Shentong

According to Ruegg, the Jonangpas attribute the doctrine of Shentong to: (*a*) Asanga and Vasubandhu, (*b*) the *stotra* (*stava*) of Nagarjuna, and (*c*) the *Brhattika*. However, when discussing the Indian origins of the Great Madhyamaka [*La Théorie* 61], he remarks that the whole of that tradition should be studied in depth before it is possible to reach conclusions touching on the whole collection of complex questions it raises.

Although at first it seems that certain formulations of Shentong doctrine such as the Parinispanna being empty of both the paratantra and the parikalpita can be usefully traced historically, it is not always easy to determine whether the view behind the formulation is Shentong or not. Not nearly enough research has yet been done, not only on the different systems in their own terms, but also on the full range and usage of Buddhist terminology.

In his commentary on the RGV, Kongtrul puts greater emphasis on Maitreya and Nagarjuna than Asanga and Vasubandhu as sources of the Great Madhyamaka (i.e. Shentong) teaching lineage (*bshad rgyud*). He also mentions Dignaga and Sthiramati, explaining [8a] that they spread the teachings of the Nitartha Madhyamaka and the three Maitreya Dharmas— *Abhisamayalamkara* [AA], *Madhyantavibhaga* [MAV], and *Mahayanasu-tralamkara* [MSA]. We are touching here, however, on a very controversial area. (More details are given in appendix 6 on the Five Maitreya Dharmas.) Tibetan commentators have been arguing for centuries over how the AA and so forth are to be interpreted and what was the final view of Indian commentators such as Nagarjuna, Vasubandhu, Dignaga, Maitreya, and

Asanga. As already mentioned, in trying to determine the source of Shen-tong doctrine, one is confronted at every turn with complex issues. Tibetan commentators disagree about who interpreted what text how, and western scholars disagree about who wrote what text anyway. Nevertheless, there are interesting patterns and rationales behind these disagreements. Although these are not the subject matter of this present work, a short discussion ensues introducing the reader to some of the issues involved.

In the SKK [om 150ba], Kongtrul talks of Maitreya's four Dharmas (excluding the AA), Nagarjuna's *Stotra* (*Stava*), Asanga, Vasubandhu, Candragomin, Santipa (also known as Santipada and Ratnakarasanti), and their followers, as the sources of Great Madhyamaka (Shentong). He explains that, although the third Dharmacakra Sutras and commentaries teaching this doctrine were translated at the early and later spreadings of Dharma in Tibet, the later spreading of the four Maitreya Dharmas through Sajjana to Ngog and the RGV to Tsen was of the greatest importance. (Details are given in Kongtrul's Introduction to his RGV commentary translated in the next section of this present work.)

He explains that gradually, though the traditions holding Madhyamaka and Cittamatra views were originally separate, documents appeared clearly accepting the Mind empty of duality, self-aware, self-illuminating and truly existent (*gnyis stong gi shes pa rang rig rang gsal bden grub*) [SKK om 151.5] as the cause of Buddha. The followers of this tradition were Tsang-nagpa, twelfth and thirteenth centuries, [see Kongtrul's RGV commentary 9a], Rangjung Dorje, Dolpopa and Longchenpa, Minling Terchen (*sMin gling gTer chen*), his brother (seventeenth century), and Tenpay Nyinche, (eighteenth and nineteenth centuries—the eighth Situ). Kongtrul calls the tradition stemming from all these the ''long lineage of the Great Madhyamaka of the Nitartha beyond Cittamatra.'' He traces the same tradition to the Indian Siddha Sri Virupa (*dPal ldan chos skyong*) the teacher of Sukhasiddhi [BA 731], who he says explained the *Madhyamakakarikas* according to the third Dharmacakra.

Having named Maitreya, Asanga, and Vasubandhu as the true Great Madhyamikas of India, Kongtrul [RGV commentary] adds that the essence of their Madhyamaka is the same as the Heart-Essence (*snying po don*) of the Siddha tradition of India and Tibet. He describes it as the Path of Direct Experience, which is the speciality of Saraha and his lineage (which includes Maitripa—see Table 8.1). In fact, from Kongtrul's account it becomes clear that Maitripa is the key figure in terms of linking the Siddha and Great Madhyamaka traditions. Kongtrul [RGV commentary 15a–b] mentions the *Tattvadasakarika* (*De kho na nyid bcu pa*) in particular as a special instruction (*man ngag*) on the Prajnaparamita that accords with Mantrayana. Maitripa wrote this after receiving special instruction (*gdams ngag*) from Saraha and his lineage. In this section, Kongtrul emphasizes the importance of special instruction and introduction (*ngo 'phrod*) to Mahamudra. As has been discussed already in this present work, special instruction and "introduction" from an experienced practitioner of the lineage is the key to Shentong doctrine and Kongtrul, like Dolpopa, does not fail to stress this point.

iv. The *Brhattika*

Kongtrul [RGV commentary 7b] mentions Vasubandhu in two connections, (*a*) his commentary on the DhDhV, and (*b*) the *Brhattika* (*Aryasatasahasrikapancavimsatisahasrikastadasasahasrikaprajnaparamitabrhattika—Yum gsum gnod 'joms*) of which he is supposed to be the author. Kongtrul [RGV commentary 7b] adds that through this and other works Vasubandhu was able to bring out the true meaning of the Madhyamaka. According to Ruegg [*La Théorie* 325], however, the *Brhattika* is more likely to be by Damstrasena (*bTsun pa mche ba'i sde*) than by Vasubandhu.

Ruegg [*La Théorie* 61] links Ratnakarasanti with the *Brhattika* of Damstrasena so, like Kongtrul, connects Shentong with Ratnakarasanti and Ruegg explains [*La Théorie* 139ff] that Nyabon Kunga Pal (*Nya dbon kun dga' dpal*) also makes this connection. Ratnakarasanti was a contemporary of Maitripa—first half of the eleventh century.[13] Shonupal [BA 842] describes how he was defeated by Maitripa in debate and that he and Asanga dwell together in Tusita, each holding a different interpretation of Prajnaparamita. Thus, although Kongtrul links the Siddha tradition of Maitripa to the Great Madhyamaka of Ratnakarasanti, it is questionable whether they held identical views. Ratnakarasanti was a harmonizer of the Vijnanavada and Madhyamaka in the manner of the synthesizing movements especially characteristic of later Buddhist thought in India [LM 122].

The doctrine of the *Brhattika* seems to be an Indian precursor of the Shentong doctrine of Tibet; particularly its doctrine of the parinispanna (Dharmata) as the base (*stong gzhi*) empty of the "diverse and relative dharmas" (parantantra and parikalpita). The Dharmata eye (*chos nyid kyi mig*) and so forth are said to be empty of the eye (*mig*) and so forth. The eye and so forth that it is said to be empty of is the imaginary eye (*kun brtags kyi mig*, parikalpita eye) and so forth, the meaning approximation (*don*) of that conceptual "eye" (*rnam brtags kyi mig*, vikalpita), and also the appearance of a subject perceiving an object. Tsongkapa in his *Legs bshad gser phreng* explains that the *Brhattika* specifies that paramartha and sunyata are empty of self-nature, which, according to him, naturally excludes the notion of a non-compounded Absolute Emptiness-of-Other. He

Table 8.1
Kongtrul's Scheme of the Transmission Lineages of the Heart-Essence

Teaching Lineage	Practice Lineage	Teaching & Practice Lineage
GREAT MADHYAMAKA	SIDDHA MAHAMUDRA	RATNAGOTRAVIBHAGA
Maitreya & Nagarjuna	Saraha	Maitripa
Asanga Dignaga	Maitripa	Anandakirti*Atisa Santipa
(Vasubandhu, Sthiramati Brhattika)	Marpa	Sajjana
	Milarepa	Zu & Tsen
	Gampopa (1079–1153)	
	(Z)Rangjung Dorje (1290–1364) — — Jonangpa Dolpopa (Z) (1292–1361)	
	(Z)Karma Tinlay (15th–16th Cent.)	
	(Z)Mikyo Dorje (1507–54)	
	(Z)Tenpe Nyinche (8th Situpa 1699–1774)	
	(Z)Kongtrul (1813–1901)	

KEY
* known to have translated RGV.
(Z) Shentongpas
— Well documented lineage connection.
= Direct Guru disciple connection.
— — Lineage connection hinted at by Kongtrul but not well documented.

Table 8.2
Transmission and Translation of RGV from Kongtrul's Account

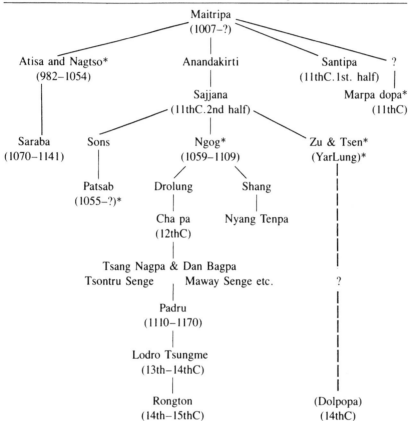

Comments:- It seems the earliest translation was by Atisa and Nagtso lotsawa, who received the transmission directly from Maitripa in the first half of the eleventh century, followed shortly after by Mardo's translation coming through the direct disciples of Maitripa. Saraba took the transmission from Atisa's line but seems later to have adopted Ngog's translation. Sajjana's sons continued to transmit the RGV, and Patsab, having received the transmission from them, made another translation. From Kongtrul's account it seems only the traditions started by Sajjana survived in Tibet (see chap.2fn.3). For Yarlung see Transl.fn.68. Kongtrul's description suggests later commentators such as Lodro Tsungme and Rongton were following Tsang and Dan Bagpa etc., but the exact line of transmission is not clear. Although Shonupal mentions a late translation by Dolpopa, Kongtrul does not.[14]

concludes that the doctrine of the *Brhattika* cannot be identified with the *itaretarasunyata* and the Shentong [f. 260b3]. Notice that he identifies Shentong and the *itaretarasunyata* in the LAS, but Dolpopa does not accept this.[15] Tsongkapa's argument is far from conclusive, however, since, as we have seen already, Shentongpas accept that, from the point of view of the conceptual mind, absolute dharmas such as nirvana, paramartha, and sunyata are empty of self-nature.

v. Nagarjuna's *Stotra* and *Karikas*

Kongtrul considers [RGV commentary 12a] the final view of Nagarjuna to be found in the *Dharmadhatustava* [DDS], and to be the Heart-Essence Great Madhyamaka.

Since this collection of hymns (*stotra* or *stava, bstod, tshogs*) are similar in style to the *Doha* of the Indian Siddhas, it has often been suggested that they were by the Siddha Nagarjuna and not the Madhyamaka philosopher. Ruegg [LM 32, 35, 44], however, does not rule out all possibility that they are by the same Nagarjuna. He [LM 35] makes the point that it is a circular argument to decide what are Nagarjuna's works by their conformity to the ideas expressed in his works, and that although the DDS, for example, at first sight seems to belong to a later Nagarjuna—there are traces of Tantric ideas therein—Ruegg accepts the possibility that at least the kernel of this work could be an early Madhyamaka work. Furthermore, he mentions that among the earlier commentaries on Nagarjunas's writings there are some by important masters of the Yogacarin/Vijnanavadin school [LM 49]:

> The existence of such commentaries on the MMK by leading authorities of Vijnanavada clearly indicates that Nagarjuna's work was not considered to be the exclusive property of the Madhyamikas . . .

Dolpopa [RC 57] quotes the *Dharmadhatustava* [DDS], explaining that the Dharmadhatu, which is the cause of samsara, is seen, when purified, to be the Nirvana Dharmakaya. Just as butter in milk is not evident, the Dharmadhatu is obscured amid the klesa. Just as, when one churns milk, butter emerges from it as the pure, essential, solid, valuable essence, or core, so the Dharmakaya emerges from the klesa. The DDS also gives the example of the plantain tree whose stem is without a heart-essence (*snying po med*) but the tree itself does have a heart-essence (*snying po*), its fruit. It explains that the mistake is to search for the heart-essence (*snying po*) in the stem, which like all dharmas, is essenceless (*snying po med*). So one must look in a completely different place and, thus, one finds the fruit which, in this case, is Absolute Reality.[16] As might be expected from the Shentong point of view, the *Stotras* emphasize the necessity for devotion (*bhakti*),[17] which relies on faith; also Absolute Reality (Dharmadhatu) is taught to be the purport of all three vehicles, which finally become one (*ekayana*) and so on. It is because these teachings conform to the Shentong interpretation of Tathagatagarbha doctrine that Shentongpas cite the *Stotra* as a source.

The question arises as to how the Shentongpas resolve the apparent contradiction between the strong emphasis on rangtong in Nagarjuna's *Mulamadhyamakakarikas* [MMK] and the Shentong teachings of the *Stotra*. Dolpopa explains that the MMK concentrates simply on the non-implicative negation of self-nature in apparent (samvrti) phenomena and does not mention the Dharmadhatu, Dharmakaya, Tathata and so forth,[18] which are doctrines concerning Absolute Reality beyond all the conceptual categories negated in the MMK. Nevertheless, in the opening lines of the MMK, dependent arising (*pratityasamutpada*) itself is described as the cessation of conceptual artifice (*prapancopasamam sivam*), which is without arising or ceasing and so forth. Ruegg points out [LM 44] that this contrasts with the usual application of the term "dependent-arising." It usually applies to apparent (samvrti) phenomena, which are ever subject to arising and ceasing. In Shentong terms, by demonstrating that all apparent phenomena arise as dependently arising concepts, Nagarjuna shows that the true nature of phenomena must be the cessation of concepts (prapanca). In other words, when one realizes dependent-arising, one realizes the cessation of concepts, the unborn, and unceasing. Dolpopa links this to the *Mahaparinirvanasutra* and its explanation of the pure essence of each of the links (*nidana*) of the *pratityasamutpada*.

Ruegg [LM 46] explains how in the MMK [xxii 16] the Tathagata and living beings are shown to have the same self-nature (*svabhava*), but this is followed immediately by the statement that both are without *svabhava*. Although a Rangtongpa might regard this as conclusive evidence of Nagarjuna's rejection of a Shentong position, a Shentongpa would disagree. He would argue that the *svabhava* that beings and Buddhas have in common is the non-conceptual Absolute with its inseparable qualities, but that both beings and Buddhas are *nisvabhava* in the sense that they do not have a conceptually graspable *svabhava*.

Because it says that one emptiness is that of the non-born and one emptiness is that of the born, the former being supreme, and the latter perishing, Dolpopa frequently quotes the *Madhyamakabhavanakrama* [RC 305 and elsewhere] as evidence that Nagarjuna followed the Great Madhyamaka. Ruegg, however, does not mention it in the *Literature of the Madhyamaka School of Philosophy in India* [LM].

Kongtrul [RGV commentary 12a] mentions that, as well as the *Dharmadhatustava* and *Cittavajrastava*, the *Bodhicittavivarana* (*byang chub sems*

'grel) is a work by Nagarjuna teaching that Tathagatagarbha is the Clear
Light Nature (a hallmark of Shentong doctrine). However, Paul Williams in
his review of Lindtner argues against its authenticity as a work by
Nagarjuna.[19]

vi. How Shentong Relates to Later Developments of Buddhism in India

When Ruegg [LM 87] discusses the Yogacara-Madhyamaka synthesis, he
relates Great Madhyamaka and Shentong to the later developments of Buddhism in India such as the Yogacara-Svatantrika-Madhyamaka and Vijnapti
Madhyamaka (*rNam rig dbu ma*). He refers [LM 102–103] to Santaraksita
(eighth century) as the founding father of this school in Tibet. The
Prasangika school was established in Tibet later and it is often said that,
whereas Svatantrika arguments are best for opposing the tenets of non-
Buddhist systems, for they present an inference of their own, Prasangika
arguments are best for debates among Buddhists, for they direct the mind
out of the tangle of conceptual thinking and beyond all views.

Ruegg explains [LM 59] that at the end of the eighth century the Tibetan scholars distinguished Sautantrika Madhyamaka (*mDo sde pa'i dbu
ma*) and Yogacara Madhyamaka (*rNal 'byor spyod pa'i dbu ma*), but not
Prasangika and Svatantrika, which are appellations that appear in the second diffusion in the eleventh century, when the Prasangika school became
established there. The Sautrantika-Madhyamaka and Yogacara Madhyamaka
distinguished Madhyamaka systems according to whether they maintained
or rejected the existence of external objects relatively (samvrti) or conventionally (*vyavahara*).

An important feature of Tsongkapa's Prasangika system is the insistence on the relative existence of outer objects.[20] However, from Ruegg's
remarks it is clear that the issue of the existence or otherwise of outer objects is not a distinguishing feature of Prasangika systems. Thus, there is no
reason for Great Madhyamikas (i.e. Shentongpas) not to accept Prasangika-
type reasoning while at the same time refuting the existence of outside objects, even conventionally. The Mind-Only view that outside objects are
none other than mind accords with the Shentong view to some extent although, in Shentong terms, it does not go far enough. Ruegg [LM 90] explains that Santaraksita regarded the doctrine of Mind-Only as a
philosophical preliminary leading up to the Madhyamaka goal of establishing the insubstantiality of all factors including the mind. Although this is
also true in Shentong terms, Santaraksita's meaning seems not to have been
in accord with the Shentong view.

This, therefore, exemplifies again the difficulty of tracing the sources
of Shentong doctrine from texts using similar sounding formulae. In the

same way, when Ruegg makes the observation [LM 96] that Kamalasila (eighth century) gave gotra and Tathagatagarbha doctrine a much more prominent place in later Madhyamaka thought than they had occupied in the works of earlier Madhyamikas—for example, the *Madhyamakaloka* discusses the gotra and Tathagatagarbha doctrine in relation to *ekayana* doctrine—one is tempted to link him with Shentong, which also combine Tathagatagarbha doctrine and Madhyamaka. However, as far as the Indian background to Shentong doctrine is concerned, Kongtrul [SKK om 149a] sees no connection between Kamalasila and Shentong. For him Kamalasila is a Svatantrika and precursor of Rongton whose commentary on RGV is Rangtong [SKK om 150].

Although Ruegg [LM 94] refers to Kamalasila's having continued Santaraksita's work in establishing Yogacara Madhyamaka in Tibet, Kongtrul regards Santaraksita also as primarily Svatantrika. The confusion seems to arise from referring to Yogacara-Svatantrika-Madhyamaka as "Yogacara Madhyamaka." Further down the page [LM 94] Ruegg refers to Kamalasila as Yogacara-Svatantrika-Madhyamaka. This Yogacara Svatantrika system was one of the two main divisions of the Svatantrika, the other being the Sautrantika Svatantrika. According to Ruegg, Vimuktasena, seventh century, the parent of Yogacarara-Svatantrika-Madhyamaka was the first Madhyamika writer to discuss gotra in his works. Again, although it is characteristic of Shentong to link gotra and Madhyamaka, there is no suggestion that Vimuktasena's view was Shentong.

vii. The Term "Great Madhyamaka"

As has been mentioned, Shentong Yogacara Madhyamaka is known as Great Madhyamaka by its adherents and Dolpopa, Rangjung Dorje, Mikyo Dorje, and others refer to Maitreya and Asanga as the Great Madhyamikas with special reference to the Tathagatagarbha doctrine of the RGV and RGVV. They regard Great Madhyamaka as the ultimate meditation experience. Rangjung Dorje expresses this sentiment in his *Mahamudra Prayer* [verse 19]:

This is Mahamudra free from conceptual artifice (prapanca).
This is the Great Madhyamaka free from positions,
This is the Great Completion (Dzogchen) that includes all,
May I gain conviction that in knowing one I realize all.

Kuijp in his book *'Contributions to the Development of Tibetan Buddhist Epistemology'* [CDTBE 36ff] explains that the earliest occurrence of the term "Great Madhyamaka" is in the Nyingma Tantric Collection (*rNying ma'i rgyud 'bum*). It is considered to be one of the "Three Greats" (*chen po gsum*) of Tibetan Buddhism together with Dzogchen and Chagchen (Mahamudra).

However, since it is regarded as the peak or summit of philosophical analysis, Great Madhyamaka is also used for Prasangika-Madhyamaka in some contexts [CDTBE 39]. According to Kuijp, Sakya Chogden regarded Madhyamaka in general as the peak of Buddhist philosophical systems; he cites him as saying there were two types of Madhyamaka: (*a*) one based on Nagarjuna's *Rigs tshogs*, and (*b*) one based on Maitreya and Asanga. The first removes the fault of taking the unreal to be real (*sgro 'dogs, samaropa*) and the latter removes the fault of denying reality to the Real[21]. Kuijp [CDTBE fn 125] quotes Sakya Chogden [TMCB] as follows:

> *gnyis stong gi ye shes gang yin pa de bsgom pas nyams su myong bya nyid du 'chad pas skur 'debs kyi mtha sel bar byed do.*
> Since this doubly empty Jnana is explained as what is experienced through meditation, the extreme of false denial is removed.

Sakya Chogden explains it is variously known as Yogacara Madhyamaka and False Aspectarian Madhyamaka (*rNam rdzun dbu ma*—a branch of Cittamatra that accepts neither outside objects nor the consciousness that apprehends them as real) and Vijnapti Madhyamaka (*rNam rig gi dbu ma*).

Kuijp explains [CDTBE 45] that, Karmapa Chodrak Gyamtso (*chos grags rgya mtsho*), 1454–1506, in his commentary on the *Pramanavarttika* explains that the two Madhyamaka traditions are not at variance with each other, for they both show ultimate reality (*mtha' thug de kho na nyid*). Asanga's Madhyamaka teaches "the very nature of the luminous mind is sunyata from the very beginning," and Nagarjuna's teaches "this sunyata is from the very beginning present in the nature of luminosity".

At first glance these two seem to be attributed wrongly. The first statement seems to be referring to Nagarjuna's establishment of emptiness and the second to the RGV's establishment of the Clear Light Nature. In such a context, the usefulness of Dolpopa's terminology is easily appreciated. What one wants to ask here is whether Chodrak Gyamtso means both Madhyamakas show the self-emptiness of apparent phenomena (samvrti) or both show the Emptiness of other of the Absolute, or whether he means one shows the self-emptiness of apparent phenomena and the other the Emptiness of other of the Absolute.

Kuijp [CDTBE 39] explains that this Great Madhyamaka differs from the Prasangika Madhyamaka, not only by being based on different texts, but also because it relates more to the meditation tradition (*sgoms lugs*), while the other relates to the listening and reflecting tradition (*thos bsam gyi lugs*). He considers it well-known [CDTBE 40] that this Great Madhyamaka is the trade mark of the Jonangpas.

Kuijp [CDTBE 41] gives both Kongtrul's and, more importantly, Taranatha's accounts of the major exponents of the Great Madhyamaka. Taranatha's list traces it back to Dolpopa and before that to both Zu and Tsen as well as Ngog. Like Kongtrul's, this is not a transmission lineage exactly, so the details remain vague. From Kuijp's ensuing comments one is led to conclude that, although Ngog spread the teaching of the RGV as a listening and reflecting tradition, he accepted the meditation tradition also. Thus, Rongton's RGV commentary, which ostensibly follows Ngog, explains the text from the Rangtong point of view, without refuting the Shentong interpretation as such.

Kuijp [CDTBE 42] mentions that later historians such as Shonupal and Sakya Chogden point to Sajjana as the ultimate source of both traditions. It suggests that, whereas Tsen got only the meditation tradition transmission and wrote his commentaries from that point of view, Ngog received both but wrote mainly from the listening and reflecting tradition point of view. Thrangu Rimpoche doubted Ngog held views akin to Shentong, however, and thought that he was called a great Madhyamaka in the general sense only.[22]

All that has been said so far confirms Kuijp's suggestion that the forerunner of the Great Madhyamaka and the Jonangpa position was the meditation tradition associated with Maitreya, that is, the one that Sajjana transmitted.

viii. Tantric Shentong

Professor Ruegg has suggested that the origin and significance of the Shentong doctrine cannot be understood without reference to the *Kalacakra Tantra* but, when asked, Khenpo Tsultrim felt Sutra Shentong stands on evidence from Sutra sources alone. In practice Khenpo Tsultrim distinguishes between Sutra and Tantric Shentong. This present work concentrates on the former, mentioning the latter merely in passing. Nevertheless, it is certainly true that the Jonangpas—famous for popularizing Shentong doctrine—were, indeed, great Kalacakra masters; their Tantric view and experience was certainly reflected in their interpretation of the Sutras.

Khenpo Tsultrim agrees that the *Kalacakra Tantra* is, indeed, one of the main pillars of Tantric Shentong. According to him the main feature of Tantric Shentong is that the Mind's True Nature is referred to as the ultimate, changeless Great Bliss (*mi gyur ba'i bde ba chen po mtha' thug*), the All-Aspected Emptiness (*rnam pa mchog ldan kyi stong nyid*), the Empty Form-Kaya (*stong pa'i gzugs pa'i sku*), or Inseparable Appearance and

Emptiness, Dhatu and Awareness, or Bliss and Emptiness. He explains that the Tantras make no attempt to establish emptiness through reasoning and argument, because it relates to meditation practice. It is taken as given that its philosophical basis is the Madhyamaka and the Tathagatagarbha doctrine of the RGV. From the Shentong pont of view the meditative experience of the true nature of the Mind, that is, Absolute Reality (Parmarthasatya) Buddhajnana with its Inseparable Qualities, is the basis for Tantric meditation. Without this "experience," Tantric Shentong is incomprehensible, for it is about how, in Tantric practice, vivid sensual experiences arise spontaneously out of non-conceptual Emptiness. In the Nyingmapa tradition they are associated with the Turgyal (*thod rgyal*) aspect of Dzogchen; *bindus* appear first as part and then as whole images and *mandalas* of Buddhas and *istadevatas* and so on. In Kalacakra these are called "Empty Form-Kaya." As Khenpo Tsultrim points out, Tantric Shentong is really only of interest to Tantric yogis familiar with these experiences and the precise manner in which they occur. To others it is merely mysterious. Nevertheless, he felt it important for something to be known about it since if one does not understand how Tantric practice is supposed to work it is difficult to develop the right kind of faith and confidence. As is well known, in Tantric practice one meditates on one's skandhas as the Deity (*istadevata, yi dam*). It is important that the practitioner be familiar enough with Tantric Shentong to know that the true meditative "experience" of the Deity (*istadevata*) is an experience of Reality and not a clever feat of mental gymnastics. Khenpo Tsultrim emphasized this point explaining that if the skandhas were not essentially pure and expressions of the *istadevata* by nature, then no amount of thinking would change them. Afterall, one cannot turn a sheep into a yak by just thinking about it.

Kongtrul expresses Tantric Shentong as follows [ZND commentary 3]:

> . . .*gzhi dngos po'i gnas lugs la lus dang sems gnyis las. sems nang gi bdag nyid bde gshegs snying po'am lhan cig skyes pa'i ye shes dang. lus nang gi bdag nyid de'i rang 'od las shar ba'i mtshan dang dpe gzhan rdo rje'i lus su grags.*
> The basic nature of existence (*bhava*) has two [aspects], the body and the mind. Of these two the inner nature of the mind is Tathagatagarbha or the simultaneously arising Jnana and the inner nature of the body is the marks and signs (of a Buddha) that shine from its own light which are known as the "Other Vajra Body."

In the Sutras and the lower Tantras, the Tathagatagarbha is, on the whole, presented as the locked up, not fully expressed power that is the true nature of an ordinary being's mind, which needs to be released or uncovered. This is illustrated in the RGV [I.96ff] in nine examples. In the higher Tantras that same power, which is also known as the Buddhajnana or the Nature of Mind, is the ever released and expressed power of the whole universe including the klesa themselves. Manifestation is an expression of the power of the Clear Light Nature of Mind, Dharmakaya. Even illusory manifestations are an expression of this. Shamar Rimpoche, when explaining the difference between Jnana and vijnana in connection with Rangjung Dorje's text *rNam shes ye shes dbye pa*, used the example of different expressions on a face. Jnana is the happy expression and ordinary consciousness the unhappy one, but in essence it is always the same face. Needless to say, however, this is a subtle point requiring careful handling or one could mistake this for the substantialist view of an underlying substratum.

8.3 Kongtrul and the Rimay Tradition

i. Kongtrul

Jamgon Kongtrul Lodro Thaye (*'Jam mgon kong sprul blo gros mtha' yas*) was a nineteenth century Lama (1813–1899). He wrote a great many works among which was a commentary on the RGV with a very important introductory section, giving a brief outline of the history of what he sees as the two main traditions of interpretation of the RGV in Tibet (Rangtong and Shentong). His introduction has been commented on at length in this present work, because of the light it sheds on a modern approach to the rangtong-Shentong controversy and because his commentary is the standard one for modern Kagyupa teachers.[23]

Kongtrul joined the Kagyu monastery of Palpung (*Palpung*, Situ's monastery) in 1833 where he quickly became valued as a highly gifted Lama.

Kongtrul had at least sixty great teachers in all traditions and lineages and his interests covered the entire field of traditional Tibetan scholarship including medicine, poetry, astronomy, history, and drama.

Jamgon Kongtrul's works number slightly more than the ninety volumes of his *gSung 'bum* (see Palpung edition). These are traditionally divided into five "*Treasures*," which are: *Shes bya kun khyab (mdzod), bKa' brgyud ngags mdzod, Rin chen gter mdzod, Grub rgyu shing rta brgyad dam ngags mdzod*, and *Thun mong ma yin pa'i mdzod*. His commentary on the RGV was one of the three appended treatises in the *bKa' brgyud ngags mdzod*. The other two were his commentary on the *Zab mo nang gi don* (Rangjung Dorje, 1284–1339), and on the root text of the Hevajra Tantra.

Nowadays, these three texts and their commentries by Jamgon Kong-trul, together with the *Jewel Ornament of Liberation* by Gampopa, are re-garded as the standard text books for the philosophical background of Kagyupa practice.

ii. The Rimay[†] Tradition

Kongtrul and others adopted what came to be known as the "Non-Partisan" approach. This movement and the writings of Kongtrul have had and are having a profound influence not only on the modern Kagyupa school, but also upon the Nyingmapas and the other major schools of Ti-betan Buddhism.

The Rimay tradition is the name given to the work of a number of nineteenth and twentieth century Lamas who strove to gather together and preserve the massive collections of Tantric transmissions and commentaries of the Kagyu, Nyingma, Sakya, Kadam, Jonang, and numerous other lin-eages. The work was directed by Jamyang Kyentse Wangpo (*'Jam dbyang mkhyen brtse dbang po*, 1820–92), who was perhaps the most important source of inspiration for Kongtrul, and a prolific writer.

Non-Partisan here means not limited by adopting a one-sided approach to the Buddhist tradition, which was the great feature of Kongtrul's life and work as well as that of his contemporaries. It should be noted, however, that the Rimay movement included very little, if any, Gelugpa material ex-cept insofar as the Gelugpas trace their origin to the Kadampas whose works are represented.

The work of these great masters in gathering together and preserving all this material was made all the more important in this century by the destruction of the great libraries and monasteries and the exodus of so many Tibetans. It has meant that these vast collections of works have been preserved and now are available for future generations.

Gene Smith gives an account of Kongtrul's life and role in the Rimay movement; Smith mentions that Kongtrul contributed his tremendous knowledge of Bon that he had gathered during his early childhood. Also he describes his deep understanding of the Palpung "synthesis" going back to Situ Panchen, who had blended the Shentong and Mahamudra and spread them throughout Kham. Gene Smith in his foreword to Situ's *Autobiogra-phy and Dairies* [p. 8] explains how Situ (1700–1774) was converted to the Shentong of the Jonangpas, giving it a new lease on life, so that the teach-ing spread throughout East Tibet, thus reversing the trend of the previous

---

[†]*Ris med*, pronounced Rimay.

century. Situ and his associates were among those thinkers who gave birth to this Rimay movement.

It is worth noting that Situ was one of the last great Tibetan *Lotsawas* (*lo tsa ba*, translators) using original Sanskrit sources. The study of Sanskrit had been declining since the day of Dolpopa and his contemporaries.

A close associate of Kongtrul was Shaluribu Tulku Losal Tenkyon (*Zhwa lu ri sbug sprul sku blo gsal bstan skyon*), a Kalacakra master from Tsang (*gTsang*). It was he who persuaded the administrator at Tashilunpo to allow him to survey the extant blocks of the Jonangpas at Taranatha's monastery and at Ngan Ring. He had impressions made of these for the first time in over two hundred years. The majority of the blocks stored in the printeries of these two establishments had been sealed by the fifth Dalai Lama who went so far as to forbid even the copying of existing prints. I have noticed that even today there is a tendency for some, though not all, Gelugpa Lamas to be reluctant to touch or refer to these works.

Other great figures of the Rimay movement were Choggyur Dechen Lingpa (*mChog gyur bde chen gling pa*, 1829–70), Mipam Gyatso (*Mi pham Gya mtsho*, 1846–1917), Dujom Lingpa (*bDud 'joms gling pa*, 1835–?), Rigdzin Pema Dupatsal (*Rig 'dzin padma 'dus pa rtsal*, 1810 or 1812–?), Lerab Lingpa (*Las rab gling pa*, 1856–?), Nyag Rongton Sogyal (*Nyag rong ston bsod rgyal*), and a number of great grammarians and Bonpo scholars. Jigme Lingpa (*'Jigs med gling pa*, 1730–98), and Patrul (*dPal sprul*, 1808–?), are also often included as Rimay masters; their works were a major source of inspiration to the movement.

Chapter 9

Traditions of Interpretation of the RGV and RGVV

9.1 Introduction to the *Ratnagotravibhaga* and
Ratnagotravibhagavyakhya and Associated Traditions.

i. Authorship and Rediscovery

The *Ratnagotravibhaga* [RGV] is a commentarial work on the Tathagatagarbha Sutras, in verse form of varied meter. Since there is scarcely any record of it in India, its exact origins are shrouded in mystery. However, it was rediscovered in India together with its commentary [the *Vyakhya*, RGVV] and the *Dharmadharmatavibhaga* [DhDhV] in the eleventh century A.D. by the Siddha Maitripa.[1]

Maitripa was an important figure of the second wave of the spreading of Buddhism into Tibet which occurred after the repressive regime of the Tibetan anti-Buddhist king, Langdarma (*glang dar ma*), reign 839–842 [BA i.Intro. 19]. Among Maitripa's disciples were many great names such as Marpa and perhaps even Atisa himself. For the Kagyupas, Maitripa is a key figure, since not only is he the Siddha source for its Mahamudra practice (*grub*) lineage, but also, through his transmission of the RGV and RGVV the source of the Great Madhyamaka teaching (*bshad*) tradition of Maitreya and Asanga [see Table 8.1 A].

However, according to Fa Tsang, (643–712), the third patriarch of the Chinese Hua-yen school, the RGV and RGVV were written by Saramati "born in Central India seven centuries after the Buddha's Mahaparinirvana".[2] He records that he heard this from Devaprajna and a monk from Khotan. Takasaki at least finds this account plausible even though there is neither the name of the author in the Chinese translation nor in any of the old catalogues. If Fa Tsang's account is correct, then the RGV and RGVV were written in the third or fourth century A.D. shortly after the *Srimaladevisutra* [SMS] from which so much of its doctrine derives.[3]

According to Ruegg [LM 56], Saramati predated or was a contemporary of Nagarjuna because he is quoted by Rahulabhadra, a contemporary of Nagarjuna. Although Nagarjuna is generally believed to have lived in the first century A.D., he has been placed one or even two centuries later by some scholars and the dates of Rahulabhadra himself are no less problematical. Rahulabhadra [LM 4 fn.11] in his *Prajnaparamitastotra* expresses ideas very close to Tathagatagarbha and especially to the SMS idea of the

Absolute being the basis of both bondage and release. Rahulabhadra refers to this Absolute as Prajnaparamita whereas the SMS refers to it as Tathagatagarbha [LM 55]. This confirms that these were ideas already held by the earliest Madhyamikas and makes the authorship by Saramati quite credible. Fa Tsang himself taught a doctrine very similar to the Shentong doctrine of the Jonangpas.[4]

Nevertheless, according to the Tibetan tradition, dating from the time of its rediscovery by Maitripa, the RGV is by the Buddha Maitreya. Johnston refers to a Saka script fragment of the RGV verses from central Asia that gives the author as the Bodhisattva Maitreya; however, he cannot date it more precisely than between the eighth and twelfth centuries A.D. It would be significant if the name of Maitreya had been associated with the text before Maitripa, but there is no evidence that it was [Study 7].

It is clearly significant that Maitripa was also a devotee of the Buddha Maitreya and, indeed, one suspects the whole tradition of Maitreya's authorship of the RGV arose from him—as long as the association of the name Maitreya with the text does not predate him.

Even though the evidence is not conclusive, modern scholarship favors Saramati as the author of RGV, for the record of his authorship predates that of Maitreya. Nevertheless, there is a sense in which the Tibetan tradition remains unaffected. According to Mahayana, (if not all) Buddhist tradition, the fact that Maitripa received spiritual authorization from Maitreya in a vision means that Maitripa's transmission lineage stems from Maitreya even if the text itself does not.

Maitripa (1007–?) also known as Advayavajra [La Théorie 340] passed on the transmission of the RGV and RGVV to his own teacher Ratnakarasanti, also known as Santipa or Santipada; he lived during the first half of the eleventh century. According to Kongtrul it was Ratnakarasanti who attributed the RGVV to Asanga [RGV commentary 7a].

ii. Maitreya

The Buddha Maitreya is held to be the next Buddha to be born into this world after the present Dharma age of Sakyamuni has been long since dead. He is believed to reside at present in the Tusita heaven awaiting the time of his advent here. Tradition has it that Asanga, A.D. 375–430, who was a devotee of the Buddha Maitreya, was able to meet Him and receive teaching from Him personally for fifty years in Tusita. Although much has been written about the true identity of Asanga's teacher, Maitreya, there is no conclusive evidence either for or against his being a historical person. It seems reasonable to suppose that had he been so there would certainly have been some evidence to that effect, because of the tremendous influence he and his disciple Asanga had on the development of Buddhist thought. Furthermore, had Maitreya been a human teacher, why should his disciple, Asanga, have concealed his identity? On the other hand, since it is widely believed that Asanga was prophesied in the *Manjusrimulatantra* as a disciple of Maitreya, this could conceivably have been the origin of the Tusita story. An undoubtedly more credible tradition is that he received the teachings on earth at night through some divine inspiration.[5]

iii. The Importance of the Maitreya-Asanga Connection

Subsequently, this ascription to Maitreya-Asanga of the RGV and RGVV respectively became of paramount importance to the Tibetan commentators. This stems from the fact that in every Tibetan tradition the Mahayana transmission is seen as two pronged: (*a*) one side coming through Maitreya and Asanga, and (*b*) the other through Manjusri and Nagarjuna.

This tradition can be traced back at least as far as the sixth century to Arya Vimuktasena, Bhadanta Vimuktasena, and Haribhadra (eighth century). Ruegg, in his chapter on the Madhyamaka Prajnaparamita synthesis [LM 101], explains that it was then seen as a union of the Prajnaparamita tradition of the *Abhisamayalamkara* [AA] ascribed to Maitreya and the Madhyamaka tradition of Nagarjuna.

It is significant here that although the basic topic of the AA is gotra, Kongtrul [RGV commentary 12a] comments that Vimuktasena and Haribhadra both explain it as a non-affirming negation, which clearly indicates that this particular Maitreya transmission was not Shentong.

Nevertheless, Kongtrul [SKK a' 282] explains that there are two Madhyamakas of the Ultimate Nitartha Heart-Essence: (*a*) that of Maitreya, and (*b*) that of Nagarjuna. Maitreya's Madhyamaka is the Jnana without the duality of perceiver and perceived (*gzung 'dzin gnyis med kyi ye shes*), and Nagarjuna's Madhyamaka is the mere nothingness of the non-affirming negation of prapanca (*spros pa'i mtha' thams cad bgag pa'i med par dgag pa tsam*).

Gampopa [*Thar rgyan* chapter 9] explains that there are two traditions for taking the Bodhisattva vow: one through the divine Manjusri by way of Nagarjuna, and the other through the divine Maitreya by way of Asanga. The former is known as the Deep View tradition (*zab mo lta ba'i lugs*) and the latter as the Vast Conduct tradition (*rgya che spyod pa'i lugs*).

Incidentally, Ruegg [LM appendix II] mentions that Ratnakarasanti's Vijnapti Madhyamaka (eleventh century) was a synthesis combining

Maitreya and Asanga's Vijnanavada with Nagarjuna's Madhyamaka. However, those who try to link the RGV and RGVV to the Maitreya-Asanga Vijnanavada tradition find it hard to explain the absence in it of any reference to the alayavijnana.

Kongtrul [SKK a'281ba], when arguing against those in India and Tibet who belittle Tathagatagarbha doctrine and the tradition of Maitreya and Asanga by calling it Cittamatrin, compares Maitreya and Nagarjuna to the sun and moon, which are the twin adornments of the sky in relation to whom other Pandits are mere stars. He urges the reader to abandon sectarianism and recognize the equalness of these two teachers and the non-contradiction between their traditions.

Kongtrul [SKK a'281ba] explains that, in order to reconcile these two traditions, Tibetan commentators have tried to show that the final view of each lineage is the same. Shentongpas argue that both traditions teach Shentong. For example, Dolpopa [RC 305 and elsewhere] quotes from Nagarjuna's *Madhyamakabhavanakrama* (*dBu ma sgom rim*); it reiterates that one emptiness is that of the non-born, and the other emptiness is that of the born—the former being supreme, and the latter perishing. Dolpopa takes this as evidence that Nagarjuna taught Great Madhyamaka Shentong.[6] Elsewhere, as we have seen, Dolpopa and other Shentongpas quote the *Dharmadhatustava* and the other hymns (*stotra* or *stava*) by Nagarjuna, which are undoubtedly very close to the RGV in doctrinal content.

Rangtongpas, of course, argue that both traditions teach Rangtong. Gyaltsab, for example, argues that Maitreya's RGV teaches the Prasangika Madhyamaka of Nagarjuna and Candrakirti. Ruegg [*La Théorie* 59] attributes this view to Tsongkapa's master Redawa and later [*La Théorie* 65] he attributes it to Atisa and Tsongkapa. Gyaltsab [*Dartik* 4a.ff.] explains that the main subject matter of the RGV is:

> . . . *chos thams cad bden pas stong pa don dam pa'i bden pa spros pa thams cad dang bral ba.* . . .
>   . . . all dharmas are empty of reality; absolute reality is freedom from all prapanca.

He adds that this is the doctrine of both the Prajnaparamita and the Tathagatagarbha Sutras and as such it represents the final view of Maitreya indifferentiable from that of Nagarjuna.

Thus, Shentongpas, although holding Nagarjuna in high esteem, laud Maitreya for his definitive explanation in the RGV, while Rangtongpas, while not denigrating Maitreya, find him hard to interpret and laud Nagarjuna as the clearest exponent of the highest view.

iv. The RGV as a Synthesis of the Tathagatagarbha
Sutras and Prajnaparamita Sutras

Although, as mentioned earlier, certain of the early Indian Madhyamikas had ideas akin to the Tathagatagarbha teachings of the SMS, the Tathagatagarbha Sutras that the RGV and RGVV are based on represent a whole separate class of literature, which has nothing to do with either Maitreya or Nagarjuna's Madhyamaka. Again, as mentioned already, the Tathagatagarbha Sutras were scarcely mentioned or commented upon in India, but moved swiftly northwards out of India to Khotan and thence to China where they were already influential by the seventh century, for example, in Fa Tsang's system.

Since evidence suggests that the Tathagatagarbha Sutras appeared in India in the Andhra region in about the third century A.D., they were probably a little later than the Prajnaparamita Sutras, the earliest of which were approximately first century B.C.[7] The *Srimaladevisutra* [SMS] is an important example of this kind of literature and is one of the principal sources for the RGV and RGVV. However, whereas the SMS seems to be mainly concerned with showing that Tathagatagarbha is something Bodhisattvas realize and Sravakas and Pratyeka Buddhas do not, the RGV goes further and answers those Bodhisattvas who accept Prajnaparamita, but want to reject Tathagatagarbha doctrine [RGV 1.150–167]. The way the doctrine of the SMS is presented gives the impression it was written before the streams of Prajnaparamita and Tathagatagarbha doctrine met, as if all Bodhisattvas accepted its Tathagatagarbha doctrine. It mentions beginner Bodhisattvas who "wander from the emptiness"[8], but not Bodhisattvas who reject Tathagatagarbha doctrine. That the RGV is addressed to those Bodhisattvas who accept Prajnaparamita, but who have doubts about Tathagatagarbha doctrine, is demonstrated in the section on the purpose for teaching the Tathagatagarbha [RGV 1.156 and RGV 5.20–24], where the dangers of rejecting the true doctrine are emphasized. The *Ratnagotravibhaga* [RGV 1.156–60] anticipates the readers' question concerning earlier teachings which seem to contradict the message of the RGV. It asks why it is that, although it is taught here and there that all knowable things are empty like clouds, dreams, and magical illusions, here in the RGV it is taught that the Buddhadhatu exists in beings. Then again RGV [1.162] teaches that those Bodhisattvas who, having given rise to Bodhicitta, feel themselves to be superior to those inferior beings who have not, are at fault. In the first case the RGV is talking about those who accept the Prajnaparamita doctrines of emptiness and the second about Bodhisattvas who have aroused Bodhicitta, but, in both cases, the individuals concerned doubt whether the Tathagatagarbha exists in all beings.

That the author of the RGV knew the Prajnaparamita literature is clear from RGV [2.59] where the *Saddharmapundarikasutra* etc. are mentioned in connection with the second stage of training of a Bodhisattva (corresponding to the second Dharmacakra).

The RGV itself does not use the term "Tathagatagarbha" but uses the term "Element" (Dhatu) instead—although it occasionally uses the term *"Buddhagarbha"* [RGV 1.28, 1.152]. The RGVV on the other hand, quotes at length from Tathagatagarbha Sutras, in which the term "Tathagatagarbha" often occurs; it also uses the term frequently itself.

The reason the RGV uses the term "Element" rather than "Tathagatagarbha" might well be that its special contribution to Tathagatagarbha doctrine is to link doctrines concerning what it calls the "Seven Vajra Bases" to the concept of a single Absolute Buddha Element. The Vajra Bases are Buddha, Dharma, Samgha, Element, Enlightenment, Qualities, and Activity [RGV 1.1]. Since Tathagatagarbha is the name for the Element, when covered by the veils of the klesa in ordinary beings, it is, perhaps, not the best name to use for pointing out the sameness of that Element in each of the Seven Vajra Bases, which include not only ordinary beings, but also Bodhisattvas and Buddhas. If the Shentongpas are correct that they all refer to the same Absolute Reality, we have an explanation for the RGV's use of the term "Element" rather than "Tathagatagarbha."

The task of the RGV is to resolve the apparent contradiction between the third Dharmacakra doctrine of inseparable, spontaneously existing Buddha Qualities and the second Dharmacakra doctrine of the mere negation of the two selves (*bdag gnyis bkag tsam*, [SKK hum 31]), which it does chiefly by means of examples drawn from the Tathagatagarbha Sutras.

The important feature of the RGV from the historical point of view is that it represents a synthesis of Prajnaparamita Sutra and Tathagatagarbha Sutra doctrine [RGV 158, 159] and, as such, it clearly expresses doctrines in harmony with the latest developments of Buddhist thought in India just before it finally disappeared there.[9]

Some of the most important verses of the RGV itself seem to derive directly from the SMS, as well as the *Tathagatagarbhasutra*[10] from which the nine examples of the Tathagatagarbha wrapped in sheaths are taken [RGV 1.95–129], the *Gaganaganjapariprccha*, [*Study* 239fn.292] from which the example of the Mind's nature being like space is taken [RGV 1.53–63], and the *Jnanalokalamkara* from which the nine examples of the Buddha Activity are taken [RGV chapter 4].

RGV [1.2] mentions that its layout follows the *Dharanirajesvarasutra*, which is either contained in or given as another name for the Sutra called the *Instruction on the Tathagata's Great Compassion* (*Tathagatamaha-karunanirdesasutra*).[11]

v. The *Vyakhya* [RGVV]

The *Ratnagotravibhagavyakhya* [RGVV] is a commentary in prose on the RGV; its most quoted source is the third chapter of the SMS on Nitartha. The RGVV is sometimes referred to as the auto-commentary on the RGV because the two texts were rediscovered together, and the verses of the RGV are interspersed with the comments of the RGVV.

The RGVV quotes at length from the *Anunatvapurnatvanirdesa* concerning the inseparable Buddha Qualities, the three stages of impure, pure and perfectly pure, inconceivability, permanence, and so on. There is also a very important quotation from the *Avatamsakasutra* about the whole of the Buddha's wisdom being present in all beings. Many other texts are quoted in the RGVV, but those mentioned above include all the most essential and characteristic doctrines of the RGV and RGVV. (For more details see Takasaki's *Study* p. 35–44).

vi. Transmission to Tibet

Fortunately for Buddhism, the time of these synthesizing developments coincided with the second wave of Tibetan translators and scholars who were reintroducing Buddhism to Tibet in the eleventh century. Thus, the Tibetans were able to preserve not only the work of synthesis already begun but also to build on that work.

At the same time the growing tension between the Pandits bringing Buddhism direct from India and those bringing it via China was reaching a crisis point. The RGV had already been popular and influential in China for over 150 years, since approximately the time that Cha'an, (called ''Zen'' in Japanese), arrived in China from India. As Chinese Buddhism fell from grace in the eyes of the ruling powers of Tibet, the influence of the RGV must also have waned.

It seems a strange coincidence that it was rediscovered in India at just this juncture. Although it is conceivable that the rediscovery story covers up the fact that the texts were reintroduced into India from China, this is unlikely for several reasons, not least among which is that Tibetans only ever use Tathagatagarbha to refer to Buddhajnana in beings, and never in inanimate objects. The Chinese Tathagatagarbha doctrine, however, applies to both the animate and inanimate. Furthermore, the Tibetan text is closer to the Sanskrit text than any extant Chinese one.

Thus, the RGV was transmitted to Tibet in a form acceptable to the supporters of the gradual approach of Indian Buddhism (Ngog's tradition) [Kongtrul's RGV commentary 8b]. At the same time, if Kongtrul's account is to be believed, a special Shentong-type transmission of the RGV was introduced into Tibet for meditators. Both transmissions emanated from Sajjana in Kashmir in the wake of the Maitreyanic revival among the Indian Siddhas (e.g. Maitripa), which became associated with Asanga.

Whether Tathagatagarbha doctrine was ever interpreted in these two ways (Rangtong and Shentong) before the rediscovery of the RGV, and whether it ever happens in traditions based on other Tathagatagarbha literature is an open question. Certainly Dolpopa shows [RC 127.6] that it was already an issue at the time the MPNS was written, because he quotes a section of that Sutra that argues against those who take Tathagatagarbha to be non-self and definite emptiness (*gtan du stong pa nyid*).

9.2   Matters Arising from the Introduction to Kongtrul's Commentary on the RGV.*

i. The Two Tibetan Transmission Lineages of the RGV (Table 8.2)

Ruegg gives an account of three different traditions of interpretation of the RGV (*La Théorie* 58ff]; these are the traditions that interpret it as Vijnanavada (Buton), as Madhyamaka (Redawa), and as Great Madhyamaka (Shentong). Kongtrul gives two traditions of interpretation—Rangtong and Shentong.

Kongtrul, in the introduction to his RGV commentary, describes how, after the Indian Siddha Maitripa (eleventh Century), found the RGV in a stupa, it was taken to Kashmir and transmitted to Sajjana from whom stem two lines of transmission—one through Ngog and the other through Zu and Tsen.[12]

Kongtrul's commentary on the RGV adopts a Shentong position and gives as its principal source the work of Rangjung Dorje, whose interpretation of the RGV it associates with the tradition passed down through Gampopa's lineage (the Dagpo Kagyu). Kongtrul gives the impression that this represents an unbroken line of transmission since the time of Zu and Tsen in the eleventh century. He also claims it accords with the Shentong (or Great Madhyamaka) interpretation of Tathagatagarbha doctrine and the meditative tradition of the Indian Siddhas, such as Saraha and his lineage, which includes Maitripa, the essential doctrine of whom is known as the Heart-Essence (*snying po don*).

Kongtrul contrasts the Shentong view with the Rangtong interpretation of the RGV, which he associates with Ngog (1059–1109), and his transmission lineage which, from Kongtrul's account, seems to include Rongton (1367–1449), the great Sakya scholar [CDTBE 16, 22].

---

*Translated in the next section of this present work.

Unfortunately, although Ngog's commentary is presumably still extant since Ruegg was able to refer to it in *La Théorie*, I was unable to acquire a copy. A detailed study of it in relation to Kongtrul's comments will therefore have to wait. Instead, Rongton's commentary has been taken as representative of the Rangtong tradition that Kongtrul refers to in his account. Kongtrul makes several references to it in his own commentary, even though he is avowedly commenting from the Shentong, while Rongton does so from the Rangtong, point of view. This may seem odd, but is consistent with his position of giving equal validity to both traditions. It is rather unsatisfactory from the point of view of this present work, however, since Kongtrul uses Rongton's commentary for two key verses in the RGV [RGV 1.27 and 1.28] and so obscures the difference between a Rangtong and Shentong interpretation of them.

ii. Questions Arising From Kongtrul's Commentary

Several questions arise out of Kongtrul's scheme. First, what text or texts by Rangjung Dorje was Kongtrul using to justify his assertion that he was mainly following Rangjung Dorje? Although Rangjung Dorje's RGV commentary seems to be no longer available, it is possible that Kongtrul was referring to some other work by Rangjung Dorje, for example, the *sNying bo bstan pa* or *Zab mo nang gi don*, which comment on the RGV.

It is curious that Kongtrul mentions his main source as Rangjung Dorje because, for the greatest proportion of his RGV commentary, Kongtrul follows almost word for word a commentary reputedly by the Jonangpa Dolpopa entitled *rGyud bla ma'i legs bshad nyi ma'i 'od zer*. Its colophon reads:

> *Jo nang dpal gyi khrod du rgyal khams phyogs med pa rton pa bzhi ldan gyis sbyar ba'o*
> The one having the four things to rely on with no allegiance to any country composed this in the mountain retreat of the glorious Jonang.

This accords with the colophon in Dolpopa's collected works [Dolpopa's *gSung 'bum* vol. 1]. The text has been printed by the Karmapa's printing establishment in Delhi and its frontispiece claims it is by the Jonangpa, Dolpopa Sherab Gyatlsen. If it is, indeed, by Dolpopa, the question arises why Kongtrul does not acknowledge him as the main source of his interpretation of the RGV? One answer might be that the text is not in fact by Dolpopa, but by Rangjung Dorje, written when he was visiting Jonang, which he certainly did. He was very much influenced by Dolpopa and his Shentong doctrine. Alternatively, he might have written a commentary almost indistinguishable from that by Dolpopa. This is conceivable since Dolpopa's commentary is little more than a synopsis of the RGVV, but even so, it is unlikely he would have followed Dolpopa quite so word for word. Another idea put forward by Khenpo Tsultrim Gyamtso is that, although Kongtrul follows Dolpopa in the main, there are one or two crucial points in which he favors Rangjung Dorje rather than Dolpopa. He does not venture to say what points these might be, however.

Tempting as it is to think that the *Legs shes nyi ma* [Dolpopa's RGV commentary] is wrongly ascribed and was indeed by Rangjung Dorje, Thrangu Rinpoche, a leading authority on Shentong, was in no doubt that it was by Dolpopa, though he produced no conclusive evidence to prove this assumption.

Conceivably, Kongtrul wanted to propagate Dolpopa's work, but knowing how the Jonangpas were maligned by Gelugpas and other scholars in Tibet, he had it printed under his own name to protect it. Most of the additions by Kongtrul are not significant; they are expanded definitions of standard terms such as Buddha, klesa, Enlightenment and so forth. The effect of these additions is to produce sentences of unwieldy length that obscure rather than accentuate their essential message. It is, however, true to the style of oral commentary and one suspects it was dictated under pressure to a scribe at some speed. Kongtrul's style of writing in others of his works, for example, the *Encyclopedia of Knowledge* (*Shes bya mdzod*), is completely different. It is clear, concise and brilliantly organized. Generally his comments on the RGV in the *Encyclopedia of Knowledge* are more illuminating than those in his RGV commentary. The interesting parts of Kongtrul's RGV commentary are the introduction, translated in the next section, and some quoted remarks by Mikyo Dorje and Karma Tinlay. As was mentioned above, besides these, he also refers several times to Rongton. Incidentally, except to say he is mainly following him, he scarcely mentions Rangjung Dorje.

Another question that arises from Kongtrul's account of the two traditions of interpretation of the RGV is to what extent it is true, as Kongtrul suggests, that the tradition stemming from Zu and Tsen corresponds to that of Rangjung Dorje. There is plenty of evidence in the *Zab mo nang don, sNying po bstan pa* and *rNam shes ye shes 'byed pa* by Rangjung Dorje that his view on Tathatagatagarbha accords with Shentong but, since the commentaries of Zu and Tsen are not available, it is not possible to compare them. Kongtrul links Rangjung Dorje's tradition to theirs, but does not trace an actual lineage. His only evidence seems to be that Zu and Tsen's tradition was famous for its meditation [CDTBE 40], and Rangjung Dorje was famous for his special understanding of the inner meaning, that is, the meaning discovered through skill in meditation.

The tradition of Zu and Tsen is not well known today and their works on the RGV have been lost. They were superseded by the work of Ngog, whose translation and commentary on the RGV became far more popular than those of Zu and Tsen or any other tradition.

Thus, although there are two well-established streams of interpretation, Rangtong and Shentong, not enough evidence has been assembled so far to establish to what extent the different Rangtong traditions correspond to each other; a similar position exists in respect to the Shentong traditions. For example, Rongton follows a Rangtong tradition that is different from the Rangtong position of the Gelugpas,[13] yet both claim to be following Ngog and both differ from Buton's DZG (also Rangtong). Whereas Ruegg often speaks of Buton's and Gyaltsab's as the two main traditions of interpretation of Tathagatagarbha doctrine—omitting to mention the Jonangpas or any other Shentong-type system—neither Buton nor Gyaltsab are mentioned by Kongtrul in his account of the commentarial traditions on the RGV; however, he must surely have been familiar with their works. Possibly he considered that neither of them followed the mainline tradition of Ngog. If this were indeed his position, it would be illuminating to know how he justified it. Since it is standard practice for Rimay masters to disregard the later Gelugpa tradition after Tsongkapa (Tsongkapa himself did not write a commentary on the RGV), this could explain the omission of Gyaltsab (as well as Sonam Tragpa and other Gelugpa commentators) but not of Buton. Indeed, Kongtrul's account of the history of the commentarial traditions on the RGV is of interest as much for what it does *not* say as for what it does. Buton was a contemporary of Dolpopa and the *mDzes rGyan* by Buton [DZG] seems to be a critique of Dolpopa's view. That he is completely ignored by Kongtrul must be significant.

iii. Other Commentators Not Mentioned in the Initial Praises

Kongtrul mentions a number of commentators in connection with the sources for the Shentong interpretation of the RGV. For example, he mentions several Karma Kagyu Lamas (that is, Lamas of the Karmapa's lineage), including Karma Konshon (*dKon gZhon*), and Karma Tinlaypa (*'phrin las pa*—late fifteenth, early sixteenth century), who both wrote on the RGV. Shonupal (*gZhon nu dpal*—1392–1481), made a very expanded commentary on the RGVV which, according to Kongtrul, agreed with their interpretation. In Kongtrul's opinion these commentaries agreed with the special system of analysis used by Dolpopa. Incidentally, Shonupal's teacher's teacher was a disciple of Dolpopa's; he saw Dolpopa in a dream about Kalacakra. Kongtrul's layout suggests Dolpopa himself was following the tradition of Zu and Tsen, but again, he gives no direct evidence for this.

Kongtrul makes special mention of the fact that the general and particular lineages following Dolpopa's line of explanation continued to the time of his writing as an unbroken transmission (*lung rgyun*). This has special significance in the light of the fact that Dolpopa's works had been sealed and banned by the Gelugpas since the seventeenth century.

Another branch of the Shentong tradition of RGV interpretation was found at Zurmang (Trungpa Rimpoche's monastery); this interpretation was based on the *tika* made by Lalung Karma Tenpel (*Lha lung karma bstan 'phel*). The name "Karma" suggests he was also of the Karma Kagyu school. According to Kongtrul, this was a later tradition but well received. Kongtrul does not mention Mipam (*Mi pham*), one of his own colleagues and disciples, presumably because Mipam wrote his commentary on the RGV after Kongtrul had written his own. Mipam's commentary offers an interesting field for future research into the RGV and Shentong.

Another source that Kongtrul mentions and quotes at length in his commentary[14] though not in his introduction—is Mikyo Dorje, the eighth Karmapa (1507–1554). He wrote the *dBu ma Shentong smra ba'i srol legs par phye ba'i sgron me*, which defends the Shentong Great Madhyamaka tradition of Maitreya and Asanga as the final (Nitartha) teaching of the Buddha.

Although Kongtrul gives a brief outline of the sources for the Rangtong and Shentong interpretation of the RGV in his introduction, it has not been possible here to study many of these sources in order to assess to what extent they agree or disagree with each other. However, in this present work, a general account of the Shentong interpretation of the RGV and RGVV is given, relying mainly on Dolpopa, Rangjung Dorje, Mikyo Dorje, and more recent Shentong scholars such as Kongtrul and my Lama informants.

iv. Gampopa and the Sutra and Tantra Mahamudra

For Kongtrul, Gampopa, the father of the four great Kagyu lineages, is the inheritor and unifier of the two lineages of Maitripa, the Siddha practice lineage, and the RGV teaching and practice lineage [see Table 8.1]. Although the layout of Kongtrul's account suggests an identity between Maitripa's Siddha tradition and Sajjana's special meditation tradition, Kongtrul does not mention any lineage connection. Similarly, he does not give the lineage details for the transmission of the RGV teaching or practice traditions to the Kagyupas. His account is impressionistic: the practice (*grub*) traditions of the Siddhas and Sajjana teach the same Heart-Essence (*sNying po don*) as transmitted by Zu and Tsen's RGV tradition.

Although the implication is that the Kagyu RGV transmission derives from Zu and Tsen, Kongtrul gives no account of the source of Gampopa's (and hence the Kagyu) RGV transmission. Although Gampopa made the famous remark that the basis of the Kagyu Mahamudra was the RGV [RGV commentary 15a], theoretically his transmission could as easily have been by way of Atisa, Marpa, or Ngog, as by way of Zu and Tsen. Perhaps it was because he received it through a number of Gurus of different traditions that Kongtrul gives no clear record of the source of Gampopa's transmission. Since Maitripa is the source of all RGV transmissions in Tibet, the only certainty is that, whatever the details, Gampopa's RGV transmission derives eventually from him.

It seems that Gampopa distinguished Sutra from Tantra Mahamudra, the latter requiring empowerment (*abhiseka*), the former not. He had accordingly a special method of teaching Sutra Mahamudra.[15] The *Blue Annals* [BA 459] states (Roerich's translation):

> Now the venerable Mi la ras pa [Milarepa] did not teach the *upayamarga* and the Mahamudra separately, but Gampopa used to preach the hidden precepts of the *upayamarga* to those only whom he considered fit to receive Tantric initiation. (On the other hand) he used to bestow the hidden precepts of the Mahamudra on those who were fit to receive the paramitas, though they did not get any Tantric initiation.

No doubt this method derived from Gampopa's integrating Atisa's Kadampa (*bKa' gdams pa*) with Milarepa's Mahamudra tradition. Perhaps, having received a Rangtong transmission of the RGV from the Kadampas and a Shentong from the Marpa-Mila tradition, he found, as presumably Sajjana had done, that both were useful. The Rangtong was useful for teaching Sutra Mahamudra and the Shentong for Tantra Mahamudra. Although at this stage we cannot be sure what Gampopa's Sutra Mahamudra was, the fact that it did not require empowerment suggests it was more Rangtong than Shentong in flavor. Among present day Kagyu Lamas, Mahamudra continues to be taught both with and without empowerment; it would be interesting to find out the exact difference.

Kongtrul sheds no light on this complex issue. He distinguishes Sutras that teach the Absolute Dharmata from those that give "detailed secret teaching" (*gsang gtam zab mo*) but this does not tell us what Sutras or what interpretation of RGV are the basis for Sutra Mahamudra. When asked, Khenpo Tsultrim explained that Sutra Mahamudra is based on the Tathagatagarbha doctrine of the RGV whereas Tantra Mahamudra derives from Tathagatagarbha doctrine in Tantric works (i.e. the same distinction as between Sutra and Tantric Shentong). This would suggest that Sutra Mahamudra is based on a Shentong interpretation of RGV.

Although it remains an open question whether Gampopa's Sutra Mahamudra was Rangtong or Shentong, he clearly was not averse to giving the RGV Tathagatagarbha doctrine a Rangtong interpretation. He does so in the opening chapter of *The Jewel Ornament of Liberation*.[16] He explains that by "Dharmakaya," emptiness is meant, and that the three reasons (or signs) that all beings have Tathagatagarbha are: (*a*) because all beings are emptiness, (*b*) because the emptiness nature of Buddhas and beings is the same and (*c*) because they have one of the five gotra, each of which is capable of bringing a being to Buddhahood. He defines gotra as:

Sangs rgyas chos bskyed pa'i nus pa
The power to give rise to Buddha qualities.

In spite of this Rangtong explanation, that is, Tathagatagarbha is the ability to develop Buddha qualities through the accumulation of merit and wisdom, Kongtrul [RGV 15b] refers to Gampopa's *Jewel Ornament of Liberation* as if it taught the "Path of Direct Experience" (i.e. Shentong). The fact that Gampopa chooses to introduce his graduated sequence of teachings (*lam rim*) in the *Jewel Ornament* with Rangtong should not be seen as a rejection of Shentong. Indeed, in the "Prajna" chapter, he stresses the importance of special instructions (*man ngag*) as given to him by his Guru Milarepa; the reader will by now make the obvious connection between special instructions and Shentong.

Broido [JIABS vol.8: 35ff] alerts us to the ways different traditions structure Mahamudra practice to suit people moving along the path at different speeds. This not only relates to how, to use Kongtrul's terms, the path of Experience can be fast or slow, but it also relates to the Path of Inference, which is obviously for the gradual type of person (*rim gyis pa*).

v. Rangjung Dorje and the Mahamudra-Dzogchen Synthesis[17]

Whereas Gampopa was famous for bringing together the Kadampa and Mahamudra lineages, which may have made his position in regard to the RGV somewhat unclear, Rangjung Dorje is famous for bringing together the Mahamudra and the Nyingmapa Dzogchen teachings. He holds the rare distinction of being included within both the Kagyu and Nyingmapa lineages. Since Rangjung Dorje was not only a colleague of Dolpopa and admirer of his Shentong explanations, but also a great Tantrika responsible for drawing together the different strands of Tantric tradition, it is understandable that Kongtrul should regard Rangjung Dorje, rather than Gampopa, as the founder of the Kagyu tradition of Shentong and follow him.

Section Three

A Shentong Interpretation of the RGV and RGVV and A Translation of Kongtrul's Introduction to His RGV Commentary

Chapter 10

A Shentong Interpretation of the RGV and RGVV—A Paraphrase With Comments

10.1 The Title and its Implications

The RGV is known in the Tibetan tradition as the *Mahayanottaratantrasastra* which translates as *The Ultimate Thread (tantra) of the Mahayana—a Commentary*. According to E. H. Johnston, editor of the Sanskrit edition, however, the real title should be *Ratnagotravibhaga*, which translates as *The Divisions of the Jewel Lineage*. In the Tibetan version, this name only occurs at the end of each section.

Tantra means "thread" and is translated in Tibetan as *rGyud*. *rGyud* is defined as "continuity" (*rgyun chags* [RC 244]). In the title of the RGV it refers to the nondual Buddhajnana that is the central thread or continuity of the Buddha's doctrine throughout all three vehicles, that is, their final or ultimate meaning (Nitartha). Since it is present in the base, path, and fruit [Kongtrul's RGV commentary 27a], it is the central thread or continuity of our experience. It is the ultimate nature of Reality itself that runs through everything and that is variously referred to in the RGV and RGVV as Tathagatagarbha, Gotra, Dharmakaya, Dhatu, Tathata, and so on. Except for its occurrence in the title, "*tantra*" appears only once in the whole text [RGV 1.160]. Nevertheless, it is worth noticing not only its appearance but also that the Tibetans adopted it as the title of the text. It reflects the place the RGV has come to occupy in the minds of the Tibetans as the bridge between the Mahayana Sutras and the Vajrayana Tantras.

In the title *The Divisions of the Jewel Lineage* the term "gotra" (lineage) takes the place of "tantra." It refers to lineage of the Buddha, Dharma, and Samgha, the three "Jewels" of Buddhism. The slight ambiguity associated with the term gotra[1] is exploited in the layout of the text so that it refers both to the lineage succession of Buddha giving rise to Dharma, which gives rise to Samgha, the members of which eventually become Buddhas and so on, and to the Buddhajnana itself that is the essence of the lineage. This is the Dharmakaya, which is compared to a wish-fulfilling jewel, the treasure hidden in filth, and so on [RGV 1.30, 1.96ff].

The "divisions" or "analysis" (*vibhaga, dbye ba*, [see *Study* 141fn.1]) of the lineage refers to the way the subject matter is handled under various subheadings. For example, when it is fully realized, it is called "Buddha";

when it is seen as that which is to be realized and the means of realizing it, it is called "Dharma"; when it is being realized in the mind of the Samgha, it is called "Samgha"; when it is simply present in the mind of unenlightened beings, it is called the "Element" (Dhatu); when it is realized, it is called "Enlightenment"; when its nature is being described, it is called "Qualities" and when its Activity is being described, it is called "Activity."

In Shentong terms, the message of the RGV and RGVV is that these seven concepts, that are found everywhere in Buddhist literature, are seen, when fully analyzed, to be aspects of the same basic Reality known by such terms as Dhatu, Gotra, Tathagatagarbha, Tathata, Paramarthasatya, Dharmakaya, Buddhajnana and Clear Light Nature of Mind. Indeed, RGVV [1.1] gives Paramartha, Dhatu, Tathagatagarbha, and Dharmakaya as synonyms.[2]

Thus, each term refers to the same subject matter from a different point of view. This is in contrast to the situation in the lower levels of the Buddha's teaching where these terms refer to disparate aspects of our experience. At first, Gotra, paramarthasatya, Buddha, Dharma, Samgha, Dharmadhatu, Enlightenment, Buddha qualities and activity all appear as clearly different and distinct phenomena. For example, paramarthasatya refers to the ultimate nature of the dharmas, which in *Abhidharma* terms means the smallest non-divisible particles of the objective world and the smallest indivisible moments of mind. We saw in Chapter 3.1 ("Progressive Stages of Meditation on Emptiness") and chapter 5.3 ("The Two Realities and the Two Visions") in this present work that as the analysis of the nature of the dharmas is refined, paramarthasatya comes to be synonymous with emptiness, but it is not synonymous with Buddhajnana until the third Dharmacakra where it is synonymous with both Buddhajnana and Emptiness.

10.2   General Introduction to the Seven Vajra Bases

The rest of this chapter paraphrases the RGV and RGVV from a Shentong point of view. Although some details vary from one Shentong commentator to another, the essential message is always the same [Kongtrul's RGV commentary 16a]. Thus, in the following exposition a generalized model of the Shentong view derived from the foregoing discussion is used. The paraphrase is interspersed with comments. These refer, where appropriate, to Kongtrul's SKK and RGV commentary, Dolpopa's RC, Rangjung Dorje's *Zab mo nang don,* and Mikyo Dorje's *gZhan stong sgron me.* In addition, explanations given by Khenpo Tsultrim and other Lama informants have been used. In fact, Kongtrul and Dolpopa's commentaries on the RGV are often not as helpful as one might have hoped in terms of bringing out the specifically Shentong point of view. The best references for this are in their other more general philosophical works, which frequently quote the RGV and RGVV. The main use of their RGV commentaries is the expansion of the rather terse phrases of the original into full grammatical sentences and the division of the work into headings and subheadings in order to clarify its basic structure.

Paraphrase. The basic structure is built around the seven Vajra Bases— Buddha, Dharma, Samgha, Element, Enlightenment, Qualities, and Activity [RGV 1–3]—which are commented on at length in the RGVV. It is explained there that they are each a Vajra Base, because: a) they each express the impenetrable Vajra Nature; b) they each are a teaching device that acts like a vajra (Indra's weapon, like a thunderbolt—invincible and impenetrable like a diamond) to destroy the ignorance of beings. The first chapter of the text—nearly half of the RGV and over three quarters of the RGVV—is devoted to the first four Bases (Buddha, Dharma, Samgha, and particularly the Element). The second chapter is on Enlightenment, the third is on Qualities, and the fourth is on Activity. The last chapter is devoted to explaining the benefits and authenticity of the teaching in the text.

The Sanskrit for Vajra Base is "*vajrapada*".* The RGVV explains that the Bases are the dwelling place of that which is realized (*rtogs pa'i don*), which is like a vajra. It is like a vajra because it is hard, if not impossible, to penetrate with the prajna of listening and reflection. This is because it must be known by Self-Awareness (*prativedhana, so so rang gis rig par bya ba*), which is beyond utterance. Nevertheless, the words of these seven Bases show the way that accords with what is to be realized (*rtogs pa'i don*); that is why they are called "dwelling places of the Vajra." The dwelling place is the words; the Vajra is the meaning that dwells in the words.

The RGVV explains that the RGV teaching on each Vajra Base derives from the Sutras. The first three derive from the *Chapter Teaching the Superior Resolve (Sthiradhyasaya-parivarta, Lhag pa'i bsam pa bstan pa'i le'u)*:[3]

> Ananda, the Tathagata is undemonstrable, cannot be seen with the eyes; Ananda, the Dharma is inaudible and cannot be heard with the ears; Ananda, the Samgha is non-compounded and cannot be honored with body and mind.

Comments. Dolpopa [RC 19] quotes this section from the RGVV, and compares it to the Tantric doctrine of the Kaya of the Absolute Deity being in

---

*Translated in Tibetan as *gnas*, dwelling place.

the body of all beings and being the Ultimate Triple Gem. He explains, that Tathagatagarbha is the Absolute Deity, Tantra and Mandala and so on [RC 40].

Paraphrase. The fourth Vajra Base, the Element, derives from the *Anunatvapurnatvanirdesa* [AAN]:

> Sariputra, the Tathagata's object (*yul*) is the Tathagata's sphere (*spyod yul*). Sariputra, this point (*artha*) cannot be known, seen, or examined by the Sravaka's or the Pratyeka's own pure prajna, so there is no need to mention ordinary immature beings. They have no recourse but to realize it through faith in the Tathagata. Sariputra, the Absolute is to be realized through faith. Sariputra, the Absolute is a word for the Element of beings. Sariputra, the Element of Beings is a word for Tathagatagarbha. Sariputra, the Tathagatagarbha is a word for Dharmakaya.

Comments. Dolpopa [RC 47] makes the following short comment of his own, having quoted this passage in full: "In case you think that the seed of Buddha or emptiness in the sense of the mere non-existence of the dharmas is meant here—it is not. It means the measureless Buddhajnana having all the Qualities." He then quotes RGV [1.25] on the inseparable Dharmas and the RGVV [25.3], which state quite clearly that the stainless Buddha Qualities are present in beings at the same time as they are defiled (klesa). The inseparable Dharmata is the same before as after and so this base (*gnas*) is inconceivable.

Paraphrase. The fifth Vajra Base, Enlightenment, derives from the *Srimaladevisutra* [SMS]:

> Bhagavan, the "Complete and Perfect Enlightenment" is a word for the Nirvana Dhatu (*dbyings*). Bhagavan, "Nirvana Dhatu" is another word for the Tathagata's Dharmakaya.

The sixth Vajra Base, Qualities, derives from the *Anunatvapurnatvanirdesa* [AAN]:

> Oh, Sariputra, the Dharmakaya that is taught by the Tathagata is the Wisdom Qualities indivisible from and endowed with the Dharmas of the Tathagata beyond the sands of the Ganges [in number].

The seventh Vajra Base, Activity, derives from the *Tathagatagunajnanacintyavisayavataranirdesa* (*Instruction on Entering the Field* (*yul*) *of the Tathagata's Inconceivable Qualities and Jnana''*):

> Manjusri, the Tathagata does not conceptualize nor think, but engages spontaneously and conceptionlessly in natural deeds (*rang bzhin gyi mdzad pa*) in each place as appropriate.

The order in which the Vajra Bases are introduced follows that of the *Dharanisvararajasutra* [DRS] [RGV 1.2]. The first three follow the order in its introductory chapter; the remaining four follow the order in its chapter on the ''Divisions of the Dharmas of the Tathagatas and Bodhisattvas'':

> Bhagavan, He completely awakens to the equalness of all dharmas. He turns the wheel of the Dharma and teaches all the many disciples . . .

The RGVV gives a fuller explanation of the above lines:

> He realizes the *garbha* of Enlightenment (*bodhi*) on the eighth, ninth and tenth levels and then the Buddha, amidst his disciples, turns the wheel of Dharma and etc . . .

After this the Enlightenment, Qualities, and Activity are explained and finally the example of purifying the lapis lazuli with a three-fold process [RGVV 1.6] is given, again taken from the DRS [21c]. The RGVV explains that the Tathagata knows the Dhatu of beings, and so teaches impermanence, suffering, non-self, and impurity to make them renounce samsara. This is not enough; he then teaches emptiness, signlessness (*mtshan ma med pa, animitta*), and desirelessness (*smon pa med pa, apranihita*); he makes beings realize the manner of the Tathagata. This too is not enough; he then teaches the irreversible Dharma wheel for beings of all sorts of natures to make them enter the field (*yul*) of the Tathagata; thus they realize the Dharmata of the Buddha (see Chapter 7 The Three Dharmacakras in this present work). There follows an example which Takasaki [*Study* 152] says is a Prakrit verse—that is apparently also in Pali, although its source is unknown—about the pure gotra. The Tathagata Dhatu is compared to the rock in which the gold is not visible but from which, by purification, it is made to appear. It is made to appear through the sixty elements of purification, which are the four Bodhisattva adornments (*rgyan, alamkara*), the eight manifestations (*snang ba, avabhasa*), the sixteen compassions, and the thirty-two activities. These sixty elements of purification result in Enlightenment, which is the next subject to be taught. After that, Qualities (the ten powers etc.) are taught, and finally Activity.[4] In this way the RGVV establishes that the order of the seven Vajra Bases follows that of the above mentioned scriptures.

Comments. From the Shentong point of view the sixty elements of purification are cause and result only in the sense that the process of the path reveals these elements. Rangtong systems explain them as elements associated with following the path. In general, it is not clear whether ''elements of purification'' means elements that emerge through the process of purification or elements by means of which purification takes place. From the

Shentong point of view both the agent and the emergent "fruit" of purification are aspects of the same Reality.[5]

Mikyo Dorje adds the following comments (*gZhan stong sgron me* 2b):

> Therefore the means to give rise to the real (*dngos*) Vajra-like realization awareness is, after the ordinary being has purified his. . . . mind by the power of listening, reflecting and meditating, then, without having to rely on listening, reflecting and meditating, the realization Jnana which is like a self-arisen Vajra like the sun . . . shining, destroys the darkness of ignorance tendencies in an instant. The meaning of "Vajra" is that the Jnana light-source has the power to destroy the mass of ignorance the instant it meets it. This is the meaning of the seven Vajra Bases of the Mahayana Uttara Tantra Sastra.

Kongtrul explains [SKK hum 43.5]: "The Dharmadhatu, stainless and Clear Light by Nature, has the seven Vajra Bases" (*chos dbyings dri ma med cing 'od gsal ba'i rang bzhin rdo rje'i gnas bdun dang ldan pa*). Khenpo Tsultrim[6] explains this as meaning the seven Vajra Bases are all complete in the Dhatu and spontaneously present (*lhun grub du ldan pa*). Thus, they are each different ways of talking about the Dharmakaya, which is the Vajra-Buddhajnana, destroying all ignorance and inpenetrable by the conceptual mind.

10.3   Vajra Bases 1–3: The Three Jewels

After the introductory verses there follow fifteen slokas [RGV 1.4–18] describing the first three Vajra Bases. They consist of three basic verses praising: 1. Buddha, 2. Dharma, and 3. Samgha respectively. Each of these verses is followed by several commentarial slokas.

1. Buddha is described:
   i. as without beginning, middle and end, that is, non-compounded,

   ii. as peace, that is, the effortless or spontaneous (*lhun grub, anabhoga*) Dharmakaya. "Spontaneous" is explained in the RGVV as meaning non-conceptual and conceptionless, literally, prapanca and *vikalpa* have ceased (*spros pa dang rnam rtog pa thams cad nye bar zhi ba*),

   iii. as "self-enlightened" (*rang rnam sang rgyas*). This is explained in the RGVV as that which is realized through self-risen Jnana. "Self-arisen" in this context means without arising or ceasing, that is, non-compounded,

> iv. as knowledge. This is explained as having the knowledge with which to liberate others,
>
> v. as love,
>
> vi. as power, that is, the power to overcome the suffering and ignorance of others.

The first three points describe his realization, which is his "own welfare"; the second three points describe his knowledge, love, and power, which are the "welfare of others." The images of a sword and a thunderbolt (vajra) are used, representing wisdom and compassion, which cut down the wall of wrong views concealed in the dark forest of doubt.

The RGVV gives a long reference to the *Jnanalokalamkarasutra* [JAAS] in connection with these verses. This Sutra deals particularly with the doctrine that the Buddha is non-arisen, non-compounded, and so on and yet acts for beings spontaneously and constantly. The RGVV [phi 6a.2] quotes this Sutra as follows:

> *chos thams cad kyi de bzhin nyid mngon par rdzogs par byang chub pa'i sgo la. gZhan gyi rkyen gyis mngon par rtogs pa ma yin pa nyid bstan to.*
>
> It is taught that the complete and perfect realization of the Tathata of all dharmas is not realized by other condition(s) (*parapratyaya*, literally, in dependence on another).

Comments. Dolpopa [RC 127.2] comments on RGV [1.6]: "non-compounded and spontaneous" (*dus ma byas shing lhun gyis grub*", *asamskrta*, *anabhoga*) saying that the permanence of the Buddha's activity cannot mean that it is a continuous stream, since then it would be compounded and here it is described as non-compounded.

Not realized by a condition other than itself (*aparapratyayabhisambodhi*, *gzhan gyi rkyen gyis rtogs min pa*) contrasts with the usual explanation that without the right conditions (*rkyen*) a being cannot realize the Tathata. Such explanations imply that ultimate realization is conditioned "by other conditions." Since ultimate realization is said in the Sutras to be nonconditioned, there is an apparent contradiction, which Shentongpas explain by saying that the removal of veils depends on conditions; however, the realization of Enlightenment that emerges is non-conditioned (i.e. it is without arising, staying, and ceasing).

Kongtrul explains [his RGV comm. 31b and 32b]:

> *So so rang gis rig pa'i rang byung gi ye shes kyis rtogs par bya ba yin pa'i phyir gzhan gyis brjod pa la sogs pa'i rkyen rtogs par bya ba min pa'o.*

Because it is what is realized through self-risen Jnana that knows through self-awareness, it is not something realized by a condition such as the utterance of another.

One may wonder how an exclusive Rangtongpa such as Gyaltsab explains the clear reference in this section to what is realized through self-realization (*so so rang gis rtogs bya* [RGV 1.7]). He explains [*Dartik* 29] that self-realization, explained as what is to be realized through self-arisen jnana (*rang byung gi ye shes kyis rtogs par bya*, [RGVV 1.8]), means what is realized by Buddhas themselves.

Paraphrase. It should be noted that the nine examples given in the fourth chapter of the RGV to illustrate the Buddha's spontaneous Activity are also taken from the JAAS.

  2. Dharma is described [RGV 1.9–12]:
      i. as the Reality that is Cessation, which is:
          a. not definable as nonexistence nor existence nor both, nor also other than existence and non-existence. It is non-conceptual and non-conceptualizable Reality (*brtag pa mi nus nges tshig dang bral . . . bsam med . . .*),
          b. known by Self-Awareness,
          c. peace,
      ii. as the Reality that is the path which is:
          a. stainless Jnana (*dri med ye shes*),
          b. luminous (*'od zer snang ldan*),
          c. remedial (*gnyen po*).

Dharma is explained in the RGV as the non-conceptual Jnana of the Path of Seeing and the Path of Meditation. It is like the sun, which is unspoilt (unstained) by the clouds which obscure it; it is luminous like the sun, making known all that is to be known; it is remedial like the sun, removing all darkness. This Jnana removes all the darkness of ignorance based on the habits of conceptual thinking. (For more details see Chapter 5.2 "Non-Conceptuality" Section iii "Nisprapanca as non-conceptuality in the RGV 1.9").

The section concerning the Reality of Cessation is explained in the RGVV from the JAAS and the SMS. RGVV [1.12 phi 7b] quotes the SMS:

bcom ldan 'das chos 'jig pa ni sdug bsngal 'gog pa ma lags so
Bhagavan the Cessation of Suffering is not the destruction of dharmas (or a dharma).

It then explains that it is the non-born, non-compounded, permanent Dharmakaya with all its Inseparable Qualities, which is called the "Tathagata garbha" when not free from the klesa.

For the Reality of the Path, the RGVV [1.12 phi 7b, 8b] explains it as the non-conceptual Jnana (*rnam par mi rtog pa'i ye shes, avikalpa jnana*), and recommends we look at the Prajnaparamita Sutras for further details.[7]

3. The Samgha is described as those who realize:
   i. the Clear Light Nature of Mind,
   ii. peace, which is the highest realization of "non-self" (*bdag med mtha'*). RGVV [1.12] explains that the ultimate position (*mtha'*) is to have perfect realization, which has two aspects: (*a*) the seeing of what is and (*b*) the seeing of what is not. This realization is called "precisely what is" (*ji lta ba bzhin yod pa nyid, yathavad bhavikataya*), and is explained in the RGVV as knowing the Clear Light Nature and knowing the veils to be unreal (without essence),
   iii. the realization called the "full extent of what is" (*ji snyed yod pa nyid, yavad bhavikataya*), which is explained as seeing this, their own nature, in all beings. This is closely related to the quality of compassion [RGVV 18 phi 10],
   iv. the supreme quality (or qualities), which is explained as their being a supreme refuge for beings.

The RGVV [1.15 phi 9] explains that the Samgha consists of those who realize the Clear Light Nature of Mind (*rang bzhin gyis 'od gsal ba, prakrtiprabhasvarata*) and so on because for two reasons their Jnana Vision is purified. Thus, they have the insurpassable qualities or quality of the Jewel (of Buddha).

The two reasons for their realization of the Dharmata of beings are:

1. seeing the unspoiled Nature of Mind
2. seeing the klesa are unreal and that they never truly existed (*gdod ma nas zad cing*).

This point is backed up by an important quotation in the RGVV [1.15 phi 9] from the SMS concerning the inconceivable nature of a mind that can be defiled and yet unspoiled (or unaffected) by those defilements. The RGVV states:

> de la sems rang bzhin gyis 'od gsal ba gang yin pa dang. de'i nye
> ba'i nyon mongs pa zhes bya ba gang yin pa 'di gnyis ni dge ba
> dang mi dge ba'i sems dag las gcig rgyu bas sems gnyis pa
> mtshams sbyor ba med pa'i tshul gyis zag pa med pa'i dbyings la
> mchog tu rtogs par dka' ba yin no.

Concerning these two, the Clear Light Nature of Mind and what is referred to as its *samklesa*, the *kusala* and *akusala* minds, when the one moves, the other (literally, second) has no connection with it and in this way the stainless (*anasrava*) Dhatu is extremely difficult to realize.

It then quotes from the SMS:

Therefore, Bhagavan, a moment of the *kusala* mind is not "troubled" (klesa) by the klesa; neither is a mind that is a moment of the *akusala* mind "troubled" by the klesa. Bhagavan, the klesa do not touch the mind, nor the mind the klesa. Bhagavan, that mind that is not a *dharmin* touched like that becomes "troubled" (*klesa*) by darkness. Bhagavan there are *samklesa* but there is no defiled ("*klesa*'d") mind; Bhagavan even so the meaning of the defiling ("*klesa*-ing") of the naturally pure Mind is hard to realize.

Comments. Although this passage is not altogether clear, it seems that the SMS is arguing against the naturally pure Mind being the mind-stream since a defiled moment of the mind stream has nothing to do with a pure moment of the same. Therefore, the naturally pure Mind talked about in the SMS and other scriptures cannot be a moment of the mind stream and the manner of its being defiled at all is totally mysterious.

If one wonders what Rangtong commentators make of this passage, Rongton seems to simply ignore these references to the inconceivability of a pure mind being defiled, although Gyaltsab tries to explain it.[8]
Paraphrase. "The Samgha's realization of the full extent of what is" is explained in the RGVV as its realizing the Tathagatagarbha to be present in all sentient beings (Takasaki traces this to a quotation in the *Avatamsaka*, [*Study* 175fn.21])

(For more detail on the expressions precisely what is (*ji lta ba yod pa nyid, yathavad bhavikataya*, [RGVV 1.15 phi9]), and full extent of what is (*ji snyed yod pa nyid, yavad bhavikataya*), see chapter 5.3 "The Two Visions (*Yathavadbhavikata* and *Yavadbhavikata*)," in this present work, and Takasaki's *Study* [p.173 fn.8]). In the RGV [RGVV 1.15 phi 9] the former is closely associated with the process of looking inwards and realizing one's Own Nature—here referred to as the "ultimate position." Realizing this, one automatically sees that the klesa are incidental and not real in essence. Then this awareness spreads out to others, and as one sees that their true Nature is exactly the same as one's own, spontaneous compassion arises. Put another way compassion is an Inseparable Quality of the realization that all sentient beings have the Tathagatagarbha. Notice that the Jnana that knows precisely and fully in this way is called the "Inner Jnana" (*nang gi ye shes* [RGV 1.14]).[9]

The RGVV explains that the realization of the Samgha is pure because it is free from the two kinds of veil. The two kinds of veil are the klesa-veil and the knowledge-veil. The RGVV explains that the knowledge-of-precisely-what-is liberates the Bodhisattva from the klesa-veil—which is referred to in the RGV as "attachment"—and the full-extent-of-what-is liberates him from the knowledge veils—referred to in the RGV as "obstruction." Although the Bodhisattva is not completely freed from knowledge veils, he is said to be free from the two kinds of veil in the sense that he has the Jnana Vision (*ye shes gzigs pa*) that realizes the meaning of the Dharmadhatu extending everywhere (*chos kyi dbyings kun tu 'gro ba'i don du rtogs pa* [RGVV 1.15 phi 9b]). Thus, not only does he see that the klesa are essenceless, which removes the klesa veil, but also that the Buddha Jnana is in all beings, which removes the knowledge veil [RGVV 1.17 phi 10]. His vision is called "pure" in comparison to the limited vision of others (*cig shos nyi tshe ba'i ye shes, itara pradesika jnana*).

The RGVV [1.18 phi 10] gives an example—which Takasaki thinks must come from a Sutra—of the Bodhisattva, like the crescent of the new moon, moving to the full moon of the Buddha's Enlightenment. Sravakas on the other hand are like the stars: they give light, but they are not the moon. In other words, they do not have direct knowledge of Buddhajnana.

The Samgha of Bodhisattvas who have reached the Path of Seeing, being at the irreversible level, have this direct knowledge, and on the Path of Meditation use that knowledge (jnana) to overcome their residual habitual ignorance tendencies. They not only have the Buddhajnana already, but, since they dwell (*nye bar gnas pa 'gyur ba, upanisadgata*) close to this utter purity, they are also a proper refuge for beings.

Comments. Mikyo Dorje [*gZhan stong sgron me* p. 2] explains that there are two aspects of the Tathagatagarbha, the primordially present Jnana and the influence (*byin brlabs*) of that Jnana that causes the freedom from veils:

> *sems can gyi rnam rig la dri ma dang bral bar byas pa'i shes pa la ye shes kyi mthu bsam gyi mi khyab pas byin gyis brlabs pa dang. dri bral gyi shes pa'i cha la'ang ye shes kyi cha yod pa gnyis ka'i nus pa las rnam rig dri med gnas gyur te. . .*

In the awareness (*rnam rig*) of beings, the inconceivable power of Jnana influences (blesses) the mind that removes stains and the stain-free aspect of mind also has a Jnana aspect. By the power of these two the awareness becomes stainless. (See below in this chapter, 'The Dhatu'-section on "Union.")

Thus, in Shentong terms, the opening verses of praise to the Buddha, Dharma, and Samgha convey the message that Buddha Enlightenment, which is non-conceptual, nondual Jnana, is the essence of the Triple Gem. It is Buddha with his Inseparable Qualities of Knowledge, Love, and Power. It is the essence of the Dharma, both when fully realized (fruit, *phala, 'bras*) and as the means for realizing it (path, *marga, lam*), and it is the essence of the Bodhisattva Samgha in that they have that Awareness and Compassion, which is the very Nature of the Buddha Enlightenment, even if it is not fully revealed yet.

Paraphrase. There follow the famous lines [RGV 1.19–22] on how the chief of all refuges is the Buddha because of the relative and temporary nature of the Dharma and Samgha. These are the concluding verses of the section on the Three Jewels.

Comments. These verses are clearly based on SMS [526]. Since in the opening verses of the RGV all three Jewels are explained as true places of refuge because they are in essence Buddhajnana, these later verses seem a little out of place. However, inasfar as they emphasize that the ultimate refuge is Buddhajnana, they back up the essential message of the earlier verses.

10.4   Vajra Base 4: The Dhatu (Element)

After the section on the Three Jewels, the first three Vajra Bases, there follows four slokas on the next four Vajra Bases [RGV 1.23–26]:

1. The Element, described as the stained Tathata
2. Enlightenment, explained as the stainless Tathata
3. Qualities
4. Buddha Activity

Causes and Conditions for Purification [RGV 1.23]

This verse explains that the Buddha, Dharma, and Samgha arise from the above four, which are themselves the field (*yul*) of those who "see" the Absolute (i.e. Buddhajnana). RGV [1.6] explains that the first of these is the cause (*hetu*) and the last three the conditions (*rkyen*) for purification. RGVV explains that the Element is the "seed of the Supra-mundane Dharma." Through proper ways of thinking (*tshul bzhin yid la byed pa'i gnas kyis*) this "seed" is purified, which results in the realization of the cause in the sense of the "stuff" (*hetu, rgyu*), of the Three Jewels. (See Chapter 6 "The Nature of Beings"—section called "Base, Path and Fruit"—in this present work). The last three are conditions in the sense that, for Buddhajnana within oneself (the "stuff" of Enlightenment) to be realized, help from "outside" is needed. In other words, there must be other beings who are already Enlightened acting upon one. Thus, in Shentong terms, the last three are Buddhajnana acting as conditions for the Enlightenment of others.

Comments. "Field" (*yul*) usually means the object of dualistic awareness and in that sense, those who "see" the Absolute, "see" that it is not a field [BCA 9.2], because they "see" without a see-er and seen. However, here "field" is not being used in a strict sense and simply means that these Four Vajra Bases are what the Buddhas and Bodhisattvas realize, that is, they are all Buddhajnana. This emphasizes the direct link, which is in fact an identity, between the Element functioning within us awakening us to its Nature (the cause—*hetu*), and the spontaneous, non-conceptual Activity of the Buddha's Enlightenment and Qualities (the conditions).

Dolpopa [RC 165.5] explains that in RGV [1.26] the Tathagatagarbha is that which must be made pure (*dag par bya rgyu'i gzhi*). The klesa are the "stuff" that must be purified away (*sbyang bya rgyu*). He explains [RC 166.6] that in the scriptures, it is the skandhas and elements and so on that are what is to be made pure (*sbyang gzhi*) because their true nature is the pure by nature (*rang bzhin dag pa'i*) skandhas that are Tathagatagarbha [MNPS].

The Four Paradoxes [RGV 1.24, 1.25]

Paraphrase. These are described in the SMS, (which is quoted at length in the RGVV).

The four paradoxes are:

1. The Buddha Element is pure and yet is defiled.
2. Enlightenment has never been defiled and yet becomes purified.
3. Qualities are the Dharmas that are inseparable.
4. Activity is spontaneous and non-conceptual.

1. The Buddha Element is pure and yet is defiled.

The RGVV again quotes the passage from the SMS about how a mind that can be defiled and pure at the same time is inconceivable. It points out that only those with great realization such as the Queen Srimala herself and high level Bodhisattvas can realize the meaning of this doctrine. Others such as the Sravakas and Pratyeka Buddhas must rely on faith [RGV 13.1]

2. Enlightenment has never been defiled and yet becomes purified.

A passage from the DRS [RGVV 1.25 phi 13.2] is used to expand on the inconceivability of the stainless Tathata, which was never defiled, becoming purified:

> *gang gi phyir sems ni rang bzhin gyis 'od gsal ba ste. de ni de kho na bzhin shes so. des na skad cig ma gcig dang ldan pa'i shes rab*

*kyis bla na med pa yang dag par rdzogs pa'i byang chub tu mngon
par rdzogs par sangs rgyas so zhes gsungs pa yin no.*
Because Mind is Clear Light by Nature, it knows precisely how
it is. Therefore, it is taught that the unsurpassable complete and
perfect Enlightenment is realized by the instantaneous wisdom
(*prajna*).

Comment. This seems to be a reference to the last moment of the Bodhisattva's path as a Buddha reaches Enlightenment. This moment of prajna is
called the "vajra-like samadhi." It is the moment when the last of the veils
is rent asunder and Buddhahood is attained. The above quotation is pointing
out that the veils are able to be rent asunder because the true nature of
Reality (Tathata) is the Clear Light Nature of Mind itself. In Shentong
terms it is the Buddhajnana itself. In a sense, therefore, this inconceivable
point is saying that, although it seems to become purified, in the last analysis all that happens is that the Clear Light Nature of Mind awakens to its
own Nature. That moment of awakening is called "purification" but in fact
its nature never changes.[10]

3. Qualities are the Dharmas that are inseparable.

Paraphrase. The inconceivability of the Inseparable Qualities is explained
in the RGVV with reference to a long quotation from the *Avatamsakasutra.*
The full explanation of this point is given in the RGVV [1.25 phi 13] as
follows:

*de la dri ma med pa'i sangs rgyas kyi yon tan ni gcig tu kun nas
nyon mongs pa so so'i skye bo'i sa la yang rnam par dbyer med
pa'i chos nyid snga phyir khyad par med pa yod pa'i phyir gnas 'di
bsam gyis mi khyab ste.*
Concerning the stainless Buddha's Qualities, this base is unimag-
inable because it is the inseparable Dharmata [i.e. Nature] that exists without difference between before and after, even at the level
of defiled (*samklesa*) ordinary beings.

The *Avatamsaka* passage quoted in the RGVV explains that Buddhajnana
pervades all beings and that it is only because of beings' perceptions ('*du
shes*) that this is not apparent. As soon as they stop clinging to concepts,
the Jnana of omniscience, the self-arisen Jnana, emerges unobstructedly.
The example given is of a great silk cloth (*dar yug*)[11], the size of the universe, painted with every planet and detail of the universe, and then put
into a single atom. Then every atom of the universe is filled with a cloth
containing the whole of the universe in this way. Eventually a wise being
with supernormal vision sees that these cloths are inside the atoms and so

rendered useless. He therefore takes them out of every single atom of the universe by cutting them open with a subtle vajra. In this way they become useful for all beings. The Sutra then states that the cloth is like the Tathagata's limitless Jnana and the atoms like sentient beings. The completeness of the Buddhajnana that is so helpful to beings is in fact within every being. RGVV [1.25] states:

> There is not a race of beings in whom the whole of the Tathagata's Jnana does not reside (*rjes su zhugs pa*). It does not manifest because of their clinging to dualistic conceptions (*'du shes kyi 'dzin pa*). Once a being is free from clinging to dualistic concepts his all-knowing Jnana, the self-arisen Jnana arises unobstructedly.

Comments. Dolpopa also quotes this section from the *Avatamsaka* in full [RC 49]. He also refers [RC 110.1] to the Tathagatagarbhasutra where the Tathagatagarbha is said to be like an eye. In beings the "eye" is present with full capacity, but closed. In Takasaki's opinion [*Study* 189 fn. 29] the Tathagatajnana in the *Avatamsaka* is identical with Dhatu and gotra and "shows the origin of Tathagatagarbha theory."[12] He is thinking here of Tathagatagarbha doctrine according to the Hua Yen (Avatamsaka) school. This school carries the doctrine further than is suggested in the above passage, in that it teaches the interpenetration of every atom of the universe by the whole of the universe and that the totality of the whole within every part is the Tathagatagarbha.[13] The above example only uses the atom as a simile and it is the Buddhajnana, not the whole of the universe, that is said to be contained in all beings. The man who cuts open the atoms with a subtle vajra is a simile for the Buddha teaching beings so that they become Enlightened and actively start benefiting others. Atoms do not become Enlightened in this sense even in Hua Yen philosophy. In Hua Yen terms, atoms are an expression of Buddhajnana and as such contain within themselves the whole of it, just as Buddhajnana contains within itself all atoms.

4. Activity is spontaneous and non-conceptual.

Paraphrase. The Buddha's Activity [RGVV 1.25 phi 14] is paradoxical because it acts everywhere at once and at all times completely spontaneously, that is, without conceptual effort.[14]

The RGVV explains more fully by quoting from the DRS in which Buddha Activity is described as completely unlimited even though according to some scriptural statements it might seem limited. It is not known by beings of the world, it is indescribable, present in all the Buddha Fields, equal in all Buddhas, completely effortless, and like space, it is completely conceptionless, and inseparable from the Action of the Dharmadhatu.

Comments. ''Dharmadhatu'' means the nature of all the dharmas and is translated into Tibetan as the ''expanse of the dharmas'' (*chos dbyings*). In other words, it is the expanse or vast spaciousness that is the true nature of dharmas and which, therefore, prevades and contains them all. Thus, according to the DRS, since Buddha Activity is the action of the Dharmadhatu, it is none other than the natural functioning of Reality itself.

The Three Reasons [RGV 1.27–28]

Paraphrase. The next section is a key verse of the text, much quoted in Tibetan works on the Tathagatagarbha. It gives the three scriptural reasons that are the basis for the statement in the *Tathagatagarbhasutra* that all beings have the Tathagatagarbha [*Study* 196 fn.1]. The verses [27, 28] read as follows:

Because the Perfect Buddhakaya radiates,
Because the Tathata is inseparable,
Because the gotra is present,
All beings have the Essence (*garbha*) of Buddha.

Because Buddhajnana is present in the mass of beings,
Because the stainless nature (*svabhava, rang bzhin*) is non-dual,
Because the Buddha gotra is named after its fruit, it is taught that
all beings have the Buddha Essence (*garbha*).[†]

In these two verses the RGV draws together three important aspects of the Tathagatagarbha doctrine—Dharmakaya, Tathata and Gotra. These three aspects are the key to the RGV and the way a commentator interprets them determines how he interprets the whole text. The first line of each of these verses refers to Dharmakaya, the second to Tathata, and the third to Gotra.
The verses resemble a passage in the *Mahayanasutralamkara* [Tib. pha 10.5 17d] attributed to Maitreya and quoted in the RGVV:

de bzhin nyid ni thams cad la. khyad par med kyang dag gyur pa.
de bzhin gshegs nyid de yi phyir. 'gro kun de yi snying po can.
The Tathata is non-differentiable in all [beings], but the purified one is the Tathagata; therefore, all beings have its garbha.

(see *Study* [288]).

[†]N.B. The order of the verses is reversed from the Sanskrit in the Tibetan version, and sometimes verse 28 is omitted altogether.

Comments. For Shentongpas Buddhagarbha is Buddhajnana. It is the true nature of beings, which must be uncovered and revealed. Kongtrul explains [SKK hum 43a.6]:

> *de bzhin nyid dam bde gshegs snying po zhes bya ba de nyid sems*
> *can dang sangs rgyas sogs chos thams cad la mnyam pa nyid du*
> *khyab cing bzhugs kyang. sems can rnams la snying po'i tshul*
> *dang. sangs rgyas rnams la mngon sum gyi tshul gyis bzhugs pas*
> *sangs rgyas kyi snying po zhes kyang bya ste ngo bo mi 'gyur ba'i*
> *phyir ro.*

That which is called "Tathata" or "Tathagatagarbha" is present pervading all dharmas, such as beings and Buddhas, equally, but in beings it is present as a "heart essense" (*garbha?*) and in Buddhas manifestly. Thus, it is called Buddha's "Heart Essence" (*snying po*) because its essence (*ngo bo*) is unchanging.

In Shentong terms there are three senses in which beings are pervaded by Buddhajnana:

1. The Buddhajnana Dharmakaya of all the Enlightened Buddhas by its very nature has the Inseparable Qualities of Knowledge (*mkhyen*), Love (*brtse*), and Power (*nus*); this radiates and pervades all beings.

2. Buddhajnana as the nature (Tathata) of beings and Buddhajnana as the nature (Tathata) of Enlightened Buddhas are one inseparable Reality. Karma and klesa and so on are not real and never affect or create differentiations in its nature.

3. Buddhajnana is present in beings as the naturally present power (gotra) that moves them spontaneously (without conceptual effort) to renounce samsara and aspire to nirvana. This gotra is inseparable from the fruit because both are Buddhajnana.

The expression "the Buddha gotra is named after its fruit" (*bauddhe gotre tat phalasyopacarat*) is explained in Takasaki's *Study* and *upacara* is explained as "a metaphor" or as "to reside in."[15] *Upacara* is translated into Tibetan as *nyer brtags*, which means "to be called" or "to be a metaphor." Thus, in the scriptures the lineage (or essence of the lineage) is called the "Buddha lineage" (or "the Buddha lineage essence") because its mature representative (fruit) is Buddha. Since beings have this lineage, it implies they have the power to become Buddha or that they have the Heart-Essence of Buddha (Buddhagarbha).

Takasaki [*Study* 198fn.3] discusses the three senses of garbha in the *Buddhagotrasastra* (known only in Chinese), and links them to the three signs or natures of Buddha *garbha* given in RGV [1.27–28]. In his notes,

Takasaki always brings out the sense of interpenetration and totality found
in the Hua Yen, so that the first reason shows beings "enveloped" in the
garbha (womb) of the Tathagata. This accords with the Sanskrit *"bud-
dhajnanatargamat sattvaraseh,"* "the mass of beings enter the Buddha
Jnana." In Tibetan it is translated as *"sangs rgyas ye shes sems can tshogs
zhugs,"* "the Buddha Jnana is present in the mass of beings." Takasaki
explains the other two reasons as beings have the *garbha* (womb) in which
the Buddha is hidden; this is reminiscent of the doctrine of the part in the
whole and the whole in the part.

By contrast Gyaltsab interprets RGV [1.27] "Because the Dharmakaya
radiates" as Buddha activity pervading and reaching out to beings in a way
that avoids the implication that Buddha Dharmakaya is in beings at the
outset. Rongton [36.3] objects to this and argues such an interpretation contradicts the scriptural authority of the quotation from the *Mahayanasutralamkara* [MSA].

Whereas Kongtrul [RGV comm. 20b] explains that each of the three
signs is sufficient in itself to show all beings have Tathagatagarbha, because
they are three ways of saying nondual Buddhajnana is in beings, Rangtongpas explain each of the three signs differently. (See Appendix 5, "Some
Points of Comparison Between Rangtong Commentators on RGV")

The Element Arranged in Ten Points

Paraphrase. The next section [RGV 1.29–1.95] deals with the main topic
(*dngos don*), the Absolute Element (*don dam dbyings*), under ten headings.
These are:

    i Essence (*svabhava*)
    ii Cause (*hetu*)
    iii Fruit (*phala*)
    iv Action (*karman*)
    v Union (*yoga*) (i.e. Qualities inseparable in base, path, and fruit)
    vi Occurrence (*vrtti*)
    vii Phases (*avasthaprabheda*)
    viii All-pervasiveness (*sarvatraga*)
    ix Changelessness (*avikara*)
    x Inseparable Qualities (*abheda*) (i.e. Qualities inseparable from
      nirvana)

i. Essence [RGV 1.29–30]

The Element is compared to a wish-fulfilling jewel, which has the power to
grant riches, to space, which is forever changeless, and to water, which is

always moist whether it is clean or dirty. The Dharmakaya is like the jewel, having the power (*mthu, prabhava*) to grant what is desired; the Tathata is like space in that it is always the same (*gzhan du mi 'gyur, ananyartha-bhava*), and the gotra is like water in that it has the moist (*brlan, snigdha-bhava*: I hesitate to say "wet") quality of compassion for beings. A jewel, space, and water are the same in that their nature is not spoiled by being mixed with impurities. In the same way the Element of the Buddha is not spoiled by being mixed with the klesa.

Comments. Snigdhabhava has meanings like sticky, slippery, smooth, and viscous as well as tender, gentle, and affectionate. Thus, from the Sanskrit the connection with compassion is more obvious than from the Tibetan *brlan*, which means wet or moist. Khenpo Tsultrim suggests that compassion is like water because it sustains and satisfies beings.

An interesting point to notice is that Gotra is characterized as compassion. Thus, we are led to understand that any expression of compassion in a being is a sign of his emerging Buddha Element, like wetness is the sign of water. This includes even the compassion that an animal shows for its young.[16]

ii. Cause [RGV 1.30–34]

Paraphrase. The RGV explains that aspiration to the Mahayana Dharma, superior wisdom (prajna), samadhi, and compassion are the four causes that remove the four kinds of obstacles had by beings. In other words, they are the conditions necessary for the emergence of Buddhajnana. However, if "cause" (*hetu*) in the ten headings refers to the nature of Buddhajnana (Paramarthadhatu, *don dam dbyings*), one would expect the four causes to somehow refer to the nature of the Dhatu and the way it functions. Perhaps such a relationship is self-evident from the images of RGV [1.30, 31], which lend themselves easily to this kind of interpretation. Just as the qualities of power, immutability, and wetness are inseparable qualities of a wish-fulfilling jewel, space, and water respectively, so aspiration (*mos pa*), prajna, samadhi, and compassion are inseparable Qualities of the Dhatu.

Nevertheless, RGVV [1.33 phi 17a] explains that four causes are given as the means for four different kinds of being to overcome their special kind of obstruction. Aspiration (*adhimukti, mos pa*) [RGV 1.34] to the Mahayana Dharma overcomes the obstacle of hostility towards Dharma had by those who lust for pleasure, and superior wisdom overcomes the obstacle of belief in self had by those of other religions that do not lead to liberation. Samadhi brings peace of mind and overcomes the obstacle of the Sravakas, which is to be overly fearful of samsara. Compassion overcomes the obstacle of the Pratyeka Buddhas, who are obstructed from the full realization of

Buddhahood due to their indifference (relative to Buddhas and Bodhisatt-vas) to the sufferings of others (*sattvartha nirapeksata*).

The RGVV [phi 16–17] then goes to great lengths to link the following verses with this structure of the four kinds of beings and their four kinds of obstacle.

Comments. One feels that, in Shentong terms, all this deviates from the essential message of the RGV. According to Takasaki's analysis the slokas of the RGV [1.32–33] that introduce this topic are not from the original RGV text.[17] The same applies for verse 1.34, which compares Mahayana aspira-tion to the father's seed, wisdom to the mother, samadhi to the womb, and compassion to the wet-nurse. He arrives at his conclusion by comparing the various texts in which the RGV verses appear in Chinese. The consistent absence from all the earlier sources of certain verses leads him to conclude they were later additions. There could be other explanations for their ab-sence, but as a working hypothesis his conclusions are interesting. It is particularly interesting from the Shentong point of view, because wherever there are verses in the RGV that fit awkwardly with a Shentong interpreta-tion, we find they are absent in early Chinese versions. That is not to say these verses do not have an early source. A similar idea to that of RGV [1.34] is expressed in the MSA [IV,11], and in other sastras, indicating that it probably has some ancient canonical source. [*Study* 206fn.62]

From the Shentong point of view, it is a little disappointing that RGV [1.32–34] misses the opportunity to expand on the idea that aspiration, pra-jna, samadhi, and compassion are the signs of the presence of the Insepa-rable Qualities of the Dhatu in ordinary beings making them give up the four kinds of obstacle (typified by the four kinds of being). Instead, they digress into a discussion about the necessity for Bodhisattvas to have these four qualities and how this makes them superior to other kinds of being. Furthermore, RGV[1.34] makes it seem as if, of the four qualities, as-piration is the prime cause, and the other three secondary conditions, for Buddhahood to arise. Of course in a sense this is true, even from a Shen-tong point of view, but the RGV and RGVV make no attempt to explain the not too obvious link, perhaps, between the three images and the four qual-ities in RGV [1.30]. For example, elsewhere in the RGV: a) Dharmakaya is linked to samadhi, which is like a wish-fulfilling jewel, b) Tathata to pra-jna, which is like space, and c) aspiration and compassion, to Gotra, which is like water.[18] RGVV [1.30–31] does indeed link compassion to Gotra in the manner suggested here and so fits awkwardly with the explanations and images concerning compassion in the following verses.

Dolpopa [RC78] quotes the MPNS, which explains that all beings have the *Surangamasamadhi* (*dpa' bar 'gro ba'i ting nge 'dzin*) but, because they are not familiarized with it (*bsgoms*), they do not see it. He also equates the *Bodhipaksikadharmas* with the primordial Reality of Cessation [RC 321, 324–325], and this [RC 326] with Tathagatagarbha, Absolute *Deva*, *Mantra*, *Tantra* and so forth. In other words, all the qualities of the path such as faith, concentration, and energy are expressions of Buddhajnana.

iii. Fruit [RGV 1.35–1.39]

Paraphrase. The Four Transcendental Qualities The Absolute Element is described as having the four transcendental qualities (*gunaparamita, yon tan pha rol tu phyin pa*) when it fully emerges as the fruit of the path. "Transcendental" here is a translation of the Sanskrit word "paramita" meaning passed over to the other side; it is often translated as "perfection."

The four transcendental qualities are, (1) transcendental purity (*subha paramita, gtsang ba pha rol tu phyin pa*), (2) transcendental self (*atma paramita, bdag pha rol tu phyin pa*), (3) transcendental bliss (*sukha paramita, bde ba pha rol tu phyin pa*), and (4) transcendental permanence (*nitya paramita, rtag pa pha rol tu phyin pa*).

RGVV [1.36] then expands on the doctrine of the four *gunaparamitas* as described in the SMS and other Tathagatagarbha Sutras, quoting at length from the SMS.

RGV [1.36] explains that the four transcendental qualities are the reverse of the four mistakes concerning the Dharmakaya. The four mistakes are, in fact, the result of four concepts produced on the earlier stages of the path to act as remedies for misconceptions concerning the nature of samsara.

This relates to the SMS doctrine of the four *gunaparamitas*. The RGVV [1.36 phi 17b] quotes it at some length, explaining that the misconceptions concerning the nature of samsara are that: (*a*) ordinary beings see their bodies as pure (i.e. good and desirable), (*b*) they are attached to their five skandhas as if they were themselves, or were owned by a self, (*c*) they cling to life in samsara as if it were happiness, and (*d*) they do all this with the underlying assumption that things have some real and permanent existence. For these people the Buddha taught the four remedies (*gnyen po*). These are the concepts (*samjna, 'dus shes*) that the five skandhas and so forth are impermanent, suffering, non-self, and impure.

The RGVV explains that it is wrong to think that these four remedial concepts apply to the Dharmakaya. To remedy the misapplication of those concepts, the four transcendental qualities are taught. It then quotes at length from the SMS [546 cha 273], explaining how even to have the concept that the Dharmakaya is permanence, self, bliss, and purity is to be better off than the Sravakas and Pratyeka Buddhas who do not see the sphere of the Tathagata even with their pure vision arrived at through meditation on emptiness.

RGVV [1.36] explains the four *gunaparamitas* as the fruit of the four qualities of the previous verses (i.e. aspiration, prajna, samadhi and compassion). Transcendental purity is the result of aspiration to the Mahayana, transcendental Self the result of prajna, transcendental bliss the result of samadhi, and transcendental permanence the result of compassion. This last is explained as Buddhas purifying beings for as long as samsara lasts, which is endless time.

Comments. Again the explanations in this section are rather disappointing from a Shentong point of view. They give the impression that the four transcendental qualities are separate results of different contributory causes of Buddhahood; even transcendental permanence is explained as continuous activity rather than non-arising, non-dwelling, non-ceasing, non-compounded and so on.

Dolpopa [RC 392], when explaining that because the Sravakas misapply the remedies, they cannot see the Tathagatagarbha properly, quotes the MPNS where it talks of monks meditating too long on non-self, and so forth and missing Emptiness by applying the remedies to ultimate Reality. Dolpopa explains [RC 390] that the worldling believes he has self, permanence, bliss, and purity; he sees these qualities in what does not have them. Those who are beyond the world also talk of Self, Permanence, Bliss, and Purity, but in their case it is meaningful because they know what really has these qualities. Dolpopa remarks [RC 374.1] that just to believe this removes many veils, thus emphasizing the power of faith. In other words, it is not wrong to believe in happiness and seek it in the right place, but it is wrong to despair or seek it in the wrong place. Thus, contrary to a lot of people's impression of Buddhism, it does not advocate the stifling of the urge to happiness but the correct channeling of it.

Khenpo Tsultrim and Thrangu Rimpoche explain that, since the fruit is beyond concepts, it must also be beyond concepts of pure and impure, bliss and suffering, and permanence and impermanence. Thus, they are "paramita" qualities in the sense of transcending all conceptual categories (nisprapanca). This accords with RGV [1.37], which explains that the fruit is the "Transcendental Self" because it is beyond the concepts of both self and non-self. It is again disappointing, from the Shentong point of view, that RGV and RGVV do not expressly extend this as Khenpo Tsultrim and Thrangu Rimpoche do to the other transcendental qualities.

Incidentally, the Rumtek version of RGVV quotes SMS [546] "*shes pa dag pa*" (pure mind) as "*stong pa nyid kyi ye shes*" (emptiness jnana). The Rumtek version of RGVV [p35] also misquotes the passage so as to omit the

assertion that the Quality Paramitas are the object of the Jnana of the Omniscient (*thams cad mkhyen pa'i ye shes kyi yul*) and are the Tathagata's
Dharmakaya that Sravakas and so forth do not see. Takasaki has the correct
version. The *sDe dge* version of SMS is the most accurate.

The Purity Paramita is Explained in RGV *[1.37]*

> de ni rang bzhin dag phyir dang bag chags spangs phyir gtsang
> ba yin.
> Because it is pure by nature and because the tendencies have been
> given up, it is purity.

Paraphrase. This line explains how the transcendental quality of purity
means to be pure (unspoiled) by nature and purified of (i.e. no longer obscured by) stains. "Stains" in this context is explained in the RGVV to mean
the stains of the ground of ignorance tendency patterns (*avidyavasanab-
humi, ma rig bag chags gi sa*). This is an important feature of the doctrine
of the SMS [530 cha 265b] quoted and explained in the RGVV [1.37 phi 19ff].
The ground of ignorance tendency patterns is the basis for the subtlest level
of conceptual thinking that underlies and gives rise to the whole conceptual
process (*mtshan ma'i spros pa kun du spyod pa phra mo* [RGV ph 19.1],
suksmanimitta prapanca).[19]

The SMS explains that the skandhas arise on a gross and a subtle level.
On the gross level mental formations (*samskara*) and ignorance arise in
mutual dependence. With ignorance as the prime cause, mental formations
act as the condition for defiled karma to arise. From this results samsara
consisting of worlds subject to birth, sickness, old age, and death. On a
subtle level, even when gross mental formations have ceased, the ignorance
tendency patterns continue to give rise to non-defiled karma resulting in the
subtle mental bodies or skandhas of a mental nature (*yid kyi rang bzhin kyi
phung po, manomaya skandha*). The SMS argues that, since Sravaka Arhats,
Pratyeka Buddhas, and high level Bodhisattvas are not beyond the ignorance tendency patterns, they have the mental skandhas and, therefore a
subtle form of birth, old age, sickness, and death. Since Nirvana is defined
as beyond these four, the SMS concludes that the Sravaka, Pratyeka Buddha
Arhats, and high level Bodhisattvas do not have Nirvana. Only Buddhas are
free from the ignorance tendency patterns; therefore, only they have the real
Nirvana—the purity paramita.

Comments. I suggested to Khenpo Tsultrim that, since the subtlest kind of
residual veil for Bodhisattvas on the pure levels (eighth–tenth) is the appearance of duality (*gnyis snang*), this must be what the ground of ignorant
tendency pattern was. While not actually committing himself, he thought

this quite possible. If it were the case, then it looks as if it is the residual tendency to experience awareness as a stream of mutually dependent see-er and seen aspects. It seems that until Buddhahood, even high level Bodhisattvas still have this subtle tendency. More research is needed, but possibly this is what causes non-defiled karma (*zag med las*). Sravakas and Pratyeka Buddhas and Bodhisattvas no longer accumulate negative karma because this has all been exhausted in the course of their path to Enlightenment. However, their samadhi is maintained as a result of their pure (non-defiled) karma produced by their subtle veils.

The Self Paramita is Explained in RGV [1.37]

> bdag dang bdag med spros pa dag nye bar zhi bas dam pa'i bdag.
> The conceptual artifice (prapanca) of self and non-self have completely ceased, so it is the supreme Self.

Comments. As we have seen the RGVV [1.36 phi 19–19b] and the SMS [530.7ff] explain how Sravakas, Pratyeka Buddhas, and even Bodhisattvas, who have attained power, are still subject to causes and conditions, are compounded, and subject to birth old age, and death, and how what is compounded (i.e. form etc.) is not permanence, bliss, self, or purity. Thus, by implication they define "Self" as non-compounded Reality that is not subject to birth, sickness, old age, and death.
Paraphrase. RGVV [1.36] explains by quoting from the SMS [546]. The Buddha's precise and perfect wisdom sees that the dharmas are not self and the self is not to be found in apparent compounded phenomena. His realization of non-self means that He realizes what is not the self. Just as He is quite clear that what is not the self is, indeed, not the self, He is also quite clear about what is the Self.[20] Therefore, His knowledge of non-self is His knowledge of the true Self. It is explained in the RGVV [1.36 phi 18b.3] that the non-self-ness is called "Self,"[21] (*bdag med pa nyid bdag tu byas pa*).

The Bliss Paramita is Explained in RGV [1.38]

> yid kyi rang bzhin phung po dang de rgyu logs phyir bde ba nyid.
> Because the skandhas of mental nature and their cause have gone,
> it is bliss.

The RGVV [p.37.3ff] explains that as long as the mental skandhas continue there will be the subtle "suffering" of change, decay, and death. "Suffering" here should be understood in its technical Buddhist sense; a state subject to change cannot by definition be true bliss, for there is always the fear of loss or deterioration; thus, it is a form of *dukkha* (suffering). Just as the Buddha is said to be free from both the concept of self held by ordinary beings and the concept of non-self of the Sravakas and so forth, he is also free from both the suffering of ordinary beings as well as the "suffering" of Sravakas and so forth. This freedom from all trace of suffering is true bliss. *Comments.* Although the RGVV describes the fruit as bliss only in the sense that it is freedom from suffering, Tantric Shentongpas go further than this since, in their experience, the bliss that arises when the mind rests free from prapanca is an Inseparable Quality of Buddhajnana. Since one cannot know this without experiencing it, such a teaching is considered self-secret. This is why in ordinary discourse bliss can only be defined as the "absence of suffering." The significance of bliss to the Shentongpa is that, since Buddhajnana is the true nature of everything and one of its Inseparable Qualities is Bliss, the true nature of everything must be Bliss. Thus, the more nearly one experiences the true nature of things the more they are experienced as bliss or happiness. Therefore, in *The Royal Song of Saraha: a Study in the History of Buddhist Thought* [110fn.35] and other sources, the remark is made that the Tantric expression "bliss-spontaneity-awareness" implies that bliss is commensurate with knowledge.

The Permanence Paramita is Explained in RGV [1.38]

> khor ba dang ni mya ngan 'das mnyam pa nyid du rtogs phyir rtag.
> Because it realizes the equalness of samsara and nirvana it is permanent.

Paraphrase. RGVV [1.36] gives three separate explanations of the quality paramita of permanence. First, it gives the SMS doctrine that the Buddha Dharmakaya is permanent because, unlike the skandhas, it is not a compounded phenomenon. Second, the Buddha as the fruit of the Bodhisattvayana is permanent because his work for the purification of beings lasts forever. Third, the RGVV gives the SMS doctrine that Buddhas are permanent because they do not have the ignorance tendency patterns, mental skandhas, birth, old age, and death. The mental skandhas arise (birth), change (sickness), decay (old age) and are destroyed (death). Death in this context is called the "inconceivable death transformation" (*bsam kyi mi khyab ba'i 'chi 'pho ba*).
Comments. Dolpopa [RC 108.6] explains that only something that never came into existence and so will never pass away can be called "permanent." Therefore in Shentong terms, the fact that the Buddha has no mental skandhas indicates that His Absolute Form Kayas are not dependently arising and subject to birth, old age, and death.

The inconceivable death transformation seems to refer both to the end of the Arhat's samadhi as well as to the way Bodhisattvas pass from life to life. Since they proceed to their next existence by the inconceivable death transformation, Aryas (both Arhats and Bodhisattvas) do not experience the "between state" (bardo). Only Buddhas have neither the ordinary death nor inconceivable transformation; they are beyond the notion of transformation and anything to be transformed.[22]

In the Mahayana Sutras the Arhat's samadhi—which he takes to be nirvana—ends when he is roused by the Buddha's spontaneous activity. For example, Gampopa says (Thar rgyan) [5b–6a]:

> de yang ji ltar bskul na.sku gsung thugs kyis bskrul ba yin te. thugs kyi 'od zer spros pas nyan rang yid kyi lus can de dag la reg pa tsam gyis. zag med kyi ting nge 'dzin las sad par byed do.
> Then how are they roused? They are roused by [the Buddha] body, speech and mind. By radiating the light of His mind—merely by its touching the mental bodies of the Sravakas and Pratyeka Buddhas, they are awakened from their samadhi without outflow.

Thus, as the Arhat's subtle conceptual samadhi ends, the non-conceptual Buddhajnana wakens him and causes him to enter the Bodhisattva path. Presumably this is his inconceivable death transformation. It is taught that he enters it at the end of the the seventh Bodhisattva level, which is the beginning of the first of the pure levels. He then proceeds to the full Enlightenment of perfect Buddhahood.

Paraphrase. RGVV [1.38] quotes a section from the SMS [545 cha 273.4] about the avoidance of the two extreme positions (mtha'), that is: a) that nothing is true, and b) that compounded phenomena are permanent. It explains that the Tathagata avoids the nihilistic position that nothing is true (chad par mtha', ucchedadrsti) because he does not diminish (anapakarsa) impermanent samsara ('khor ba mi rtag mi 'brid) [Study 219].[23] The SMS gives a more detailed explanation, explaining that the nihilistic position is the view of those who do not believe in any other life than this one—which to a Buddhist implies they are heedless of the effect of their actions in terms of their results in future rebirths. In other words, it is to underestimate the significance of apparent reality. The Tathagata avoids the eternalistic position that compounded phenomena are permanent because He does not overstate[24] a permanent Nirvana.

According to the SMS definition, the eternalistic position is to not be aware of the momentary nature of the stream of dualistic consciousness, which arises and perishes moment by moment. Because of this non-awareness, one believes that the stream of consciousness is eternal and the true Self. This is an overstatement, giving permanence to what is not permanent. The Buddha does not fall into either of these positions, for His view concerning the impermanent and the permanent is correct. The SMS [545 cha 273.6] explains that to hold the view that things are impermanent, far from being a nihilistic position, is in fact the correct view; the view that Nirvana is permanent, far from being an eternalistic position, is the correct view.

Comments. It should be noted here that the RGVV [1.38][25] has the opposite, that is, to hold the view that samsara is impermanent is the nihilistic position, and to hold nirvana as permanent is the eternalistic position. This is doctrinally incorrect by any Buddhist standard and is plainly contradicted in the ensuing explanations given in the SMS.

Dolpopa [RC 382] quotes the SMS at length giving the doctrinally correct version, that is, that seeing apparent things as impermanent is not a nihilistic view and so forth. The *sDe dge* version of the SMS has the doctrinally correct formulation. However, the *Dartik* gives a long and complicated explanation of the meaning of the "wrong" version in order to make it doctrinally correct.

Paraphrase. This whole discussion is ostensibly an explanation of the line in the RGV [1.38] that says that the Buddha is permanent, for he realizes the equalness of samsara and nirvana. In fact, the SMS doctrine that the RGVV quotes to explain this line says samsara is impermanent and Nirvana permanent, which demonstrates their unequalness rather than equalness.

It would seem that the RGVV takes "equalness" to mean that the Buddha has a balanced attitude that takes proper account of both samsara and nirvana. This is backed up in the next verse of the RGV [1.39], which describes how Bodhisattvas do not dwell in samsara because of their wisdom realizing non-self, and do not dwell in nirvana because of their compassionate involvement with beings.

RGVV [1.38] explains that the Buddhas rest in the non-dwelling Nirvana (*apratisthitanirvana, mi gnas pa'i mya ngan las 'das*) because of their equanimity. They have equanimity because, on the one hand, they have given up desire which means they are not attached to samsara. On the other hand, their compassion for beings prevents them abandoning them and passing into the nirvana of the Arhats and Pratyeka Buddhas. This is another way of saying they are permanent because of their compassionate involvement with beings.

Comments. Thus, in spite of all the discussion in the RGVV of the SMS doctrine of permanence, which conforms to the Shentong view, it ends by explaining permanence as the continuity of the Buddha's compassionate concern for beings.

Although it is true that it is taught that Buddhas act forever for the benefit of beings, from the Shentong point of view, the special message of

the Tathagatagarbha Sutras is that this action is inherent in the nature of
Buddhajnana; it is always active whether Buddhas arise in the world or
not. Its permanence derives from its being non-compounded, unborn, and
undying.

A Shentong interpretation of the line in RGV [1.38] that refers to the
Buddha's realizing the equalness of samsara and nirvana might be that since
both samsara and nirvana are conceptual creations neither should be accepted nor rejected. The true nature of phenomena is Buddhajnana and
when one realizes this, nirvana (in the sense of mere cessation) and samsara
are both seen to be distorted versions of the inseparable Buddha Qualities.
Since the Buddha realizes this, he is not afraid of samsara nor attracted to
nirvana (as cessation). Unfortunately (for Shentongpas) the RGVV explanation that the Bodhisattvas are not attracted to samsara because of having
renounced desire through prajna, and that they are bound to beings because
of their compassion, suggests a conceptually based equanimity—not the inherent equanimity of Buddhajnana.

In Shentong terms Buddhajnana is permanent, for it has none of the
characteristics of what is impermanent. On the other hand, since both permanence and impermanence can be shown by Madhyamaka reasoning to be
conceptually incoherent, one can say, as Khenpo Tsultrim and Thrangu
Rimpoche do, that it is beyond permanence and impermanence, therefore, it
is the Supreme-Perfect-True (*Sat*) Permanence.

Paraphrase. One of the final comments of the RGVV on this section could
be read in a Shentong way:

> *chos kyi dbyings kyi tshul gyi sgo 'dis ni don dam par 'khor ba
> nyid mya ngan las 'das par brjod pa yin te. gnyis ka ltar rnam par
> mi rtog pa mi gnas pa'i mya ngan las 'das pa mngon du byed pa'i
> phyir.*
>
> This way of being of the Dharmadhatu explains that, in Absolute
> Reality, samsara itself is Nirvana. According to both [reasons] the
> non-abiding Nirvana which is non-conceptual is realized.

Comments. Given the context, it is doubtful that the intention here was
particularly Shentong. What is beginning to emerge in this present analysis
of the RGV and RGVV is that the basic verses, in Takasaki's terms, and the
Tathagatagarbha source materials on which they are clearly based, favor a
Shentong interpretation, but the commentarial verses of the RGV and the
RGVV explanation on them lend themselves to various interpretations,
sometimes highlighting the Shentong view and sometimes obscuring it.

As has been discussed in the Chapter 5.3 "The Two Realities and the
Two Visions," Dolpopa objects to nirvana and samsara being equated, but

here the RGV says they are seen as equal; the RGVV says that samsara actually is nirvana. Dolpopa's explanation of this is given in RC [215] where he makes it clear that they are equal because the Absolute (Nirvana—Buddhajnana) is the base (*gzhi*) of both samsara and nirvana (apparent nirvana), which are both conceptual distortions of Ultimate Reality. Presumably he takes the RGVV statement that samsara is Nirvana as looseness of language. What it really means is the apparent phenomenon, samsara, is in essence a distortion of the Ultimate Reality, Nirvana. He makes a firm and clear distinction here [RC 218.2] between the apparent phenomena of samsara and nirvana being conceptually created and samsara and nirvana being direct but distorted manifestations of Absolute Mind.

iv. Action [RGV 1.40–1.41]

Paraphrase. This topic is covered by the second half of RGV [1.35] and in RGV [1.40–41] and, again, is mainly derived from the SMS [548 cha 274.5b], which is quoted in the RGVV. The action of the Element is to produce disgust with samsara and aspiration for nirvana [RGV 1.40–41]:

> If there were no Buddha Element one would not become sick of suffering and want to seek after or aspire for nirvana.
> Seeing the fault with existence, suffering, and the virtue of nirvana bliss, happens because of having the gotra; it does not happen in those without it.

Comment. As has been explained in Chapter 4.3 "Buddha Activity" the Shentong view is that it is the haunting awareness of something else makes one disenchanted with samsara. One has a natural tendency to seek for happiness, and without this tendency one would never aspire to nirvana. This natural tendency is a function or expression of the Buddhajnana itself.

The fact that RGV [1.4] mentions that those without gotra are not aware of the suffering and bliss of samsara and nirvana respectively seems to contradict the essential message of the RGV, which is that all beings have the gotra. Khenpo Tsultrim explains that it means only sentient beings have Tathagatagarbha and not non-sentient things. Other commentators suggest that it is referring to the expanding gotra. (see Chapter 6 "The Nature of Being" Section 6.4 "Gotra".)

Paraphrase. The RGVV takes this latter view and adds the observation that, though some beings do not seem to have the gotra because it is so obscured by their bad karma and klesa, in fact it is taught that as soon as they develop the aspiration to nirvana it starts to expand; they are then said to belong to the Buddha lineage (*gotra*). Thus, it is only those without the expanding gotra that are without aspiration to nirvana.

The RGVV [1.41 phi 21b] quotes a passage found in the *Avatamsaka* and the *Jnanalokalamkarasutra* (JAAS) [*Study* 223] about how the Tathagata is like the sun; its rays being like wisdom, which penetrate all beings, benefitting them and making the cause of their future (i.e. Enlightenment) grow, nourished by virtue.

Comments. The example of the Buddha being like the sun is a recurrent theme in the RGV. In the basic verses of the RGV, that is, the verses that Takasaki finds in all the early Chinese sources, sun and space are the most common images used to describe the Buddha. A notable exception occurs in verse 4.97 where the image of the earth is described as the most fitting image of all. This is in spite of the fact that it occurs only once in the whole text.

The whole question of the relationship between the naturally present and the expanding gotra is not clarified at all in the RGV and the RGVV, so that later commentators such as Mikyo Dorje felt the need to add comments of their own. Mikyo Dorje (*gZhan stong sgron me*, [13b]) raises the question of whether the urge to Enlightenment arises from the defiled or the naturally pure mind; he concludes that the nonexistent contingent stains produce disgust with samsara and aspiration to nirvana through the truth and influence (*byin rlabs*) of the non-compounded Tathagatagarbha Dharmadhatu. The SMS [548] raises, and answers a slightly different question, which is how a defiled mind (i.e. the vijnana) could experience suffering (*sdug bsngal myong ba ma lags*) because it is momentary and non-abiding.

Superficially it looks as if Mikyo Dorje is in disagreement with the SMS. However, it should be understood that he is making a distinction between the conceptual process of renunciation and aspiration, which is a function of the deluded conceptual mind, and the non-conceptual impulse, which is a function of the Tathagatagarbha Dharmadhatu. The SMS only concerns itself with the initial impulse coming from the Tathagatagarbha, pointing out that a moment of dependently arising consciousness could not produce this impulse because it is either a moment aware of pain or a moment aware of happiness. Since it cannot be aware of both at the same time, it cannot suffer in the deeper sense of wishing itself free of suffering or wishing itself the experience of happiness.

This seems to contradict the argument that the skandhas cannot be the self because they are *duhkha* (suffering). The SMS does not address this problem. Presumably, the answer is that they are not the self because, although they are pervaded with unsatisfactoriness, they do not themselves experience the tension between the apparent and the Real. Incidentally, throughout this discussion one should remember that suffering (*duhkha*) in

Buddhism includes the all-pervading unsatisfactory nature of impermanent phenomena (*viparinamaduhkha*).

The SMS argues [quoted in RGVV 1.40] that only an awareness capable of not suffering can experience suffering in the sense of developing an aversion to it. Thus, only the naturally blissful Buddhajnana is sensitive and responsive in a nondual way and so can "experience" suffering and move beings to renounce it and seek nirvana. Thus, Dolpopa, when he defines gotra [RC 24.4], describes [RC 39] how it is that the Dharmakaya becomes sick of suffering and longs for nirvana, giving some convincing arguments for Dhatu being Dharmakaya.

v. Union (*Yoga, ldan*) [RGV 1.42—1.44]

Paraphrase. This section emphasizes the inseparable nature of the Qualities in the base to be purified (i.e. an ordinary being's mind) and in the fruit, which is the purification of that base (i.e. the Enlightened Buddha's Mind). The Qualities in the base are compared to an ocean in which there is a limitless supply of precious jewels and an exhaustless supply of water. The ocean is a common scriptural metaphor for anything in vast quantities and it is a well established tradition (presumably Indian) that oceans conceal great treasures in their depths.

Verse [1.43] explains that the Dharmakaya is like an ocean, and wisdom and compassion are like jewels and water respectively. Thus, two of the same symbols that are found in verse [1.30] are used here with a slightly different slant. The RGVV [1.43 phi 21b] explains that the Buddha Element is the union of three causes:

1. aspiration (*mos pa*) to the Mahayana, which is the cause of the purification of the Dharmakaya,
2. meditation that combines wisdom with deep concentration, which is the cause of attaining the Buddhajnana,
3. the Bodhisattva's compassion meditation, which is the cause of the Tathagata's great compassion.

The first is like the ocean because it contains wisdom, concentration, and compassion, which are like water and jewels; the second is like jewels because it is conceptionless, which means it has inconceivable and powerful qualities; and the third is like water because it has the single taste that is the supreme moisture (tenderness) for all beings.

It is because it has the three causes for these three qualities that it is said to be "yoga" (united or connected, in Tibetan translated here as *ldan*,

having). Aspiration, wisdom, concentration, and compassion have already
been discussed in verses [1.30–1.34] in connection with the Element as
"Cause." In "Union" the emphasis is not on causality but on the way that
the qualities associated with causing Buddhahood are inseparable from the
nature of the Element, just as water and jewels are inseparable from the
nature of the ocean. In other words the aspiration to attain the Dharmakaya
arises from the Dharmakaya present in beings (i.e. the Element present in
beings). Wisdom, concentration, and compassion are inherent functions of
the Element.

Comments. Khenpo Tsultrim, following Patrul Rimpoche (*dPal sprul*), explains that since all sentient beings are aware at some level, since they must
have some degree of concentration in order to survive, and since, as mentioned above, few beings do not feel an instinctive protective compassion
for their young, all sentient beings show signs of the Buddhajnana's Inseparable Qualities (the gotra).

However, the explanation in the RGVV [1.43 phi 22] suggests that this
section is about the expanding gotra and echoes the preceding verse about
those without the gotra not having aspiration. It seems "yoga" (*ldan pa*)
compares the expanding gotra to an ocean that has in its depths the treasures and water of Buddhahood.

Thus, Khenpo Tsultrim's explanation emphasizes that all beings have
the Buddha*gunas* naturally, and the RGVV emphasizes that the Qualities that
become evident as the gotra expands are expressions of or are inseparable
from the Buddha*gunas* of the fruit. In other words, aspiration, wisdom,
concentration, and compassion in ordinary beings are expressions of the
Inseparable Qualities of the Buddhajnana.

Paraphrase. The second part of verse [1.42] and verse [1.44] deal with
yoga in terms of the fruit. The Buddha Element "has" the fruit, as well as
the cause. The RGV explains that the Element is like the flame of a lamp
because in the stainless base (*gnas*) there is super-normal knowledge (*mngon shes, abhijna*) and stainless Jnana; they are inseparable, just as the
color of a flame is inseparable from its light and heat. The RGVV [1.44 phi
22] explains that "super-normal knowledge" refers to the five super-normal
knowledges of a Buddha [*Study* 227fn.210] that overcome the darkness (i.e.
the obstacles to experiencing the true Nature). "Stainless Jnana" here
means the Buddhajnana when it is completely free from defilement; at that
time it is like fire burning up all defilements. The quality of inseparability
is the exhaustion of defilement. In other words, it is the Clear Light Nature,
which has Inseparable Qualities, as does the color (or form) of the flame in
the revealed lamp, which has the inseparable qualities of heat and light.
The RGVV also quotes the example of the lamp and its light, heat and color

as well as the jewel with the inseparable qualities of light, color, and shape from the *Anutvapurnatvanirdesasutra* (AAN) [*Study* 228] The example is given later in the RGV itself [RGV 3.37]. In this quotation from the AAN, the doctrine of the Inseparable Qualities of the Dharmakaya as countless as the sands of the Ganges is reiterated and called the ''Inseparable Jnana Qualities.''

Comments. This section echoes the lamp in the pot example in the *Anguli-malasutra* and the *Dharmadhatustotra.* Just as when the pot has been completely broken, the color (or form) of the flame is revealed, so when the veils are removed the Qualities of Knowledge, Love, and Power that have always been inseparable from the Mind are fully revealed.

In Shentong terms, the headings ''cause,'' ''action,'' and ''yoga'' are very similar in import since all point to the dynamic nature of the Element that moves beings to action and causes the removal of obstacles to their Enlightenment. Since the expanding Gotra is in essence none other than the naturally present Gotra, the fact that the RGV does not distinguish them clearly presents no particular problem. The ''cause'' section corresponds to ordinary beings as an expression of Buddhajnana; the first section of ''yoga'' corresponds to Bodhisattvas as an expression of Buddhajnana, the second section of ''yoga'' to Buddhas as an expression of Buddhajnana. The section on ''action'' links the two, saying that, because of the Element and that Element emerging (expanding), the three-fold category of beings, Bodhisattvas, and Buddhas arises.

vi. Occurrence [RGV 1.45–1.46]

Paraphrase. This follows on from the comments made above. Verse [1.45] states that the Tathata is divided into three. It occurs in ordinary beings, Bodhisattvas, and Buddhas; that is why all beings are said to be the Buddha *garbha.* (Notice that here the Tibetan word ''*can*'' signifying ''having'' is omitted in the Tibetan so that all beings are said to be Buddhagarbha and not just to have it).

Verse 1.46 elaborates by saying that beings are deluded; the Aryas remedy this delusion of beings, but it is only Buddhas who are completely without delusion since only they are entirely beyond conceptual artifice (prapanca). The RGVV [1.46 phi 22b] refers the reader to the Prajnaparamita and its references to the non-conceptual Jnana (*mi rtog pa'i ye shes*). There the Tathata of all dharmas, which is the pure general characteristic, is taught. Ordinary beings do not see it, Bodhisattvas only partly see it, and Buddhas see it completely since they are free from the tendencies and the two kinds of veil. In other words, the nature of all three is the Tathata: the only difference between them being the extent to which they know it.

Comments. Dolpopa [RC 385] argues against those who say that Tathata when released from the klesa is not Tathagatagarbha. He explains that the RGV says that the Tathata pervades all three phases, and therefore the essence of the Tathagata is Tathagatagarbha. He gives a long list of scriptural evidence for this.

vii. Phases [RGV 1.47–1.48]

Paraphrase. Verses [1.47, 48] repeat the same point about the three phases or guises of the Element as impure, pure, and perfectly pure. RGVV [1.48 phi 23b] gives a long quote from the *Anunatvapurnatvanirdesa* saying that the Dharmakaya, when it is wrapped in the klesa, is carried away by the endless process of birth and death in samsara. Thus, samsara itself is called the "Element of beings." When it enters the Bodhisattva path, it is called "Bodhisattva." When it is completely free from the veils and so forth, and dwells in the pure Dharmata—while still being able to be seen by beings— it is called the "Buddha."

Thus, we have here a very clear reference to the Dharmakaya itself as the one Reality that is variously called the "Element of beings" (or samsara), Bodhisattvas, or Buddhas.

There is little difference between the section on "Occurrence" and the section on "Phases" since the former explains that the Element occurs in three guises and the latter that it is known by a different name each time. This division of the Element into three is an important feature of the RGV around which the next three points are structured.

Comments. In Shentong terms the three stages are equivalent to the division of the Clear Light Nature of the Mind into base, path, and fruit Mahamudra in Tantric treatises. (See Chapter 6 "The Nature of Beings" section 6.1 "Base, Path, and Fruit".)

viii. All-pervasiveness [RGV 1.49–1.50]

Paraphrase. This and the next section are again almost entirely based on the *Anunatvapurnatvanirdesa*. According to Takasaki's analysis (see *Study* Appendix), it is all part of the original verses of the RGV.

The Mind's Nature is compared to space that is the same everywhere. It is no worse or better in an inferior pot than in a mediocre or good one. This section does no more than emphasize that the Element of beings is the Dharmakaya and that the Dharmakaya is the Element of beings. One should not be confused by the terminology and think that it is ever anything other than the same Element whatever its name or guise.

Comments. Dolpopa [RC 35] quotes this section of the RGV and RGVV at length on how Mind's Nature is like space and is the same in beings, Bodhisattvas, and Buddhas.

ix. Changelessness [RGV 1.51–1.83]

Paraphrase. This is a very long section divided into three. The first section deals with the changelessness of the Element in beings [RGV 1.52–65], the second with its changelessness in Bodhisattvas [RGV 1.60–78], and the third with its changelessness in Buddhas [RGV 1.79–83]. Thus, changelessness is to be understood in three different senses. The Element is changeless in beings because it is the changeless fundamental Nature of all things without which even delusion, karma, and samsaric rebirth could not take place. It is changeless in Bodhisattvas because they are no longer subject to gross birth and death arising from delusion. Buddhas alone are entirely changeless (as has already been explained in the section on the Permanence Paramita).

The Changelessness of the Element of Beings [RGV 1.52–1.65]

The simile of space is used following the *Ganganaganjapariprccha*, (see *Study* 239fn.292). Space is described as that subtle element that is the basis for the worlds to arise and perish. They rest on space and depend upon space, but space rests and depends on nothing. The image used is taken from an Indian version of the creation myth: wind arose in space and created a rain that formed an ocean. The wind then churned the ocean until the earth emerged from it like butter from milk. The RGV uses this image to show how the wrong-way-of-thinking (*ayonisamanasikara, tshul bzhin ma yin yid la byed pa*) moves like wind in the space of the non-conceptual, non-arisen Mind, producing the water of mental poisons and karma. Khenpo Tsultrim suggests they are like water in that they bind everything together. The mental poisons and karma are like an ocean that is churned by the wind of the wrong-way-of-thinking. As the ocean is churned the earth emerges—this is like the skandhas arising from mental poisons and karma through the action of the wrong-way-of-thinking [RGVV 1.64 phi 25b.6]. RGV [1.62] explains:

> The nature of Mind is like space, being without cause and condition, non-created, non-arisen, without perishing and without staying. The Mind's nature that is Clear Light is changeless like space. It is never troubled by the adventitious stains such as desire, which arise from the wrong way of thinking.

This verse is much quoted in Tibetan commentarial literature and is very significant from the Shentong point of view.

The RGVV [1.64 phi 25.4] quotes the whole passage from the *Ganganaganjapariprccha* from which this section of the RGV is taken. Verse 1.65 refers to the fact that the fires of death, sickness, and old age, which are like the fire at the end of time, hell fire and ordinary fire respectively, do not affect the Element. The RGV quotes at length from the SMS [548 cha 274b] to explain this point.

Comments. Incidentally, it is this section of the SMS that is quoted in the *Lankavatarasutra*, telling how birth and death are just conventional terms for the arising and perishing of the sense faculties, but the Tathagatagarbha never arises and perishes like this because it is beyond conditionality.

Paraphrase. RGVV [1.64 phi 25b] concludes that the root of all dharmas is completely cut (*yongs su chad pa*), their root is without essence (*snying po med pa'i rtsa ba can*), their root is not abiding (*mi gnas pa'i rtsa ba can*), their root is pure (*dag pa'i rtsa ba can*), and their root is rootless (*rtsa ba med pai rtsa ba can*).

The Changelessness of the Bodhisattvas who are at the Stage of Being Both Impure and Pure [RGV 1.66–1.78]

It has been explained above that Bodhisattvas are impure because they are not free from the ground of ignorance tendency patterns. It has also been explained that because they are free to some extent of both the klesa and knowledge veils, they know: a) the Clear Light Nature of Mind, b) the adventitious nature of the unreal klesa, and c) the fact that all beings have the Tathagatagarbha [RGV 1.13]. Therefore, they are partly pure and partly impure. This is the doctrine according to the SMS [530.7ff] and RGVV [phi 19b.7].

Since they are free from the wrong-way-of-thinking (*ayonisomani-skara*), they do not have birth arising from the klesa and karma. Although their body of mental nature undergoes the subtle arising, aging, and death mentioned in the section on the transcendental qualities, this is almost imperceptible (*shin tu snang ba med par* [RGVV 1.67 phi 22b.1]). Nevertheless, they do appear to take birth and so on in the world for the sake of beings. The RGVV [1.68 phi 26b] quotes some long passages from the *Sagaramatipariprccha* telling how the Bodhisattva takes birth in the world, because of his/her own deliberate intentions, by means of virtuous karmic roots and the "klesa" that go with these. These "klesa" are thirst for accumulating merit, attachment to taking rebirth deliberately and so on. The example found in the *Sagaramatipariprccha* of the boy who falls into the pit of filth and is saved by his father who plunges in after him is also given in the RGVV. The boy represents sentient beings, and the mother and relatives, who fail to rescue him, the Sravakas and Pratyeka Buddhas. The father is, of course, the compassionate Bodhisattva.

Comments. From the Shentong point of view, this emphasis on the conditionality of the Bodhisattva's state is beside the point in the context of the changelessness of the Element in the Bodhisattva. The main thrust of Tathagatagarbha doctrine is that as soon as, and as long as, the Bodhisattva directly realizes the non-compounded Nature of Mind, he/she is already freed from the process of ordinary karmic birth and death, for he realizes the dharmas are essenceless and that there is no birth and death in the Tathagatagarbha. This is implied by RGVV [1.68] and one is led to the conclusion that the reason for the Bodhisattva's still being subject to subtle birth and death at all is the incompleteness of his/her realization [RGV 1.36].

Paraphrase. There follows yet another quotation from the *Sagaramatipariprccha* in the RGVV [1.68 phi 27b.5] that explains how the Bodhisattva realizes the dharmas are essenceless (*snying po med pa*) and so forth. Thus, he/she is neither impatient in the sense of rejecting anything nor does he/she become attached to anything. In this way, he/she is able to dwell in the world in order to help beings. Because he/she sees that the mind of beings is like a precious jewel caked in mud, he/she endeavors to clear away the mud, for it is contingent, powerless, and not the true nature of beings.

The next section of the RGVV explains what samsara means to a Bodhisattva. It states that the Bodhisattva's mental skandhas, which are of three kinds for the three realms in which they appear like reflections, do not arise from klesa and karma; so they could, in that sense, be called non-compounded, non-arisen and non-ceasing. However, they do arise from good karmic roots so technically they are compounded. Thus, sometimes it is said that there is a compounded and a non-compounded samsara and a compounded and non-compounded nirvana. It is because the Bodhisattva arises from a mixed compounded and non-compounded mind that he/she is called "impure-pure."

Comment. The SMS is quoted to support the point about the compounded and the non-compounded samsara and nirvana, but in fact, this section of the SMS [542 cha 271b] is demonstrating a slightly different point. In the case of the SMS, compounded samsara and nirvana are samsara and nirvana as understood by the Sravakas and Pratyeka Buddhas, and the non-compounded samsara and nirvana as understood by the Buddhas.

Paraphrase. The RGVV continues by introducing further details about the Bodhisattva path and how the Bodhisattva turns away from nirvana in order to benefit others, sometimes even taking on the form of an animal. All this discussion is a digression from the main theme of the section, which is the changelessness of the Bodhisattva.

Comments. From the Shentong point of view the important point is simply that the Bodhisattva realizes the nature of the nondual Jnana, and therefore is no longer deluded by apparent phenomena. That is why he can remain in the world without being stained by it like a lotus growing out of mud [RGV 1.71–72].

Paraphrase. RGV [1.69–78] describes how the Bodhisattva's action in the world is continuous, ever-active, conceptionless samadhi. The samadhi is maintained by the force of the former practice of the Bodhisattva, and his action for others is very precise, giving every being exactly what he needs in terms of teaching at precisely the right time, place and manner. In this way his action in the world is just like that of the Buddha but, in fact, in terms of his realization (*rang don,* own good), he is as different from a Buddha as the amount of water in a hoof print compared to the water of the ocean, or a speck of dust compared to the dust of the whole earth. This reminds us of the vast difference created by removing the ground of ignorance tendency patterns described in the SMS [530ff cha 265b ff.]. However vastly the Bodhisattva's awareness extends, as long as it is limited by the subtle conceptual tendency, it will be minute compared with the limitless Awareness of the Buddha.

The RGVV describes in some detail how, of verses 1.69–78, the first two apply to the first level (*bhumi*) Bodhisattvas, the third and fourth to Bodhisattvas on the second to the seventh bhumi, the fifth to those on the eighth bhumi, the sixth, seventh, and eighth verses to Bodhisattvas on the tenth bhumi, and the ninth and tenth verses to a comparison of the tenth bhumi Bodhisattva with the Buddha. This section is yet another example of a digression into general Mahayana doctrine with no particular attempt to relate it to the main theme of the text (i.e. Tathagatagarbha doctrine).

The Changelessness of the Perfectly Pure Buddha [RGV 1.79–1.83]

This section adds nothing to the doctrine of the Buddha's permanence discussed in the opening verses in praise of the Buddha and the verses about the transcendental permanence of the fruit. The RGVV [1.82 phi 30] refers again to the SMS, telling how the Buddha does not have the ground of ignorance tendency patterns and mental skandhas associated with it. Thus, He is beyond all conceptual tendencies, non-arisen, non-perishing and so forth. The doctrine about the Inseparable Qualities occurs in this section too and is mentioned in the section of the *Anunatvapurnatvanirdesa* quoted in the RGVV.

Comment. In the Tibetan version, RGVV [30b.3] is made into a verse and included in the root text [*Study* 258].

x. Inseparable Qualities [RGV 1.84–1.94]

Paraphrase. The RGV and RGVV do not develop the concept of Inseparable Qualities in the manner explained in Chapter 4.1 "Inseparable Qualities" in this present work. Instead, their main concern here seems to be to refute the idea held by Sravakas and Pratyeka Buddhas that nirvana (the cessation of suffering) is simply the ceasing of the klesa, karma, and rebirth. It seems that even some would-be Bodhisattvas also thought this. The proof that the RGV (following the SMS) puts forward for this not being the true Nirvana is that the Inseparable Qualities are not evident. In verse 1.84 the example of the sun and its rays is given. Just as one cannot say that all the clouds have gone until the rays of the sun are seen, so one cannot be satisfied that all suffering has gone and Nirvana has been attained until complete and perfect Buddhahood with its Inseparable Qualities is seen.

Verses 1.84–87 expound the SMS doctrine of the Dharmakaya, which the SMS refers to as the Tathagatagarbha, as the Aryan Truth of the Cessation of Suffering (i.e. Nirvana). Though ostensibly commenting on the explanations of the two kinds of Aryan Truths in the SMS, neither the RGV nor RGVV really develop the doctrine as found in that Sutra concerning the compounded and the non-compounded versions of each of the Four Aryan Truths. The SMS [542 cha 271b] explains that the compounded is the nirvana which is the result of removing the klesa and so forth (i.e. it is produced). The non-compounded is the Nirvana that is non-arisen, eternally present Absolute Reality. The compounded nirvana was taught for the fainthearted Sravakas and Pratyeka Buddhas, but has finally to be abandoned in favor of the real Nirvana, which is Buddhahood.

Verses 1.88–92 give an example taken from the *Ratnacudasutra* which, again, is not particularly helpful from the Shentong point of view. It is one of the very few sections of the RGV that makes any reference whatever to the practice of the six paramitas and their relevance to the realizing of Buddhahood.

The example given in the RGV is that of a king wanting his portrait painted and six different painters being commissioned for the task, each specializing in their own part of the portrait. If one of these artists does not turn up, the picture cannot be completed. The painters are the six paramitas. The picture is said to symbolize the All-aspected Emptiness.

Comments. "All-aspected Emptiness" is a key expression in Tantric texts but this is its only occurrence in the RGV or RGVV. It is used by Santideva at the end of chapter XV of *Siksasamuccaya* and Ruegg [LM 97] mentions it in connection with Kamalasila on the "emptiness endowed with all excellent modes", (*sarvakaravaropeta*), that is, emptiness inseparable from the six paramitas as means.

Even though the whole message of Tathagatagarbha doctrine—from the Shentong point of view—is that liberation arises from realizing the Buddhajnana that is the true nature of all sentient beings [RGV 1.154], Dolpopa in the RC and Mikyo Dorje in the *gZhan stong sgron me* repeatedly stress the need for the different practices, such as the six paramitas, for removing the different obstructions because, in practice, it helps to think in these terms. However, they help only in the sense that they trigger the emergence of the naturally present gotra.

In Shentong terms, the image of the six painters could be understood to mean that generosity, discipline, patience and so forth are expressions of the Buddha Qualities and as such represent aspects of the Buddha Himself, which is only fully realized when all the paramitas are present and especially the paramita of wisdom. This is not made clear in the RGV and RGVV, however, and the example suggests development rather than the emergence of something originally present.

Paraphrase. In verse 1.93 the example of the sun and its rays is used in an almost identical way to the example of the flame of the lamp and its heat, light and shape given in verse 1.44.

Incidentally, RGVV [1.86] quotes from the SMS on the Inseparable Qualities as countless as the sands of the Ganges, although the RGV has so far only mentioned wisdom, compassion, and power and their expression in beings as faith or aspiration, renunciation, and samadhi. The exact meaning of the countless qualities is nowhere explained in the RGV and RGVV. This is one of the aspects of Tathagatagarbha doctrine that is developed in the Chinese Hua Yen and related interpretations of Tathagatagarbha doctrine where the doctrines of Interpenetration and Totality take up this theme.

In the example of the lamp with its light, heat, and color, and the example of the sun with its light and rays, the Inseparable Qualities are given as different aspects of wisdom itself. For example in verses 1.93 and 1.94 the Mind of the Buddha is said to be like the light of the sun, His wisdom like its radiance, and His freedom from veils, its clarity. The RGVV explains that the mind of the Buddha sees the true nature of Reality and is like light dispersing darkness—like precise knowledge (*ji lta mkhyen pa*) in verse 1.14. The wisdom of the Buddha radiates, for it expands out to pervade all things—like knowledge of the full extent (*ji snyed mkhyen pa*) in verse 1.14, so it is like the sun's rays. The Buddha's quality of freedom from veils is like the clarity or purity of the sun that enables it to dispel darkness and radiate in this way. Just as the sun, its light and its rays are one and the same reality, so the knowing of the true Nature and the extension of this knowledge to all things and the nondual Jnana that is the source of these two kinds of knowledge, are one and the same Reality [RGV 1.13]. Therefore, until those Inseparable Qualities are revealed, the goal (Nirvana) has not been attained.

Comments. The significance of this is that the knowledge of all things (omniscience, *thams cad mkhyen pa*) is a special quality of the Buddha alone; Sravakas and Pratyeka Buddhas do not even aspire to it. They only aspire to know the true nature of reality, not to know all things. They think that they see the true nature of reality when they attain nirvana. The RGV points out that, since they do not have the knowledge of all things, they also do not see the true nature of Reality, for they are one and the same.

In terms of the path, it is always stressed that the Bodhisattva path combines wisdom and compassion. The reason for this is explained here. Buddhajnana has two Inseparable Qualities: one is to see the true nature of Reality (*ji lta mkhyen pa*), and the other is to see this in all things (*ji snyed mkhyen pa* or *thams cad mkhyen pa*). To see it in all things is to see that all beings have that Buddha Nature and to see no distinction between self and others, which is the essence of compassion. Therefore, to have at least the concept that all beings have the Buddha Nature is to start to love them as oneself [RGV 1.167]; this is an expression of the Inseparable Quality of the full extent of the Buddha's knowledge, which starts to become synonymous with compassion.

Paraphrase. Thus, although the Inseparable Qualities are described as countless, the RGV sums them up as three—knowledge, love, and power—[RGV 1.4].

The Nine Examples [RGV 1.95–1.152]

These verses describe the nine examples of how the Tathagatagarbha is hidden in the sheath of the klesa until it is removed by the action of the Buddha, thus allowing beings to emerge as fully enlightened Buddhas who can act for the benefit of others. These examples all come from the *Tathagatagarbhasutra* and the way they are presented in the RGV is in metered verse interspersed with, and explained by, nonmetered verses. The RGVV itself makes scarcely any comments on this section, until the end of verse 1.152.

The examples are as follows:

1. *Buddha in a Faded Lotus* [Verses 1.99–101] is compared to the Buddha's dharmata, present even in beings in the worst hell. In verse 1.130 the lotus is compared to the klesa of desire that at first makes things look so attractive, but which quickly turns into disappointment. The Buddha that is in the lotus is said to represent the Buddha Dharmakaya, which only the perfection of the Buddha himself can symbolize [verse 1.145].

2. *Bees Swarming Around Honey* [Verses 102–104] The honey is compared to the Gotra Element, which is non-defiled Awareness (*zag med pa'i shes pa*) in beings. The bees are compared to the klesa of hatred [1.130] and the honey to the single and unique taste of the profound teaching Dharmakaya [1.145].

Comments. Here we have the doctrine of the teaching Dharmakaya with its two aspects, the profound and the manifold. The honey represents the profound Nature that is demonstrated everywhere at all times, spontaneously without effort. The next example illustrates the manifold aspects of the teaching kaya, which flow out from this and demonstrate the profound Nature to different beings differently according to their character and ability to understand. This is also a spontaneous and natural expression of the Dharmakaya.

Paraphrase.
   3. *Grains in Husks* [Verses 105–107]. Just as the kernels (*snying po*) of grains are not usable until freed from their husks, so the Buddha Nature does not express itself as the helpful Dharma Teacher carrying out the Buddha activity, until it is released from the klesa. The many grains with their many tastes are compared to the teaching Dharmakaya of the manifold aspects and the husks that have to be removed are compared to the klesa of stupidity.
Comment. In Shentong terms, this means that the manifold and various teachings of the Buddha are a spontaneous expression of Buddhajnana and not carefully devised conceptual contrivances. Like the rain example in RGV 4.46, the water is, in fact, of a single taste, but tastes differently according to the type of ground it falls on. Thus, however a teaching may sound superficially, when fully understood it is always the same in essence.

Paraphrase.
   4. *Gold Fallen Into Filth by the Wayside* [Verses 1.108–111]. The gold is described as the imperishable subject matter (*dharmin, chos can,* literally, dharma-haver), the quality of beings and the perfect precious Buddha that is explained in verse 1.145 as the Tathata. The filth is attachment, which is the cause for all the klesa to arise.
   5. *Treasure Under the Poor Man's Hovel* [Verses 112–114]. The treasure is an exhaustless treasure that is compared to the stainless Dharmata in the minds of beings (*manas, yid*), to which there is nothing to add and nothing to take away. The subtle ground of ignorance tendency patterns that prevents a man knowing that this treasure is there, and which prevents the treasure revealing itself, is like the ground in which the treasure is embedded. In verse 1.145 the treasure is compared to the naturally present gotra. The ground that obscures it is like the subtle veils of the Arhats, that is, the ground of ignorance tendency patterns.
   6. *The Germinating Seed of a Mango Fruit* [Verses 115–117]. The germinating seed is an imperishable substance (dharma). It is referred to as the

Element of the dharmas (Dharmadhatu, translated as *chos khams* instead of the usual *chos dbyings* in Tibetan). Dharma Vision grows like a tree fertilized and nourished by good actions. It grows from the seed of the Dharmadhatu. This is an example of the expanding gotra defined here as the growing Dharma Vision. The seed is used as an example of the imperishable essence of the fruit, that does not wither and die, but is the power (gotra) that maintains the continuity of the lineage (gotra). Although the Dharma Vision increases, the Dharmadhatu itself is beyond increase and decrease.

Comment. Of all the verses in the RGV this is perhaps the one that lends itself best to a Rangtong interpretation. It might give the impression that one aspect of the gotra remains unchanged while another aspect develops from the coming together of the right causes and conditions on the path. From the Shentong point of view, however, the simile should not be over interpreted.

Dolpopa [RC 155–156] discusses the question of the expanding gotra (*rgyas pa'i rigs*) being like a seed of liberation fertilized by roots of virtue, and points out that one has to distinguish between the teaching about the Dharmata being primordially the exhaustion or relinquishment of stain and the teaching about the removal of these stains by means of a remedy. He explains beings are Absolute Buddha but not apparent (samvrti) Buddha. Absolute Buddha is self-born Jnana (*rang byung*), whereas apparent jnana is born of others (*gzhan byung*), and gives rise to the apparent form-kayas. In the same way, there are the two accumulations, the Absolute and the apparent, and similarly two kinds of gotra. RGV [4.6–4.9] compares the two accumulations to the sun. This image is appropriate for the primordially existent Absolute Accumulations, but not for the apparent ones, which have to be newly created from causes and conditions.

Kongtrul explains [RGV comm. 87b]:

> By completing the accumulation of wisdom and getting rid of all the incidental stains, the naturally-present gotra attains the doubly-pure Dharmata, the first kaya, the *Svabhavikakaya*. By the completion of the expansion of the expanding gotra and the accumulation of merit, the second two kayas that appear to ordinary beings and Bodhisattvas (i.e. Nirmanakaya and Sambhogakaya) are obtained.
>
> On this occasion the Honorable Lord Tinlay [said]: "These days most who follow the Maitreya Dharmas accept that the expanding gotra is compounded (*'dus bya*). The reason they give is the expression "the perfect proper adoption" (*yang dag blangs pa mchog nyid do*). Quoting this, they say properly adopting roots of

merit is the expanding gotra. This is nothing but the noise of the
rabbit's crying "Oh dear!"*

The great Rangjung said in his *Zab mo nang don;* "Moreover if
anyone thinks the expanding gotra is newly arisen, it is not like
that. . . . ," and in this text [i.e. the RGV], since it has the same
intention (*dgongs pa*), it does not say the proper adoption of roots
of merit is the expanding gotra. It is primordially present, but being obscured by veils at the sentient being stage, the ripening and
activity are not expanded (*rgyas pa*), so it cannot perform the vast
benefit of beings. On the path of training, by the proper adoption
of the roots of merit, that gotra's power (*nus pa*) spreads and so at
the Buddha stage, since the veils are cleared away, the activity of
the form kayas spreads.

Karma Tinlay is saying here that everyone has just been blindly following everyone else in saying that the expanding gotra is none other than the
gotra of proper adoption. The gotra of proper adoption is compounded. (See
this present work Chapter 6.4 "Gotra.") Rangjung Dorje says [ZND 5a.5]:

It is said that the expanding gotra is newly arisen, conditioned by
the patterns/traces/tendencies/habits (*vasana*) of listening etc. (to
Dharma).

He then refutes this position.

In RGV [1.130] the example of the fruit around the seed is explained as
the veils that are removed on entering the Path of Seeing. At that time the
Element is seen directly for the first time and from then on the vision develops as the Path of Meditation is traversed. The vision is increasing as
more and more veils are removed, so that from the Shentong point of view,
the example of the growing tree is not totally appropriate. It implies some
sort of growth and development as does the example of the poor woman
with the Cakravartin in her womb. This symbolizes the Bodhisattva emerging from the impure to the pure levels. Thus, both of these "development"
examples occur in connection with important moments of the Bodhisattva
path when a major breakthrough occurs. Maybe, this is why they are chosen. A tree emerging from a seed and a baby from a womb mark great

---

*N.B. This is an allusion to the tale of the rabbit who, when a fruit (or branch)
fell on his head or into a nearby pool, thought that it was a sign that the world
was coming to an end. He rushed off into the forest telling everyone and causing
a mad panic.

moments of transition, as does the Bodhisattva breaking through to the first level at the Path of Seeing, and through to the pure levels at the end of the seventh level of a Bodhisattva.

Paraphrase.

7. *Precious Buddha Image in Filthy Rags* [Verses 1.118–120]. The precious image is explained as the *Sugata's* substance (*bde gshegs dngos po*) that is even in animals. The filthy rags are compared to the veils removed in the course of the path of meditation—levels one to ten of the Bodhisattva path. The Buddha image itself is like the naturally-present Gotra, which attains the *Svabhavikakaya*. It is completely genuine and non-adulterated so it is changeless and of great value like the *Svabhavikakaya*.

8. *The Poor Woman with the Cakravartin in Her Womb* [Verses 1.122–123]. Like a woman who thinks herself destitute and without a protector, yet carrying the greatest protector of all within her, beings wander in samsara unaware of the stainless Dhatu within them. The embryo is like the expanding gotra, which attains the Sambhogakaya. The Sambhogakaya rules the Dharma Realms like a Cakravartin. The womb itself is like the veils that are removed at the end of the impure levels, that is, at the end of the seventh level.

9. *The Golden Image in a Clay Mould* [Verses 1.124–126]. The golden image is described as natural peace and as the Clear Light Nature. Just as a skillful craftsman knows that inside the clay mould the golden image is finished and ready to be chipped out of the clay, so the Buddha sees that beings are like a treasure trove, for they have the peaceful Mind (*zhi ba'i yid*) that needs to be freed from the klesa. Verse 1.142 explains that the clay is like the veils of the pure levels that fall away at the end of the tenth level and are finally removed by the Vajra-like Samadhi. Verse 1.152 explains that the golden image is the expanding gotra, which attains the Nirmanakaya. The Nirmanakaya is like a mirror reflection, and that is why it is presented as a golden image.

Thus, each image is particularly identified with one kind of klesa and one aspect of the Element. They are also linked with the four kinds of beings, so that examples one to four "Buddha In a Faded Lotus" up to "Gold Fallen into Filth by the Wayside" are said to correspond to ordinary beings; "Treasure Under the Poor Man's Hovel" corresponds to Arhats; "The Germinating Seed of Mango Fruit and Precious Buddha Image in Filthy Rags" correspond to training Bodhisattvas (on the impure levels) and the "Poor Woman with the Cakravartin in her Womb" and "The Golden Image in a Clay Mould" to the wise Bodhisattvas on the pure levels [see RGV 1.133].

In fact, the klesa are limitless in number [see RGVV comments after verse 1.132]. They are sometimes categorized as 84,000 and the Buddha's Dharmas (teachings) are also 84,000—one Dharma to remedy each of the 84,000 klesa. The RGVV points out that in the *Tathagatagarbhasutra* it is clearly stated that this is a mere teaching device and, in fact, the klesa are countless.

Comment. The slight lack of clarity in the RGV and RGVV concerning the relationship between the naturally-present and the expanding gotra is nowhere more clearly demonstrated than in this section of the nine examples and their explanation.

If the expanding gotra is the naturally-present Gotra emerging, why does verse 1.50 make a clear distinction between the naturally-present gotra as what attains the *Svabhavikakaya*, and the properly adopted gotra as what attains the form-kayas? From the Shentong point of view, one would expect all three kayas to be attained by the same naturally-present Gotra, and the process of attaining all three of them to be called the expanding gotra. In fact, in Shentong terms the *Svabhavikakaya* is a name for the three kayas as one, and the naturally-present Gotra is what attains this [RGV 1.150].

Paraphrase. The RGVV [following verse 1.152] explains that the form-kayas are, in essence, simply the Buddha Element itself. Their apparent arising from causes and conditions is not really the Buddha at all [RGV 2.52]. Thus "the properly adopted gotra attaining the form-kayas" simply means that by properly adopting roots of merit, the naturally-present Gotra emerges as the expanding gotra, which gives rise to the attainment of the form-kayas. The removal of veils takes place through causes and conditions produced from good karmic actions, but the Element itself does not develop from causes and conditions. When it is fully emerged, the Buddha Activity can function and by means of this the form-kayas appear in the world.[26]

Comments. When Gampopa [*Thar rgyan* 174b] quotes from the *Mahayanasutralamkara* [9:62],[27] he does not seem to make a great distinction between the *Svabhavikakaya* and the Dharmakaya. In fact, the development of the three kaya doctrine in Shentong and Tantric systems is a whole new area of research. In brief, the essence of the three kayas is explained as three Inseparable Qualities of the Clear Light Nature of Mind, and as such can be experienced directly through non-conceptual Awareness right from the beginning of the path. For example in the second point of "*Seven Points of Mind Training,*" Atisa says, "Contemplating the manifestation of illusion (error) as the four kayas is the supreme way of guarding Emptiness."

Paraphrase. At the end of the section on the nine examples [after verse 1.152] the RGVV expands on an important doctrine from the *Mahayanabhidharmasutra* and the SMS. First of all, it explains that the last five examples teach that the Tathagata Element is the Essence (*garbha*) of beings in terms of its being their lineage (gotra). The Tathagata's Element is the Tathagata's lineage that gives rise to the three kayas. So in this sense the Element is a "cause" here.

Comment. In Shentong terms, the Element is the "stuff" (*hetu, rgyu*) of Buddhahood and in that sense it is its prime cause. In another sense, it is not a cause at all since Buddha lies outside the whole conceptual framework of causality.

Paraphrase. The RGVV continues by quoting from the *Mahayanabhidharmasutra* as follows:

> *thog ma med dus can gyi khams. chos rnams kun gyi gnas yin te.*
> *de yod pas na 'gro kun dang. mya ngan 'das pa'ang thob pa yin.*
> The Element that primordially exists is the base for all dharmas.
> Since this exists all beings and nirvana are possible.

This reminds us of the *Gaganaganjapariprccha* [RGV 1.52ff], which compares the Element to space on which everything depends. Then RGVV [1.152] defines the Element by quoting the SMS:

> Lord, the Tathagatagarbha is the *garbha* of the supra mundane Dharma(s), the *Dharmagarbha* that is pure by nature.

It then explains "the base for all dharmas" (see above) by the following quotation from the SMS:

> Lord, for this reason the Tathagatagarbha is the dwelling place, base and support for the connected, inseparable, irremovable, noncompounded dharmas. Lord, the Tathagatagarbha is the base, dwelling place and support for the unconnected, separable dharmas that are removable and compounded dharmas.

Comments. The wording of SMS [548] differs from the RGVV, which suggests either the RGVV is misquoting the SMS, or there are alternative versions of it:

> *bcom ldan 'das de lta lags pas de bzhin gshegs pa'i snying po ni*
> *tha dad du mi gnas shing 'brel la sbubs nas grol ba'i shes pa can*
> *dag gi gzhi dang. rten dang. gnas lags so. bcom ldan 'das di ltar*
> *de bzhin gshegs pa'i snying po ni 'brel pa ma mchis shing tha dad*
> *du gnas la shes pa grol ba ma lags pa phyi rol gyi 'dus byas kyi*
> *chos rnams kyi gzhi dang rten dang gnas kyang lags so.*
> Bhagavan, thus, since this is so, the Tathagatagarbha is the base, support, the dwelling place of the minds [literally, havers of

knowledge or mind] free from the sheath (*sbubs*) that are not apart
and are connected.

Bhagavan, like this the Tathagatagarbha is also the base, support,
and dwelling place for the outer compounded dharmas, the non-
free knowers/knowledge/minds which are unconnected and dwelling apart.

"Since this exists all beings" is explained as: Lord since the Tathagatagarbha exists there is the term samsara.

"Nirvana is possible" is explained as:

Lord, it is explained at length that, if the Tathagatagarbha did not
exist there would be no disgust with suffering and no desire for,
seeking after, or aspiration for, nirvana.

Comments. It is significant that the RGVV reminds us of this doctrine at this
particular point. In Shentong terms the last five examples, which concern
the gotra as the cause, should be understood in connection with the verses
on "Action" [RGV 1.40, 41]. Because the naturally-present Gotra exists,
the expanding gotra is activated, manifesting disgust with samsara and aspiration to nirvana and finally giving rise to the three kayas.

Although the reference to the two kinds of gotra, with the *Svabhavikakaya* arising from the naturally-present Gotra and the form-kayas arising from the properly adopted gotra, agrees with the Rangtong view, the
RGVV does not suggest that the Jnana aspect of the Dharmakaya arises from
the properly adopted gotra. This is important because in Rangtong terms
not only are the form-kayas produced by causes and conditions but the
jnana and associated mental qualities of the Buddha's mind also arise in
this way.

In Shentong terms, there are three senses in which the naturally-present
Gotra is a cause without its being in any way conditioned by cause and
effect itself:

1. It is the nature of beings, the Buddhajnana, that is, their innate potential to attain the three kayas.

2. It is the "stuff" of Reality, primordially present and without which
nothing would be possible [see RGV 2.18–20].

3. It is the dynamic quality of Buddhajnana that sets the movement
towards Buddhahood in motion as the expanding gotra.

(Gotra is also discussed in Chapter 6 "The Nature of Beings" section 1
"Base Path and Fruit" and 4 "Gotra" of this present work.[28])

The Essence of the Doctrine [RGV 1.153–155]

Paraphrase. These are three key verses of the RGV, based chiefly on the SMS but also on the *Mahaparanirvanasutra*. Both of these Sutras are quoted at length in the RGVV. RGV [1.153–155] states:

> This, the Absolute, the Self-Arisen One, is realizable through faith. The disc of the sun blazing with light is not visible to those without eyes.

> Here there is nothing to clear away and nothing to set up. See Reality perfectly, and from seeing Reality there is liberation.

> The Element is empty of the adventitious that is by nature separable. It is not empty of the supreme dharmas that are by nature inseparable.

The RGVV begins this section with a discussion of Dharmata *pramana* (see Chapter 5 section 1 "Faith" in this present work). In verse 1.154 the "Reality" is the Dharmata (the nature of the dharmas). "Looked at properly" means with the yogi's *pramana*. Thus, when one uses the non-conceptual Jnana of the yogi to look at the Dharmata, when it is seen properly one is liberated (from the subtle conceptual tendencies of the ground of ignorance tendency patterns).

The RGVV [40.1] explains that, according to the *Tathagatagarbhasutra*, the Dharmata is the same whether Buddhas arise in the world or not, and that beings always have the Tathagatagarbha. The RGVV raises the question of what is the validity (*rig pa, yukti*), connection (*sbyor ba, yoga*), and means (*thabs, upaya*) of realizing it? Sure realization (*nges pa rtogs pa*) and perfect knowing (*yang dag par shes pa*) are the realization of the Dharmata or Dharmata valid cognition. This is the unthinkable (*bsam par mi bya*) and unnamable (*brtags par mi bya*), that can only be the object of devotion of a superior kind (*lhag par mos pa,* [RGVV 40b.1]).

Thus, since one cannot know the Dharmata through conceptual reasoning, and one does not have the non-conceptual realization of the yogi, the only recourse is to devotion. Traditionally, devotion (*mos pa*) in Buddhism means faith combined with a longing for realization. See Kongtrul's commentary [89.1]:

> *yid ches pa'i lung la brten nas dad cing mos la yid ches pa nyid kyis don spyi'i tshul du rtogs par bya ba yin gyi. . . .*
> . . . They realize it as a meaning approximation through belief associated with faith and longing (devotion) based on trustworthy scriptures.

The RGV is reiterating in [Verse 1.153] the doctrine of the SMS [545.2 cha 273] concerning the means of knowing the Absolute. In the SMS the example is given of the sun, which can neither be seen by: a) the blind or b) those who have just been born and therefore have not yet been outside; this is reminiscent of Plato's Cave. Ordinary beings, who do not even understand the impermanence of compounded things, are the blind; Sravakas and Pratyeka Buddhas, who do not understand the permanence of Nirvana, are like those who have been born, but have not yet emerged from the house of their birth. Those beings who have faith and believe that the Buddha is Permanent, Bliss, Self, and Purity have the right view and those who "see" it are the sons of the Buddha.

The RGVV quotes the passage from the SMS [549 cha 275] about how the Tathagatagarbha is not the sphere of three kinds of person. The three kinds of person are those fallen into the views concerning (what is subject to) destruction, those with perverted desires, and those whose minds wander from emptiness (*stong pa nyid las sems rnam par gyengs pa*, the definition of this term appears a little further on in this section [RGVV 1.155]). The RGVV then elaborates on the doctrine already mentioned in the "Fruit" topic (on *"The four Transcendental Qualities"*). However, the RGVV mentions four kinds of person, ordinary beings, Sravakas, Pratyeka Buddhas, and "those who have newly entered the vehicle." Although the format here has changed slightly from that of the earlier verses, the RGVV explains that those fallen into the views concerning (what is subject to) destruction are the ordinary beings, those with perverted desires are the Sravakas and Pratyeka Buddhas, and those whose minds wander from the emptiness (*stong pa nyid las sems gyengs pa rnams*) are the Bodhisattvas who have newly entered the Mahayana vehicle and have the tendency to see emptiness as something less than the Tathagatagarbha. The RGVV explains that there are two basic kinds of mistake concerning the Dharmata. One is to see the Dharmata (or emptiness) as the destruction of something with the idea that nirvana is the cessation of something, so that meditation on emptiness is for bringing about that destruction. The other is to think that emptiness is something other than form, sound, smell, taste, feeling, and thoughts, and so on, but which is, nevertheless, something (*dngos po*) that should be used as a support or object (*dmigs pa*) of meditation.

The SMS [545.2] says that Sravakas and so on merely see Reality in the same way that the light of the sun is seen by a babe from the house of its birth, that is, indirectly, and implies Bodhisattvas see it directly. On the other hand, the RGV [1.153] uses the same example to show how even Bodhisattvas are like babes in the house of their birth and only Buddhas see Reality directly. As has already been mentioned, the SMS shows how the

Bodhisattva vehicle is superior to the Sravaka and Pratyeka Buddha vehicles and emphasizes that Tathagatagarbha is the base, that the path is to see it properly, and the fruit is when it is seen in its completeness. The RGV teaches the same, but for the benefit of Bodhisattvas who, while accepting Prajnaparamita, want to reject Tathagatagarbha. The direct seeing (*yang dag mthong ba*) of the Bodhisattvas in the SMS [547.1] is like experiencing the base Jnana. The SMS emphasizes it is the same Jnana as the Buddha Jnana, and the RGV uses the same example to emphasize that it is not as pure, that is, free from veils, as when Buddhahood—the fruit—is reached.

Thus, the RGV [1.153] explains that there is nothing to clear away or get rid of (the first mistake mentioned), and nothing to set up as an object of meditation (the second mistake mentioned).

The RGVV explains verse 1.154 as meaning that there is no sign or mark (*nimitta, rgyu mtshan*) of the klesa that must be removed, and no sign or mark of something pure that must be set up or established. It explains that this is because the klesa do not exist at all and that the purity of Mind is the Nature (Dharmata) of inseparable Dharmas. "Signless" means that something cannot be grasped by the conceptual mind. Klesa cannot be grasped because they do not exist. The Inseparable Qualities cannot be grasped because they cannot, by definition, be the object of the conceptual mind.

The RGVV then quotes the SMS to support Verse 1.155:

Therefore, the Tathagatagarbha is empty of all the klesa sheaths that are separable and removable. It is not empty of the inseparable and irremovable inconceivable Buddha Dharmas beyond the sands of the Ganges.

Again the words of this quotation differ from the SMS.

The RGVV then gives an important definition of the meaning of emptiness discussed already in this present work:

Something in which something else is absent is empty of that. If one proceeds then to look properly, what remains is ever present and known perfectly.

The RGVV explains that these slokas, since they are free of the two positions, which are to deny reality to what is true, and to assign reality to what is false, teach the nature (*mtshan nyid*) of the non-mistaken Emptiness.

Concerning this, whoever does not rest the Mind evenly and one pointedly without letting his/her mind wander off from this manner of the emptiness into mental proliferations (prapanca) is said to be someone whose mind has wandered from the Emptiness. Concerning this, without the Jnana of the Absolute Emptiness it is not possible to realize or to think of (*'du bya*) the non-conceptual pure Dhatu.

The SMS is quoted to illustrate this point:

> The Tathagatagarbha's Jnana is the Tathagata's Emptiness Jnana. Therefore, the Tathagatagarbha is not seen or realized beforehand by Sravakas and Pratyeka Buddhas.

Comments. Here it is clearly stated that Sravakas and Pratyeka Buddhas do not realize the same Emptiness as the Buddhas. It should also be noted that the SMS does not say that Bodhisattvas do not realize the Jnana of the Tathagata, but that their problem is the wandering of their minds from the Emptiness into subtle conceptual activity. In other words their problem is that, although they have the realization, they cannot maintain a steady awareness of it. The Sravakas and Pratyeka Buddhas on the other hand have never even had it.

Paraphrase. RGVV [1.155] continues:

> As for the question of how the Tathagatagarbha is the Dharmakaya *garbha*, it is as follows: it is said to not be the sphere of experience of those who have fallen into the accumulation of views concerning [what is subject to] destruction. The Dharmadhatu is the remedy for all views. How is the Dharmakaya the *garbha* of the supra-mundane? It is said that it is not the sphere of experience of those who delight in error. The supra-mundane Dharmakaya is taught to be the remedy for the mundane dharmas that are impermanent etc. How is the Dharmakaya the perfectly pure Dharma *garbha*? It is said that it is not the sphere of experience of those whose minds have wandered from the Emptiness. Those who have distinguished the supra-mundane Dharmakaya of inseparable Dharmas by virtue of their purity are of the Nature empty of accidental stains. Therefore, by the unique means of realizing the Dharmadhatu's inseparable Jnana, the Bodhisattvas on the ten levels who see the natural purity of the supra-mundane Dharmakaya see the Tathagatagarbha just a little. It is held that the perfect and precise Jnana sees all.

Comments. Although the frequent use of "*garbha*" in this context seems to introduce a slight complication, the gist of the paragraph is that the Dharmakaya is both the remedy for the mundane dharmas and the essence (*garbha*) of the supra-mundane Dharmas. There is only one way of realizing it and this is possessed by the Bodhisattvas on the ten levels. It is not the sphere of Sravakas and Pratyekas and even by the Bodhisattvas it is not known completely. Only Buddhas know it completely. Thus, the Tathagatagarbha is possessed by all beings and it is what remedies all conceptual views, but it is not the "sphere" of all beings.

The term "sphere" (*spyod yul*) occurs frequently in Buddhist literature. It is the field or sphere of experience of a being in the sense that it is where he exists and it is what he experiences and enjoys. The term *yul* is sometimes used like *spyod yul,* but *yul* is more typically used in the sense of an object on which one can focus or even grasp (see Kongtrul's RGV commentary [13b], *lta ba'i yul*).

Compare this with Tsongkapa's view that emptiness as the object (*yul*) of the meditation of the Sravakas, Pratyeka Buddhas, Bodhisattvas, and fully Enlightened Buddhas is the same; it is the mode of cognition that differs and makes the realization of the Buddha special.[29] Shentongpas do not argue that the Buddha's realization is not special, but from their point of view, there is a very real sense in which the Bodhisattva experiences the same way of knowing, and is able to use this as the basis for his practice in a way that Sravakas and Pratyeka Buddhas cannot.

The Purpose of the Instruction [RGV 1.156–167]

Paraphrase. These verses explain why it is necessary to teach this doctrine of Tathagatagarbha to ordinary beings when, as the RGVV points out, it is quite clear that not even Bodhisattvas at the highest level realize it fully, let alone Sravakas and Pratyeka Buddhas.

Verse 1.156 raises the question by asking why, after having been taught in various places in the scriptures that all knowable things (*shes bya*) are empty like clouds, dreams, and magical illusions, does the Buddha teach here that all beings have the Buddha *garbha.* RGV [2.58–59] refers to the Prajnaparamita doctrine of the *Saddharmapundarikasutra* and this is clearly the doctrine referred to in RGV [1.156] that explains that it is taught that klesa are like clouds, karma like experiencing dreams, and the skandhas like a magical illusion.

Comments. Clouds are given as an example of klesa because they appear and disappear for no apparent reason and, although they seem to mark or stain the sky, when one examines them closely—as when one walks in them or tries to grasp them in the hand—there is nothing there. Khenpo Tsultrim explains that magical illusion here means the kind of illusion created by a magical spell that creates a whole world in which one lives, maybe for years. On being released from the spell, one finds oneself back in one's original world with, sometimes, only a few moments having elapsed. It is the kind of magical illusion that is encountered in fairy stories worldwide.

Paraphrase. The RGV [1.157–167] explains that the supreme thread (*tantra*) or Element (dhatu) is taught in order to overcome five faults that develop if beings do not realize they have the Buddha Nature. The five faults are:

1. *Faintheartedness.* Some beings feel so inadequate that they do not presume to aspire to supreme Buddhahood. Thus, they do not take the Bodhisattva vow to bring all beings to Enlightenment, which is essential for developing Bodhicitta. The remedy for this kind of faintheartedness is for them to know that they and all beings belong to the Buddha lineage. This knowledge should give them confidence, and encourage them to try to attain Buddhahood.

2. *Looking down on others.* Some beings suffer the opposite fault. They bravely and confidently take the Bodhisattva vow and then feel that since they now belong to the Buddha lineage, they are naturally superior to those who do not. Knowing that all beings naturally belong to the Buddha lineage undermines this kind of arrogance.

3. *Attachment to what is not real.* Those who do not know that the true nature of beings is Tathagatagarbha take their faults and imperfections to be their true nature. In this way, they fall into the position of setting up the unreal as real.

4. *Denial of what is real.* By being attached to this unreality, they overlook completely the reality that beings have Buddhajnana. They deny that beings have the perfect and unspoiled Qualities of the Buddha and thus fall into the position of denying reality to what is real.

5. *Not loving others as oneself.* Without the knowledge that all beings have Tathagatagarbha (Buddhajnana) as their essence, it seems that self and others are separate and distinct. With such a view point it is impossible to feel equally strongly for oneself and others. On the other hand, when one understands the doctrine of Tathagatagarbha, one knows that self and others partake of the same undifferentiable Reality so that one naturally identifies with others and, from feeling their happiness and suffering as one's own, love and compassion naturally arise.

The teaching of Tathagatagarbha can, thus, be seen to provide five remedies for the five faults. The five remedies are confidence, respect for others, prajna (in the sense of not taking the unreal to be real), Jnana (in the sense of knowing the Real to be real), and Great Compassion. With these five virtues one is able quickly to attain Buddhahood.

This ends the first section of the RGV on the Tathagatagarbha. This first section comprises over half of the RGV and almost two thirds of the RGVV. The remaining sections of the text will be summarized much more briefly because most of the important doctrines have already been touched on in this first section.

10.5 Vajra Base 5: Enlightenment

The Ten Sections

This section begins with two lists of headings, one with ten [RGV 2.1] and one with eight items [RGVV 2.1:43b, RGV 2.2] and these two lists correspond. Takasaki [*Study* 401] points out that both these lists and the lists of topics for the other chapters are exactly equivalent to lists in other texts, suggesting a standard format into which material was traditionally organized. The headings are as follows:

1. Purity	1. Essence (i.e. the essence of transformation, the purified Tathagatagarbha)
2. Attainment	2. Cause (the cause of transformation, supra-mundane conceptionless Jnana and the after-attainment Jnana)
3. Freedom	3. Fruit (freedom from klesa and knowledge veils)
4. Own Welfare	4. Action (accomplishing own welfare and others' welfare)
5. Others' Welfare	5. Union (having the base of own welfare and others' welfare)
6. Profound (Dharmakaya)	6. Occurrence (*'jug, vrtti*—as the three kayas)
7. Vast (Samboghakaya)	
8. Magnanimous (*Mahatma*—Nirmanakaya)	
9. Duration	7. Permanence
10. Exact Nature	8. Inconceivability

The first six of the second list are identical to the list in the first chapter. RGVV [2.1: 43b] gives the more detailed account of all eight ("Essence" up to "Inconceivability")

1. Essence and 2. Cause (Purity and Attainment) [RGV 2.3–2.7]

RGV [2.3] again describes the Clear Light Nature as like the sun and space. The adventitious stains are like clouds, which are removed by the two kinds of jnana—non-conceptual (*mi rtog*) and discriminating (*rnam 'byed*).

The image of the sun and sky indicates that at the moment of Enlightenment two things occur: the full realization emerges, and all veils fall away. This double action is the result of two kinds of jnana—non-conceptual and discriminating.

In this context [RGVV 2.1: 43b 6] the two kinds of jnana are linked to the two kinds of veil—the klesa veil, and the knowledge veil. Therefore, one deduces that they correspond to the two kinds of knowledge—precise-knowledge and knowledge of the full extent [RGVV 1.17]. RGVV [2.1–7] explains the two kinds of jnana as the supra-mundane, non-conceptual jnana (*akalpana* [2.3] or *avikalpa* [2.7], *mi rtog*) and the mundane discriminating jnana (*pravicaya, rnam 'byed*) attained thereafter (*tatprsthalabdha, rjes thob*) [2.3].

Comments. It is taught that the supreme siddhi (accomplishment) of Buddhahood is accompanied by the mundane siddhis by means of which one can help sentient beings. Thus, mundane *jnana* here seems to correspond to the power to help beings and is, therefore, associated with compassion, as is knowledge of the full extent. Except for this connection the use of ''mundane jnana'' here is rather curious.

Paraphrase. The RGVV interprets the discriminating jnana—the jnana attained afterwards [RGV 2.7]—as the knowledge associated with seeing Tathagatagarbha in all beings, thus linking it with spontaneous compassionate Activity—in the manner suggested for ''mundane jnana'' above. In general, ''discriminating wisdom'' in this context refers to the Buddha's ability to know phenomena—as opposed to merely knowing the empty essence of all things.

Comments. Attained-afterwards Jnana is not mentioned at all in the first part of the RGV; it is for this reason one feels it is not introducing any new doctrine at this point. Bodhisattvas on the path to Buddhahood develop non-conceptual jnana in their sessions of meditative equipoise and attained-afterwards jnana in between sessions. The term ''attained-afterwards'' usually refers to between-session practices in which the meditator sees the world as unreal like an illusion as he acts in the world for the benefit of others.[30]

It is thought by many Mahayana schools that during the meditation session it is necessary for the meditator to lose his power to discriminate the dharmas, and simply to rest in the equalness of their empty essence. It is in the after-session period that he again can discriminate the dharmas, but this is thought necessarily to involve him in subtle conceptual discrimination. By means of his activity in the between-session period he is able to accumulate the merit he needs to progress towards Enlightenment. It is only the Buddha that can go beyond this distinction between meditative and post-meditative jnana.

The Mahamudra and Dzogchen traditions, however, do not make this radical distinction between meditative and post-meditative jnana. They neither consider it necessary to block off the impressions of the senses in the meditative equipoise, nor do they consider that acting in the world necessarily involves conceptualization. According to them, one constantly has the opportunity to have flashes of the non-conceptual state, even if one is not actually able to maintain constant awareness of it. In other words, in Shentong terms, it makes sense to equate the attained-afterwards jnana in RGV [2.7] with the knowledge of the full extent that sees Tathagatagarbha in all beings, rather than with the somewhat conceptual jnana of the Bodhisattva described above.

Just as, in Shentong terms, the two kinds of knowledge are actually two aspects of the same Buddhajnana, the same is true for the two kinds of jnana here.[†]

Paraphrase. Non-conceptual jnana removes klesa veils so the Mind's Clear Light Nature is revealed like the sun [RGV 2.4, 8, 10]. The attained-afterwards discriminating jnana removes the knowledge veils [RGV 2.11] so that the Clear Light Nature is seen in all beings like the sun is seen to shine everywhere throughout the clear sky [RGV 2.4].

Comment. In Shentong terms, this is not saying that each kind of knowledge removes a different kind of veil, but that both kinds of knowledge are the results of the removal of both kinds of veil.[31]

It is significant that when RGV [2.4] says the Buddha's Enlightenment is divisible into the inseparable and the pure Dharmas, it is the inseparable existent aspect of the realization that is mentioned first (the sun). Based on this realization the true nature of all the dharmas is realized (the clear sky). Thus, the Buddhajnana with its Inseparable Qualities is seen first and from this comes the realization of the empty nature of the dharmas [as in RGV 1.13ff]. In Rangtong terms, the empty nature of the dharmas is seen first and from this arise the inseparable qualities of Buddhajnana.

[†]N.B. The two kinds of jnana are referred to in RGVV [2.1: 43b.6, 2.17: 44b.6] and RGV [2.3, 2.7, 2.10, 2.11, 2.21].

The Shentong Buddhajnana is realized as the last veils go; it is only then that the true "pure" nature of the dharmas is seen. However, the RGV and RGVV do not go so far as to say— as Shentongpas do—that the dharmas are then seen to be expressions of Buddhajnana. RGV [2.4] says only:

> The Buddha is divided into the inseparable and the pure dharmas. They are of the nature of jnana and relinquishment. Like the sun and the sky.

Compare this with SMS [535 ca 268.3]:

> *bcom ldan 'das nyon mongs pa dang nye ba'i nyon mongs pa de dag thams cad spang shing sangs rgyas kyi chos bsam gyis mi khyab pa gang g'a'i klung gi bye ma las 'das pa snyed brnyes pa. de bzhin gshegs pa rnams kyi chos thams cad la sgrib pa ma mchis pa'i mngon par mkhyen pa brnyes te thams cad mkhyen pa dang. thams cad gzigs pa dang. skyon thams cad spangs pa dang. yon tan thams cad dang ldan pa dang. chos kyi rgyal po . . .*
>
> Bhagavan, giving up all the klesa and *upaklesa* and finding the Buddha's unimaginable Dharmas, the extent of the sands of the River Ganges, he finds the knowledge of all the Tathagata's Dharmas, unveiled and evident, this is Omniscience and All-seeing, and the relinquishment of all faults, the having of all Qualities, the Dharma King . . .

Since in Shentong terms there is no real difference between non-conceptual Jnana and the discriminating Jnana, Mikyo Dorje in the *gZhan stong sgron me* [p. 15] says:

> *de na de bzhin gshegs pas mi slob pa mngon du pyas pa de'i spang rtogs kyi yon tan thams cad kyang de bzhin gshegs pa'i snying po dang dbye ba med do.*
>
> Therefore, all the Tathagata's relinquishment and realization Qualities from the actualization of Non-learning are inseparable from the Tathagatagarbha.

"Non-learning" refers to the stage of Buddhahood. In the same way that the sun, when completely freed from veils pervades the whole of space with its light, the realization of the Inseparable Qualities (precise knowledge) is simultaneous with the removal of all veils from everywhere. Thus, everything is seen to be pervaded by the Buddhajnana with its Inseparable Qualities (knowledge of the full extent).

Paraphrase. RGVV [2.7] explains that the fruit is two-fold purity. "Two-fold purity" means:

1. The natural or innate purity (*prakrtivisuddhi*) which means the Clear Light Nature of Mind in essence is always free or separate from the adventitious stains. Nevertheless, it is not doubly pure as long as it is not freed from association with them.

2. The purity of stainlessness (*vaimalyavisuddhi*), which means having undergone the process of being freed or separated, like water and so on, freed or separated from sediment and so on, because the Mind's Clear Light Nature is separated from all the adventitious stains.

3. Fruit (Freedom) [RGV 2.8–17]

RGV [2.8] introduces two new images. The conceptionless jnana is described by three examples that illustrate its three inseparable qualities of samadhi, compassion, and wisdom (jnana) respectively. By means of His samadhi, compassion, and wisdom, the Buddha acts spontaneously for others.

Comments. In Shentong terms, samadhi, compassion, and wisdom are all the functioning of the inseparable Buddha Qualities as Buddha Activity on the one side, and the innate nature of beings on the other. Thus, the Buddha Nature and emerging samadhi, compassion, and wisdom of beings and the spontaneous Activity of the Enlightened Buddhas are one inseparable Reality.

Paraphrase. The RGV explains that beings counter attachment by meditation, counter hatred by developing compassion and counter ignorance by developing understanding, inspired by the spontaneous Activity of the non-conceptual Buddhajnana. The example is given of a lotus pond whose pure water makes the lotuses bloom. The pure water is like the samadhi of non-conceptual Jnana and the opening lotuses are like the disciples giving up their attachment and desire.

Comments. Kongtrul expands the meaning a little [RGV commentary 100.4], explaining that the result of removing the impurities from one's own Mind (Own-Welfare) moistens beings (Others' Welfare).

Paraphrase. The second example is that of the moon being released from Rahula after an eclipse. In Indian mythology, an eclipse of the moon is caused by the planet Rahula—seen as a demon—swallowing the moon. It is the spontaneous compassion of the non-conceptual jnana that releases beings from the grip of hatred, like the moon escaping from the jaws of Rahula.

The third example is once more that of the sun emerging from behind clouds. The sun is like the spontaneous wisdom of the non-conceptual jnana, which is stainless, has qualities, and is luminous. It lights up the ignorance of beings like the sun emerging from behind the clouds.

The nine examples that illustrated the Tathagatagarbha inside its sheath of klesa in chapter 1 are referred to again in chapter 2 [RGV 2.15–17].
Comments. From the Shentong point of view, the fact that the RGV says the nine examples are specifically said to illustrate the effect of the attained-afterwards jnana does not need to imply that they are not the effect of the non-conceptual jnana as Rangtongpas might think it does.
Paraphrase. In RGV [2.9] the nine examples are given again. The Buddha in the bad lotus illustrates the teaching Dharmakaya; the honey the single taste of the profound Dharmakaya; the grains the manifold aspects of the vast teaching Dharmakaya; the gold the pure (unadulterated) nature and quality of the Tathata; the treasure the naturally-present gotra removing poverty; the tree the gotra producing fruit; the Buddha image the precious Dharmakaya; the Cakravartin the Sambhogakaya, and the golden image the Nirmanakaya.
Comments. It should be borne in mind that as in chapter 1 of the RGV, these images are very much associated with the idea of Buddha Activity emerging from beings, so in some ways this section is simply reminding us of what has been said already. In my opinion, from the Shentong point of view, the first three examples (the lotus pond, Rahula, and the sun) illustrate the Vajra Base of Qualities very well and the nine examples illustrate the Vajra Base of Activity, although of course both Vajra Bases concern the one inseparable Reality.

4. Action and 5. Union (Own Welfare and Others' Welfare) [RGV 2.18–37]

Paraphrase. Action (Own Welfare) [RGV 2.21]. In RGV chapter 1 "Action" referred to the action of the Tathagatagarbha as the naturally-present and the expanding gotra, which inspires beings to give up suffering and aspire to nirvana. In RGV chapter 2 "Action" refers to the action of the two kinds of jnana at the moment of Enlightenment. The non-discriminating jnana removes the veils and the ignorance tendencies so that the Buddha realizes Nirvana or freedom from suffering, which is his Own Welfare. This is referred to here as the "Liberation Kaya." The effect of this is that he realizes the extent of the true Nature of all things (knowledge of the full extent), which is referred to in this section as the "purification of the Dharmakaya." This is associated with the welfare of others because it is this knowledge that allows the Buddha to act spontaneously for the benefit of others.
Union (Others' Welfare) [RGV 2.29]. The topic "Union" emphasizes the "base," which is the space-like Absolute Nature of Buddha and RGVV [2.28] quotes from the *Vajracchedikasutra* [*Study* 322fn.69] that if the Bud-

dha could be recognized by the thirty two marks of a superman, then even the Cakravartin would be a Tathagata.

RGV [2.18, 2.22–37] describes the Dharmakaya as non-defiled, all-pervading, and imperishable. It is imperishable because it is non-compounded, which means it is everlasting (primordially existent), peace, permanent, and non-transferring. It is also a base (*gnas*) though at the same time being causeless (*rgyu min*). RGV [2.26] explains "base" here as the base or the source for all good qualities (literally white dharmas). In Kongtrul's commentary [RGV 105] he explains that this is why it is the base (*gnas*) for the perfect and complete Welfare of Others. The realization comprising relinquishment and the manifestation of Jnana is the source or base for the special or white qualities to arise in the minds of beings according to their karmic capacity. The question is how can something that is beyond the divisions of cause and effect be a base or a source for anything?

RGV [2.18] hints at an answer to this question. Enlightenment is like space, which, although it rests on nothing and is non-compounded, functions as a base and a cause for everything else in the universe.

Comments. Kongtrul [RGV commentary 105] explains how space gives the opportunity (*go 'byed pa'i sgo nas*) for the eye faculty to see form, the ear to hear sounds, and so on for all the senses. Khenpo Tsultrim explains that without space between the eye faculty and its object nothing is seen, and the same is true for all the senses—though what this means in terms of the mind faculty and its object has to be carefully considered.

Paraphrase. RGV [2.18–21] deals with this very important doctrine as follows:

> The non-defiled, all-pervading, imperishable *Dharmin* is everlasting, peaceful, permanent and non-transferring. The Tathagata, like space, is the cause of the Pure Ones (*dag pa*)[††] experiencing the objects of the six sense faculties. He is the cause of the samadhi faculties (*dbang 'byor*) seeing form, hearing the pure, good speech, imbibing the pure fragrance of the Tathagata's discipline and savouring the great Arya Dharma. He is the cause of experiencing the bliss sensation of samadhi and the realization of the profound manner of one's own essence. Yet, when one makes a minute examination, that creator of the Absolute Bliss is signless like space.

[††]N.B. The Rumtek RGV root text has *dam pa* and *'byung med* instead of *dag pa* and *dbang 'byor* in the above quotation. This does not change the meaning.

Comments. In terms of how Buddhajnana functions, we saw in RGV chapter 1 that it causes beings to become aware of the unsatisfactory nature of samsara and aspire for nirvana, thus functioning as the expanding gotra.

Now we see that, from the point of view of the Pure Bodhisattvas, it functions like space, allowing the objects of the refined senses resulting from samadhi to appear and inspire them.

Kongtrul [RGV commentary 105] explains that this is what causes the high level Bodhisattvas to give rise to the non-defiled Qualities of the form-kayas through seeing the apparent form-kayas, and all the non-defiled Qualities of the Ten Powers and so forth from seeing the Ultimate Dharmakaya. However, he does not give any explanation of how this occurs.

Thinking about it, one could say that, from the Shentong point of view, because it exists as Absolute Form, it is visible to Bodhisattvas who have realized Emptiness and glimpse Absolute Form directly. Although the RGV does not explicitly say that the Pure Bodhisattvas are experiencing the Sambhogakaya, this seems to be the case. The RGV explains that it manifests to the Bodhisattvas as form resulting from samadhi. They are able to receive teaching from it—pure speech (*gtam bzang gtsang ma mnyan*), and appreciate its subtle mental discipline—fragrance (*dri gtsang snom*). They can taste or experience the Dharma (*chos ro myong*) that it teaches and gain experience of the feeling of bliss (*reg bde nyam myong*) in samadhi. Above all, they are able to realize this Nature in themselves. In Shentong terms, the experiences of the refined faculties of the Arya Bodhisattvas are, in fact, the spontaneous Activity of the Buddha's Enlightenment.

Paraphrase. RGV [2.28] refers to the two kayas as the cause for the arising of the non-defiled Qualities in the faculties of the Bodhisattvas who are free from veils. However, this does not appear to be referring particularly to the two kinds of form-kayas (Sambhogakaya and Nirmanakaya), but to the Liberation and Dharmakaya mentioned at the beginning of this section.

The topic "Union," like "Action" covers both Own Welfare and Others' Welfare. Verses 2.29–2.37 on "Union" are not much more than a reiteration of all the doctrines raised in the first chapter about the inconceivable qualities of the completely pure level of perfect Buddhahood. The example from the SMS of the child in the house of his birth is repeated and the permanence that is a result of having overcome the ground of the ignorance tendency patterns is again referred to in some detail.

6. Occurrence (Profound, Vast, and Magnanimous (*Mahatma*)) [RGV 2.38–2.61]

The topic "Profound" [RGV 2.38–39] deals with the nature of the Dharmakaya in much the same terms as elsewhere in the text. This is elaborated on again in RGV [2.43–48]. No new doctrine is introduced at this point.

The topics "Vast" and "Magnanimous" deal with the Sambhogakaya and the Nirmanakaya respectively. Verses 2.40–41 are of interest in this connection:

> The energetic activity (*brtson pas mdzad*) of the kaya with the light rays of various True Dharma (teachings) is like the wish-fulfilling king of jewels, because it accomplishes the liberation of beings. Although [manifesting as] various things (*dngos*), these are not its Nature.
> The form [kayas] which cause the entering of the path that calms the world, cause the maturing and the giving of prophecy, ever dwell in this as the form realm rests in space.

Here the RGV is talking about the relationship between the Vajra Base of Activity, which is the Buddhajnana thought of as Absolute Buddha Activity, and the form-kayas. Although their essence is beyond all conditionality, the form-kayas, as they appear to beings, arise dependent on causes and conditions. Their essence is like space, for it supports the form-kayas as space supports the various worlds that arise and perish in space. "The kaya with the light rays of the various True Dharmas (i.e. Teachings)" seems to be a general reference to the teaching Dharmakaya that was referred to in RGV 1.145.

RGV [verses 2.49–52] describes the Sambhogakaya. In the verse above, the form-kayas are described as the cause for ordinary beings to enter the path of liberation, for Sravakas and Pratyekas to be matured by entering the Mahayana, and for Bodhisattvas to be prophesied as Buddhas on reaching the pure levels. The verse is very terse but this is a well-known Mahayana categorization.

Comments. The idea is that an ordinary being will see the Buddha as an ordinary man and be inspired to follow His example and enter the Hinayana. Aryas, who are still on the impure levels, will see Him as a complete and perfect Buddha; they will be inspired to follow His example by entering the Mahayana. The Bodhisattvas of the three pure levels will see Him as a Sambhogakaya form; they will receive from Him the prophecy of when they will become Buddhas themselves. Thus, the Buddha, who is at all times and everywhere the same, appears variously to the eyes of the beings who are to be trained.

Paraphrase. This point is illustrated in verse 2.51:

> Just as the various colors appear even though they are not of the nature of that jewel, so by the various conditions associated with beings, the All-Pervading One appears as what He is not.

The image behind this example is that of a multicolored cloth on which
stands a crystal. The colors on the cloth are reflected by the crystal; it
sends different colored lights out all around. In reality, it is clear and col-
orless by nature although it has the power to act in this way.
Comments. Rangtongpas might interpret this verse as meaning that the
form-kayas are essentially conditioned and only relatively real. Shentongpas on the other hand would be very careful to distinguish the Absolute
Form-Kayas and the apparent form-kayas that appear to beings.

Dolpopa [RC 56] discusses the differences between the Absolute Dharmakaya signs and marks and the apparent form-kayas signs and marks; the
former are known only through the Guru's instruction. He adds:

> Furthermore, it is taught that the Tathagatagarbha Dharmadhatu
> has by nature completeness with the signs and marks, these are the
> Qualities of the Absolute Dharmakaya and not of the form-kayas.

and

> Therefore, in apparent reality there are the qualities of apparent
> phenomena and likewise in Ultimate Reality there are the Qualities
> of the Absolute.

He then explains that, since these are inseparable from Absolute Reality,
they are called "Inseparable (*mi 'bral*) Qualities as vast in number as the
sands of the Ganges" [RC 399.7]. RC [401.4] quotes the RGV on the two
kayas and the sixty-four qualities; then it introduces an interesting discussion concerning the freedom fruit, which is the Dharmakaya, changeless,
Parinispanna, and the Tathatakaya. The freedom Qualities of the powers
and so forth are complete; it is taught that in the developed fruit (*bskyed
'bras*) Form-Kayas there is the non-mistaken Parinispanna, pure Jnana, and
the developed Qualities (*bskyed pa'i yon tan*) of the signs (*mtshan*) and so
forth. He explains that some say the Dharmakaya is also the apparent developed fruit and some say the form-kayas are also the Absolute freedom
fruit—one wonders who he is referring to here. On page 402, he says that
some say the Dharmakaya is not primordially in beings. He calls all this a
mistake and quotes from the *Mahayanasutralamkaya* and *Suvarnaprabhasottamasutra* and so on that there is one Absolute Kaya and two apparent
kayas. He also mentions scriptural authority for saying there are four kayas,
but this he says is merely because sometimes the Absolute Kaya is divided
into the *Svabhavikakaya* and Dharmakaya and sometimes not. That is all, it
does not matter (*skyon med*).

Dolpopa explains that the two apparent form-kayas and the one Absolute Kaya as one or two and so on are all common to Mahayana (*theg pa
chen po la thun mong*).

The uncommon Mantra tradition, however, is the Vajrakaya or Mantrakaya. This is the Tathata, Self, the Pure Self, Vajradhara, or Vajrasattva, or the single sameness of knower and known Kaya (*cig nyid shes dang shes bya gcig pa'i sku*) that is the union of Emptiness and Compassion; this can be divided into two kayas, such as wisdom and means or into three kayas of body, speech, and mind or the three Jewels, and so on, or into four kayas of the four Vajras, or the five kayas of the five wisdoms and so on thus making one, two, three, four, or five naturally-present gotras.

He then quotes the Tantras to show that even though in this way there can be a hundred or thousands of naturally-present gotras in fact they are all of the same Nature (*rang bzhin gcig*). However many are numbered, one must remember they are all inseparable in their base and fruit (*gzhi 'bras dbyer med*). On page 404.7 Dolpopa gives a description of the Absolute and apparent form-kayas and on page 405 he discusses how the Absolute Sambhogakaya, so famous in Mantrayana, is the Dharmata and Tathata. It is the inseparable Tathagatagarbhakaya. The Buddha's Vajrakaya has no perceiver and perceived (literally object and object-haver, *yul* and *yul can*). The three Absolute Kayas are inseparable from the Parinispanna Buddha; they are not to be confused with the samvrti form-kayas.

On page 439 he quotes the *Suvarnaprabhasottamasutra* where the three vijnana are purified and become Nirmanakayas. *Manas* is purified to become Sambhogakaya and the *alaya* is purified to become Dharmakaya. This kind of doctrine is referring to the Absolute Form-Kayas, not the apparent ones. He gives a number of similar examples.

Thus, for Shentongpas the crystal would be the Absolute Form-Kayas and the colors the apparent form-kayas. (See Appendix 3, "Further Details on the Three Svabhava and the Three Kinds of Emptiness as Found in the SNS".)

Incidentally, Geshe Wangchen explains the inseparable qualities of the Tathagatagarbha as the ability had by a perfectly clean and polished crystal to reflect different colors. He says that, although the Tathata or emptiness has no self-nature in the sense of an ultimately real nature that can be understood conceptually, this emptiness is like a crystal with a power (*nus pa*) to manifest qualities when clean. For him, the whole difference between Rangtong and Shentong is that Rangtongpas make the point that the qualities are not complete from the beginning because until the crystal is clean and polished it cannot reflect colors; whereas Shentongpas make the point that the crystal's nature does not change and so its qualities must have been there in their completeness from the beginning. If this were, indeed, the sole difference between Shentong and Rangtong there would be no need for controversy. Both sides would be accepting that the form-kayas seen by beings were samvrti and both would be accepting that the power of the crystal was there from the beginning.

However, I am doubtful that this is Gyaltsab's view. In the *Dartik*, it seems the power (*nus pa*) that gives rise to the qualities is an aspect of mind other than its emptiness:

> *sems kyi steng na yod pa'i 'jig rten las 'das pa'i chos skye rung ba'i nus pa.*
> A power in the mind capable of giving rise to supra-mundane dharmas.

Paraphrase. RGV [2.49–52] describes the qualities of knowledge, love, and power of the Sambhogakaya. Then it describes [2.53–59] the acts of the Nirmanakaya. The Nirmanakaya looks on the world and, without moving from the Dharmakaya, takes birth in various forms, which are emanations by nature. The perfect Nirmanakaya performs the twelve acts as the Buddha Sakyamuni did. These are to leave the paradise of Tusita (*dGa' ldan*), take birth from His mother's womb, be educated in the arts and sciences of His day, enjoy His wife and courtly life, renounce the world, undergo austerities, sit under the Bodhi tree, overcome evil, become Enlightened, teach Dharma, and pass into *Parinirvana*. Thus, as long as samsara lasts, the Nirmanakaya appears again and again in the impure worlds.

Comments. Impure worlds are worlds such as our own in contrast to pure worlds such as that of Sukhavati (Dewachen) in which the Sambhogakaya form of the Buddha appears. The acts of the Nirmanakaya take place dependent on causes and conditions and are apparent phenomena. In the RGV [2.62] the "permanence" of the apparent nirmanakaya refers simply to its endless continuity, which in Shentong terms, is not true permanence at all. The true permanence of the Nirmanakayas is the inseparable Qualities that are seen by beings as the apparent Nirmanakayas but in essence never move from the Dharmakaya (see RGV 4, on Activity).

Paraphrase. RGV [2.57–59] refers to the stages of the Buddha's teaching. First He teaches impermanence, suffering, non-self, and nirvana (cessation), causing beings to renounce the world and enter nirvana. He then teaches the *White Lotus Sutra* (*Saddharmapundarika*), and so forth, causing the renunciation of one-sided nirvana in those who, having entered the one-sided nirvana of the Sravakas and Pratyeka Buddhas, think it the true Nirvana. Having given up their attachment to it, they enter the Mahayana path, which unites wisdom and compassion. This is called the "ripening" or "maturing" process. Finally, they are given the prophecy on the three pure levels of a Bodhisattva.

Comments. On the pure Bodhisattva levels, the Bodhisattva is given a specific prophecy about when and where he will become Buddha. Although there is no explicit link between the giving of the prophecy and the third cycle, Khenpo Tsultrim considers the teaching that beings are primordially Buddha as a prophecy that they will definitely attain Buddhahood.[32] In both cases the inevitability of Buddha Enlightenment is expressed; the general effect of the teaching is to encourage the disciple and give him the confidence that goes with relaxation of mind.

Paraphrase. RGV [2.61] reiterates the doctrine that the two form-kayas are based on the Dharmakaya, just as forms are based on space. This emphasizes again that the apparent form-kayas as they appear to beings are dependent on causes and conditions and arise and perish as worlds arise and perish in space.

7. Permanence (Duration) [RGV 2.62–68]

RGV [2.62] sums up this topic. This verse is one of the verses Takasaki considers to be original. It reads as follows:

> Because the Lord of the World is of unlimited cause, because beings are endless (*zad med*), because of His having complete and perfect love, miracles and knowledge, and because He is Master of the Dharma and defeater of the demon death, and because He is essenceless, He is permanent.

The following three verses explain the meaning of this. The "unlimited cause" is the deeds of the Bodhisattva on His path to Enlightenment, the giving up of His body and possessions innumerable times, and so on for the sake of the Dharma, which earns Him inexhaustible merit. Beings being "endless" means the Bodhisattva, having made the promise to save all beings, does not cease in His activity until all beings are saved. Since they are endless, so is He. "Complete and perfect love and miracles" means He is able to behave as if dwelling in the world in order to help beings. "Complete and perfect knowledge" means He is free from perceiving samsara and nirvana as a duality. "Master of the Dharma" means He is ever abiding in blissful samadhi, even when appearing to act in the world. "Defeater of the demon of death" means that He has attained the abode of peace free from death. "Essenceless" is the primordial peace of being noncompounded by nature.

The first seven of these ten points are explained [RGV 2.68] as reasons for the form-kayas being permanent and the last three for the Dharmakaya being permanent. Thus, we have "permanence" used in two different senses. The first seven points explain how the activity of the Buddha's form-kayas is continuous and endless in the way it appears to beings in the world. The last three points explain how the Buddha's Dharmakaya is changeless because it is non-compounded, conceptionless, and spontaneous. *Comments.* In this section, the form-kayas are clearly the apparent kayas that appear to beings; there is no hint of the doctrine that they are Absolute Form in essence. Like form in space, they are somewhat incidental to the Dharmakaya though based on it and unable to manifest without it.

Generally in RGV chapter 2 there is very little to suggest that the Nirmanakaya is in essence Buddhajnana, although RGV chapter 4 is more explicit. This reflects the overall lack of clarity in the RGV concerning the exact relationship between Buddhajnana and the world as it appears to beings. Since, in Shentong terms, the world that beings experience is a distorted view of Buddhajnana in which there is no inside and outside, the Nirmanakaya that appears to beings as external to themselves is a distortion of the real inseparable Qualities of Buddhajnana. In other texts, especially in the Mahamudra and Dzogchen traditions, the three kayas are explained in terms of the three inseparable Qualities of Mind. Each tradition explains these Qualities in slightly different terms, but the principle is the same. For example, in the second point of the "Seven Points of Mind Training," Atisa calls emptiness "Dharmakaya," clarity "Nirmanakaya," and both of these being inseparable the "Sambhogakaya." Other texts[33] explain the emptiness as "Dharmakaya," the clarity as the "Sambhogakaya," and the unimpeded nature (*ma 'gags pa*—sometimes referred to as "the variety of appearance"—*so so char ba*) as the "Nirmanakaya."

Thus, "Nirmanakaya" to ordinary beings means emanations of the Buddha that appear to them in material form, but for the meditator, who understands the true nature of Mind, it means the Inseparable Quality of Buddhajnana that speaks to him directly in the way he experiences the world. Thus, the world of his experience becomes his teacher. In the higher Tantras even the klesa are understood as expressions of Buddhajnana, but there is no hint of this kind of doctrine in the RGV.

8. Inconceivability (Exact Nature) [RGV 2.69–73]

Paraphrase. Verses 2.69–73 explain how the Dharmakaya and the form-kayas are inconceivable. The Dharmakaya is inconceivable for all the reasons given above and the form-kayas are inconceivable because they belong neither to samsara nor nirvana. They appear in the world but they are not what they appear to be.

Comments. Here again the RGV is simply talking about the apparent form-kayas. In Shentong terms, it is the Absolute Form-Kayas that are inconceivable [RGV 4.83] and, although they may understand the RGV to be referring to the Sutra doctrine of the Absolute Form Kayas, it is not explicit on this point; often (as here) it conspicuously omits to give such an explanation. This ends the second chapter of the RGV which is on Enlightenment.

10.6   Vajra Base 6: Qualities

Paraphrase. RGVV [p.47b.6] introduces the topic of the Qualities based on the stainless Tathata with the example of the jewel with its inseparable qualities of light, color, and form—its utterly inseparable, perfectly pure, and stainless qualities.

Although there are thirty-nine verses in this chapter, verse 3.1 is the only one that is included in Takasaki's basic verses. It reads as follows:

> Own Welfare and Other's Welfare is the Absolute Kaya and the apparent kayas based on it. They are the fruit of freedom and maturation and are the sixty-four divisions of the qualities.

Here "freedom" seems to correspond to the removal of veils from the Absolute Kayas, and maturation to the actual manifestation of the apparent form-kayas (also referred to as symbolic kayas) to the vision of beings. The remaining verses of this chapter [verses 3.2–39] describe the sixty-four qualities of the body, speech, and mind of a Nirmanakaya Buddha as He appears and acts in the world. These qualities are described according to the standard categorization of the thirty-two qualities of the Dharmakaya and the thirty-two qualities of the form-kayas. The first are the ten powers, four fearlessnesses, and the eighteen exclusive properties. The ten powers are compared to a vajra that destroys the veils of ignorance [RGV 3.4]. They consist of the different kinds of knowledge possessed by a Buddha such as knowing what is and what is not a source of good karma, the way karma ripens, the aspirations of beings, and their constitution. He knows where different spiritual paths lead, how klesa are purified, His former births, and He has the divine eye (*divyacaksus, lha yi mig*), that is, He has various super-normal faculties and foreknowledge. Finally, He knows the cessation of the defilements (*asravaksaya*). These are called the "ten powers of the Dharmakaya."

Comments. Although these are called the "powers of the Dharmakaya," they are actually the mental powers of a perfect Nirmanakaya Buddha. A perfect Nirmanakaya Buddha is one such as Sakyamuni, the historical Buddha, who comes into the world and sets the wheel of the Dharma in motion again for the first time after the Dharma of the previous Buddha has completely ceased. A perfect Nirmanakaya always performs the twelve deeds of a Buddha as described above, leaving the heavens, entering his mother's womb and so on.

Paraphrase. As well as the ten powers [RGV 3.5–7] there are the four fear-lessnesses [RGV 3.8–10], which refer to the Buddha's fearlessnesses when delivering the teaching of the Dharma. He is so self-assured that He is like a lion who fears no other forest creature. This is because He is in no doubt that He knows and can make known what is to be known (i.e. suffering), and He knows and can make known what is to be given up (i.e. ignorance). He knows and can make known what is to be attended to (i.e. the path), and He knows and can make known what is to be attained (i.e. nirvana).

The eighteen exclusive properties [RGV 3.11–16] are qualities of the Buddha's body, speech, and mind, such as His perfect mindfulness and faultlessness of speech and conduct. Since no other beings can compare with the Buddha in perfection, His qualities are said to be exclusive to Buddhas. Just as space has qualities exclusive to itself, which are not pos-sessed by any other element, so the Buddha's Qualities are not possessed by any other being.

The two kinds of form-kayas (Sambhogakaya and Nirmanakaya) are compared to the moon in the sky and its reflection in water respectively [RGV 3.4, 3.26]. The moon is visible to those who look up into the sky, and the moon's reflection is seen by those who look down into the water. In the same way the Sambhogakaya is seen by high level Bodhisattvas who have the high view and are near to Enlightenment, whereas the Nirmanakaya is seen by ordinary beings who are at a lower level and are farther from En-lightenment. Thus, the Sambhogakaya is like the real thing—the actual moon in the sky—and the Nirmanakaya merely a reflection of that (the moon in water).

The thirty-two qualities of the perfect Nirmanakaya [RGV 3.15–23], which are called the thirty-two qualities of maturation in this context, are His physical attributes such as having wheels on His feet and hands, eye-lashes like a bull, an amazingly long tongue capable of perfect tasting, a voice like Brahma, and so on.

Comments. These thirty-two attributes, variously listed in Buddhist texts, are in fact the classical Indian signs of physical perfection and are also the signs of a Cakravartin. A Cakravartin is a superman who rules the whole world of Mount Meru with its four surrounding continents and so on. He is called the Cakravartin (who turns the wheel of dominion, [McDonells San-skrit English Dictionary]) because he travels on a wheel that conveys him around the world in a day at will. He also possesses other magical and wonderful agents of power and wealth and he epitomizes the ideal of earthly happiness.[34] The Buddha is said to have been born with all the signs, which meant He would become either a Cakravartin or an Enlight-ened being, and it was in order to hasten the former possibility that Gautama's father tried to shield him from the sufferings of the world, which might have caused him to renounce all worldly ambition. Because his father failed to do so, Gautama saw the three signs of suffering and renounced the world in order to find nirvana.

Paraphrase. RGV [3.27] mentions that the sixty-four qualities and the causes for their attainment are to be found in the *Ratnasutra*, which the RGVV identifies as the *Ratnadharikasutra*. The causes are the meritorious acts that are the karmic cause for these qualities to manifest. Concerning the first set of thirty-two qualities, RGV [3.37] reads as follows:

> These thirty-two qualities are divisions of the Dharmakaya, but like a precious jewel and its light, colour and shape they are inseparable.

Comments. In Shentong terms, one could say that even the apparent qualities of a Buddha, that is, those qualities that appear to the distorted faculties of beings, are versions of the inseparable Qualities of the Dharmakaya. Dolpopa [RC 342–43] explains that there are an Absolute Ten Powers and so on that are the non-compounded Empty Ground (*stong gzhi*), that is, the ultimate Reality of Cessation, and the apparent ten powers and so on that are the impermanent, compounded path reality, which is self-empty.[35] RC [351] gives more details on the Jnana Skandhas and the vijnana skandhas, the Jnana Elements, and the vijnana elements, and [350] on the *pratityasamutpada* as Tathagatagarbha. This doctrine is elaborated on in great detail in the Tantras where the body as well as the mind of beings is taught to be Tathagatagarbha. This very body we have now is taught to have the thirty-two marks of perfection as its Absolute Essence. What exactly is meant by the thirty-two marks of perfection in this context needs to be carefully investigated, however. From the Shentong point of view, RGV [3.37] can be read as hinting at this kind of doctrine. It is easy to see how the mental qualities of the Nirmanakaya are expressions of the inseparable Qualities of the Absolute Dharmakaya. It is harder to see how the physical qualities of the Nirmanakaya are expressions of inseparable Qualities of the Absolute Form-Kayas. Nevertheless, in Shentong terms, this must be so since there is never any real distinction between mind and matter, see-er and seen, quality and qualified and so on.

The following verses [RGV 3.28–36] lend themselves to a Shentong interpretation.

Paraphrase. RGV [3.28–36] explains that the ten powers are heavy, solid, firm, and unbreakable like a vajra, the fearlessnesses as self-reliant, firm, and powerful like a lion, and the eighteen exclusive properties as being subtle, sustaining, and yet without any characteristic either mundane or beyond the mundane. It (i.e. the Dharmakaya with its eighteen exclusive properties) is compared to space, for it has qualities peculiar to itself.[36]

However, RGV [3.38] concludes the chapter on Qualities by explaining that the thirty-two qualities that beings see and that bring them such joy and satisfaction are based on (i.e. belong to) the two form-kayas which, far from being permanent, stable and inconceivable, arise in dependence on the beings who see them.

10.7   Vajra Base 7: Activity

The RGVV introduces this chapter by pointing out that the Buddha's Activity has two important aspects that must be considered. These are that it is effortless and that it is uninterrupted.

RGV [4.1] explains how the Buddha Activity is effortless and yet at the same time acts with perfect appropriateness to the time, place, aspirations, and capacities of beings. Verses 4.2–12 present and explain six examples to illustrate the different aspects involved in the continuous and spontaneous Activity of the Buddha. These are that Buddha Activity:

1. Is like a lake of jnana water with valuable jewels lying in its depths.
2. Is like a rising sun, since it is merit and jnana accumulated by Bodhisattvas on the path.
3. Is like space, because the Buddha Himself, having traversed all vehicles, is vast without limit.
4. Is like a mine of treasure, because Buddha Activity acts on beings.
5. Is like removing clouds, because the veils that are removed by Buddha Activity are without substance and are ephemeral.
6. Is like the wind, because the Buddha's compassion blows the clouds away.

Comments. In Shentong terms, the first example illustrates how the samadhi at each level (*bhumi*) of a Bodhisattva is Buddhajnana with inseparable Qualities, like water with treasures in its depths. These then emerge more and more as each level is traversed. Thus, although the Bodhisattva path consists of the double process of accumulating merit and jnana, in fact, what is really happening is that the Buddhajnana emerges like the sun from behind the clouds. Looked at in this way the accumulations are, in fact, nothing but the spontaneous action of the Buddhajnana itself.[37]

Kongtrul [RGV commentary p.136ff] follows Rongton by emphasizing how these express the uninterrupted nature of Buddha Activity. Thus, he explains that Buddha Activity is continuous and uninterrupted because: the *cause of deliverance* (qualities and jnana—example 1) and the *cause of teaching* (jnana and punya—example 2) are complete and perfect; the *fruit* Enlightenment without limit is attained (example 3); the *deeds* are directed at beings who are an exhaustless treasure (example 4); the *need* for its continuity is to remove the veils (example 5); and the *power* (*nus pa*) that provides the continuity is the Buddha's compassion (example 6).

From the Shentong point of view, he could have exploited the imagery of these verses more, as Mikyo Dorje does in his *gZhan stong sgron me* [p. 3]. Nonetheless, the images are there and one wonders if Kongtrul, feeling their meaning self-evident from the Shentong point of view, chose to follow Rongton in order to bring out a further detail that might otherwise have been missed.

The image of the Buddha being like space, which makes all things possible without the slightest effort, occurs often in the RGV and has already been discussed at length. Since the space-like Buddhajnana pervades all things and since, from the Shentong point of view, it is one and the same Reality as the essence of beings, they are like a great treasury waiting to be exploited. Then, just as clouds are spontaneously dissipated by the conceptionless wind, so the veils of beings are removed by the conceptionless action of the Buddhajnana.

In Shentong terms this means that as a disciple opens up in appreciation of the Buddha, the more directly will he feel the effect of the Buddha Activity, which is continuous with his/her own awakening gotra. Thus, Buddha Activity cannot help but respond quite spontaneously and precisely to the capacity of the person's mind to understand; doing this at exactly the moment that he/she is able to understand and, in precisely the way, he/she is able to understand it.

Paraphrase. RGV [4.12], however, reminds us of another sense in which the Buddha's Activity is continuous. We return to the theme of the seven Vajra Bases, which represent a temporal continuity as well as a continuity of essence. The Buddha acts for the benefit of beings because of his initial aspiration, and the power engendered by having given up all in order to attain Enlightenment. Loving others as Himself, and intent on carrying out His task of saving others, His action must continue as long as beings last. They are endless and so is His activity. His activity is to teach Dharma, which gives rise to the Samgha. In the Samgha is the Element, which becomes Enlightened; the spontaneous Qualities and Activity then act to liberate beings in just the same way as the activity of previous Buddhas has done.

Comments. The reason the action is able to occur continuously in this temporal sequence is because of connections established within the illusion of time. Without the connections created by Buddhas on their path to Enlightenment there would be no way for beings to become connected to the process of spontaneous Enlightenment.[38] In order to establish such connections, the Buddha appears in the world as any kind of creature or object that will produce the maximum and most positive connections between beings and their means to liberation.

Paraphrase. RGV [4.1] describes the Buddha's Activity as "spontaneous" (*lhun gyis grub*), which, as we saw [Chapter 4.2 "Inseparable Qualities" in this present work] means non-arisen, non-ceasing, and causeless. RGV [4.2] introduces the six examples listed above.

Comments. Takasaki includes these in his basic RGV verses. As always with such verses, they lend themselves easily to a Shentong interpretation. They seem to refer to the spontaneous Absolute Nature of Buddha Activity. The other two verses of RGV [4] that Takasaki takes to be basic are 4.13 and 4.41 (see below).

Paraphrase. Nine examples are given to illustrate how the Buddha Activity is both exact, appropriate, precise, and continuous as well as spontaneous and conceptionless. The RGV points out that in ordinary terms this is not possible, for precise action requires conceptual thought and intention. It is, therefore, a difficult doctrine for ordinary beings to understand; therefore, it is necessary to give examples in order to help them.

The examples are as follows:

1. The image of Indra [RGV 4.4–20] and his court is reflected in the earth, which has been made into shining lapis lazuli as a result of the meritorious deeds of beings. Even though that image is not real, seeing it inspires beings to gather merit so that they too can be reborn like Indra. The images appear, but Indra remains without the intention to do anything. He is unmoving yet effects this great deed for the benefit of others. The images appear and disappear according to the purity or otherwise of the minds of beings.

In this example Indra is like the Buddha and the clear ground created by the previous karma accumulated by beings is like the purity of mind created by beings through their good karmic actions. Just as the purity of the lapis lazuli enables beings to see Indra, so the pure mind of a being enables him to see the Buddha. In both cases the vision causes beings to aspire to follow the teaching in order to become like Indra or Buddha, even though they do nothing more than simply appear to beings.

Comment. In Shentong terms the Buddha here is the Absolute inseparable Qualities of the Dharmakaya.

2. *Paraphrase.* The drum of Indra [RGV 4.21–25] plays spontaneously, warning the gods of suffering and impermanence. It is created by the good karma of the gods, plays automatically without deliberate intention and is

heard by the gods who have faith. Thus, they abandon their distractions and seek the true Dharma.

In the same way, the voice of the Buddha is heard by beings through their good karma and faith, even though the utterances of the Buddha are spontaneous and without conceptual effort.

Verses 4.34–40 are included under the section comparing the Buddha's speech to the drum of Indra, but are in fact related to another example with an intention different from the first. It is the example of the heavenly instruments of the gods, which play to distract and enchant the gods and other beings. Even though this music is wonderful, it is not as wonderful as the Buddha's speech, which brings true peace and happiness. Takasaki[39] points out that there are various inconsistencies in this passage. RGVV [4.35: 51b.6] elaborates on this example at length. It explains that the drum of Indra is not like these other heavenly instruments of the gods, but has in fact the same four qualities as the voice of the Buddha Himself. These four qualities are non-restrictedness (i.e. lack of *pradesikatva, nyi tshe ba nyid*, [RGVV 4.40]), benefit, bliss, and deliverance. In other words, it penetrates the whole universe; it brings true benefit, because it makes beings give up distractions; it brings true bliss because it distinguishes between what is truly conducive to happiness and what is not; and it is deliverance because it teaches impermanence, suffering, and non-self. The other instruments of the gods have the corresponding four faults of being restricted only to the ears of the gods, harming them rather than benefitting them, bringing them unhappiness, and not helping them find deliverance.

After RGV 4.40 the RGVV [p. 52.7] again makes a lengthy comment about the nature of the Buddha's speech, which is summed up in the next verse (another basic verse in Takasaki's terms):

> Just as the gods do not hear everything because they do not experience subtle sound that is beyond their hearing, the most subtle Dharma is the sphere of experience of only extremely refined jnana. However, it can be heard by the ears of a few people, but they must be free from the klesa.

The RGVV [p. 52.7] comments that three kinds of miracle are taught. The Buddha's Body pervading all the world spheres is the "Miraculous Manifestation Miracle." The Buddha's Mind knowing deeply the mental behavior of beings is called the "Miracle of All Utterance." The "Miracle of his Teaching After Enlightenment" is the fulfilment of his vow made at the beginning of his path to deliverance. Thus, the voice sphere (*mandala*) of the Buddha pervades everywhere, unimpeded in all its aspects, like space, completely uninterrupted. However, it can never be perceived in all its aspects. This is not the fault of the Buddha's voice but of those who cannot perceive it.

Verse 4.13 lists the nine examples; verse 4.41 describes the true Dharma-teaching as so subtle that it is known completely only to Buddhas, although it is known to some extent by others who are free of the klesa. The RGVV [p. 52b] comments on this in terms of the Buddha's speech Activity being all-pervasive and unimpeded like space.

Comments. This sounds more like the Shentong Absolute Speech Activity than ordinary sound.

3. *Paraphrase.* The rain falling from a cloud [RGV 4.42–4.52] which, without the intention to do so, makes crops grow is like the cloud of the wisdom and compassion of the Buddha from which falls a rain of Dharma that causes virtue to increase in the world. Compassion is like a wind in the cloud that causes it to condense and fall like rain. The cloud is like the fullness of the Buddha's samadhi and mystical incantations (*dharanis*).

As in the previous examples, two aspects of the Buddha Activity are described. On the one side, the Buddha's Activity acts everywhere spontaneously and equally, while on the other it seems to vary and manifest differently due to the different conditions created by the beings who are the beneficiaries of it. To illustrate the latter point, beings are compared to the ground on which rain falls. Depending on the kind of rock on which it falls, water tastes differently. In fact, it even falls on those who hate it. The impartiality of the Buddha's Activity is illustrated by the example of rain falling on men and flightless birds at the end of the dry season that is welcomed by them, but hated by the hungry ghosts who get rained on just the same. Again as lightning strikes the mountains and plains alike, the Buddha's Dharma strikes every kind of being whether they like it or not. Even beings who believe in the self-views, and those whose tendencies are lying dormant are struck by it.

Comments. The mention here of beings who actually hate the Dharma is interesting. Could it be that the author of the RGV is pointing a finger at those who are hostile to Tathagatagarbha doctrine, making the point that the fact that one does not like it, makes it no less authentic?

Paraphrase. Verses 4.50–52 seem quite out of place here because they are included in the verses explaining the cloud example, but in fact introduce a completely new example. They compare the Buddha's doctrine to medicine that cures the sickness of suffering in the five kinds of rebirth experienced by beings. It gives the cause of the suffering, its cure, and the means to this end (in other words the four Aryan Truths).

4. Brahma [RGV 4.53–4.57], without moving from his sphere, appears among beings by emanating forms of himself effortlessly. On seeing these, the gods are inspired to try to attain the same level and so give up attachment and so forth. The Dharmakaya acts in the same way, arising in the world as the Nirmanakaya, performing the twelve acts and disappearing again as the positive karma of beings is exhausted.

Comments. This is an interesting example in that the Buddha's action seems to function exactly like Brahma's, insofar as the samvrti Nirmanakaya appearing in the desire realm is concerned. Thus, even Brahma is able to benefit beings who have the right karmic connections, by formulating aspirations and accumulating merit to give these aspirations the power of fulfillment. However, compared with the Buddha, of course, the degree of benefit Brahma can bestow is limited.

5. *Paraphrase.* The sun [RGV 4.58–4.66], at one at the same time, causes day-flowering blooms to open and night-flowering blooms to close. It does this without any concept of benefitting or not benefitting either kind of flower. In the same manner, the sun opens lotuses and ripens crops and so on. It does all these different things spontaneously without any intention; in the same way, the Buddha acts on beings, opening them up and ripening them. The Dharmakaya and the form-kayas are like the sun of omniscience shining in the sky, sending out rays of wisdom to beings. At one and the same time, the sun can be reflected in limitless vessels of water. Again, just as the rising sun first illuminates the highest mountains, and gradually the lower ones, until the whole world is flooded with light, so the sun of the Buddha's Enlightenment gradually illuminates all beings.

However, the sun only illuminates this world and only gives ordinary light. The Buddha's compassion, by means of various forms and colors, reaches all realms, and sheds the light of wisdom and understanding everywhere.

6. Just as a wish-fulfilling jewel [RGV 4.67–4.70], spontaneously and at once, grants all the different wishes of beings, so the Buddha's teaching can satisfy the wishes of all beings spontaneously. Also a wish-fulfilling gem is rare and hard to find, just as it is hard for those with bad karma to find the Buddha.

7. Like an echo [RGV 4.71–72], the Buddha's speech arises from others' concepts (*vijnapti, rnam rig*) and, while being itself effortless and without conception, it rests neither inside nor outside, like the sound of an echo.

Comments. Presumably, the point of this example is that an echo cannot be traced either to the rock from which it seems to come, nor to any other source. In the same way, the Buddha's speech cannot be traced to Him nor to any other source.

Kongtrul [RGV commentary 160] explains that the rock and so forth has no intention and makes no effort to say anything and the sound is neither inside nor outside the rock and so on, but is heard by others according to what they themselves say. In the same way the Buddha has no intention and makes no effort to teach, and the sound comes from neither within nor without his body, yet it is heard by his disciples each according to his own thinking. This idea is echoed in a common Tibetan saying that if you think of the Buddha as a Buddha you get the blessing of a Buddha, and if you see him as an ordinary man you get the blessing of an ordinary man. However, this dependently-arising speech of the Buddha that is heard by beings cannot be the Shentong Absolute Speech. Nonetheless, the former must be based on the latter.

The RGV uses the image of the echo to express the effortlessness and absence of concepts in the Buddha's speech, which is how the Shentong Absolute Speech of the Buddha is described. In Rangtong terms, however, the echo image expresses the dependently-arising nature of the Buddha's speech. Nevertheless, we have already seen how, in Shentong terms, what is dependently-arising is not beyond concepts.

8. *Paraphrase.* Just as space [RGV 4.73–74] is invisible, based on nothing and formless and yet from the relative point of view appears to have higher and lower spheres, so the Buddha appears to have higher and lower manifestations; however, He does not really. This example illustrates how the form-kayas of the Buddha make Him appear manifold, but in fact He is the single undifferentiable Reality.

Comments. This example illustrates very well the principle of the Absolute Form-Kayas as opposed to the samvrti form-kayas, which do indeed manifest variously according to the point of view of beings.

9. *Paraphrase.* Just as the earth [RGV 4.75–76] is the base for all things to grow and flourish, the Buddha without conception makes the roots of merit of beings grow and flourish.

Comments. "Roots of merit" refers to the good deeds done by beings, which are like roots planted in the ground and which, supported by the earth, give rise to good results.

Paraphrase. These nine examples are said in the RGV [4.78] to come from a Sutra; Takasaki identifies this Sutra as the *Sarvabuddhavisayavatarajnanalokalamkarasutra.* Verses 4.77–98 give the purpose for giving these examples, a summing up of their meaning, and an assessment of which is the most apt example of all.

The example of Indra illustrates how the teacher (the Buddha) appears in the world of men like a reflected image. The drum illustrates how the voice of the teacher spreads peace and virtue while not being the actual voice of the Buddha at all. The rain cloud illustrates the pervasiveness of compassion and wisdom of the Buddha, which are the real power behind His activity. The example of Brahma illustrates the power to emanate while remaining unmoved and unchanged by this activity. The example of the sun illustrates the radiance of the light of Jnana. The next three examples—the jewel, echo, and space—illustrate what is referred to as the three secrets of the Buddha's Mind, Speech, and Body respectively. (From the Shentong point of view, these seem to relate to the Absolute Mind, Speech, and Body of the Buddha). The last example, earth, is said [in verse 4.96] to be the best example of all, because it shows how the Buddha not only is causeless like space, but also is the base or support for all that is good and wholesome.

Comments. This concluding remark about the Buddha being the support or base for the good and wholesome suggests a Shentong interpretation. Had the intention of the RGV been to teach primarily a Rangtong doctrine concerning the emptiness of samvrti dharmas, space would have been the most apt example. The fact that space is rejected in favor of earth makes it clear that more than just a mere absence of substance is being taught here. On the other hand, had the primary intention been to teach a very advanced doctrine of Interpenetration and Totality, as in the Chinese Hua Yen traditions concerning Tathagatagarbha doctrine, the emphasis on the Buddha being the source of the good and wholesome would not have been so appropriate. Tathagatagarbha as the support and base of all things (as found in the SMS for example), not just the good and wholesome, would have been more apt.

Paraphrase. The final verse of this chapter explains how the good and wholesome is the basis for meditative absorptions, which in turn lead to the path to Enlightenment. It also explains that it is in this way that the Buddha's nurturing and sustaining activity produces the final harvest of fully Enlightened Buddhas.

Comments. In Shentong terms, this could be understood in two ways. First, it could refer to the fact that the Buddha's appearing in the world and teaching beings, makes them give up bad karmic actions and perform good ones, which results in their being able to enter meditative absorption, and finally reaching the supra-mundane path to Enlightenment. Second, it could also refer to the fact that the very qualities of appreciation, faith,

confidence, wisdom, concentration, compassion, and so forth, which moti-
vate a being to make good karma and enter the path to Enlightenment, are
the functioning of Buddhajnana.

10.8   The Benefits

Nearly all of the twenty-eight verses of this section are basic in Takasaki's
terms. These verses explain that by knowing that; a) the Tathagatagarbha is
present: b) one is able to "attain" it; and c) when "attained" it has these
qualities, the Bodhisattva is always full of aspiration, diligence, mindfulness, concentration, and prajna and so on. Thus, to believe in and aspire
to realizing the inconceivable Qualities of the Buddha outshines all other
virtues, such as generosity and so on. It is a direct cause of increasing
one's prajna, which in the end is the only thing that removes the two
kinds of veil. The knowledge veil is defined [RGV 5.12] as the tendency to
divide see-er, seeing, and seen (trimandala, 'khor gsum, see Vajra Base 7
Activity).

Verses 5.16–24 raise the question of the authenticity of the doctrine put
forward in the text.
Comments. Takasaki considers these verses basic, which suggests that from
early times the doctrine was subject to criticism and attack.
Paraphrase. Verse 5.18[40] states that what is meaningful, connected with
Dharma, causes the klesa to be relinquished, and shows the benefits of nirvana is the teaching of the *Rsi* (i.e. the Buddha). What is other than this is
not. Again what is simply the Buddha's doctrine, taught with non-distracted
faculties, and is in accordance with attaining liberation, is the *Rsi*'s doctrine and should be respected as such.
Comments. In other words, the authenticity of the doctrine should be
judged by its contents regardless of its source. If the doctrine can be shown
to be in harmony with the Buddha's doctrine, to function to remove ignorance, and to aid the course of liberation, then by definition it is the Buddha's doctrine. This suggests that the writer of these verses suspected, or
knew, there was something somewhat dubious about the historical origins
of the text, but felt sufficiently confident in the doctrines expressed in it to
suggest this was no ground for rejecting it. In fact, in Shentong terms, the
doctrine of the text itself suggests this view. If the action of removing veils
and bringing beings to Enlightenment is an Inseparable Quality of the Buddha, then that Activity, wherever it occurs, is an expression of the Buddha.
Buddha is this and this is the Buddha.
Paraphrase. The next verse argues that since the Buddha is the all-wise
one, lesser mortals should not interfere with his teaching, for this is tanta-

mount to trying to destroy the Dharma—which is one of the most heinous of crimes. It is worse than crimes against the Buddha and one's parents and so on, because without the Dharma, there is no chance of repentance and purification. For this reason one should fear rejecting the Dharma more than one fears fires, snakes, enemies, or lightning. In fact it is only prejudice and preconceptions that cause people to reject the true doctrine. Such people are like a cloth dipped in oil that cannot be dyed. Only clean pure cloth can be successfully dyed.

Verse 5.25 dedicates the merit of expounding on the seven Vajra Bases to the end that all beings may see Amitayus, endowed with boundless light, and seeing him they may quickly obtain Enlightenment. The last three verses of the text are not counted as basic by Takasaki. They simply summarize the last chapter.

Chapter 11

Translation of the Introduction to Kongtrul's RGV Commentary

Theg pa chen po rgyud bla ma'i bstan bcos snying po'i don mngon sum lam gyi bshad srol dang sbyar ba'i rnam par 'grel pa phyir mi ldog pa seng ge nga ro zhes bya ba bzhugs so. By Jamgon Kontrul Lodro Tayay (otherwise known as *Karma ngag dbang yon tan rgya mtsho*).

Herein is contained *The Unassailable Lion's Roar, which is a commentary on the Mahayana Uttara Tantra Sastra linked to the Explanatory Tradition of the "Path of Direct Experience" of the Heart-Essence Meaning (snying po'i don, garbha artha).*

This explanation of the *Mahayana Uttara Tantra Sastra* linked to a good and faultless tradition is called the *"Unassailable Lion's Roar."*[1]

Respectfully I salute the lotus feet of the Compassionate Lord, the glorious Guru Maitreya.

I honour and worship with clouds of offerings the Guru, inseparable from (*dang dbyer med*) the Lord of Love (*Byams mgon*) [an epithet of Maitreya]. He is the one with the Jnana of precise and all-inclusive knowledge* free from the stains of attachment and obstruction, who, having crossed over to the far side of the ocean-vast way of Dharma, resides fearlessly as the Regent [literally on the level of the Regent].[2] His three secrets,[3] like the young moon, are beautiful midst the revolving stars of the Aryan Assembly,[4] and the hundred divine beings.[5]

I bow to those whose hearts brim with the stream of the true Dharma nectar issuing from the Lord of the Tenth Level, the Unconquerable [another epithet of Maitreya], the Arya Asanga and his brother [Arya Vasubandhu]. I bow also to the long tradition of followers who uphold that tradition without fault. I thoroughly praise the Lord Maitripa, who revealed that which was hidden, and the holders of the special instruction lineage (*gdams ngag brgyud 'dzin*), Zu and Tsen. I thoroughly praise also the Great Charioteers who bring its meaning to ultimate accomplishment and the Golden Rosary of the Dagpo lineage.[6] May the one among the wise who is of genuine omniscience,[7] the Lord of the Doctrine, incomparable among the holders of the doctrine, the Conqueror [Buddha] Rangjung Dorje [the

---

* NB Translated elsewhere as knowledge of the full-extent.

third Karmapa], who is the Lord of Sages[8] of the Land of Snows, and Tenpe Nyinche [the 8th Situpa],[9] enjoy the lotus lake of my heart.[10]

2b   I salute the fundamental nature (*gshis lugs*) of the whole of samsara and nirvana that is the stained Heart Essence that pervades all like space and which, when free from the accidental stains, manifests and through this eternally performs the Activity of the Buddha.

This text expresses the ultimate meaning intended by the Conqueror, the Heart-Essence (*snying po'i don*), well commented on by the Regent Maitreya. Although the explanation of this subject matter by the System of Inferential Reasoning (*rjes dpag rigs pa'i 'chad tshul*) is greatly renowned, the Path of Direct Experience (*mngon sum lam byed*) is the way the Buddha Vehicle is; it is not the lot of inferior dialecticians.[11] It is the speciality of the Saraha father-and-son lineage. The analysis will be done according to the meaning truthfully taught by the Sublime Charioteers of the Heart-Essence that is the definitive meaning (Nitartha). It is a commentary that presents the teaching on the Heart-Essence, the Unassailable Lion's Roar, which is supreme over all the perfectly taught Dharma systems of the Lord of the Sakyas—the Perfect and Complete Buddha, who is the Omniscient One; it is the highest summit of the whole *Mahayana Pitaka*.

Concerning the explanation of this king of all sastras there are two [parts].

3a   (A)   A general synopsis for giving a definite idea concerning the text to be explained [i.e. the whole introduction translated here. It is in eight parts]:

       i. Recognizing the essence (*ngo bo, svabhava*) of what is being explained.
      ii. The sources on which it is based.
     iii. The teacher who composed it.
     iv. The series of lineages from which it arose.
      v. The meaning of that which is to be explained.
     vi. How it is explained.
    vii. A synopsis of the text from beginning to end.
   viii. An explanation of the purpose and relevance of what is being explained.

(B)   An extended commentary on the meaning of the words of the text itself [i.e. the main body of Kongtrul's commentary, which is not translated here]

i. Recognizing the essence of what is being explained

In general the nature of the gotra is the all-pervading nondual Jnana, which is the Dharmadhatu. This same, when it is doubly pure, having given up the two incidental veils, is the nature of Dharmakaya. The means to attain it is the Path, the nature of which is the view free from all conceptual artifice (prapanca), and the non-conceptual meditation (*rnam par mi rtog pa'i sgom pa*).

The perfectly taught instruction of the Buddha which is the means to reveal these three is supreme scripture (*gzhung bla ma*). If this scripture is examined minutely, it is three-fold: there are: a) the Mahayana Sutra collections, which are an aspect of nondual Jnana, that makes all things manifest (*rnam pa thams cad par shar ba*). They are the self-manifesting melodious voice/or speech[12] of the Buddha—the ultimate scripture. This is the Absolute Speech aspect.[13] This is the same in essence (*ngo bo gcig*) as the natural purity (*rang bzhin rnam dag*) and the fruit of becoming liberated—the Dharmakaya (*bral bras chos sku*); b) the Mahayana Sutras having names, words, and letters that appear as verbal approximations[14] in the minds of Aryas and ordinary beings; and (*c*) that which corresponds to the above: this is called the "continuity" (*rgyud*) of the Mahayana Nitartha Sutras— that is, the scripture expressed in terms and words of speech.

The latter two are very different from the essence (*ngo bo*) of the Nature (*rang bzhin*), Fruit, and Path; but they arose from the wishing prayers of the Buddhas and are in accordance with the Dharmakaya (*chos kyi sku yi rgyu mthun pa*) because they have the power to make the veils be given up. Therefore, they should be understood as included in the non-defiled (*anasrava*) dharmas,[15] the discerned object that brings about purification (*rnam par byang ba'i dmigs pa*) and perfect Existence(*yongs grub, parinispanna*).

All such Mahayana collections of scriptures are gathered into two collections, the Word (*vacana*, bka'), and the Commentaries (sastra). As stated in the *Devaputrapariprcchasutra* (*Lha'i bus zhus pa'i mdo*):

> All the dharmas are gathered in the Word and the Commentaries which are the good teachings and the commentaries on their intended meaning (*dgongs'grel*). By means of these the doctrine of the Sakya will remain long in this world.[16]

If one wonders how the text explained here, the *Uttara Tantra Sastra* should be recognized, from one point of view, it is possible to recognize it as words [bearing] the authorization (*rjes su gnang ba*) or blessing [of the Buddha] (*byin gyis brlab pa'i bka'*) since the Conqueror himself, having placed the crown on his head, granted [Maitreya] the regency as teacher of the Dharma. As is stated in the *Mahayanasutrasamuccaya*:[17]

> All the rivers that flow in the world (Jambudvipa)[18] and all the flowers, fruit trees, medicines and forests have as their stable rest-

3b

4a

ing place the lord of the nagas, the powerful naga residing in Ma-
nasarovar (*Ma dros gnas pa'i klu dbang*). They are that naga
king's power and glory. All the utterances of the Conqueror's disciples when they teach, explain or reason about Dharma, and the
causing of the supreme Aryan bliss (*mchog 'phags bde byed pa*)
and the obtaining of the fruit by this means, is all the creation of
the Enlightened being (*Purusakara*), the Tathagata.

However, the Lord (*rje btsun*) himself [i.e. Maitreya] said, in relation to its
being a commentary on the intended meaning of the Great Muni's speech:

4b   The whole of the main body of the sastra in short . . . [RGV 1.1].

Thus, he held it to be a sastra, and like a sastra it has the two qualities of
restoring (*'chos*) and protecting (*skyobs*).[19] Concerning this, from among
all the countless commentators on the intention of the Buddha there is no-
body in the world like the Regent Lord of the Tenth Level, Maitreya, and
the Lords of the Three Families (Rigsum Gonpo).[20] So, since their speech
is inseparable from the Buddha's speech, all the scholars and accomplished
ones of the Aryan Land (India) and of Tibet put their hands together at the
crown of their heads saying, "It is a Bodhicitta commentary." This is the
nature (*ngo bo*) of the great sastra that is to be explained here.

ii. The sources on which it is based

The fathers, Conqueror Rangjung Dorje and the Omniscient Dolpopa and
their [spiritual] sons held that it rested mainly on the Nitartha Essence
Tathagatagarbha Sutras of the last Wheel (Dharmacakra). Furthermore, the
perfect Buddha in his omniscience saw that the Element (dhatu) of Buddha
was in all beings. Since beings do not know they have the Buddha Element,
because they are veiled by the four veils of "anger at the Dharma" and so
forth [RGV 1.32], they have the five faults of "being disheartened with
themselves," and "scorning others," and so on.[21]

5a   Thus, they go round and round in the ocean of samsara. Having seen
this Buddha Element in all beings, and that the only means to clear away
the stains that veil it is the progression of teachings matching the faculties
of the disciples, he taught approaches to Dharma that were less clear, clear,
and very clear Dharma teachings; among these this is the supreme or ultimate one.

As regards those Bodhisattvas with sharp and fully matured faculties,
who have already purified their minds (*rgyud*) through having properly entered all the vehicles, He taught various Nitartha Sutra collections such as:

Sandhinirmocana (*dGongs pa nges 'grel*)
Lankavatara (*Lan kar gshegs pa*)

Ghanavyuha (rGyan stug po)[22]
Avatamsaka (Phal po che)

These are the four well-known Cittamatrin Sutras. They all show the Dharmata to be the truly existing Absolute by common or ordinary reasoning (*chos nyid don dam bden grub tu ston pa rigs pa thun mong ba rnams*).[23]

The extra-ordinary tenets that are the detailed secret explanations (*gsang gtam*) are:

Tathagatagarbhasutra (De bzhin gshegs pa'i mdo)
Mahabheri (rNga bo che)
Angulimala (Sor mo'i phreng ba la phan pa)
Srimaladevisutra (Lha mo dpal phreng gis zhus pa)
Dharanirajesvara (gZungs kyi dbang phyug rgyal pos zhus pa)
Mahaparinirvana (Mya ngan las 'das pa chen po)   5b
Ratnamegha (dKon mchog sprin)
(Pasanta?) (Rab zhi rnam nges)
Suvarnaprabhasa (gSer 'od dam pa)
Mahamegha (sPrin chen po)
Ratnamegha (dKon mchog sprin)* etc.,

These tenets teach the Tathagatagarbha, the True Dhatu (*yang dag dbyings*), the Changeless Dharmakaya, and the permanent everlasting unchanging Absolute Qualities that are primordially and inherently present (*rang chas su bzhugs pa*). It is the field of the Omniscient Ones alone, even those [Bodhisattvas] on the [ten] Arya levels do not realize it exactly, not to mention the dialecticians and Sravakas. As is said [RGV 2.31–33]:

Since Buddhahood, the sphere of the Jnana of the Omniscient, is not the sphere of the three wisdoms,[24] one should understand this Jnana to be inconceivable for beings. Since it is subtle it is not within the sphere of listening. Since it is Ultimate Truth it is not within the sphere of reflection. Since the Ultimate Nature (*chos nyid,* dharmata) is profound it is not within the sphere of mundane meditation and so on. The reason is that this has never been seen before by the immature, just like form in the case of someone blind from birth, or even by the Aryas, just like the form of the sun in the case of a tiny baby in the house of his birth.

Therefore, for those held in care[25] who are of inferior lot and whose faculties are dull, in order to make them get rid of their veils from not under-   6a

---

*NB. Repetition seems to be an error.

standing or misunderstanding, it is held that the whole subject matter of
these profound Sutra collections was condensed into seven Vajra Bases and
made into this clarifying sastra.

Rongton Shecha Kunzig[26] and the others hold that it is not a commentary on the intention of merely the last Wheel but a general commentary on
the Nitartha teaching Sutra class. These are in fact about fifteen in number
(*dngos su bco lnga tsam bgrangs par mdzad do*):

> *Mahakarunanirdesa* (*sNying rje chen po bstan pa*)
> *Adhasayanirdesa* (?) (*Lhag bsam bstan pa*)
> *Saddharmapundarika* (*Dam chos pad dkar*) etc.[27]

iii. The teacher who composed it

Of those whom the erudite call best, medium, and inferior commentators,
this present one is not only praised as erudite in the field of knowledge and
a seer of the Truth of the Dharmata, but in the ultimate sense (*nges pa'i
don tu*), for as many previous kalpas as dust particles in a Buddha field, he
had already been a complete and perfect Buddha. He manifested by taking
the form of a Bodhisattva on the tenth level, which is called the "Cloud of
Dharma," having only one more rebirth (*skye ba gcig gis thogs pa*). He
6b   was then empowered as the great Regent. He purifies the Buddha-realms,
ripens beings and, by perfecting the conduct of the ten Paramitas, he prepares to come as the fifth saviour of the Good Kalpa.[28]

The Lord Maitreya, the Unconquerable, is an actual Conqueror, who
like the present Buddha has mastery of inconceivable miracles and is also a
close son [of the Buddha, i.e. a Bodhisattva]. He declared in the "Great
Lion's Roar," in the presence of the Great Muni [i.e. Sakyamuni], that he
would hold, protect and cause the increase of the True Dharma. Then, with
vision free from [the veils of] "Attachment" and "Obstruction" concerning the meaning of the Buddha's Word and with his special cognition,[29] he
first composed the *Abhisamayalamkara*, which teaches the Nitartha Great
Madhyamaka Dharma in an approximate and concise form. Then in the *Mahayansutralamkara*, the *Madhyantavibhaga*, and the *Dharmadharmatavibhaga* he explains it clearly at length. Finally, in the RGV he firmly
establishes the meaning of the Tathagatagarbha Sutras, which comprises the
detailed tenets not common to other systems.

7a   Concerning this, the teacher Haribhadra[30] holds that five volumes of
Maitreya's Dharmas were composed for the benefit of the teacher Asanga.
Abhaya[31] explains that they were composed at the time of the councils
(*bka' bsdu'i dus*).

According to the teacher Santipa,[32] the one who made these sastras
appear in the world was the Arya Asanga, who is said in the *Madhya-*

makalamkara to dwell on the third level [of a Bodhisattva], which is called the "Illuminator." The *Manjusrimulatantra* (*'Jam dpal rtsa rgyud*) prophesied:

> The *bhiksu* called Asanga will be erudite in the meaning of these sastras and will distinguish well the Sutra classes of Nitartha meaning and also the many kinds of neyartha meaning. He will take on the form of a masterful teacher of knowledge to the world and a composer of treatises. That by which he will attain knowledge is called the Salay Ponyamo.[33] The power of this mantra will make his intellect develop to excellence. He will compose a condensed explanation of the meaning of the True Nature (*de nyid*, Tathata) of the Sutras in order that the doctrine remain long. He will live for 150 years and when he passes away, he will go to the god realms. Having enjoyed for a long time happiness in existences in samsara, finally the Magnanimous One (*bdag nyid chen po*) will become Enlightened.

Thus, this prophesied one, having perfected the practice directed towards invoking Arya Maitreya over the course of twelve years, was accepted as a follower and dwelt for the duration of fifty human years in Tusita. There he listened to the whole *Mahayana Sutra Pitaka* from Maitreya.[34] In particular he was given the *Five Dharmas* of Maitreya; he introduced them into the world. He composed many sastras, such as the five collections on the Levels (*Sravakabhumi, Bodhisattvabhumi* etc.) and, especially in the commentary on the RGV, he clarified and expanded on the extraordinary tenets; this is famed as the system of the "Path of the Great Charioteers." 7b

The supremely erudite Vasubandhu, who had internalized the essence (*bcud*)[35] of the ninety-nine hundred thousand sections [of *Prajnaparamita*], also composed extensive commentaries, among which was the commentary on the *Twenty Thousand* [*Prajnaparamita*] called the *Brhattika*, (*Yum gsum gnod 'joms*). His commentary on the *Dharmadharmatavibhaga* skillfully brings out (*rtsal du bton par mdzad*) the Nitartha Madhyamaka tenets. Thus, he was a great clarifier of this tradition. However, nowadays nothing remains of this lineage.

iv. The series of lineages from which it arose

In this way, the general tenets of the Nitartha Madhyamaka and the three Maitreya Dharmas (i.e. *Abhisamayalamkara, Madhyantavibhaga* and *Mahayanasutralamkara*) were spread widely by many pure/good disciple lineages such as that of Dignaga[36] and Sthiramati.[37] 8a

The extraordinary [doctrine], since it is hard for the minds of others to accommodate, was passed from the ear of one superior disciple to the next, and the texts of the RGV and the DHDHV were concealed as hidden treasures (*gter*).[38] Therefore, the *Madhyantavibhaga* and the doctrine of the two *Alamkaras* were translated and explained by the translators Paltseg (*dPal brTsegs*) and Shang Yeshe De (*Zhang ye shes sde*) in the period of the Earlier Spreading of the Doctrine.[39]

Concerning the RGV and the DHDHV root texts and their commentaries, some time later a light was seen through a chink in a stupa by the Lord Maitripa. When he went to investigate what it was, he found the two volumes (*glegs bam*) of the sastras. He then prayed to the Lord Maitreya, who appeared to him directly in the midst of a cloud, and granted him the authorization (*lung*)[40] in the proper way. He gave it to pandit Anandakirti (*dGa' ba grags pa*) who went in the guise of a beggar to Kashmir.[41] He was known as a "holy being." Sajjana,[42] the elder son of the one called pandita Sugata, recognized him as being erudite and listened to the two sastras [from him].

8b   Pandita Sugata was the son of the Brahmin Ratnavajra (*Rin chen rdo rje*) who was one well acquainted with the knowledge and secrets of the pandits of many noble lines of great erudite scholars (*mkhas pa chen po*) of Srinagar (*dPal grong khyer dpe med*). He was known as the first of the "Great Central Pillars" because he was both a pandit and a siddha (*mkhas shing grub pa*) in all the outer and inner tenets.[43]

Then the great Bodhisattva Ngog Lo Loden Sherab,[44] when he was learning and practising the Dharma in the country of Kashmir (*kha che*), having listened to them [i.e. the RGV and DHDHV], he translated them into Tibetan in that same country; he then spread the exposition of them far and wide in Tibet.

Previous to this, Neten Changchub Jungne of Yer made a request of the Bodhisattva of the Good Kalpa, the great erudite scholar, the Lord of Lords (*Jo bo rje*) Atisa Dipankara,[45] which led the translator Nagtso Tsultrim Gyalwa[46] to translate them. Although the great Sharawa[47] made his explanation based on these, later, due to the translations of Ngog being so popular with most disciples, it is known that he explained it twice based on [Ngog's translations]. Later, many people such as the translator Patsab,[48] Marpa Dopa,[49] and others translated it [i.e. RGV] but it appears that no long [tradition] of explanation and learning arose based on this.

The great translator Ngog made a minor commentary (*tika*) on the commentary on the RGV and, based on this, his own disciples, Lodro Jungne of Drolung,[50] and Shangtse Pongpa Choki Lama[51] each made a mi-
9a   nor commentary (*tika*). Based on these two, Shang's disciple Nyang Tenpa made a commentary.[52]

Later Chapa Choseng's[53] disciples Tsang Nagpa Tsontu Senge,[54] Dan Bagpa Mawe Senge[55] and so on made many commentaries and their followers, the many erudite scholars such as Lodro Tsungme,[56] Drogon Pamo Dru Gyaltsen Zangpo,[57] Rongton Shecha Kunzig and so on covered the whole of Tibet with volumes of commentaries. These were all followers of the great Ngog in spite of many unimportant discrepancies in the Dharma language.[58]

On the other hand, the pupil of Trapa Ngonshe (*Grwa pa mNgon shes*) known as Tsen Kawoche[59] went to Kashmir together with the great translator [Ngog] and requested Sajjana:

Since I wish my "death dharma practice" to be from the dharmas of Bhagavan Maitreya, please bind me to your heart with a special instruction: . . .[60]

[Sajjana] taught all five *Maitreya Dharmas* with Zu Gawe Dorje (*gZus dga ba'i rdo rje*) acting as translator. Furthermore, he gave special instruction (*gdams pa*) on the RGV very properly to Tsen Drime Sherab (*bTsan dri med shes rab*)[that is, Tsen Kawoche], who went to Tibet and taught it in U (*dBus*) and Tsang (*gTsang*). Zu Gawe Dorje made a minor commentary   9b (*tika*) on the RGV that accorded with Sajjana's teaching and also translated the root and commentary on the *Dharmadharmatavibhaga* [DHDHV]. This [i.e. the system of Zu and Tsen] was famous as a meditation system on the *Dharmas of Maitreya*. It was not the usual explanation and was an especially elevated line of exposition and practice, so a [separate] tradition arose from it.

The Omniscient Rangjung Dorje, who was someone who realized precisely the intention of the Unconquerable One (Ma Pham, Ajita) [an epithet of Maitreya] by means of his (jnana) vision, made a summary of the contents of the RGV. Karma Konshon[61] and son commented at length and the great Karma Tinlaypa[62] made a commentary by inserting minor corrections to the latter. The great translator from Go, Shonupal,[63] also made a very expanded commentary on the commentary by Asanga [i.e. RGVV] in accordance with this extraordinary system introduced by the great Omniscient Dolpopa; he also commented on it. Following the system introduced by him and his commentary, his disciple lineage in general, and especially that of Taranatha[64] and so on, established a system through explanation and experience. The transmission (*lung*) of these commentaries continues up to   10a the present day.

Later, Kunzig Choki Jungne (*Kun gzigs chos kyi 'byung gnas*) listened to the great and glorious Choki Dondrub,[65] and from the stream of his repeatedly given teaching arose that of the great master Lalung Karma Tenpel (*Lha lung karma bstan 'phel*) of Zurmang,[66] who composed a short explanation (*mchan, tika*); it also was well received.

Of all these [traditions], the one followed here is mainly that of the Victor Rangjung Dorje.

v. The meaning of that which is to be explained

The real meaning of the Heart-Essence, the teaching of the Bhagavan [i.e. Maitreya] that states, "All beings are ever possessors of the Buddha*garbha*" [RGV 1.28], is taken as the basis of this exposition. As for the manner of expounding this, there were many different systems in both India and Tibet, each following its own tradition of scriptural authority (*lung*), reasoning, and meditation; however, the teachers of the Nitartha Madhyamaka accept the following points.

The whole final meaning (Nitartha) of the three Dharmacakras is contained within the two non-selves.[67] When one reaches the ultimate meaning of this, since in terms of the individual and of phenomena there is emptiness of the duality of perceiver and perceived (*gzung 'dzin gnyis kyis stong pa*), their Emptiness is not a non-implicative negation.

As is said in the *Madhyantavibhaga*:

10b   Here the non-existence (*dngos po med pa*)[68] of the individual and the dharmas is emptiness. That Existence (*dngos yod*)[69] that is that non-existence (*dgnos med*) is Emptiness itself.[70]

In this context the Emptiness that is not nothing (*ma yin dgag*), which is the Essence (*ngo bo*), the Self-Aware Self-Illuminator (*rang rig rang gsal gyi ngo bo*), is taught as the Tathagatagarbha; this is the Vajra of the Nitartha. When this very Vajra is divided into phases it becomes three. As is stated [RGV 1.47]:

The non-pure, pure and the very pure, are called beings,[71] Bodhisattvas and Tathagatas respectively.

In the context of samsara, which is when the adventitious stains are not purified away, [the Vajra] is called "beings" and in this case the Element (*dbyings, dhatu*) is called the "Gotra or Dhatu (*Khams*) Tathagatagarbha". In the context of its having both purity and impurity [the Vajra] is called "individuals who have entered the path," and by the Element aspect (*dbyings kyi ldog cha*) [the Vajra] becomes the Dharma and the Samgha. For example, from the point of view (*ldog*) of its having just the Jnana of the Path of Seeing, it is the Samgha, and from the point of view of its being the

11a   Path of Non-Obstruction (*bar chad med lam*)[72], it is the Path Reality (*lam bden*). Because of its aspect of being associated with the special Path of

Liberation (*grol ba'i lam khyad par dang bcas pa'i cha nas*), it is the Reality of Cessation (*'gogs bden*). In the context of the very pure Buddha, [the Vajra] is called "Sugata" and so forth, and, furthermore, that Element (*dbyings*) is called the "Dharmakaya." When this is divided into aspects,[73] there are three, the Enlightenment, Qualities, and Activity. Therefore, by subdivision, it is taught as seven Vajra Bases.[74] Although it is easy to understand that the teaching of the Nitartha of the two later Wheels are included in these [seven Vajra Bases], one may ask how the first Nitartha, which is the "not-self of the person," is included. It is included because all the three, that is, the base to be purified (*sbyong gzhi*), the means to purification, and the fruit of purification of the inferior path (*dman lam*, Hinayana), are included within the stained Tathata.[75]

Therefore, the main thing to be taught by this sastra is the way the Tathagatagarbha exists. All the Nitartha of the three Dharmacakras should be known as being included in this. One may wonder what this *garbha* is. In general, in the Buddha's words (*gsung rab, pravacana*) it is:

1. The emptiness, that is, "absence of conceptual artifice" (*spros pa dang bral ba'i stong pa nyid, nisprapancasunyata*).

2. The Clear Light Nature of Mind (*sems kyi rang bzhin'od gsal ba, cittasvabhavaprabhasvara*).

3. The "base consciousness" (*kun gzhi 'i rnam par shes pas, Alayavijnana*).   11b

4. Bodhisattvas and beings.

Arising from these same [above] that are said to be *garbha*, the following four points are explained:

The three things that have their own characteristic are (*a*) the Dharmakaya, (*b*) the Tathata, (*c*) the Gotra, and the general characteristic is, (*d*) non-conceptualization (*mi rtog pa*).

Also there are the ways of expressing the [Buddha's] intention concerning the three phases mentioned above, and the neyartha and Nitartha. If one wonders from where these are expounded and what individuals established them, [see the following]:

1. *Absence of conceptual artifice (nisprapanca) being the Tathagatagarbha*:
This is the Nitartha of the second Wheel onwards and is clarified through many means using scripture (*lung*) and reasoning by Arya Nagarjuna and his followers. However, that which is characterized (*mtshan gzhi*) as emptiness, self-nature and so forth, that is the nothingness of a non-implicative negation (*med par dgag pa nyid*) discovered by the power of reasoning, arrived at through the exposition of the *Madhyamaka Collec-*

tions of Reasons (*rig tshogs*), is favored by almost all Aryan Land and Tibetan Prasangikas and Svatantrikas who emphasize only this negation (*med dgag kho na nan gyis bsgrubs*).

12a   Concerning that kind of emptiness being the Tathagatagarbha, Bhavaviveka[76] in the *Tarkajvala*, Arya Vimuktisena,[77] and Haribhadra all explain the gotra and the *Svabhavikakaya* to be the emptiness that is a non-implicative negation. In effect Candrakirti[78] also held this view. Again, Jnanagarbha[79] explains the Dharmakaya to be this, so it is indeed held to be the *garbha*.

Nevertheless, it is taught that the Bodhisattva's great sickness is the emptiness that is the non-implicative negation found through valid cognition through inference (*rjes dpag tshad ma*), because this very thing becomes a great bondage of concepts (*rnam rtog pa*). Therefore, due to the fact that the last Wheel [i.e. the third Dharmacakra] is for entering into the non-conceptual (*rnam par mi rtog pa la 'jug pa' i don*), it is also especially supreme.

    2. The Clear Light Nature of Mind Being the Tathagatagarbha:
This [doctrine] is clearly taught in both the middle and last Wheel and in the Mantra-Tantra, and in the RGV and the *Mahayanasutralamkara*, the *Dharmadhatustava* and *Cittavajrastava*. It is clearly explained at length that this is the *garbha*, also in the *Bodhicittavivarana* (*byang chub sems 'grel*) and so forth by Nagarjuna.

12b   *3. The Alayavijnana Being the Tathagatagarbha:*
This doctrine occurs in the *Lankavatara, Ghanavyuha* (*rGyan stug pa*), SMS, and the *Vajra Tent* (*rDo rje gur*) [probably a misprint for *rDo rje mgur, Vajra Songs* or *Doha*] and so forth and the teachers of the Cittamatra took it literally according to their usage of the terms.

    4. Beings Being the Tathagatagarbha:
In the *Pradipodyotana* (*tika*) (*sGron gsal*), it is stated that: "All beings are Tathagatagarbha." Also from the text itself [RGV 1.48], "The Dhatu (*khams*) is taught at the three phases by three names." The meaning of what is said here will be explained at length below but here it will be said in short: "Because the Buddhajnana resides in the mass of beings, and because that stainless nature is not two, and because the Buddha gotra is a name for (*nyer btags, upacara*)[80] the fruit, all beings are said to have the Buddha *garbha*" [RGV 1.28, Skt. ed. 1.27].

13a   First, because the Buddhajnana resides in the mass of beings, that Buddhajnana that resides in beings is called the "Tathagatagarbha." Second, because the Mind's Nature (*svabhava*), the Tathata without stain, is not different in Buddhas and beings, it is taught as the Tathagatagarbha. Third, because the skandhas and so on in beings that are the like-aspect (*'dra ba'i cha*) to Buddha, are the Buddha gotra and because gotra means "what is very similar," this gotra, having been given the name (*ming btags*) of Tathagata, is explained as *garbha* (*snying po*).

For the [above] reasons it is taught to be the Dharmakaya, Tathata, and gotra respectively. The Go translator [Shonupal] maintains that the first one [i.e. the Dharmakaya] is the actual Tathagata and the Heart-Essence (*garbha*) of beings is named after [the Tathagata], and the middle one [i.e. Tathata], since it possesses the aspect of both Buddha and beings is both [the actual Tathagata and the actual Heart-Essence (*garbha*)] and the final one [i.e. gotra] is in fact, the Heart Essence (*garbha*) of beings and is named after the Tathagata.

Non-conceptualization (*rnam pa mi rtog pa*) should be known as applying generally to all four points.

"Gotra", "dhatu" (*khams*), "seed" and so on are given as synonyms. Though dhatu does not mean *hetu* (*rgyu*, basic cause), since the term does contain the meaning *garbha* in the sense of "that which is not revealed" (*ma gsal ba'i tshul*), it is called "dhatu" (*khams*). Since the nine examples of the Buddha in the spoiled lotus and so on are about an Essence (*ngo bo*) really Existing, veiled by something else outside that obscures, they exemplify the Dhatu (*khams*). Thus, the Dharmadhatu is taught to be the Element (*Dhatu*) as well as the Gotra. The term *garbha* is used because it is applied to what is in the centre wrapped around by skins; the Tathata, at the time of the base, is veiled by adventitious stains from amidst of which it appears. "*Hrdaya*" (Skt. for *snying po*) is used because it is applied to the pith or the best, and the Tathata is the pith or the best [part] of the dharmas. "*Sara*" is used because it is applied to what is hard and stable; Tathata is to be taken as meaning never changing.[81]

13b

vi. How it is explained

In general, all three, the base (*gnas*) to be known at the "base time" (*gzhi dus*),[82] the field of the view (*lta ba'i yul*) at the "path time," and the Svabhavikakaya at the "fruit time" apply to the Dharmadhatu Jnana; this is how it stands in all the texts by the Lord Maitreya. For example in the *Abhisamayalamkara*:

> The nature (*rang bzhin*) of the Dharmadhatu is the support for accomplishing (*sgrub pa yi rten*) and . . .[83]

Thus, the attainment of the Dharmakaya is explained as the fruit of relinquishing all the things to be relinquished, occurring on the base to be purified (sbyang gzhi). The agent of purification is explained as the four accomplishments (sgrub pa bzhi)[84] or the four ways of acting (sbyor ba bzhi). That which is removed on purification is what is removed (sbyang bya)[85] on the Path of Seeing and the Path of Meditation. Here the base to be purified is the Element, the Sugatagarbha; the means of purifying are the four [things] named "Aspiration for Dharma" and so forth, and the "Sixty Perfect Purifications."[86] The thing to be removed (sbyang bya) is the nine stains, that is, attachment and so forth, the three veils, and the four (obstacles), that is, hostility to Dharma,[87] and so forth. The "fruit" of freedom [i.e. the fruit of this process of purification] is the Dharmakaya with its Qualities and Activity becoming manifest. In these two explanations [i.e. in the Abhisamaya and RGV], there is merely a difference in Dharma language. In fact, their meaning comes to the same thing (gcig tu 'babs pa).

Therefore, having explained at the base time the presentation of the alaya (which is the support—rten) in which the separate traces (bag chags) of samsara and nirvana are put ('jog),[88] and at the path time, the adventitious stains that are to be given up, there is no difference between accepting the natural purity, the self-aware Jnana as the aspect to be experienced, and establishing the existence (yod par bsgrub) of the ultimate wisdom of transformation (gnas 'gyur)[89] at the fruit time. This being the basis of this text, there have been two ways of explaining it: the explanation by means of: 1. the Path of Inference (based on the Madhyamaka texts), and 2. the Path of the Direct Experience (of the meaning of the Heart-Essence).

1. The Path of Inference. This is the system of explanation of Ngog, the great translator and his followers. The Tathagatagarbha is held to be the absolute truth. It is held to be the emptiness that has the characteristic of being a non-implicative negation as is explained in the *Collections of Reasoning (Rigs pa'i tshogs).*[90]

The great translator and Tsang Nagpo say of that absolute reality:

It is not even a subtle conceived object,[91] let alone the real object of terms and concepts (sgra dang rtog pa'i dngos yul).

The teacher Chapa [see fn. 53] holds that:

Absolute Reality which is a non-implicative negation (med dgag) is things (dngos po) being empty of reality (bden pas stong). It is also held to be an object able to be grasped by words and concepts (sgra rtog gi zhen pa'i yul).[92]

14a

14b

Further, the meaning of the expression "having qualities by nature" applies to the fact that when one discerns the emptiness, all qualities are naturally gathered there. The reason for being completely pure is that, regarding the two non-selves, the object of completely pure jnana, they are not to be newly added. In terms of the reason for being complete klesa (*kun nas nyon mongs pa*),[93] the self of the individual and the dharmas, being falsely established by the klesa, these objects of the klesa never existed, so there is nothing to be removed that existed previously.[94] The meaning of "pervaded by the Dharmakaya" is explained as the Dharmakaya being attainable by beings.[95]

15a

2. The Path of Direct Experience. Marpa listened to those who belong to the tradition of meditation on the *Maitreya Dharmas* (*byams chos sgom lugs pa rnams*), stemming from the lineage of the translator Zu and Tsen, and the *Tattvadasakatika*[96] and so forth which is a special instruction (*man ngag*) on the Prajnaparamita that accords with the Mantra [tradition], which the Lord Maitripa composed after having received special instruction (*gdams ngag*) from the father, the Great Brahmin Saraha, and his sons; then Marpa said:

> The Dharma that is free from limits (*mtha'*) and is not a mental construction, the Heart-Essence of the Ultimate Vehicle, introduced me (*ngo sbrod*)[97] to the Mahamudra.

and the Lord Gampopa said: "The Text for our Mahamudra is the *Mahayana Uttara Tantra Sastra* composed by Bhagavan Maitreya."[98] This has been clarified in the teachings of the *Jewel Ornament of Liberation* (*Thar pa rin po che'i rgyan*) and so forth composed by himself.

After that the Glorious Pamo Drupa father and sons and the second Conqueror Rangjung, and so forth who are "Lords of the Tenth Level" who directly see the Heart-Essence, were united in following this (*gcig tu 'brang bar mdzad*). Kyoba Jigten Sumgi Gonpo[99] also commencing from this same Heart-Essence turned the wonderful Dharma Wheel. Also this same [Kyoba Jigten],[100] in his next incarnation as the Omniscient Dolpo Sangye [i.e. Dolpopa],[101] composed the Heart-Essence of the Nitartha, *The Fourth Council* (*bka'i bsdu ba bzhi pa*). The great Silung (*Zi lung*) Pandit, the Omniscient Taranatha and the Omniscient Tenpe Nyinche [the 8th Situpa] and so forth, all come to the same crucial point (*gnad*) concerning the view; the only differences are some small points in the manner of expression. Furthermore, the explanations of Maitripa's direct disciple, Pandit Vajrapani, on the root text and commentary on the *Tattvadasakatika* that spread far and wide in Tibet are also the oral tradition of the Mahamudra, which teaches the meaning of the same. Maitripa's direct disciple, Dampa

15b

Sangye, having given the name "The Holy Dharma Pacifying Suffering"[102] to the Mahamudra Dharma that accords with the Essence (*ngo bo*) Prajnaparamita and Secret Mantra, also agreed with the above earlier teaching in Tibet.

16a   Thus, in short, all the oral traditions (*bka' srol*) of explanation and instruction (*gdams ngag*) of the lineage from Maitrigupta[103] (except for certain expressions) come to the same meaning.

For them, the Heart-Essence Tathagatagarbha is the Mind's Nature (*rang bzhin*), the Clear Light. So, since this is called "gotra" when in the continuum (*rgyud*) of beings, beings are called "possessors of the Buddhagarbha." Like the example of the naga King ascending from the depths of the ocean to the heavens, it hastens towards the Path and Fruit dharmas. When Buddhahood arises, the Heart-Essence called the "Dharmakaya" becomes manifest and, like the example of Brahma's emanations descending to the earth, it pervades (*'gebs*) all the dharmas of samsara.[104]

At the same time as these [two kinds of action, i.e. upwards out of and back down into samsara], except for the difference of being impure or pure of contingent stains, the Element of beings and the Dharmata of the Dharmakaya are the same in their Tathata from the point of view of unchangingness and quality.

16b   It is taught through the example of the Bhagavan [the Buddha] dwelling on the earth and pervading the three realms with the manifestations of his body [RGV 4.14–30; 4.53–57].

If these two [the Tathata of beings and of Buddha] are slightly distinguished, there are the two gotra, that is, the one "present by nature" (*rang bzhin gnas pa*) and the "expanding" (*rgyas 'gyur*) one. The former is present, like the Heart-Essence, from beginningless time in the continuum of beings, "Like the treasure in the poor man's home" [RGV 1.112–114]. The latter is the power (*nus pa*) of the gotra present in the base. In the same way as the fruit bearing tree that, after being newly planted, grows [RGV 1.115–116], the qualities increase by properly engaging in the positive activity (*dge ba*) of listening and so forth on the Path of Learning. Thus, the former [gotra] acts as the cause of attaining the *Svabhavikakaya* and the latter of the Sambhogakaya, and Nirmanakaya.[105]

The Omniscient Rangjung Dorje maintains that the expanding gotra is present as the base (*gzhi*) or "basic cause" (*rgyu, hetu*).[106]

The Dharmakaya has two aspects: (1) the actual Dharmakaya, and (2) what accords with the realization of the Dharmakaya (*de rtogs pa'i rgyu mthun*).

The first is the doubly pure, genuine Dharmakaya and the latter is the teachings of the Buddha that demonstrate the way of the "Profound Absolute" and the "Diverse Samvrti."

In the general teachings of the Buddha on the Tathata, the Absolute Tathata and the samvrti tathata are taught.

The great translator of Go [Shonupal] maintained that there is a general   17a
division into the samvrti and the Absolute in the three Heart-Essences,[107]
which makes six divisions altogether. Concerning the intended meaning of this text, that which is inseparable from the Tathata, from beings up to Buddhas, is the constantly present gotra-likeness (*rigs 'dra*) that is the Mind's Dharmata or Nature (*rang bzhin*).

The Clear Light that is the Mind's Nature (*rang bzhin*), which is "like space, perfectly unchanging," [RGV 1.63] and "As it was before, so it is after, the changeless Nature (Dharmata)," [RGV 1.51], is taught by means of various verbal signs and examples. In the Sutras, it is the Prajnaparamita, the Absolute Reality, the Highest Limit, the Nature of the True State (*gnas lugs rang bzhin*), the changeless Perfect Reality (*parinispanna*), the Dharmata, the Mind Itself (*sems nyid*),[108] the Emptiness and so forth.

In Mantrayana it is taught by many synonyms—the Primordial Protector (*adinatha*), simultaneously arising Jnana, the Great *Bindu*, the Clear Light Nature, the Mahamudra and so forth.

The Mind's Nature, the Clear Light, is veiled by the adventitious stains that   17b
veil like clouds. Therefore, simultaneously with the Pure Nature, like gold and dross (*g.ya*), the mind that arises together with it, and that makes subject-object duality appear, is what is named by many names, such as the *alayavijnana*, the dependent nature, illusory samvrti, and ground of ignorance tendency patterns and so forth.[109]

From that, the Four Veils of "anger towards the Dharma"[110] and so forth arise and one is bound in samsara through not realizing the True State. By properly realizing the True State by means of the Four Basic Causes of "aspiration towards the Mahayana Dharma,"[111] and so forth, the adventitious stains are rooted out and the *Buddhagarbha* manifests. This is called the Dharmakaya. Since the Clear Light Nature has primordially never been spoiled by stains, there is nothing to be removed, and since the stains are artificial and adventitious, the Dhatu is empty of them (*khams la stong pa*). Since the Qualities are the inherent essence (*rang chas kyi ngo bo*)[112] [of the Dhatu], there is nothing that did not exist before that is to be newly added.

Thus, since these are inseparable characteristics, the Dhatu is not empty of   18a
them. It is like the example of someone sick with jaundice seeing a conch as yellow. In the actual conch there is an emptiness of yellow, but not an emptiness of white.[113]

When one is establishing certainty (*gtan la 'phebs pa*) concerning the meaning of this [doctrine] by listening and reflecting; the Highest Limit (*yang dag mtha'*) is isolated from all the aspects arising from compoundedness. Shentong reasoning makes its analysis according to this and [RGV 1.4]:

> Without beginning, middle and end, inseparable, without duality, free from the three, stainless, and without conceptualization, the realization of the Nature of the Dharmadhatu is the Vision of the Yogi in meditational equipoise.

and so on. The thing experienced (*myong bya*) through the meditation on these is held to be the "Jnana-empty-of-two." The Lord Sakyapa[114] said:

> Having established it as (*gtan la phab*) the freedom from limit (*mtha' bral*),[115] practice it [in the manner of] "Both-at-once."[116]

The great beings who hold to the tradition of explanation of the Single Crucial Point (*gnad gcig*) are called Madhyamaka Shentongpas. Furthermore, Emptiness of other (*gzhan kyis stong pa*) is actually taught in the Sutras by certain hints.

18b   Here in Tibet the great Siddha, Yumo[117] composed the *gSal sgron skor bzhi* and a system of exposition arose from it. The wide diffusion of that term [i.e. Shentong] arose from the Omniscient Dolpopa father and sons. In the crucial points of their view and meditation, there is no disagreement, but sometimes there are a few differences in the way they formulate their tenets when ascertaining the "view." This is especially so concerning how the Omniscient Jonangpa takes the term "Tathagatagarbha" literally as being the Paramita of True Purity, Permanence, Bliss, and Self.[118] All the Tibetan commentators refuted him because they understood [him to be referring] to a real existence established by the intellect (*blos bzhag pa'i bden grub*). However, the meaning he intended was that this Permanence etc. refers to the changeless Element (*dbyings*), and that it is free from all conceptual artifice and signs. It is held to be beyond terms and concepts and is the object of the non-mistaken, non-conceptualizing Jnana. Since, if this same could stand up to analysis by reason, it would by its own analysis be mistaken, it is taught to be the same thing as the "Empty Image (*stong gzugs*) having All the Supreme Aspects" (*rnam kun mchog ldan gyi stong pa'i gzugs*), which is called "Mahamudri" (*phyag rgya chen mo*)[119] and so on, which are taught in the Kalacakra.

19a   In short the key point [literally the root] of the explanatory systems of both the Inference and Direct Experience Paths is whether the Tathagatagarbha is existence or non-existence (*yod med*). It concerns the meaning of [RGV 1.154–155]:

> Here there is nothing whatever to clear away and not the slightest thing to add. When the Real is properly looked at, when the Real

is seen, there is Liberation. The Element is empty of that which has the characteristic of being separable, the contingent [stains], and it is not empty of the Supreme Dharmas, which have the characteristic of not being separable.

Thus, through one understanding arising from focusing outward and one arising from focusing inward, a division between the object (*don*) of intellectual analysis and that of meditation has arisen.

vii. A synopsis of the text from beginning to end.

    1. The Actual Synopsis.
    2. Incidental Commentarial Explanation of the Path.

1. The Actual Synopsis.

"Buddha, Dharma, Assembly . . . etc.," [RGV 1.1] gives a synopsis of the text is given from beginning to end. "From the Buddha, the Dharma . . . etc." [RGV 1.3] teaches the relationship between the items in progression from the first to the last.

Of all knowable things, the Perfect Buddha alone is the thing (*dngos po*)   19b
that is beyond rival and unfailing. Having become the Self-Arisen, All-Seeing One by the power of His having purified the contingent stains, the Buddha is the chief subject matter.

The True Dharma is that which the Conqueror has seen exactly (as it is) and taught to others as a path, out of compassion.

Concerning the Samgha, as it is taught "On the Path that you have trodden, the disciples also follow . . . ," so they are simply the ones who enter and learn this Path.

Thus, the whole of the Buddha's word and sastras explain the Nature (*ngo bo*), Qualities, and Activity and so on of the Triple Gem, so this text starts with a brief explanation of the meaning of these as a basis.

Further, Buddha is non-compounded, spontaneous, and not realized through any other conditions [RGV 1.5]. These are the three qualities of Enlightenment that are One's Own Welfare.

Knowledge, Love, and Power are the three qualities that are the Welfare of   20a
Others. By adding these two Welfares, which are the basis of the division, to the six essential divisions, the total number of qualities becomes eight.[120]
Concerning the Dharma as the Reality of Cessation, it has three qualities, which are inconceivability, non-duality, and non-conceptuality. As the Path Reality, it has three qualities, which are purity, clarity, and remediality.
Concerning the Samgha, it has three qualities of awareness (*rig pa*), which are precision (*ji lta*), all-inclusiveness (*ji snyed*), and self-awareness (*so so*

rang gis rig pa), and three qualities of liberation, which are freedom from veils of attachment (*chags*), of obstruction (*thogs*), and of inferiority.[121] By adding to these the basis of the division as is done above, the total number is eight. Thus, the Three Supreme Ones have their essence explained in terms of eight qualities each.

They are presented as three provisional Refuges and established as one ultimate Refuge, the Buddha alone. Thus, by this [explanation] together with the meaning of the term "Rare and Precious" (*dkon mchog*), the Rare and Precious Ones, which are the goal to be attained, are clearly presented.[122]

After that, concerning that [Element] through the existence of which the mundane and the supra-mundane goal, the Rare and Precious Ones, is achieved, there is an expanded explanation of the branches of the way of attaining it, which are the four Bases (*gnas bzhi*), that is, the stained Tathata, the stainless Tathata, the stainless Buddha Qualities, and the Conqueror's Activity.

20b   Furthermore:

1. the Base (*gnas*) to be realized, "*The Stained Element (khams) Pure by Nature,*"
2. the Base that is the Essence of that Realization itself, "*The Enlightenment that is Free from All the Stains,*"
3. the Base that is the extensions [literally, branches] of that Realization, "*The Qualities Associated with Enlightenment,*" and
4. the Base that makes others realize, "*The Activity, that is the Power of the Qualities.*"

These four sum up all that is to be known.

1. The Stained Element (khams) Pure by Nature.

In terms of the Tathata together with the gotra of this Triple Gem, all beings have the Tathagatagarbha. In order to teach this, three reasons are set out in one verse, namely, "Because the perfect Buddha's kaya radiates. . . ." [RGV 1.27]. Although by each reason alone, the existence of the Tathagatagarbha can be established, for the sake of the individuals to be tamed three equivalents have been taught.[123]

21a   All that follows is merely an elaboration of the meaning of this. Concerning this, the heart (*snying po*) of the summarized presentation that establishes and analyses the intended meaning (*dgongs pa'i don*), that is, the Dharmata Absolute Reality, the pure nature of the Dharmadhatu, includes:

(a) the establishment in ten points[124] according to the intention of various collections of Sutras, (*b*) the application of the nine examples,

(*c*) the way it is ascertained, and

(*d*) the need for teaching the *garbha* according to the intention of the Tathagatagarbha Sutras.

From these the first is:

a) *The layout as ten.*

"Essence, cause, fruit, . . . etc." [RGV 1.29]

• *The essence point* is the Base Dharmakaya, the Tathata, the Gotra, the Element (*khams*), and Pure Nature.

• *The cause point* is the Path Dharmakaya—the means for removing the contingent stains in the Element, that is, the "aspiration for Dharma" etc..

• *The fruit point* is the Fruit Dharmakaya—the attainment of the Four Quality Paramitas when this same Element (*dbyings*) is free from adventitious stain.

• *The action point* [concerns the fact] that it is because the Gotra exists that [it happens that] a): from seeing the fault of samsara, renunciation arises, and b) from seeing the benefits of nirvana, the desire to attain it arises.

• *The possessing point* is the Element's having the "cause" qualities of "aspiration" and so forth, and the "fruit" qualities of "special cognition" (*abhijna, mngon shes*) and so on.   21b

• *The division point* is that because the individuals, who are the vessel (*rten*) having the quality (*chos can*),[125] are different, the thing they contain, the Dharmata, is divided into three phases.

• *The occurrence point* is the teaching that the division into three phases is merely a nominal division, for even though there are three kinds of individual, there is no difference in their Nature.

• *The omnipresence point* is the Dharmadhatu pervading these three as their common aspect (*rang spyi'i sgo nas*)[126] like space.[127]

• *The changlessness point* is that, although dharmas (*chos can*) arise, cease, increase, and decrease, the Dharmata (*chos nyid*) is free from these.

• *The inseparability point* is that, like the sun and its rays, the measureless Qualities of freedom and ripening cannot be said to be other than this itself in any phase, be it base, path, or fruit.

By means of these ten points it is taught that in any individual the base, path, and fruit for accomplishing Buddha are complete.

b) *The Nine Examples.*   22a

This is the teaching by means of "The Buddha in the spoiled (*ngan*) lotus . . . and so on," [RGV 1.99–104]. This is explained by applying the nine examples of the discolored (*mdog ngan*) lotus and so on to the veiling stains, that is, the klesa and knowledge veils (*klesavarana* and *vidyavarana*) that exist in all beings, from the immature ordinary beings up to the ultimate end of the continuum (*rgyun mtha'i bar du*) [i.e. to the end of the Tenth Level of a Bodhisattva and the moment before Perfect Buddhahood], and the nine examples of the Buddha and so on that are what is veiled, the Dharmadhatu, that is, the three natures [of Dharmakaya, Tathata, and Gotra]

c) The way it is ascertained.

This is the teaching that immature ordinary beings with the assemblage of [wrong views concerning what is subject to] destruction (*satkayadrsti*),[128] the Sravakas and Pratyeka Buddhas with wrong views, and the beginning Bodhisattvas whose minds wander from [or are distracted by?] the emptiness, though they have developed faith, do not realize precisely[129] the True State of the Dharmata, the Absolute Reality itself. It is realized from deep wisdom (*shes rab*) in which there is no removing or augmenting.

d) The Need to Teach Tathagatagarbha.

This is the necessity for teaching to ordinary beings the *Sugatagarbha* that is hard to realize by the Aryas, which is to get rid of the contradiction between the teaching of the middle Dharmacakra, which is absence of essence (*ngo bo*), and the teaching of the last Dharmacakra, which is the existence of the *garbha*. (This ends the the first chapter.)

2. The Enlightenment that is Free from All the Stains

22b   [The second chapter] consists of eight points. In relation to the stainless Tathata, this Dharmadhatu, by being free from all the stains, is the complete transformation of the whole base (*gnas ma lus pa yongs su gyur pa*) in the non-defiled (*zag pa med pa'i*) Element (*dbyings*) [or Expanse] of the Buddhas. This is the essence (*ngo bo*) of the Realization, Enlightenment. This is taught by "Purity, attainment . . ." and "Essence, cause . . ." [RGV 2.1].

• The ESSENCE (*ngo bo*) point is the Dharmadhatu pure by nature when, being free from all contingent stains, it is the doubly pure[130] complete transformation.

• The CAUSAL CONDITION point is the means for obtaining this which is: (1) the supra-mundane, non-conceptual jnana of meditational equipoise, and (2) the mundane jnana of the "post-attainment (*rjes thob*)."[131] Meditation in which these two are combined (*zung 'brel tu sgom pa*) is the causal condition for transformation.

• The FRUIT point is the perfect completion of "Relinquishment" and "Realization" on the exhaustion, removal, and non-arising of the stains of the two veils, together with the traces, by means of bringing to perfection the meditation practice (*goms*) on these two wisdoms (jnana).

• The ACTION point is the accomplishment of the complete and perfect Own Welfare through: (*a*) being free from the klesa veils and so being beyond all defiled continuity (*zag bcas kyi rgyud pa*), and through (*b*) having obtained stainless, limitless endowments (*zag pa med pa'i 'byor mtha' yas pa*). It is the complete and perfect Welfare of Others, which engages everywhere unobstructedly, through being free of knowledge veils.

• The POSSESSING point is having the base (*rten*) for the accomplishment of these two Welfares, that is, the limitless Freedom and Maturation qualities.

• The APPEARANCE point is the division into the three kayas, which are that very Englightenment that has those qualities. They are: a) the profound Dharmakaya, hard to fathom and not realized by even the great Aryas, b) the Sambhogakaya that is vast since it pervades all, and c) the Magnaminous Nirmanakaya (*bdag nyid chen po*) that performs only the good of others in accordance with their lot.

• The PERMANENCE point is the three kayas abiding (*gnas pa*) and pervading the limits of space, and the realms (*khams*) of beings as long as time lasts.

• the INCONCEIVABLE point is the difficulty of realizing the Buddha Nature (*rang bzhin*) which is the "Three Secrets of the Body, Speech, and Mind," because it is not the sphere of experience of any other than the Buddha himself.

These eight points comprise the second chapter. The *Dharmadharmatavibhaga* is like a commentary on this chapter. What is taught there as the "Dharmata" and here taught as the "stainless Tathata" is the same thing. The synopsis into six points begins with: "The characteristic of the Dharmata . . ." The synopsis is threefold:

(1) the thing to be known (*shes bya*),
(2) the four things to be meditated on,
(3) the fruit.

For the details one should refer to the DHDHV. [This ends the second chapter.]

3. *The Qualities Associated with Enlightenment.*

The third chapter explains, together with a detailed discussion of the examples, the special Qualities of the branches (*yan lag*)[132] of the Realization

23a

23b

summed up as the "Fruit of Liberation" and of "Maturation", which are present in the great Enlightenment. On the basis of this, "Own Welfare and Other's Welfare . . ." [RGV 3.1] teaches the sixty-four qualities. The sixty-four qualities comprise (sdoms): a) the thirty-two qualities of liberation had by the Absolute Dharmakaya, which are one's "Own-Welfare," and b) the thirty-two qualities of "Maturation" had by the apparent (samvrti) form-kayas, which constitute "Other's Welfare." Thus it enumerates their application to the two kayas.

24a   Then, "The powers [that are like a vajra] to the veils of ignorance . . ." [RGV 3.4] teaches the Dharmakaya's Qualities, arising from the purifying away of what has to be abandoned, that is, the Ten Powers, unshakeable like a Vajra, the Four Fearlessnesses, like a fearless lion, and the Eighteen Distinctive Qualities which, like space, are not common to others.

"Well set, wheel marks . . ." [RGV 3.17] teaches the qualities of the form-kayas, which are the thirty-two Good Signs (mtshan bzang) that are obtained through perfecting the qualities.

4. The Activity that is the Power of the Qualities.

On the basis that the Conqueror's Activity is spontaneous and uninterrupted through the power of having obtained these qualities, concerning the activity that makes others realize [Buddhahood], "[Knowing] the nature (khams) of beings. . . ." [RGV 4.1] teaches that the Activity engages spontaneously
24b   with no effort to conceptualize about the trainees for whose sake it engages in activity, or about the means by which they are to be trained, what the task of training should be, which land inhabited by trainees should be gone to, or what is the right time for it.

Then "Deliverance . . ." [RGV 4.5] teaches Activity through the following six points:

1. the cause, that is, deliverance, which gives rise to the Activity ('phrin las 'byung ba'i nges par 'byin pa'i rgyu),

2. the condition that precisely demonstrates it (nye bar ston pa'i rkyen),

3. the way the fruit is accomplished from this cause and these conditions,

4. the field in which the Activity of this fruit engages,

5. the veils to be given up by those [who are the field of their Activity],

6. the condition for cutting them off.[133]

The Activity, that is permanent for three reasons, is taught to be continuous, by means of linking it to examples, showing how it engages [itself] while in the state of non-conceptuality (*rtog pa med par ngang gis 'jug*). In order to remove doubts as to whether it is not contradictory that permanent and all-pervading Activity should arise from what is non-conceptual, the nine examples of Indra, the drum, the cloud, and so forth, are given; though these provide partial similes for Body, Speech, and Mind Activity, they are not comparable in all aspects. Thus, [Buddha-Activity] is taught to be beyond example. This ends the fourth chapter.

Thus, having come to the end of the main body (*dngos gzhi*) of the sastra, a synopsis (*bsdus don*) is added; it is made clear how the virtue of the mere aspiration to the "Four Inconceivable Points" is far superior (*khyad par 'phags*) to the three virtues of giving, discipline, and meditation.

Then [comes] the aside (*phros don*) about the way it was composed. Finally, the synopsis is again made clear in the dedication wishing prayer.   25a

This is the extremely vast and wonderful Buddha's teaching and the single meaning associated with it that is repeated again and again through the three [means], which are example, meaning, and signs (*dpe don rtags gsum*).

2. Incidental Commentarial Explanation of the Path.

Because the resolve to Enlightenment (*byang chub tu sems bskyed, bodhicittotpada*)[134] on the path of the Supreme Vehicle is like the guide going on before, [the order of the chapters] is in accordance with the order of the proper adopting of that Mind (*sems*). Since the Bodhicitta arises through the cause (*rgyu*) of listening to the Buddha Qualities, and the condition (*rkyen*) of going for refuge in the *Triratna*, these are taught first. Concerning that which is aimed at by the resolve [to Enlightenment] (*sems bskyed pa'i dmigs pa*), it is the Welfare of Others and Enlightenment. Since "Others" means beings for whose sake the resolve is made, the stained Tathata is taught first, even though the real Welfare of Others is taught under "Activity."

The cause of this [Activity], Enlightenment, and the "branches" (*yan lags*)   25b
of this by means of which the Welfare of Others is accomplished, that is, the Qualities, are taught in separate chapters.

All seven should be understood in terms of the two truths (*bden gnyis*).

• The Absolute Rare and Precious One is the Buddha and the apparent (*samvrti*) Rare and Precious ones are the Dharma and Samgha.
• The Absolute Sugatagarbha is the Clear Light and the Emptiness. The apparent Sugatagarbha is the properly adopted gotra.
• The Absolute Enlightenment is the *Svabhavikakaya* and the apparent Enlightenment is the two form-kayas.

• The Absolute Qualities are the "Liberation Qualities" and the apparent qualities are the "Maturation Qualities."
• The Absolute Activity is the Dharmakaya's Activity and the apparent activity is the activity of the form-kayas.

One should be able to distinguish them in this way.[135]

viii. An explanation of the purpose and relevance of what is being explained

Concerning this, if one wonders what is the subject matter and so forth of this great sastra, it is [to present] the Triple Gem, the Element, the Enlightenment, together with the Qualities and Activity, which comprise the whole meaning of the Mahayana Heart-Essence Sutras; they are the seven Bases unchanging like the Vajra and extremely hard to realize through hearing and reflection.

26a   The point of these words is [26a]:

First, through the wisdom of listening, the words that are the means of expressing are understood. Second, through the wisdom of reflection, having found certainty as a meaning approximation (*don spyi tshul*), which is like the treasure present in the poor man's house being opened, by relying on the "Three Valid Cognitions"[136] and the "Four Confidences",[137] the Nitartha Heart-Essence Buddha-Word (*gsungs rab*) is easily entered into; this is the purpose (*dgos pa*) [of these words].

Having entered in this way, with the three kinds of faith[138] as a preliminary, when one has developed the wisdom-of-meditation with respect to the Heart-Essence, one experiences how the Heart-Essence Dharmata abides, at first, in an approximate way; this is like having in one's hand a treasure from under the ground.

Having become progressively clearer, finally the stainless Jnana that realizes directly, unmistakenly and without conceptualization arises, and the Pure Nature free from the adventitious stains, which is the Dharmakaya, manifests. This is the ultimate purpose (*nying dgos*).[139]

26b   Since the ultimate purpose (*nying dgos*) [i.e. to make the Dharmakaya manifest] depends on the purpose (*dgos pa*) [i.e. to gain certainty indirectly] and the purpose depends upon the subject matter, without the earlier [stage] the later [stage] cannot arise. The relationship between them is a cause and effect (*de byung*) relationship like fire and smoke, and the two aspects of the same thing (*bdag gcig*),[140] such as the sun and its light.

Chapter 12

Conclusion

In this chapter, I shall make a brief comparison between Tathagatagarbha doctrine according to the Shentong interpretation of the RGV and according to several other interpretations. I shall try to show how they relate to practice. I shall adopt a Shentong view in the way I present them as a natural progression from the least subtle view up to the most subtle and highest view.

In doing this I am conforming to the Tibetan custom of arranging the tenets of different schools in the form of a progression. However, as far as I know, it is unusual to present the various ways of interpreting Tathagatagarbha doctrine in this way.

Gyaltsab's View

According to Gyaltsab's interpretation, [*La Théorie* 292], Tathagatagarbha is actually the state of an ordinary being who has the possibility of becoming a Buddha, but is not yet one, in any sense. Such an individual has the ordinary mind of an ignorant being full of mental poisons and veils of ignorance. These impurities, however, can be removed and the mind transformed so that the qualities of the Buddha's wisdom are acquired. Some of the qualities of a being's mind are like a rudimentary form of the Buddha's qualities, but are in no way the same thing. Buddha qualities arise gradually on the path as the Bodhisattva focuses his/her mind on emptiness. Because the nature of his/her mind is emptiness, it has the power to transform into wisdom. In other words, if the ignorant mind were not empty, ignorance would be its permanent unchanging nature and transformation impossible. This emptiness of mind cannot itself be Tathagatagarbha, otherwise Tathagatagarbha would also be present in Buddhas. Since, in Gyaltsab's system, Tathagatagarbha is defined as the state of a being in whom emptiness is obscured (*samala tathata*), Buddhas by definition do not have Tathagatagarbha. According to Geshe Wangchen, since it is the name of a state of a being, it can also loosely refer to the being's mind, but technically the Tathagatagarbha is only the stained (i.e. obscured) emptiness of a being's mind. By implication, the emptiness of a being's mind is in some way different from the emptiness of any other dharma—otherwise all dharmas would be Tathagatagarbha since they are all empty.

Thus, by meditation on emptiness the mind-stream becomes purified, good qualities develop and finally the being sees the emptiness in a completely full and perfect way. This means a person's mind can then transform, the qualities of complete Enlightenment can arise, and eventually the experience or realization of Enlightenment occurs; it is something only that person experiences. In this sense it cannot be expressed properly in words (i.e. it is ultimately inconceivable etc.), because it must be experienced directly and personally. According to this system, this is what self-awareness (*so so rang rig*) means. The Shentong explanation of the term is completely rejected.

Buddhahood is characterized as the union of wisdom and compassion and, according to Gyaltsab, these qualities arise from causes and conditions. These causes and conditions are generated by accumulating merit and wisdom as one traverses the path to Enlightenment over a period of aeons. When Buddhahood is finally realized, it is automatically accompanied by countless good qualities. This is what "inseparable qualities" means.

Thus, from the practical point of view, Tathagatagarbha doctrine means that beings should develop their accumulation of merit in their everyday life, and meditate on emptiness in their meditation sessions in order to accumulate wisdom. They should do this, confident in the knowledge that within them is the power and ability to become Buddha. By meditation on emptiness they will be adopting the right means to eventually realize what the Buddhas realize. Since emptiness is always present even on the path, it is possible for beings to realize it, but it is never possible to realize or experience Buddhajnana in any sense until one reaches Buddhahood.

Rongton's View

Rongton does not limit Tathagatagarbha so definitely to the state of an ordinary being as Gyaltsab does. For him it is the self-emptiness of the Dhatu. For him there is a sense in which the mind of a being is by nature the jnana of the Buddha, but it is obscured. Tathagatagarbha is simply emptiness and the gotra is this emptiness and the obscured wisdom aspect of a being's mind. This obscured wisdom aspect of a being's mind is purified by focusing on the emptiness. This stainless power of the mind is then freed from the veils that impair it, and Enlightenment is attained. The stainless power of the Buddha's mind, as well as the emptiness, are both accessible to the practitioner from the beginning of the path but, as in Gyaltsab's system, the qualities develop and are acquired during the course of the path. Rongton seems to accept that the "light" quality is there from the beginning, but not the countless Qualities.

In practice, there is not a great deal of difference between Gyaltsab and Rongton. Compared with Gyaltsab's RGV commentary, however, in Rongton's commentary there is less emphasis on establishing the relative existence of the mind-stream and there is no explicit refutation of the Shentong position.

The Shentong View

From the Shentong point of view, a Rangtong interpretation of Tathagata-garbha doctrine leads to the very mistake the RGV and RGVV warn us against. That is to think that the Buddha is a compounded phenomenon, which implies it is impure, impermanent, suffering and non-self [RGV 1.35–39].

From the Shentong point of view, those with merely a Rangtong understanding of Tathagatagarbha doctrine have the problem of having to make constant mental effort in order to see the emptiness of apparent phenomena and to develop compassion. Although, in the Shentong view, mental effort helps to remedy wrong concepts, it does so by replacing gross by ever more refined subtle concepts. These then must be removed. The danger is, however, that they may have become deeply entrenched and hard to detect by the time one comes to remove them. The practical advantage of the Shentong approach is that more emphasis is put on relaxing conceptual effort at an earlier stage than in a Rangtong system.

The danger of the Shentong approach is that by stressing confidence and relaxation too much, the students might be swept away by distraction, and in their confusion lose their confidence and with it all other good qualities. In such circumstances, they might have been better advised to have built up the discipline of a more goal-oriented approach.

Nowadays, it seems most Tibetan Shentong teachers like to combine both these methods so that disciples have the maximum opportunity to realize the Heart-Essence teaching by receiving oral instruction as soon as possible, while at the same time, having a firm grounding in more goal-oriented practices that help establish in the practitioners the wholesome mental tendencies that will keep them on the path.

The Hua Yen View

The Hua Yen doctrine of Fa Tsang seems in essence to be indistinguishable from Shentong although it develops the doctrine further than the RGV and RGVV do. The Chinese developed the aspect of the doctrine that accords well with the long quotation from the *Avatamsaka* [RGVV 1.25] in which the example of the silk scroll is given.

The whole universe is painted on a scroll as large as the universe that is then enfolded within an atom. If one took the example of the universe in every atom literally, one would have the doctrine of Interpenetration and Totality of the Hua Yen school, in which Tathagatagarbha, as the Dharma-dhatu, is actually the Totality of all that is and penetrates in its totality

every minutest part of the whole. This doctrine is expressed by Garma
C. C. Chang [*The Buddhist Teaching of Totality* p.160ff] when he gives Fa
Tsang's explanations of the *Hua Yen* (*Avatamsaka*) Sutra and the metaphor
of the lotus flower. This doctrine reminds one of modern physics and the
infinite possibilities existing at every point of space.[1] Thus, for certain
masters of the Hua Yen school not only does every being have Tathagatagarbha but also every rock, grain, and atom of the universe. Ruegg [*La
Théorie* p. 152n.1] gives a detailed account of which Buddhist schools accept that material things can have Buddha Nature and which do not.

The Tantric View

From the point of view of practice, this interpretation of the Tathagatagarbha doctrine, like the Shentong, emphasizes "non-doing." It corresponds to
the higher rather than the lower Tantras in flavor because the emphasis is
not on purity so much as on wholeness and sameness. The RGV Tathagatagarbha doctrine, however, finds its expression in the lower Tantras where
one believes oneself to be the nature of the Deity (*istadevata, yi dam*); however, one is in need of purification. In the higher Tantras, one is already the
Deity and all one's seeming impurities are actually expressions of the Jnana
of the Deity. The Tathagatagarbha Sutras are far more precise on this point
that the RGV itself. They lend themselves easily to a full Shentong interpretation as explained by Dolpopa in the RC.

Although the higher Tantric views such as Dzogchen and Mahamudra,
like Hua Yen, regard the whole of experience as being and always having
been Enlightenment, the Tibetan character, unlike the Chinese and Japanese, did not develop this principle in terms of aesthetics. Although, according to Khenpo Tsultrim, the Nyingmapas have a practice that involves
seeing Buddha in everyday objects, in general the Tibetans never quite
adopted the Chinese and in particular the Japanese extension of this in respect to their aesthetic appreciation of everyday things (except maybe the
Shambhala tradition).[2] The Chinese, and thence the Japanese, might see
Tathagatagarbha expressed in a flower or a rock and use this heightening of
their aesthetic sense as an integral part of the path to Enlightenment.

Rangjung Dorje in his important explanatory text on the Tantras called
the *Zab mo nang don* clearly elucidates the Tathagatagarbha doctrine in the
Tantras. He explains [112] how the stains arise and cease with the *prana*,
which is the movement of Mind when it starts to proliferate (prapanca).
This obscures the Clear Light Nature of Mind, even though the movement
is not an entity and not something other than the Clear Light. The example
of waves in the ocean is often given. The essence of waves is the ocean and
in the same way the essence of thoughts is the Clear Light Nature.

Dolpopa describes the stopping of the *prana*, binding of the *nadis*, and so on and the pointing-out instruction (*ngo 'phrod*) [171.2]. He explains that even ignorance is pure; however, special instructions are required in order to understand this [RC 297.3]. Again he explains [RC 372] that profound Mind instructions are needed since merely knowing things (*dngos po*) are self-empty is bondage; one must be freed from the movement of *prana* and mind.

In the *Zab mo nang gi don* [ZND] Rangjung refers to *garbha* (*snying po*) as the inner Nature of mind and body; he explains that it is *garbha* because it is the Nature (*rang bzhin or ngo bo*) of all the Buddhas. It is taught in general terms in the RGV by the four inconceivable points [RGV 1.24–25], but in the ZND it is taught according to the extraordinary Vajrayana.

Concluding Remarks

In conclusion I leave the reader with the following thoughts. On the one hand we have the somewhat discouraging news that we can hope for no end to this debate concerning the nature of Buddhajnana.
Milarepa said:[3]

> *ye shes bya ba yang de ltar shes pa bzo bcos ma phog pa 'di la yod med dam. rtag chad sogs tsig dang blo las 'das pa 'di rang yin. 'di la ci ltar brjod kyang 'gal ba ma yin pas. Ye shes kyang di lta bu yin te. mkhas su re ba'i blos byas pas. sangs rgyas rang la zhus kyang phyogs gcig pa cig gsung du yod mi snyam. chos sku blo 'das skye med spros bral yin. nga la ma dri. sems la ltos dang. de 'dra cig yin gsungs pas de ltar du bzhed pa med yin no.*

> It is called Jnana but in this which cannot be reached ('*phog*, literally, touched) by the contriving (*bzo bcos*) mind (*shes pa*) like this, is this actuality (*rang*) beyond words and ideas (*blo*) such as existing or not existing, and permanence or annihilation (*rtag chad*): whatever one says about it is refutable and since Jnana is like this, even if one were to ask the Buddha Himself, do not think He would take one side or another. The Dharmakaya is beyond thinking (*blo*). It is non-born and free from conceptual creation (nisprapanca). Do not ask me; look at your Mind. It is not something about which one can say, "It is like this."

Gampopa said [*Thar rgyan* 73]:

> *chos kyi sku zhes pa de yang. chos kyi dbyings stong pa nyid kyi don rtogs pas. nor pa thams cad zad pa'am. 'khrul ngo na* (Khenpo Tsultrim suggests this is a misprint for '*nor*'] *ba'i rang*

bzhin log pa tsam zhig la. chos kyi sku zhes tha snyad btags pa
tsam yin gyis. don gyi ngo bo la chos kyi sku dang. chos kyi sku'i
mtshan nyid dang. mtshan gzhir grub pa gang yang mi mnga' ba'i
phyir. bla ma mi las gsungs pa de ka ltar yin no.
Concerning that which is called Dharmakaya, since when the
meaning of Emptiness, the Dharmadhatu, is realized it is merely
that all error is exhausted or [all that is of a] mistaken nature
ceases, Dharmakaya is in fact merely a technical term. In fact, just
as the Lama Mila says: ''In essence there is no Dharmakaya, either
as quality or qualified.''

On the other hand let us take heart from Seng Chao [*Chao Lun* 51]:

The varying passages of all the Scriptures, the contrasting sayings
of all the schools, if you can penetrate to the point where they all
agree, their divergence cannot confuse you.

Restatement of the Three Main Conclusions of This Work

First, it is hoped that the reader will now understand how the term ''Emptiness of other'' as popularized by Dolpopa can be seen to correspond to
the doctrine of the Tathagatagarbha Sutras as commented on in the RGV and
RGVV; it is important that a great deal more attention be paid to these Sutras
in trying to establish the link between the Sutras and the Tantras.

Second, it should be very clear by now that Emptiness of other can
only be properly understood when it either follows, or is accompanied by, a
proper understanding of self-emptiness. It is not a question of either/or, but
of both being necessary.

Third, it is also hoped that this present work has contributed to the
removal of confusion concerning the Rangtong and Shentong approaches to
the teaching of Tathagatagarbha. One must differentiate between those
commentators who, from pedagogic considerations, present Tathagatagarbha in a Rangtong way, and those who reject on principle the Shentong
doctrine of a conceptionless Absolute, the nondual Jnana as presented in
the Tathagatagarbha Sutras. From the Shentong point of view, the latter are
rejecting the Nitartha of the third Dharmacakra on which rests all the highest teachings of the Buddha. If the Shentongpas are right, to reject this is a
very serious matter indeed.

Appendix 1

Works by Western Scholars

Most of the work done so far by Western scholars on the Tibetan traditions of interpretation of the RGV and RGVV over the last fifty-five years or so has been based on Gyaltsab's *Dartik* (*rGyud bla ma'i dar tik*). This is a commentary on the RGV and RGVV written by a scholar of the Gelugpa school in the fifteenth century. It interprets the text as a Prasangika Madhyamaka work; it strongly criticizes Shentong. Although it purports to be following the Ngog tradition [CDTBE p. 43], Kongtrul does not mention it in his RGV commentary.

From the academic point of view, although the Rangtong interpretations of the RGV according to Gyaltsab and Buton are well described by Professor D. Seyfort Ruegg, a more detailed comparison of these with the Rangtong interpretations of other Tibetan scholars such as Rongton is required. As for the Shentong interpretation, it has hardly been touched on as yet.

Professor Takasaki, at least at the time of writing his study, seemed unaware there were two kinds of commentarial tradition existing in Tibet and that neither of them corresponded to the Chinese tradition of interpretation.

Dr. E. Obermiller's RGV and RGVV translation [1931] makes frequent reference to the *Dartik*. His translation is entitled *The Sublime Science of the Great Vehicle to Salvation being a Manual of Buddhist Monism, the work of Arya Maitreya, with commentary by Aryasanga.* [Acta Orientalia vol. IX parts ii, iii, and iv.]

Interestingly, Obermiller [106] gives an outline description of the doctrine of the RGV which accords (in general terms) with the Shentong view. Nonetheless, while agreeing that this is the view presented by the RGV, he believes that such a view is non-Buddhist. He therefore approves of Gyaltsab's modifications. Consequently, Obermiller's translation becomes an odd combination of statements, implying that the Absolute, with all the Qualities, exists in all beings from the beginning, and statements (clearly influenced by explanations from the *Dartik*) opposing such assertions. For example RGV [1.12] reads as follows:

De yang ji lta bur yongs su btsal ba na de'i rgyu mtshan ma dmigs pa 'ga' yang mi mthong ba de lta bar bya'o. gang gi tshe rgyu mtshan nam dmigs pa mi mthong ba de'i tshe yang dag pa mthong ba yin te.

So how is it properly sought? It is to be viewed by not focusing on any sign (*nimitta*) of it—by not seeing anything. When one does not see any sign or object of focus, then one sees the truly Real.

Obermiller (following Gyaltsab) translates this [Obermiller translation 137] as:

Now, how are we to search (for the Absolute Truth)? (Answer): It is to be perceived through complete negation (of the separate reality) of every object and characteristic feature. As soon as we cease to perceive the (separate reality) of the objects or their characteristic marks, we come to perceive the Absolute Truth.

In a footnote he refers to the *Dartik* [45a 1]:

At the time when we no more perceive a differentiation into subject and object, we come to the intuition of the Absolute Truth.

Thus Obermiller's so called translation becomes an attempt to incorporate Gyaltsab's comments into the original text and therefore, distorts it.

Dr. E. H. Johnston edited the Sanskrit text of the RGV (1935) using mainly two fragments of the Sanskrit text found in Tibet. One of these was in an early Sarada script and dates back to about the tenth century. Therefore, it predates the rediscovery of the RGV by Maitripa in the eleventh century. The other was in a Nepali script of the eleventh century that was surprisingly poorly copied for a manuscript of that period. There was another manuscript discovered together with these, which was a summary of the RGV written in the eighth century and other Sanskrit fragments of the RGV in a Saka transliteration had been found in Central Asia by Professor Bailey a few years earlier; however, these were of no use to Johnston in the preparation of his Sanskrit edition. This edited Sanskrit version corresponds closely to the Tibetan rather than the Chinese version of the RGV.

Professor J. Takasaki published (1964) a study called *A Study on the Ratnagotravibhaga Being a Treatise on Tathagatagarbha Theory of Mahayana Buddhism*. It contained a translation of the RGV and RGVV from the Sanskrit, using the Tibetan and Chinese versions for reference. The underlying assumption behind his translation and comments was that the Tathagatagarbha doctrine expressed in the RGV corresponded to the most widely held Chinese interpretation of the doctrine, which differs markedly from any Tibetan version. See for example the first paragraph of section III of his introduction [*Study* 20]. It gives an interpretation very reminiscent of the Hua Yen doctrine of Interpretation and Totality found in *The Awakening of Faith* and other works.

In his *Study,* Takasaki analyzes various Chinese texts that incorporate verses from the RGV, to find which verses occur most consistently in the early sources. The resultant so called "original verses" are interesting, for they lend themselves easily to a Shentong interpretation with the images of space and sun figuring prominently.

J. W. de Jong wrote a detailed review of Takasaki's *Study* in *Buddhist Studies* published by Asian Humanities Press in 1979 [p. 563]. In it he mentions a detailed study by Ui Hakuju published in 1959 containing a complete translation and Japanese-Sanskrit glossary and various other works and articles by Japanese scholars. De Jong's review is important for its detailed critique of Takasaki's work, and its discussion of the authorship of the RGV and RGVV among other issues.

In 1969 Professor Ruegg's *La Théorie du Tathagatagarbha et du Gotra* was published. This contains a study of the RGV giving a brief analysis of the RGV [*La Théorie* 247–264] in which he makes several references to Gyaltsab's *Dartik*. He presents [291–296] Gyaltsab's interpretation much more consistently and accurately than does Obermiller because he adheres strictly to paraphrasing Gyaltsab's interpretation, and does not try to incorporate it into a purported translation of the original text of the RGV or RGVV. Part 3 of *La Théorie* is called "The Theory of Tathagatagarbha." Chapter I of Part 3 is the analysis of the RGV mentioned above; chapter II is about *Garbha* and Dhatu in the RGV; chapter III is about the doctrine of Tathagatagarbha in the RGVV; chapter IV is about notions akin to the Tathagatagarbha and Dhatu in the RGV and RGVV [291–96] giving Gyaltsab's observations; chapter V is about the inexpressible and unknowable nature of the absolute (there are many references to the *Dartik* in this section); chapter VI is about the indispensible qualities for the understanding of absolute reality (again references to the *Dartik*); and chapter VII is about Tathagatagarbha and sunyata.

Professor Ruegg's translation of Buton's *mDzes rGyan* was published in 1973. Its full title is *De bzhin gshegs pa'i snying po gsal zhing mdzes par byed pa'i rgyan.* It is also known as *bDe snying gsal rgyan.* As a commentary on the Tathagatagarbha doctrine based largely on the RGV, it is taken to be a refutation of the Jonangpa Shentong position. Interestingly, although a Rangtong interpretation, it differs markedly from that of Gyaltsab.

More recently, there has been an upsurge of Western interest in the text due to various Tibetan Lamas, particularly Kagyupas, teaching the RGV to their Western disciples. The disciples have in their turn published translations with the help of their Lama's comments.

For example, Ken and Katia Holmes published (1979) a translation of the RGV based entirely on the Tibetan, called *The Changeless Nature.* They were influenced by the explanations of living Tibetan Lamas, especially Khenpo Tsultrim Gyamtso and Thrangu Rimpoche. It does not attempt to explain either the Rangtong nor the Shentong point of view.

Also in 1983 a commentary on the RGV by Thrangu Rimpoche, translated by M. Kapstein and edited by Brian Beresford, was published (though apparently without Thrangu Rimpoche's and possibly without Kapstein's knowledge). Some attempt is made to explain the Shentong position but unfortunately insufficient care was taken over the editing of the translation.

In 1988 a book was published called *Buddha Nature* by Ven Thrangu Rimpoche translated by Erik Pema Kunsang and subtitled *Commentary on the Uttara Tantra Sastra*.

In 1989 a book called *A Commentary on the Uttara Tantra* by Thrangu Rimpoche was produced from a series of lecturers translated by Ken and Katia Holmes. Again the difference between a Rangtong and Shentong explanation is not clearly elucidated. Some of his explanations seem to favor a Rangtong and others a Shentong point of view.

Appendix 2

Prakritisunyata, Svabhavasunyata, and *Parabhavasunyata* in Rangtong and Shentong Terms.

To reiterate, the Tibetan term "rangtong" (if the term existed in Sanskrit it would translate something like *svasunyata*) is not to be confused with the Sanskrit terms *"svabhavasunyata"* *(rang bzhin stong pa or ngo bo nyid stong pa nyid)* and *"prakrtisunyata"* *(rang bzhin stong pa nyid),* which occur in Prajnaparamita literature.

Rangtong is a shortening of the term *"rang rang gi ngo bos stong pa"*—each empty of its own essence. It refers to each conceptually created dharma being empty of an essence (or self-nature) of its own, that is, form is empty of form, eye of eye, and so on for all dharmas; they are listed in Prajnaparamita literature as beginning with form and ending with the Buddha's Omniscience.

Prakrtisunyata

Prakrtisunyata translates into Tibetan as *"rang bzhin stong pa nyid,"* which is also the translation for *svabhavasunyata. Prakrtisunyata,* emptiness of self-nature, is the twelfth of the sixteen emptinesses found in Prajnaparamita literature.
Kongtrul explains [SKK hum 32a]:

> *bcu gnyis pa rang bzhin ni chos rnams kun rdzob kyi ngo bos stong pa de nyid la bya ba yin te. chos rnams kyi don dam pa'i ngo bo yin pa'i phyir. 'di dang stong nyid bzhi pa'i stong gzhi'i chos can gyi don ldog la khyad par med kyang. stong nyid du zhen pa dang. stong nyid de la rang bzhin du zhen pa dgag pa'i phyir so sor tha dad du bshad pa yin no.*

The twelfth is self-nature *(prakrti, rang bzhin)* because it is the absolute essence of the dharmas, that is, the emptiness of [i.e. absence in] dharmas of apparent essence. The *dharmin* of the empty base [i.e. the particular instance of emptiness] of this and the fourth emptiness [i.e. the emptiness of emptiness] are not different from the point of view of meaning, but in order to stop attachment to emptiness and attachment to that emptiness as a self-nature *(prakrti),* they are explained separately.

In this passage Kongtrul explains that the emptiness of (i.e. absence in) phenomena of apparent self-nature (*kun rdzob kyi ngo bo*) is the self-nature (*prakrti, ngo bo*) of the dharmas. The twelfth emptiness is called "emptiness of self-nature" because it is the emptiness of self-nature of self-nature. In other words, since self-nature (*prakrti*) is a concept, it also is empty (self-empty). Therefore, this *prakrti*, although it is referred to as the absolute essence of dharmas, is only the apparent absolute essence of dharmas (see Khenpo Tsultrim's comments on NTC cassette 4). The absolute, absolute essence of the dharmas, from both the Rangtong and Shentong point of view, is nisprapanca.

From this account it is clear that *prakrtisunyata* does not refer to apparent dharmas being empty of self-nature and so does not correspond to the term "rangtong."

Svabhavasunyata and Parabhavasunyata

Kongtrul explains each of the sixteen emptinesses, including *abhavasvabhavasunyata*, first from the Rangtong and then from the Shentong point of view [SKK hum 31–34]. (See chapter 5 "Own Nature and Other Nature" of this present work.)

He says that having explained the sixteen emptinesses, the middle length and expanded Prajnaparamita Sutras sum them up as four: (1) existence (*bhava*) is empty of existence (*bhava*); (2) non-existence (*abhava*) is empty of non-existence (*abhava*); (3) own nature (*svabhava*) is empty of own nature (*svabhava*); and (4) other existence (*parabhava*) is empty of other existence (*parabhava*). Kongtrul [SKK hum 32b] explains *svabhavasunyata* as follows:

> *kun rdzob kyi chos rnams gdod ma nas yod ma myong ba yin gyi.*
> *de med par ye shes kyis gsar du byas pa ma yin pa'i rgyu mtshan*
> *gyis stong pa nyid kun rdzob thams cad kyi rang bzhin tu bstan.*
> Although apparent dharmas primordially never existed, that nothingness was not newly created by jnana; for this reason emptiness is taught to be the self-nature (*svabhava*) of all apparent phenomena (samvrti).

He then goes on to explain other existence (*parabhava, gzhan dngos*) by contrasting it to apparent dharmas, which are objects of the mind that know apparent phenomena (samvrti). Other existence is what is not such an object and not an object expressible in words (*brjod pa dag gi yul du mi rung*). Kongtrul adds that Candrakirti, in his commentary on the MA, explains other existence as different from apparent existence in three ways: (1) the latter is impermanent and the former is permanent; (2) the latter is not known by jnana and the former is what is realized by jnana; and (3) the latter is not beyond suffering (nirvana) and the former is beyond suffering (nirvana). Khenpo Tsultrim [NTC cassette 4] adds that apparent dharmas are known by vijnana and emptiness is not known by vijnana.

Kongtrul explains that apparent reality includes *bhava* and *abhava* phenomena. He also explains that Absolute Reality has two conceptually distinguishable aspects of a single essence, *svabhava* and *parabhava*. Both aspects are self-empty in as far as they are conceptualizable. In other words, they are not found by reasoning that makes an ultimate analysis or analyzes the absolute (*don dam dpyod byed kyi rigs pas dpyad pa*). This discounts Ruegg's suggestion [*La Théorie* 330] that *parabhavasunyata* could be a source of Shentong doctrine.

Khenpo Tsultrim explains [NTC cassette 6] that both Rangtongpas and Shentongpas accept *parabhavasunyata* and that, in terms of the ultimate meditative realization, both arrive at the same understanding. The difference is in the way they try to avoid extreme positions in their presentation of tenets when establishing what is true through listening and reflecting [SKK hum 34a].

Kongtrul explains that, in Shentong terms, by means of the *abhava-bhava* distinction, the two extreme positions of permanence and nihilism are avoided. The permanence extreme is avoided because the *dharmin* (i.e. all conceptual dharmas) is self-empty. This is *abhavasunyata*—the imaginary nature (parikalpita) is non-existent (*abhava*). The nihilistic extreme is avoided because the *dharmin* (i.e. the Dharmata Dharmas and Dharmata Persons or the primordial Nature of dharmas and persons) is nondual Jnana, which is the Emptiness of what is Existent (*bhavasunyata*).

SKK [34a.5] explains the Shentong interpretation as follows:

dgag bya de bkag pa'i shul na chos nyid kyi chos dang gang zag gi dngos po yod pa'i cha nas dngos po med pa'i ngo bo nyid stong pa nyid du bzhags.

In the empty place left by refuting what had to be refuted is the Existent aspect, the Existent (*bhava*) Dharmata Dharmas and Persons, which is laid down as the *Abhavasvabhavasunyata*.

Ultimately Dharmata Dharmas and Dharmata Persons are equally (*mnyam pa nyid du*) the nondual Jnana and not separate (*so so*) [NTC cassette 6]. Khenpo Tsultrim adds that exclusive Rantongpas, who falsely deny the existence of that which is to be purified (made clean) or that which is to be liberated (i.e. the nondual Jnana), fall into the nihilistic extreme.

Incidentally, at one point [SKK hum 32], Kongtrul explains the sixteenth emptiness (*abhavasvabhavasunyata*) as rangtong:

bcu drug pa dngos po med pa'i ngo bo nyid ces pa ni. dngos po dngos po nyid kyis stong pa la bya ba yin la. de 'ang de nyid kyis

stong pa la ni dngos po med pa'i ngo bo nyid stong pa nyid ces bya'o.
The sixteenth, called the nature of non-existence (*abhavasvabhava*), is the name for existence (*bhava*) being empty of existence (*bhava*). This [*abhavasvabhava*] also being empty of this [*abhavasvabhava*] is *abhavasvabhavasunyata*.

Having shown how each of the sixteen emptinesses can be described as a self-emptiness (e.g. emptiness empty of emptiness, self-nature of self-nature etc.), Kongtrul describes how they can each be understood as Emptiness-of-other (Shentong). Thus, the twelfth emptiness, Emptiness of Self-Nature (*prakrtisunyata*) means Emptiness is the primordial Nature of the Dharmas and that Emptiness is their Absolute Nature, which is Empty-of-other (Shentong)—the nondual Jnana [SKK hum 33.4] called the "Dharmadhatu." In the same way, for each of the fourteen Emptinesses the *dharmin* (or empty base) is nondual Jnana. The manner of emptiness (*stong pa'i tshul*) is condensed as two (making the full list of sixteen emptinesses altogether). SKK [hum 34] explains that the first four bases are for showing the ultimate nature of all apparent dharmas is Emptiness (i.e. non-dual Jnana), and the next two are for showing that the Absolute is Emptiness (i.e. nondual Jnana). The last four are for showing that the ultimate nature of all the dharmas that the Bodhisattva has to practice and accomplish on and through the path to Buddhahood are Emptiness (i.e. nondual Jnana).*

Madhyantavibhaga [MAV 1.19] [SKK 34.2] explains *svabhavasunyata* as the naturally present gotra (*prakrtisthagotra, rang bzhin gnas rig*) [RGV 1.149]. Again from the Shentong point of view this is nondual Jnana. In Kongtrul's account [SKK hum 31–34], although *svabhavasunyata* is one of the four emptinesses that sum up the rangtong list of sixteen emptinesses, it does not occur in his list of Shentong Emptinesses.

Thus, for Kongtrul, in Shentong terms, all fourteen emptinesses (including *prakrtisunyata* and *abhavasvabhavasunyata*) mean self-emptiness when applied to the conceptual dharmas (i.e. when the *dharmin* or empty base is a conceptual dharma), and Emptiness of other when the empty base is nondual Jnana. It is clear, then, that rangtong and Shentong are terms for the mode of emptiness and should not be confused with terms such as *svabhavasunyata* and *parabhavasunyata*, which are specific instances of something (a *dharmin* or empty base) that is empty (either in a rangtong or Shentong manner).

_____

* N.B. The lay-out of Kongtrul's explanation follows MAV [1.17ff] and Vasubandu's *Bhyasya*.

Appendix 3

Further Details on the Three *Svabhava* and the Three Kinds of Emptiness as Found in the SNS

Dolpopa follows the SNS analysis [RC 194.1] and explains [RC 279] that parikalpita is emptiness of essence (*ngo bo nyid kyis stong pa nyid*), that is, it is what is merely apparent (*kun rdzob tsam*) in the sense of being mere delusion (*log pa'i kun rdzob*): it is not apparent reality (samvrtisatya). Paratantra is emptiness of true existence (*de bzhin du yod pa ma yin pa'i stong pa nyid*), that is, it has essence (*ngo bo*) only in relation to something else but not in itself: it is therefore apparent reality (samvrtisatya). Parinispanna is emptiness by/of own nature (*rang bzhin gyis stong pa nyid*), that is, the base, or ground in which there is absence of essence (*ngo bo nyid med pa'i gzhi*): it is Reality—the Absolute Absence of Essence (Paramartha *Nihsvabhavata, don dam ngo bo nyid med pa*) [RC 281], which is "empty of any other essence" [RC 21].

Sandhinirmocanasutra [SNS VII.6] explains that emptiness of essence means that there is no self of the person in the skandhas because such a self does not exist at all in reality; it is imaginary (parikalpita). Emptiness of true existence means there is no arising of an independently existing essence (or self-nature) of phenomena (dharmas). Dharmas do not arise by self-nature (*utpattinihsvabhava, skye ba ngo bo nyid med pa*). They arise from the power of some condition other than themselves [SNS VII.5] (*gzhan gyi stobs kyis byung ba yin*), like magical illusions [SNS VII.7]. This is the paratantra, empty of self-nature (i.e. of parikalpita). Absolute Absence of Essence (Paramartha *Nihsvabhavata*) is non-compounded and abides eternally [VII.9]: it is Parinispanna.

The changeless Absolute *Nihsvabhavata* might easily be mistaken for the *alayavijnana*. This was done by some writers who refuted Cittamatra, saying, it taught a creator like Indra and so forth. However, the *alayavijnana* is taught to be paratantra. Kongtrul argues that since *alayavijnana* is dependently-arising like a flowing river, it cannot be a self or a creator God like Indra.

According to the *Sandhinirmocana* only the Parinispanna is Absence of Essence (*Nihsvabhavata*) in the Absolute sense [SNS VII.6]. Then it adds [SNS IX.26]:

Oh, Avalokatesvara, although I do not say that essence (*ngo bo nyid* or *ngo bo nyid med pa nyid*)* perceives essence, however, since one is not able to demonstrate the non-essence, non-letter (*yi ge med pa*) self-awareness that cannot be demonstrated by letters [words?], I say that [Prajnaparamita] perceives absence of essence.

It also asks whether the Prajnaparamita perceives the non-essence of dharmas, and whether it is itself with, or without essence. This suggests that the debate as to whether Prajnaparamita is the perceived object (*visaya, yul*) or the perceiving awareness (literally, object-haver, *visayin, yul can*) is an ancient one [see Seng chao in the *Chao lun* p. 71]. Dolpopa [RC p. 178–179] argues against those who take Prajnaparamita to be referring to emptiness simply as the object of jnana, and not as Jnana itself. He considers this to be a grave mistake with no justification either according to scripture or reasoning.

Kongtrul [SKK om 150ba] explains that the MAV, DDV, and MSA describe the three natures, and thus make the distinction that the SNS makes between three different senses of emptiness, a feature of third Dharmacakra commentaries. Dolpopa [RC 195] remarks that the MSA and so forth distinguish the Mind as truly existing (Parinispanna) and mind as paratantra. He gives long detailed extracts with some very interesting parallels deserving more thorough investigation.

The Dependent Nature (Paratantra)—Base Consciousness (*Alayavijnana*)

Paratantra in Tibetan is *gZhan dbang*, which means other-powered. Kongtrul explains it is called other-powered because the subject and object aspects (*gzung 'dzin cha*) arise from the power of previous traces, are momentary, and power the arising of future moments. Kongtrul [SKK a'252na] gives the Cittamatra definition of paratantra as all the dharmas that arise from the *alayavijnana*. He explains that the *alayavijnana* is dependently-arising and momentary by nature (*rten cing 'brel 'byung skad cig ma'i rang bzhin*). The *alayavijnana* is a base or substratum like an ocean; the subject and object aspects are like the waves. Both the subject and object aspects are the same substance (*rdzas*) as the *alayavijnana* from which they arise. Since both the apparent outer object and the inner perceiving mind share the same nature, it is in this sense that all phenomena are of the nature of mind (*rnam rig tsam*) [SKK a'252na]. SNS [VII.13]

---

*Alternative reading.

explains that the paratantra is the mind (*shes pa*) not soiled by conventional labels (*tha snyad btags*).

According to Kongtrul [SKK a' 251–252na] the main difference between ordinary Samvrti Cittamatrins and the Paramartha Cittamatrins (Shentong Yogacara Madhyamakas) is that the former accept that vijnana (*rnam shes*) is truly existent (*bden grub*) and the latter do not. The latter only accept the nondual Jnana as truly existent (*bden grub*). However, even though Samvrti Cittamatrins say vijnana is truly existent, they do not mean that vijnana is not dependently-arising and momentary. Just as the Hinayana schools accept moments of consciousness as absolute (paramartha) in the sense of being the end point of their analysis of mind, so Samvrti Cittamatrins accept the moments of the stream of vijnana as paramartha and truly existent.

The *Sandhinirmocana* does not teach that the *alayavijnana* (i.e. the paratantra) is paramartha. Indeed, it cannot be the paramartha as defined by this Sutra, since it says the paramartha is that focus for consciousness that is completely pure (*rnam par dag pa'i dmigs pa*) [SNS IV.8, VII.6]. "Pure" means that by means of focusing consciousness on it, consciousness becomes pure, free from delusion, awakened and liberated. The paratantra is not a suitable focus for purifying consciousness, for it is impure (at least to begin with).

The nub of the criticism the Madhyamikas level against Samvrti Cittamatrins is their application of the term "truly existing" to mind-moments which, since they are held to be momentary, do not have the characteristics of something that truly exists. The Samvrti Cittamatrin view is that klesa arise from conflicts in regard to self and other, or self and the world. Once the emptiness of the paratantra of the parikalpita is realized, these subside and the stream of consciousness becomes a stream of simple self-knowing, self-illuminating moments of consciousness. This stream is the pure mind that eventually transforms into the Buddhajnana.

Madhyamikas refute the Cittamatrin "self-illuminating self-awareness" (*rang rig rang gsal*). They argue that if a perceiver needs self-awareness in order to be aware of itself, by what means is self-awareness aware of itself? If the answer is "self-awareness" the objection is that an infinite regression arises. Thus, self-awareness is rejected entirely by some Madhyamikas (e.g. Tsongkapa, [see *dKa' gnas chen po brgyad*]), but others, who accept self-aware Jnana (*rang rig pa'i ye shes*) as Paramartha, simply refute the Cittamatra position that a vijnana can be Paramartha. They maintain that Awareness, though called "self-aware Jnana" (*rang rig pa'i ye shes*), is in fact non-compounded and nondual, the perceived and perceiving aspects being simply a mistaken appearance. They argue that for something to be Paramartha it must exist independently, but the self-knowing, self-illuminating awareness of Samvrti Cittamatrins only exists in dependence on another *ad finitum* [BCA 9.8]. There can be no ultimately existing self-aware vijnana.

Paul Williams refers to this controversy in his paper "On *Rang Rig*" in *Proceedings of Csoma de Koros Symposium*, 1981. (See MA and BCA for refutation of *rang rig*; see also Obermiller's *'Sublime Science'* [p. 99] for more detail on the Yogacara concept of *alaya*.)

The Imaginary Nature—Parikalpita

For both ordinary Cittamatrins and Yogacara Madhyamakas the parikalpita is the nonreal appearance of the subject-object aspects (*gzung 'dzin cha rnam par snang ba yang dag ma yin*). More specifically this means the appearance of an inner perceiving subject different in substance (*rdzas*) to the outer perceived object in any moment of perception. Ordinary Cittamatrins think the vijnana mind "substance" itself is truly existent (*bden grub*), but that the idea of a world outside or beyond the senses is purely imaginary. Yogacara Madhyamikas hold that the Parinispanna Jnana is truly existent (*bden grub*) and that both the idea of a world beyond the senses and the "substance" of a dependently-arising stream-of-vijnana is imaginary (parikalpita).

The Truly Existing Nature—Parinispanna

Parinispanna is defined in SNS [VI.6] as the Tathata of the dharmas, which has to be meditated on until Enlightenment is attained. In general parinispanna means the truly existent nature of things and refers to the object of focus of wisdom, prajna [SKK ah 253 ba]:

> *gzung 'dzin gnyis stong gi shes pa/ rnam par mi rtog pa/ rnam par dag pa'i dmigs pa de las gzhan du med par yongs su grub pa*
> The pure non-conceptual focus of the mind empty of subject and object is the only truly existent nature (parinispanna).

The mind focused in this way is prajna, the perceiving awareness (*visayin, yul can*). In Samvrti Cittamatra this is sometimes called the "non-mistaken parinispanna" (*phyin ci ma log pa'i yongs grub*). According to Kongtrul [SKK], for Cittamatrins the clarity aspect of mind (*rig gsal*) is the non-mistaken truly existent nature, but it is not and never becomes the changeless parinispanna (*'gyur med yongs grub:* see *La Théorie* [101] for the double parinispanna of the Cittamatrins). Prajna transforms into liberated Buddhajnana when it is purified, but Buddhajnana is not the changeless parinispanna. Prajna is purified by focusing on the pure non-compounded object of consciousness, which is the truly existent nature of things (i.e. the changeless parinispanna). It seems that here we should understand prajna to be the pure stream of self-illuminating self-awareness.

When I asked Khenpo Tsultrim whether Samvrti Cittamatrins took the non-mistaken truly existent nature to be compounded, his answer was that, since they count it as a vijnana, one must assume they accept it is compounded. In his opinion, since it is dependently-arising, it would be more appropriate for them to call it "ultimate paratantra" rather than parinispanna. He said that this lack of clarity concerning the exact status of the clarity aspect of mind is removed by Madhyamaka reasoning.

General Comments

SNS [VII.10] explains that problems arise because an imaginary nature (parikalpita) is attached to the paratantra and the parinispanna. SNS VI.8–9 explains the three natures with the image of a crystal standing on different colored cloths. The colors in the crystal that make it appear as sapphire, emerald, ruby and so forth, are not its nature and this is the parikalpita; the crystal and the cloth are the paratantra; and the absence of the colors in the essence of the crystal is parinispanna (RGV [2.51] uses the same example).

In general terms, therefore, one can say the solution is to cut through the parikalpita by focusing on the parinispanna (i.e. the completely truly existent nature of the paratantra), like cutting through the deception of a magical illusion by seeing that the true nature of the various manifestations is emptiness. Dolpopa [RC 192] explains that the Cittamatrin view, of the paratantra being empty of parikalpita, is a step towards seeing the Parinispanna empty of parikalpita and paratantra.

Indeed, the SNS can be interpreted as moving towards a Shentong position. The SNS stresses the difference between saying the parikalpita is without essence and the paratantra is without essence because some "dishonest" beings try to interpret the Buddha's doctrine of "all dharmas are without self-nature etc.," to mean that parikalpita, paratantra, and parinispanna natures do not exist [SNS VII.20]. The Sutra emphasizes that this is a wrong view and that the parikalpita, paratantra, and parinispanna natures do exist (*yod*). The effect of this is to emphasize that paratantra is a functioning reality—like a dream or a magical illusion—whereas parikalpita is purely imaginary—like a sky flower or a hare's horn. In order to realize the Absolute Dhatu, one must accept the reality of the mind, otherwise one will slip into a negative extreme. SNS VIII.7 and 8 explain that the appearance of form and so forth as a mental image is none other than mind, and that ordinary beings make the mistake of not realizing that the focus or objects of their consciousnesses are mere mind (*rnam par shes pa'i rnam par rig pa tsam, vijnaptimatra*). In this way, great emphasis is put on the existence of the paratantra (albeit dependent existence). The Shentong view is directed towards a misunderstanding of this emphasis on the existence of the paratantra.

To correct this, Shentong adds that the Parinispanna is empty of the paratantra. It makes it clear that ultimately the paratantra does not exist at all and that Parinispanna is a Reality independent of paratantra. This does not contradict the SNS in as far as the paratantra is indeed empty of the parikalpita, and parinispanna is indeed Absolute Nihsvabhavata [see RC 192]. Also the SNS itself states that the paratantra is empty of essence and without arising, ceasing, or dwelling [SNS VII.1].

The SNS itself emphasizes the danger of clinging to views and that emptiness of parikalpita and paratantra were both taught in order to make it possible to realize the Absolute Dhatu—called ''Absolute Nihsvabhavata.'' This it claims was the real intention behind all the Buddha's teaching. SNS VII.28 and 29 give the example of the same substance being made up into different medicines and elixirs, or the same paint into different pictures, or melted butter into different sauces, or space pervading everywhere. In the same way, the teaching of the Nitartha pervades all neyartha Sutras. The first and second Dharmacakras are neyartha, but nonetheless imply the Nitartha. Thus, everyone has finally to realize the real intention of all His teachings, which is the Absolute Dhatu.

Both the Prasangika and Svatantrika Madhyamikas [LM 80] attack what we are calling here ''Samvrti Cittamatrins'' who, from the philosophical point of view at least, cling to the paratantra (i.e. the mind-stream) as existing.

Some Madhyamakas (e.g. Tsongkapa) maintain there is a definite difference in nature between mind and matter (*phyi don,* literally, outside objects). For Tsongkapa the only nature they hold in common is absence of self-nature [see *dKa' gnas chen po brgyad*]. However, Yogacara-Madhyamikas accept (as Samvrti Cittamatrins do and as is found in SNS VIII. 7 and 8) that the outer world, that is, perceived objects, are none other than mind, that is, that there is no real mind-matter dichotomy. Thus, contrary to what is often supposed, the difference between Madhyamaka and Cittamatra is not necessarily about the status of external objects as mind or not.

The subtle pure mind of the Rangtong interpretations of the RGV, and the Gelugpa explanations of the subtle subjective clear light mind in the Tantras, sound to a Shentongpa suspiciously like the stream of pure moments of dependently-arising awareness of Samvrti Cittamatra. However, Gelugpas do not accept that moments of awareness are the same substance (*rdzas*) as the object. Whether they are justified in their suspicion or not is something requiring very careful research. This is undoubtedly a very subtle point indeed.

The Great Madhyamikas believe the Absolute, referred to as the Dhatu in the SNS (e.g. *zag pa med pa'i dbyings*) [SNS VII.24], the Pure Mind or Clear Light Nature in the RGV and so on, and the pure self-illuminating, self-knowing awareness experienced by the Cittamatrins, are all the primordially Existent, nondual Buddha Jnana. It is always pure in the sense of unspoiled. The wrong ways of thinking never affect it [RGV 1.63]; they merely obscure it.

Incidentally, in the *Trimsaka* [*La Trentaine* 115], Vasubandhu explains that the parinispanna is the state of the paratantra when free from the parakalpita—parakalpita being the imagination of perceiver and perceived. It is the "*essencité*" of the paratantra. Later on the *Trimsaka* [*La Trentaine* 121] describes the mind as fixed in the "*essencité d'ésprit.*" It explains [*La Trentaine* 17] that although the paratantra is *dravya* it is still empty of self-nature. It mentions [*La Trentaine* 121] the revolution (transformation) of the *Alaya* and that Dhatu has the sense of cause because it is the cause of the Aryan dharmas, which are inconceivable, since they are arrived at not through reasoning but through the individual self-awareness (*so so rang rig*) [*La Trentaine* 122]. It is not immediately clear whether Vasubandhu speaks from a Rangtong or a Shentong point of view and a number of opposing commentarial traditions have arisen from his work.

For further discussion on the topic of the three natures, see LM [95] for Kamalasila's view and *La Théorie* [442] for a comparison of Shentong with the Sino-Indian school of Paramartha, which also holds the view that the parinispanna is empty of both the parikalpita and the paratantra.

Appendix 4

The *Sandhinirmocanasutra: Résumé*

SNS [I] establishes the ineffable Nature (*anabhilapya dharmata, brjod du med pa'i chos nyid*) that is neither compounded nor non-compounded [SNS 1–3] and which, furthermore, is referred to in SNS [1.4] as *dravya* (*dngos po*). SNS [I] then emphasizes that terms such as "compounded", "non-compounded", "real", and "false" are used simply for the benefit of the immature [SNS I.4–6]; although they use them in order to teach the immature, the Aryas do not really believe in them.

From this detailed and often repeated statement, made at the very outset of the Sutra, it is reasonable to assume that any later statements about the paratantra and Parinispanna existing are not to be taken too seriously.

• SNS II is about the Paramartha that is known by *pratyatmavedaniya* (*so so rang gi rig pa*), and is the character beyond all concepts.[1]

• SNS III discusses whether the Paramartha is the same as or different from the compounded (*samskara*), and establishes it is the subtle characteristic beyond same or different [SNS III.1].

• SNS IV exposes the ignorant, who teach diverse aspects of the Dharma, such as the skandhas, truths, the *bodhipaksika* dharmas and so forth, without knowing the Paramartha, which is the single taste of all the dharmas. All dharmas have this Absolute same taste characteristic.

• SNS IV.9 refers to the *bhiksu* yogacaras, who realize this and IV.10 calls this Paramartha the "*dharmanam dharmata* dhatu" (*chos rnams kyi chos nyid dbyings*) that is permanent and eternal whether the Tathagatas arise in the world or not. SNS IV.11 compares it to space.

• SNS V teaches about the nature of the *citta, manas,* and vijnana, describing the *alayavijnana* and so forth. SNS V.6 explains that Bodhisattvas are called "skillful" (*mkhas pa*) at knowing the secret of the *citta, manas,* and vijnana because they do not see the various aspects of mind (including the *alayavijnana*), or the sense organs or their objects. They are therefore skillful at the Paramartha (*Paramarthakusula*); this is what being skillful at knowing the secret of the *citta, manas,* and vijnana really means. It is not enough just to recognize these aspects, one must also know their true nature.

Thus, whatever else the SNS might say about the *alayavijnana*, it is not disputing its ultimate lack of true existence. If it truly existed the Aryas would see it in their final realization and according to the SNS they do not.

• SNS VI teaches the three natures, the parikalpita, paratantra, and Parinispanna in some detail.
• SNS VII.1 addresses itself to the question of why, having taught all the categories of the path as having the characteristic of own nature (*svalaksana*), arising (*utpadalaksana*) and so forth, the Buddha now says they are without self nature (*nihsvabhava*) and not arising (*anutpanna*) and so forth. The question is asked, using the expression *ci la dgongs nas* (with what in mind); the Buddha answers by teaching in detail the three kinds of absence of self-nature (*nihsvabhavata*).

• SNS VII.4, 5, and 6 make it very clear that not only the parikalpita, but also the paratantra and Parinispanna are *nihsvabhavata*. Parikalpita is *laksananihsvabhavata*, the paratantra is *utpattinihsvabhavata*, and Parinispanna is *Paramarthanihsvabhavata*.
• SNS VII.9 teaches that the *Paramarthanihsvabhavata* is non-compounded and abides eternally and so forth. However, one should bear in mind that in SNS [I], such terms are merely teaching devices; in reality the Paramartha is beyond such conceptually created dualities as compounded and non-compounded and so forth.
• SNS VII.14 seems to say that although the *nihsvabhavata*—taught in the preceding section—is the doctrine of all three vehicles, which makes all vehicles one, there are three kinds of being who understand according to their own level, so that each level can also be said to have its own vehicle.
• SNS VII.15 explains that those Sravakas, who have little compassion and much fear of suffering, have by nature only an inferior gotra. Professor Ruegg informed me that this is quite unusual for single vehicle (*ekayana*) Sutras, which normally teach the one gotra by means of which followers of all three vehicles attain Buddhahood eventually. The fact that the SNS mentions, albeit in passing, an inferior gotra is made much of by commentators who regard the SNS as a non-*ekayana* Sutra.
• SNS VII.16 explains that there are Sravakas who will transform into Enlightenment and this occurs at the point when they remove the knowledge veils. It is not clear whether the passage means that all Sravakas eventually become "Sravakas who will transform into Enlightenment" or whether SNS VII.16 is distinguishing another type of Sravaka to the kind in SNS VII.15. Obviously those who interpret the SNS as a non-*ekayana* Sutra take the latter view.
• SNS VII.17 teaches that it was in reference to (*samdhaya, dgongs nas*) the three kinds of *nihsvabhavata*, that the Buddha taught all dharmas were without essence, non-born, and so forth in neyartha Sutras.

• SNS VII.18–24 then explain that the Buddha's intention in speaking as he did (*samdhayavacana, dgongs te bshad pa*) was not always fully understood.

• SNS VII.20 teaches that those who do not distinguish the three *nihsvabhavatas* fall into a nihilistic view.

• SNS VII.22–23 deal with those who do not believe what is said in VII.20.

• SNS VII.24 sums up by saying that all panditas agree that the Buddha's intended meaning (*samdhi, dgongs pa*) was dharmas being without essence and non-born and so forth. However, it is those panditas who correctly understand His intended meaning (*dgongs pa shes pa*) to be the three kinds of *nihsvabhavata* who understand the single path to purification and the single purity. At this point, the Buddha declares that this is why he taught the single vehicle (all this is referring back to what was already said in SNS VII.14).

However, He stresses again that He is not denying there are various types (*dhatu, rigs*) of beings. This section seems to emphasize that in the neyartha Sutras that teach absence of essence of the dharmas, the intended meaning behind the Buddha's words is the Nitartha teaching of the three kinds of absence of essence; it is this latter teaching that constitutes the single vehicle. What is not clearly stated is whether all the beings of the various types (*dhatu, gotra*) end up following this single vehicle. This has again led to some commentators questioning whether this Sutra is truly an *ekayana* Sutra or not.

• SNS VII. 24 ends by reminding us that the Element without outflow (*anasravadhatu, zag pa med pa'i dbyings*) is subtle (*suksma, phra*), unthinkable (*acintya, bsam kyis mi khyab*), equal (*sama, mnyam*), indivisible (*nirvisesa, bye brag med*), all accomplishing (*sarvarthasiddhi, thams cad don grub*), relinquishment of all suffering and klesa, nondual, inexpressible (*anabhilapya, brjod pa ma yin*), and a lasting treasury (*bang*).

• SNS VII.28, 29, 31, 32, and 33 all explicitly state that the teaching of the absence of essence of all dharmas is Nitartha. It is compared to space in the sense that it is present in all neyartha Sutras without being obscured by the clarifications (?) (*nirvrtti* (?), *bsal ba*) of the Pratyeka, Sravaka, and Mahayana vehicles.*

---

* N.B. the term *dgongs pa* is not used at all in these sections.

• SNS VII.30 teaches that the Buddha turned the Wheel of the Dharma three times. The first time, He taught the Four Noble Truths and this was a neyartha teaching. The second time, He taught all dharmas were without essence; this was also a neyartha teaching. The third time, He taught all dharmas were without essence; this time it was the Nitartha teaching.

• SNS VIII teaches the details of the path and fruit of *samatha* and *vipasyana*.

• SNS VIII.7–8 teach how outer objects are the mind. The example is given of how we imagine, when images arise in our minds, that they are reflections of outer objects, as if the mind were a mirror and the images reflections of things outside the mind. The SNS implies that it is wrong to imagine this.

• SNS VIII.29 discusses the sixteen emptinesses and the obstructions that they remove.

• SNS VIII.31 reaffirms sunyata as the doctrine of the Mahayana and that the *sunyatalaksana* of the Mahayana is the characteristic of separateness of the paratantra and Parinispanna from the parikalpita and to not see the latter in the former two.[†]

• SNS IX teaches the eleven *bhumis*. SNS IX.26 teaches *nihsvabhavata* and Prajnaparamita. SNS IX.32 reaffirms the teaching of one vehicle explaining that it teaches the Dharmadhatu *ekayana*.

• SNS X teaches the Buddhakayas.

Additional Notes on the Term "dgongs pa"

Although Gelugpa scholars take the term *dgongs pa* as a signal indicating neyartha teachings, generally speaking *dgongs pa* in Tibetan is the honorific for "to think" or "to have in mind." It is also used to translate various Sanskrit terms (see below). Khenpo Tsultrim explains that the meaning of *dgongs pa* in the title of the SNS is that the neyartha and Nitartha intentions of the Buddha are clearly laid out. However, in SNS VIII.33 the Bodhisattva Paramarthasamudgata asks why the teaching given here is called *Samdhinirmocanadharmaparyaya*. The Buddha replies that it is because it is the *Paramarthanitarthanirdesa*.

Clearly, therefore, the authority for interpreting the term "*dgongs pa*" to mean neyartha teachings does not come from the SNS.

[†] N.B. SNS VI.8, 9 and VII.10,13,20,25, and 26 all explain the Parinispanna to be the absence of the parikalpita in the paratantra and the absolute absence of essence (*paramarthanihsvabhavata*) to be the absence of the parikalpita in the paratantra and Parinispanna.

dGongs pa is used to translate the terms *samdhaya* [CD, BHS], *samdhi*, *samdha* [Lamotte, CD], *abhipraya* [Lamotte, BHS, CD]. *dGongs nas* [CD] is *abhipretya*. *dgongs pa'i* [CD] is *abhiprayika*. Monier Williams' *Sanskrit English Dictionary* [MW] gives *samdha*, *samdhi*, and *samdhaya* as all having a sense of union or uniting, although *samdha* also means to aim. *Abhipretya* means "intending, meaning by." In the *Buddhist Hybrid Sanskrit* [BHS], *abhipraya* is given as meaning intention or difference; and *samdhaya* as the real meaning of a Buddhist text or doctrine, opposite to its *prima facie* or superficial meaning. (For more discussion on the meaning of these words see Ruegg's article JIP 1985 and Broido's articles mentioned below.)

According to these meanings, SNS IX.32 for example, would read as follows:

> Lord, when [you] Lord taught saying, "the Sravakayana and the Mahayana are one yana," what was your intention (aim or "real" meaning)?

The Buddha replies that his intention or real meaning was to remove the dispute of those who took his earlier teachings too literally and thought the Sravakayana, since it taught the various natures of things like the skandhas and so on, must be different to the Mahayana in which only (*ekanaya*) the Dharmadhatu was taught.

Ruegg suggests that the use of the term *dgongs pa* here somehow restricts the sense in which the Buddha spoke of the two vehicles as one. In other words, he is suggesting that the Buddha only meant it in reference to one particular point. He did not mean it as a general statement. Buton [DZG 12a] considers neyartha to mean what is *dgongs pa,* which he takes to mean taught for a purpose, and not to be taken literally.[2]

The foregoing discussion illustrates the complexity of the task, first of unraveling, and then evaluating, the special interpretation that Buton, Ketrub, and others put on the Sutras of the third Dharmacakra. Ruegg has produced monumental works that give us a good idea of the kind of intricacies of reasoning, interpretation, and shifts in the use of terms that have been and are being used. There are many issues involved and all one can hope to do here is to draw the reader's attention to alternative interpretations and uses of terms and await future research in order to evaluate them. Since little work has been done as yet by way of tracing the precise usage of terms throughout the whole range of Buddhist literature, it is not always possible to state categorically which are the most standard.

Appendix 5

Some Points of Comparison Between Rangtong Commentators on RGV

Kuijp [CDTBE 43] remarks that, in general, the Gelugpas and especially the Gandenpas (*dGa' ldan pas*—those from the Gelugpa monastary of Ganden) are taken to be following Ngog's interpretation of Tathagatagarbha, yet, as we shall see below, there are important differences between Gyaltsab and Rongton who is supposed to be following Ngog. Kongtrul [RGV commentary 44] quotes Ngog on the three kinds of *Sugatagarbha*; the words are identical to Rongton's commentary, substantiating to some extent that Rongton is true to the Ngog tradition.

For both Gyaltsab and Rongton, Dhatu, Tathagatagarbha, and Gotra are not synonyms. For Rongton (as for Buton), the actual Tathagatagarbha is the actual doubly-pure heart-essence (*garbha*) of the Buddha (i.e. the Dharmakaya, the final realization of emptiness). The emptiness of the defiled mind is also called "Tathagatagarbha," but this is figurative, since it is more precisely the nature (*garbha*) of beings [Rongton 28.3]. Notice he takes *garbha* here to mean simply essence or nature—this is not very satisfactory in philological terms, since it does little justice to the term *snying po* in Tibetan and even less to *garbha* in Sanskrit. The Dhatu is emptiness and awareness inseparable (see Rongton's comments on RGV 1.40) and gotra is twofold [p. 36]—the pure nature and the mind of a being (the knower of that pure nature). By "pure nature" Rongton means that nature that is the object (*dmigs pa*) focused on in order to purify the mind-stream [his commentary p. 94ff].

So let us take, for example, the key verses RGV 1.27–1.28:

27. Because the Perfect Buddhakaya radiates,
    Because the Tathata is inseparable,
    Because the gotra is present,
    All beings have the essence (*garbha*) of Buddha.
28. Because Buddhajnana is present in the mass of beings,
    Because the stainless nature (*svabhava, rang bzhin*) is non-dual,
    Because the Buddha gotra is named after its fruit, it is taught that all beings have the Buddha essence (*garbha*).

Rongton explains that the first sign refers only to the fruit Tathagatagarbha, the Dharmakaya and so is Tathagatagarbha in the true sense. The Tathagatagarbha is said (figuratively) to be present in, or to enter (*antargamat, gzhugs*) beings as their heart-essence (*garbha*), for it is obtainable by them (*thob tu rung ba*). Rongton also explains [34] that "the perfect Buddhakaya radiates" (*spharanat, 'phro ba*) to mean obtainable—a somewhat idiosyncratic piece of etymology that does not accord with the RGVV explanations.

Rongton [35] states that the cause of gaining the transformation (*gnas gyur thob ba'i rgyu*) into the realization Dharmakaya and Teaching Dharmakaya is the pure nature aspect and this (not the Dharmakaya) is what pervades all beings.

According to Rongton, the second sign refers to the nature (Tathata) of Buddhas and beings, which is emptiness. Because of this emptiness, transformation can occur. It is called "natural purity" (*rang bzhin dag pa*), the likeness of the Buddha. He explains [32.6] that, although it may seem unfitting to compare the Dhatu with a seed—because it is emptiness, which one might think is inert—in fact emptiness is dynamic because it has the power to transform. He refers us to the *Mulamadhyamakakarikas* [MMK chapter 24] and *Vigrahavyavartini* (*rTsod pa bzlog pa*), where it clearly states that what is able to be empty can be anything: (*gang la stong pa nyid rung ba, de la thams cad rung ba yin*). Thus, for Rongton Dhatu (element) has the power (*nus pa*) of emptiness, which means it can become anything. Rongton [33]:

> If the practitioner's form were existent (*dravya, dngos po*), it could not become non-existent (*dngos po med*), and the Great Vehicle could not surpass the gods, men, anti-gods and their worlds. The emptiness (non-existence, *dngos med*) of beings is not the formlessness of the formless gods. A formless god is not non-existence (*dngos med*) and he becomes a formless god because he does not realize non-existence (*dngos med*). The Buddha's disciples know non-existence (*dngos med*) and so can become non-existent (*dngos med*) and have the kayas of Buddha.

The third sign in RGV 27 and 28 refers to gotra, the power (*nus pa*) in the mind of beings that enables them to reach Buddhahood. This is the ever present, non-defiled mind referred to in RGV 1.104 and compared to bees' honey. He calls this [34] the "Dharmakaya gotra."

This is the cause Tathagatagarbha as opposed to the fruit, the actual Tathagatagarbha. It is the cause (*rgyu*) of the Tathatagata and so it is called the "*Buddhagarbha*" because it will be Buddha (the fruit) although at present it is actually the essence (*garbha*) of beings. He comments as follows:

In the skandhas of beings dwells the Buddhajnana. Since the whole base and fruit are pervaded inside and out by the emptiness of true essence (*bden pa'i ngo bo nyid kyid stong pas*), the gotra pervading it is the mind's power (*nus pa*) that is awakened by supporting conditions (*rkyen*) which is the approximate cause (*nyer len rgyu*) of Buddhajnana.

Rongton explains the statement in RGVV [1.25], which quotes the *Avatamsakasutra* on Buddhajnana abiding in the skandhas (*phung po*) of beings. This "Buddhajnana" is the stainless, nondual nature, the Buddha gotra (*nus pa*); and this is the essence of beings. It is not actually Buddha, but it is called "Buddhagotra" because it is what will transform and become Buddha. He also quotes a commentary in which this is mysteriously referred to as the essenceless substance (*snying po med pa'i rdzas*).

In contrast to Rongton, Gyaltsab takes Tathagatagarbha to mean the power to attain Buddhahood; it only refers to beings when they are veiled. The three signs that beings have Tathagatagarbha are:

1. The activity of the Buddhas acts on all beings so they can awaken.
2. The emptiness (i.e. nature) of beings' minds is inseparable from them.
3. They have the causes and conditions (inner and outer) to reach Buddhahood (gotra).

In other words, the three signs express the undoubtedly true doctrine that, although beings have the potential to become Buddha (Tathagatagarbha), the potential alone is not enough. There has also to be Buddha activity on the one side and the right causes and conditions on the part of the beings themselves, on the other. Thus, according to Gyaltsab, the essential message of the RGV is that Dharmakaya is not Tathagatagarbha.

Gyaltsab argues that "Buddhakaya radiates" means the Buddha activity (i.e. the jnana aspect of the Dharmakaya) penetrates to all beings and would teach them if they responded; this would give them the power to reach Buddhahood. It is not clear how this gives all beings the power to attain Buddhahood. It simply gives all beings the theoretical possibility of attaining the power to reach Buddhahood. Ruegg presents Gyaltsab's view [*La Théorie* 293].

> . . . *la capacité potentielle du functionnement de l'action du Dharmakāya dans la Série du sattva*. . . .

Ruegg [*La Théorie* 295] sums up how, in Gyaltsab's view, Tathagatagarbha is the cause of Enlightenment only in the sense that it is the *alambana* (object) of the jnana (*samahitajnana*) of Arya Bodhisattvas, which is the principal productive cause of Buddhajnana. It is a productive cause in the sense that by focusing on it the mind-stream is purified.

Although Kongtrul quotes Rongton's explanation of RGV 1.27, 1.28, in fact, he takes Dharmakaya, Tathata, and Gotra as all referring to Buddhajnana:

1. Buddhajnana is the Dharmakaya pervading all dharmas. Therefore, it pervades the five skandhas of beings.

2. Buddhajnana is the Tathata of Buddhas and beings, that is, base, path, and fruit are inseparable.

3. Buddhajnana is the Gotra present in the skandhas, enabling beings to reach Buddhahood, that is, it is the Tathagatagarbha.

As we have seen (Chapter 4.2 "Inseparable Qualities" of this present work) Rongton explains that Dharmakaya is the result of a transformation and, therefore, strictly speaking compounded (*'dus byas*). Since the RGV clearly says it is non-compounded (*'dus ma byas*), Rongton must explain this discrepancy. He does so by saying that the Dharmakaya, unlike the form-kayas, does not arise and perish for the benefit of beings; that is why it is called uncompounded. He explains spontaneous (*lhun grub*) as referring to the *dharmin* (i.e. the Buddha's mind), which is at peace, free from the two kinds of veil. He explains inconceivable [30ff]—in the context of the SMS discussion of how the Tathata that is pure by nature can be stained—as inconceivable for Sravakas and Pratyeka Buddhas because being pure by nature contradicts having klesa. By this interpretation "inconceivability" means that Sravakas and Pratyeka Buddhas cannot conceive of it rather than that its inherent nature is inconceivable in the Shentong sense. In other words, since Sravakas and Pratyeka Buddhas do not realize the emptiness of the klesa, they cannot understand how they are empty (pure) from the beginning. Whereas from Rongton's explanation, the solution for Sravakas and Pratyeka Buddhas would be to realize emptiness, the SMS makes more of a problem out of it, saying their only solution is to rely on faith. Rongton does not mention faith at all in this context.

Although Rongton does not address himself to the rangtong-Shentong controversy, Gyaltsab in his *Dartik* does. He states categorically [*Dartik* 19, 23] that the RGV and RGVV are only rangtong and not Shentong. He accuses [*Dartik* 23b] Shentongpas of making the absurd assertion that the doubly pure Dharmakaya is in beings. He draws this conclusion from the fact that they accept the pure by nature Dharmakaya is in beings. Pure by nature is defined by Gyaltsab as the "doubly pure Dharmakaya," meaning the Dharmakaya free from the two kinds of veil. Obviously this cannot be in beings.

What Shentongpas mean by pure by nature is the Dharmakaya nature that is never stained in the sense of being spoiled in essence. For them double purity means both pure by nature and also unveiled [RGV 1.47ff and RC 155]. RGVV [2.7:44b] clearly supports this interpretation.

Because, as we have seen above, Gyaltsab does not accept that stainless can mean unspoiled in essence, he argues [*Dartik* 24] that examples (as in the SNS) of the mind of beings being like stainless gold and so on cannot mean the Tathata is stainless in beings. He concludes, therefore, that they mean that they cannot be stained by others. In other words, beings stain their own minds through their own klesa and so forth. If and when they stop doing that, their minds will be stainless like stainless gold and so on.

Nevertheless, there seems to be a sense in which other Rangtongpas, such as Rongton, when referring to the clear light nature of mind, use "stainless" in the sense of unspoiled. This requires more detailed research as does the Gelugpa Tantric teaching on objective and subjective clear lights [see RGVV 2.7 *prakrtivisuddhi* and *vaimalyavisuddhi* and Takasaki's *Study* 315 fn.15].

Rongton explains that the stainless Tathata is primordially pure in the sense of being empty, but the stains, which were never the nature of the element, must be removed like the impurities from gold. Curiously, Kongtrul follows Rongton [Rongton's commentary 30.6] rather than Dolpopa here; he uses the example of impure gold that has no shine, but when it is clean the shine is seen to be an inseparable quality of the gold, not a newly acquired quality.

Whereas Shentongpas use the example of the gold and its impurities to show that the quality of brightness was there from the beginning, Rongton uses it to show that, at the stage of an ordinary being, the qualities are not present. Thus, it simply becomes a matter of terminology and intention. Does one say butter is in the unchurned milk, or does one categorically deny the term "butter" to mean that which will be butter when it emerges? In some circumstances, it is important to stress the butter is always in the milk and sometimes that it is not really functional as butter until it is churned out of it.

As we have seen, in Shentong terms, all seven Vajra Bases refer to non-conceptual Buddhajnana. However, just as the Dharmakaya, Tathata, Gotra, Dhatu, and Tathagatagarbha are not different terms for the same thing for Rangtongpas, so, for them, each of the seven Vajra Bases refer to something different. Since, in Rangtong terms, of all phenomena, only the truth of the self-emptiness of the dharmas is unchanging and indestructible, this is the Vajra. Buddha, Dharma, Samgha, Dhatu, Enlightenment, Qualities, and Activity are self-empty and so they are Vajra Bases. Gyaltsab

[*Dartik* 7b] explains that the Vajra bases "Buddha," "Dharma," and "Samgha" refer to what is already accomplished by others and "Enlightenment," "Qualities," and "Activity" refer to what arises in one's own mind. The Dhatu-Tathagatagarbha, which is the stained tathata (not possessed by Buddhas) and the power within the mind to give rise to supramundane qualities, refers to the causal phase (*rgyu'i gnas skabs*). Thus, for him, the seven Vajra Bases are the causes and fruit of the purification process. Gyaltsab adds:

> The seven Vajra Bases cannot be realized through terms and concepts because they are not just the paramarthasatya, but also its realization. One can create an idea (*yid byas*) of the Dharmata from terms and concepts that express it accurately, but one cannot realize it as the Aryas do in meditation.

Since Gyaltsab does not accept Buddhajnana in the Shentong sense, he must find an alternative explanation for the non-conceptuality of the seven Vajra Bases. According to him, the Vajra (self-emptiness) referred to here as "paramarthsatya" is conceptualizable—this is consistent with his overall view—but to truly realize it in meditation is another thing. One cannot conceptualize what someone else is experiencing—one must experience it for oneself. This is not the same as saying (as do the Shentongpas) that paramarthasatya is not accessible to the conceptual mind at all.

Although Rangtongpas take "Tathagatagarbha" to refer to emptiness, they do not accept that rock and trees, and so forth which are also empty, are also Tathagatagarbha. For example, Rongton states that the pure nature can only apply to the mind continuum. In other words, it is the emptiness of the power (*nus pa*) of a sentient being's mind. This does not necessarily contradict the Shentong position because both accept Tathagatagarbha as the emptiness of "something." From the Shentong point of view, Rongton's use of the term "emptiness" in this context is ambiguous. It could mean merely the self-emptiness of the mind-stream, or it could mean the power (*nus pa*) of the mind that is empty of prapanca. If one could rest in the power of the mind without prapanca, this would (in Shentong terms) be Buddhajnana. In other words, when the apparent phenomenon of the mind-stream is seen to be self-empty, the power (*nus pa*) of the mind itself is realized to be Ultimate Emptiness (Shentong), which is Tathagatagarbha.

Rongton's main concern seems to be to distinguish between the base, path, and fruit in order that the position of saying all the qualities of the Buddha exist at the time of the base is avoided. If emptiness (Tathagatagarbha) is the same in beings and Buddhas, what is the difference between them? Rongton explains that the Dharmata (emptiness) is the same in all three (Buddhas, Bodhisattvas, and beings), but the *dharmin* (*chos can*), in other words that which has the quality of emptiness, in this context the mind, differs. Thus, although the naturally pure aspect of the qualities, the Dharmata, is present in beings, beings are not Buddhas because of the difference in the *dharmin* (i.e. the mind having it). Gyaltsab's interpretation, on the other hand, seems to try to remove this ambiguity in the use of the term "emptiness." Hence his insistence that Tathagatagarbha can only be applied to the stained Tathata and never to Buddha.

Appendix 6

Five Dharmas of Maitreya

Critical scholarship cannot assume, as do all major Tibetan traditions of exegesis, either that the five great works attributed to Maitreya (the *Five Maitreya Dharmas*) are indeed by that or any other single author or whether an author by that name ever existed as a historical person at all. Admittedly the Tibetan tradition does not claim he was a historical person of this world since he is represented as dwelling in the realm of Tusita. This means that the actual penmanship for these treatises is attributed to Asanga which again cannot be accepted uncritically by the serious scholar. Nevertheless, for our present purposes, it is not necessary to enter into the whole mass of controversial issues involved in trying to establish the historicity or otherwise of Maitreya, and what his view was if he did indeed exist and what each of his five works were trying to establish and how they relate to each other in terms of Nitartha or neyartha teachings. Tibetan scholars have written much on these issues due to the tremendous importance the figure of Maitreya plays in Tibetan Buddhism of all schools.

As has already been explained [Chapter 9.1, iii "The Importance of the Maitreya-Asanga Connection"], Maitreya is regarded as the founder of one of the two major traditions of Madhyamaka in Tibet, so each Tibetan commentator has to give an account of his works that accords with his status and with his own overview of what Madhyamaka is about. Various ploys are adopted and Kongtrul's account in his introduction has to be seen in that context. For other accounts see *La Théorie* [39fn.2], BuC (transl. by Obermiller 11p.137) [f.103b7ff and f.20b (1p 53) and 19b (1p 51), khG (tsa f17a–b)], *Legs bshad gser phreng* by Tsongkapa [1 f 15b 3ff], *rGya gar chos 'byung* by Taranatha [87]. (See also Obermiller's introduction to his transl. of RGV and Buton's *mDzas rgyan* etc.)

Since Kongtrul's [RGV comm. 6b] and, indeed, any of the Tibetan accounts of the place the five treatises hold within the Buddhist philosophical framework rest on the assumption that all five of these texts were by the same author, Maitreya, it is interesting to see how Kongtrul accounts for this tradition. One senses that he is aware of the doubtfulness of its origins. He traces the tradition of five Maitreyanic treatises as far back as Haribhadra (750–800) who holds that they were composed for the benefit of Asanga (early fifth century), the great founder of the Yogacara school. (Kontrul also mentions in passing that according to Abhaya—presumably

Abhayakaragupta—late 11th, early 12th century, they were composed at the time of the council/s (*bka' hsdu'i dus* - is this the Council of Samye, 792–94?).

From Shonupal's account [DN] it is clear that the tradition of linking the RGV to Maitreya and Asanga stems from the time of Maitripa and late developments in northern India in the 11th century. This casts doubt on whether the RGV was included in the five treatises mentioned by Haribhadra. Certainly the RGV in a summarized form existed in his day (see Johnston's foreword). Kongtrul does not give any details about where Haribhadra mentions the five treatises and according to Ruegg [*La Théorie* 35] the five works of Maitreya are mentioned in Sanskrit sources from only the 11th century onwards, the RGV often being mentioned as one of them. He refers specifically to the *Sakarasiddhisastra* by Jnanasrimitra and the *Panjika* of the *Bodhicaryavatara* [9.42] by Prajnakaramati (which cites verse 5.18 of the RGV).

According to Shonupal, the DHDHV was discovered together with the RGV, but exactly how they came to be associated in this way is curious and warrants further investigation. For example, is the evidence that the latter was originally from the Maitreya-Asanga tradition stronger than that for the former? Neither the RGV nor the DHDHV are in the *Denkarma* [*lDan dkar ma*], the catalogue of texts conserved in the royal palace of Tsongtang Denkar (*sTong thang ldan dkar*) at the beginning of the 9th century, whereas the MSA, MAV and AA are [see *La Théorie* p.39]. Again, Shonupal [BA 349] observes:

> In general it seems to be true that the Ven. Maitripa had rediscovered these two basic texts of the Maitreya doctrine, for the *Abhisamayalamkaraloka* and other works contain numerous quotations from the *Madhyantavibhanga* and the *Sutralamkara*, but do not contain any quotations from these two later sastras.

Since in this present work my main argument is that the RGV is to be judged, primarily, as a summary of the doctrine of the Tathagatagarbha Sutras, the question of how it relates to other texts attributed to Maitreya is not of immediate importance.

ABBREVIATIONS

AA	*Abhisamayālaṃkāra*
AAN	*Anūnatvāpūrṇatvanirdeśaparivarta*
BA	*'The Blue Annals'* Transl. of DN BY Roerich.
BCA	*Bodhisattvacāryāvatāra*
BHS	*Buddhist Hybrid Sanskrit* (Edgerton)
BL	*'Buddhist Logic'* by Stcherbatsky
BSOAS	Bulletin of the School of Oriental and African Studies
BuCho	*Chos 'byung* by Bu ston
CD	Candra Das' *Tibetan English Dictionary*
CDTBE	*'Contributions to the Development of Tibetan Buddhist Epistemology'* by Kuijp
Dartik	*Theg pa chen po'i rgyud bla ma'i tika* by Gyaltsabje
DDS	*Dharmadhātustotra*
DHDHV	*Dharmadharmātavibhāga*
DN	*Deb ther sngon po* by 'Gos lo tsa ba
DRS	*Dharanesvararajasūtra*
DZG	*mDzes rGyan* by Bu ston
F	*Fundamentals of Buddhist Tantras*: Translation of *rGyud sde spyi'i rnam par gzhag par brjod pa* by F. D. L. Lessing and A. Wayman
JAAS	*Jñānālokālaṃkārasūtra*
JAOS	Journal of the American Oriental Society
JIABS	Journal of the International Association of Buddhist Studies
Kuijp	See CDTBE
LAS	*Laṅkāvatārasūtra*
La Théorie	*'La Théorie du Tathāgatagarbha et du Gotra'* by D. S. Ruegg
LM	*'The Literature of the Madhyamaka School of Philosophy in India—A History of Indian Literature'* Vol. VII, by D. S. Ruegg
MA	*Madhyamakāvatāra*
MAC	McDonell's *Sanskrit English Dictionary*
MAV	*Madhyāntavibhāga*
MMK	*Mūlamadhyamakakārikās*
MPNS	*Mahāparinirvāṇasūtra*

MSA	*Mahayanasūtrālamkara*
MW	Monier Williams' *Sanskrit English Dictionary*
RGV	*Ratnagotravibhāga*
RGVV	*Ratnagotravibhāga-vyākhyā*
RC	*Ri chos nges don rgya mtsho* by Dolpopa
SKK	*Shes bya kun khyab (mdzod)* by Kongtrul
SMS	*Śrīmālādevīsūtra*
SNS	*Sandhinirmocanasūtra*
SOED	*Shorter Oxford English Dictionary*
Study	*A Study on the Ratnagotravibhāga being a Treatise on the Tathāgatagarbha Theory of Mahāyana Buddhism*, by J. Takasaki
TMBC	*Tshad ma'i mdo dang bstan bcos kyi shing rta'i srol rnam ji ltar byung ba'i tshul gtam-bya ba nyin mor byed pa'i snang bas dpyod ldan mtha' dag dga' bar byed pa* in the collected works of Gser mdog Panchen Śākya mchog ldan
Toh	*Tohoku Catalogue of the Tibetan bKa' 'gyur* and *bsTan 'gyur*
Traité	*Traité de Bu ston* by Ruegg
ZND	*Zab mo nang gi don* by Rangjung Dorje

NOTES

Chapter 1

1. See de Jong's review of Takasaki's *Study* p.564ff.

2. See Appendix 1 of this present work for more details on works by Western scholars.

3. See Chapter 2 and Appendix 2.

4. The following is extracted from the *Collected Works of Dolpopa* p.779.

5. The prayer continues for another two and a half sides equating it with all the different names for Ultimate Reality (paramarthasatya) in the Tantras.

Chapter 2

1. See *Jewel Ornament* p.101.

2. See in this present work the translation of introduction Kongtrul's RGV commentary 8a.

3. See Kongtrul's RGV commentary 5a.

4. BA reference in Kongtrul's RGV commentary, 8b–9b.

5. See SNS 7.6, 7.7.

6. See RGV 1.52, 1.64, and SNS iv.11.

7. See SKK *om* 50.4 *sgrubs pa'i bka' babs.*

8. See *La Théorie* p.320 for this kind of idea in the *Culasunnatasutta* of the *Majjhimanikaya* 121 tome III p.104–105. The same idea is found in the *Mahaparinirvanasutra.*

9. See *Kindness, Clarity and Insight* p.203.

10. See, for example, Rongton's commentary on the RGV.

11. *dbu ma'i zab gnas snying por dril ba'i legs bshad sgrub dgongs rgyan* by dGe 'dun chos 'phel. Published in 1983 at Rigzin-Khyilpa Room 155 Dharma Cakra Centre P. O. Rumtek, Via Ranipul, Sikkim, 737 135, India.

12. Kongtrul's RGV Commentary 19a.

Chapter 3

1. *skandhas*—see Nyanatiloka's Dictionary (for Pali *khandha*) and Stcher. *Central Conception of Buddhism* p.5. The mind-body continuum is broken down into its component elements in various ways in the Buddhist analysis. The five skandhas are one of the standard ones, deriving from the Sutras, and systemized in the various Abhidharma traditions. Briefly they are form, feeling, perception, habitual mental patterns, and consciousnesses (Skt. *rupa, vedana, samjna, samskara, vijnana*).

2. It should be noted that, when Tibetan scholars discuss Cittamatra in relation to other systems of tenets, they are somewhat vague about exactly whose system of Cittamatra they are taking as a model. Nevertheless, the generalized version of Cittamatra presented in this kind of literature is of interest insofar as it presents a possible Mahayana Buddhist view, lying between the Sravaka and Madhyamaka views in its degree of subtlety.

3. See Mikyo Dorje's *gZhan stong sgron me*.

4. See RGV 1.35–38 on the *Gunaparamitas*.

5. SKK hum 32 and 33 na.

6. See Kongtrul's commentary on RGV 17a–18a.

7. See Chapter 7.1 iv. and v. later in this present work.

8. See SKK hum 32b.2 and discussion in Appendix 2.

9. See also Stcher.BL Vol.2 p.101 *pratisedha* = *vyavaccheda* and p.77 *The Principle of Negative Judgements*, RC 158 and 434, and Hopkins *Meditation on Emptiness* for more details.

Chapter 4

1. Paul Williams, *Some Aspects of Madhyamaka Philosophy in Tibet* p.72.

2. See *Practice and Theory of Tibetan Buddhism* by Sopa & Hopkins p.138.

3. See *The Open Door to Emptiness*.

4. See Kongtrul's RGV commentary p.18a.

5. See Garma C. C. Chang *The Buddhist Teaching of Totality: The Philosophy of Hua Yen Buddhism* Section 3, 'The Doctrine of Mind-Only' p.183–184: '. . . the mutual projection and containment of Buddha's Mind and man's mind' and Section 2: p.16 'The Philosophy of Totality' and p.157: 'Inconceivable Dharmas can

be preached through the truth of this One Mind. Men are thus led eventually to the realm of the Absolute, which is beyond words and thoughts . . .' and p.125 '. . . there is a mystic conviction that the True Mind, the transformed *Alaya* consciousness, like a great mirror, is limpid, serene and illuminating, literally capable of reflecting or perceiving all things in a spontaneous manner'.

6. Taken from the *Melanges Chinois et Bouddhiques* 1,394: see Takasaki's *Study* p.300fn.53.

7. See also SKK om 150ba.

8. Kongtrul's RGV commentary 19a; SKK a'280na.

9. See quotes from the MPNS in the RC p.189; see also Ruegg's comments in *La Théorie*, p.347ff.

10. See Gyaltsab's *Dartik* p.152.

11. See earlier and later discussions in this present work for the Shentong defence of their position.

12. RGV 1.6, *Thar rGyan* 176b, chap. 20 in Guenther's Translation.

13. E.g. Mahasanghikas, Bareau p.59–60.

14. E.g. permanence of the form kayas in the *Thar rGyan* 176b is described like this.

15. For this argument see SKK a '280na and RC 127.

16. NTS Tutorial 8/85 cassette 2.

17. See RC p.56 where Dolpopa discusses the difference between the Absolute Dharmakaya signs and marks and the apparent form-kayas' signs and marks.

18. See Mikyo Dorje, *gZhan stong sgron me* p.12b.

19. See Mila's comments quoted by Gampopa, *Thar rgyan* p.73.

20. CD 'Miraculously sprung or grown, formed all at once'; *Tib. Skt. Dictionary Satapitaka Series* 3[12] *lhun grub lhun gyi grub pa*, Skt. *sahajasiddha*, or *lhun gyis grub pa*, Skt. *anabhoga*, effortless. See RGV 1.5 *'dus ma byas shing lhun gyis grub*, uncompounded and spontaneous explained in the RGVV as free from prapanca and *vikalpa*.

21. See also *Tantric Practice in rNying ma* ed. Hopkins p.191. *The Tib-Chinese Dictionary* 1985 has *'bad med rang bzhin gyis grub pa*—effortless, natural existence.

22. NTS Tutorial 8/85 where he explains SKK hum 43.

23. SNS chapter II.3.

24. See *Thar rgyan* in the last chap. on the Buddha Activity.

25. RGV 1.35, 40 and 41

26. See Stephen Batchelor *Stone Lion: An Introduction to the Buddhism of Korea* p.15.

Chapter 5

1. Pali, *saddha*.

2. See Kuijp CDTBE p.287fn.125.

3. See Kongtrul's RGV comm. 18a.

4. See Beyer *Cult of Tara* p.138 where he refers to the Clear Light that shines through the 'shifting interstices' in any stream of events, and that there is an intermediate state between two moments in the movement of a single thought.

5. See Kongtrul's comm. 15a.

6. See Takasaki's '*Study*' p.22 and RGV 1.49.

7. See allusions to this in the song of dKon mchog yan lag in the Nalanda Translation Board's '*Rain of Wisdom*' p.50.

8. 546 cha 273b, quoted in RGVV 1.36 phi 18.1.

9. See Khenpo Tsultrim—*bLo rtags kyi rnam gzhag rig pa'i mun sel*.

10. *La Théorie* 310 305ff and chap. VI 309ff.

11. See SKK hum 43b and NTC cassette 2.

12. See *Nges don sgron me* by Kongtrul, p.55.

13. See *Nges don gron me* 54ff for *hrig ger, rjen lhag ger, lhan ner, lhang nger, lhod de*, etc..

14. *Practice and Theory of Tibetan Buddhism*.

15. Itself a simplified summary of the *Grub mtha' chen mo* by Jamyang Shepa.

16. *Concept and Reality* p.16.

17. RGV and RGVV 1.84, 1.94.

18. See Ruegg, JIP 1977 p.1. It is a common formulation in the *Upanishads*.

19. RGV commentary 19

20. RC 56b.

21. LM 75fn. 241.

22. RC 88.2: see also RC 47 which quotes from the LAS—p.60 of D. T. Suzuki's translation: see also SNS II.2.

23. See Ruegg's LM p.122.

24. See M. Broido's paper at the Oxford IABS 1982 and his particularly useful article in JIABS vol.8 no.2.

25. See JIABS p.24ff for Padma Karpo's use of samvrtisatya for the Vajra-body. etc.

26. See the *Vajradoha* of the Indian Siddhas and also *La Théorie* 340 and Broido JIABS vol.8, no.2 for more details on the history of this practice.

27. See Gampopa's discussion on omniscience—*Thar rgyan* 168a.

28. Thrangu Rimpoche uses both the distinction between seeing Absolute and relative as well as this distinction—see his *A Commentary on the Uttara Tantra* translated by Ken and Kalia Holmes [p. 41–43].

29. See Johnston's RGV and RGVV Sanskrit edition [p.14] for *taccittaprakrti-prabhasvarataya*.

Chapter 6

1. See explanation of RGVV 1.25 and Chapter 7.1 of this present work

2. Kongtrul's RGV comm. 12b. The *alayavijnana* is a concept developed by the Cittamatrins in order to explain how perception and memory work. It also serves to explain how karma is stored and how it ripens within the same individual. The idea is that the mind-stream is impregnated with impressions created by past actions which will ripen in the future. Each impression or trace (*bag chags*) is like a seed which will, when conditions are right, manifest as both a rebirth consciousness and the world into which it is reborn. If the trace is good, it will ripen as a rebirth within a situation conducive to progress towards nirvana; if not it will ripen toward samsara.

The *alayavijnana* is thought of like a great ocean in which all these traces are stored. It is described in the *rNam shes ye shes 'byed pa* by Rangjung Dorje and Kongtrul's commentary on it p.16b.ff.. Ruegg [*La Theorie* p.101ff and 488] describes the difference between *bija alayavijnana* and *alayavijnana* proper. The *alayavijnana* must transform (*gnas 'gyur*). This word occurs in RGV [5.7]—*gnas dang de ni gyur pa*—the base and its transformation. In the *Trimsaka* by Vasubandhu, this means the *alayavijnana* transforms in nature from a stream of impure moments of ordinary consciousness into a stream of pure Buddha awareness. This is referred to in *La Théorie* [102]. The RGV only uses the term *gnas 'gyur* once [RGV 5.7] and Shentongpas take it to mean that, as the Tathagatagarbha emerges, there is an apparent transformation of the essence. Dolpopa [RC 396] explains that one must distinguish between the different meanings of transformation (gnas 'gyur).

Kongtrul [SKK hum 323ba] gives Candragomin's explanation of how the emptiness aspect of the alayavijnana transforms into the Dharmadhatu, the clarity aspect into Mirror-like Wisdom, the klistamanas into Equalness Wisdom, the manovijnana into Discriminating Wisdom, and the five sense consciousnesses into All-accomplishing Wisdom.

Only once in the RGV and RVGG is Enlightenment referred to as a transformation (asrayaparavrtti, gnas yongs su gyur pa). [RGV 5.7. For details see Transl. fn.94, 96]. This term is important in Cittamatrin works about the alayavijnana and means the transformation of the alayavijnana in a very literal way. However, from the Shentong point of view, there is never any real transformation, so that the term is used somewhat loosely to indicate that moment when the base or basic nature of beings is finally and fully revealed [see Mi bskyod rdo rje gZhan stong sgron me p.2]. In other words, it is when the Dharmakaya is not only naturally pure, but also it is no longer obscured by incidental defilements. For more details, see L. Schmithausen, Alayavijnana; Origins and Early Developments of a Central Concept of Yogacara, Studia Philologica Buddhica Monograph Series IV. Tokyo, IIBS: 1987.

3. LAS LXXXII p.190 and LXXXVI of Suzuki's translation.

4. La Théorie 102.

5. LAS translation 191.

6. LAS p.55 of Suzuki's translation.

7. See Rangjung Dorje's Song of Mahamudra verse 11, Khor 'das kun gyi gzhi.

8. See Suzuki's translation p.282 verses 748–768.

9. See Suzuki's translation p.268 and 565—the doctrines of self and non-self, the former of which is true and the latter faulty—see also comments below.

10. LAS p.69.

11. His RGV commentary p.13a.

12. Dartik 4aff.

13. La Théorie 447.

14. See also Kindness, Clarity and Insight p.208ff.

15. See La Théorie 267 for the Gelugpa view.

16. See 'Fundamentals of Buddhist Tantras' p.51.

17. La Théorie 510–513; Traite 53ff.

18. See Ruegg's article BSOAS 39 p.352.

19. SXXVIII 1–10, see *Path to Deliverance* p.21.

20. See ref. in *Samyutta Nikaya Path to Deliverance* p.22.

21. See Steve Collins *Selfless Persons* 98.

22. See *Literature of the Pudgalavadins* by Bhikkhu Thien Chau Tich at the Fifth Conference of IABS, Oxford 1982, JIABS 7.1.

23. See Ruegg's article JAOS 83.

24. *Thar rgyan* chap 1.

25. Takasaki's *Study* 21; *La Théorie* Part One esp. p.143 for Nya dbon's etymologies of the word 'gotra.'

26. BSOAS vol 39 1976 'The Term Gotra and Textual History of RGV.'

27. See Obermiller *Sublime Science* p.97 for the Hinayana interpretation of gotra.

28. See *Thar rgyan* chap. 1 where the signs of the Mahayana gotra are given as natural kindness, honesty, aspiration to the Mahayana etc..

29. *Thar rgyan* chap. 1.

30. See *Thar rgyan* chap. 1.

31. *Thar rgyan* chap. 1.

32. See Bareau *Les Sectes Bouddhique du Petit Vehicule* p.297 and also p.59ff for the Mahasanghika doctrines on the nature of Buddha.

33. BSOAS (1976) 348.

34. See *La Théorie* 262, 278, 294 for discussion concerning the Tathagatagarbha being *hetu*, *karana* or *asraya*.

35. See MAC *hetu*—primary cause, nature.

36. See title chosen by Thrangu Rimpoche for Holmes's translation of RGV

Chapter 7

1. SKK hum 10na ff.

2. RGV commentary 7a; SKK hum 9ba.

3. Chapter IX, the chapter requested by Avalokitesvara.

4. Chapter VII, the chapter requested by Paramarthasamudgata.

5. See *Thar rgyan* chapter 1.

6. SMS 543 cha 272.

7. See Kongtrul SKK hum 9ba.

8. For the same position see Buton's discussion in DZG 83ff. esp. Ratnakarasanti's explanation on p.89.

9. Kongtrul reiterates this on SKK hum 3b.

10. See Wayman's Introduction to the *Lion's Roar of Queen Srimala*. SMS 16.

11. See SKK hum 12ba and *La Théorie* p.58ff for Ruegg's discussion of how the RGV is placed by the different Tibetan masters.

12. See Kuijp p.151fn. for further discussion of neyartha and Nitartha.

13. *Religions of Tibet* p.35.

14. See Rongton's commentary p.18.

Chapter 8

1. Tucci *The Religions of Tibet* p.259fn.8.

2. See Mikyo Dorje in his MA commentary and elsewhere.

3. See Karma Thinley's *History of the Sixteen Karmapas of Tibet*.

4. See *La Théorie* p.60.

5. For a more detailed account of the kind of criticism levelled against the Jonangpas see Ruegg's article in JAOS 83 and *La Théorie* p.60fn.3.

6. See references to the *sNying po don* in the Tibetan *Doha* tradition; e.g. in the Song of Konchok Yanglag in the *Rain of Wisdom* by the Nalanda Transl. Committee p.52–23.

7. See *La Théorie* for references to the *prabhasvaracitta* in the Pali Canon and its treatment by the Theravadin tradition. See also references to the Pudgalavadins, who might also have had a similar view, and how their predominance was followed by obscurity.

8. See RGVV 1.25 and Takasaki's 'Study' p.36fn.60; also his article in *JIBS* Vol.7 Ne 1 Tokyo 1958 p.48–53, "The *Tathagatotpattisambhavanirdesa* of the *Avatamsaka* and RGV, with special reference to the term *tathagatagotrasambhava*—an important term in Hua Yen philosophy."—RGV 2.8–9.

9. See Ruegg's article JAOS '83, Tucci's *The Religions of Tibet* p.69, Ketrub's *Fundamentals of Buddhist Tantra* p.51, Hopkins' *Meditation on Emptiness Part 1 1973 p.226 & 271*.

10. MAV 1.20 p.43.5, Kongtrul's RGV comm. 10b. The reader should also see JIABS 1983 ''Original Purity and the Focus of Early Yogacara'' by John P. Keenan p.13. In this article Keenan links Yogacara to Tathagatagarbha Sutras which according to him began to appear ca.150–ca.250, shortly after the time of Nagarjuna.

11. See also Ruegg *La Théorie* p.322–337 & 431ff for his discussion of this passage.

12. See Ruegg's comments *La Théorie* p.320ff, together with his notes in *errata et addenda* p.4, on the problems of translation and interpretation of this passage.

13. See Ruegg '*Prajnaparamita*' p.284.

14 See Chapter 11 endnotes 58–66. Ruegg gives an account of the RGV lineage (*La Théorie* 36). In fn.7 he mentions that in Taranatha's *Zabmo gzhan stong dbu ma'i brgyud 'debs, Ka che ba* (the Kashmiri) Jungnay Shi wa is put between Anandakirti and Sajjana.

15. RC 201.2

16. RC 476 for further comments on DDS.

17. See LM 31 for *Bhakhti*.

18. See LM 46 for more details.

19. See Lindtner *Nagarjuna* re. 180ff and Ruegg's LM p.104.

20. See his *Eight Difficult Points, rTsa ba shes rab kyi dka' gnas chen po brgyad.*

21. *skur 'debs, apavada*—falsely denying reality to the real. *Apavada* means, literally, to speak ill of.

22. See Thrangu Rimpoche's *Buddha Nature* translated by Erik Pema Kunsang 1988.

23. For details of his life see Gene Smith's *Introduction to the Index of the Shes bya kun khyab* [SKK] and his foreword to the *Autobiography and Dairies of Situ Panchen*. See also the introduction to the version of the SKK printed in China, 1982.

Chapter 9

1. See introduction to Johnston's edited Sanskrit text for an account of discovered fragments of the text.

2. See Takasaki's *Study of the Ratnagotravibhaga and Vyakhya* p.9 and de Jong's review of Takasaki's *Study*.

3. See Wayman's *The Lion's Roar of Queen Srimala* p.2.

4. See La Vallee Poussin's *Reflexions sur le Madhyamaka* p.64–66, *La Théorie* 56 and p.60fn.3.

5. See Tucci's *Maitreyanatha* and Prof. Ui on the author of the *Mahayanasutralamkara* in *Zeitschrift fur Indologie und Iranistik*.

6. This text is not mentioned at all by Ruegg in the LM.

7. See Conze *The Prajnaparamita Literature* p.9 and also John P. Keenan "Original Purity and the Focus of Early Yogacara," JIABS 1983 No.17 p.7. According to Keenan the earliest Tathagatagarbha Sutras began to appear shortly after the time of Nagajura ca.150–ca.250.

8. See RGVV 1.155 which is based on the SMS.

9. See Ruegg's LM chaps. on the Madhyamaka-Yogacara synthesis and Madhyamaka-Vajrayana synthesis.

10. See M.Nakamura, *Acta Asiatica* 7 p.66 where he gives this as the oldest Tathagatagarbha Sutra.

11. See Ruegg's *La Théorie* Bibliography, Obermiller's *Sublime Science* p.115fn.4 and Takasaki's *'Study'* p.146fn.32 where he says that the Tibetan and Chinese versions of this Sutra call it by that name.

12. See Kongtrul's RGV commentary p.8a and Kuijp p.32–48 for more details.

13. See Gyaltsab's *Dartik* for example.

14. p.94a of his RGV commentary.

15. See BA p.724–5 of Roerich's translation and more importantly M.Broido JIABS Vol.8 no.2 p.12 for his translation and further comments throughout the article, especially p.13ff and 36.

16. See *Thar rgyan* p.3b where he explains verses 1.27–28 of the RGV.

17. See Kongtrul's RGV Commentary 9b & 10a.

Chapter 10

1. See Chapter 6 "The Nature of Being," section 6.4 "Gotra".

2. Quoting from the *Anutvapurnatvanirdesa* - see SKK a'279na where Kongtrul gives Parinispanna, Dharmata, Dharmadhatu, Tathata, Paramartha and Nisprapanca Jnana as synonyms: see also *La Théorie* p.126 and 139ff where Ruegg refers to Nyabon Kungapal's (*Nya dbon kun dga' dpal*) *Yid kyi mun sel* and commentary on the AA in which, following the Jonangpas, he assimilates Gotra, Tathagatagarbha, Dharmadhatu and Dharmata.

3. See Takasaki's *Study* p.143fn.15.

4. See Takasaki *Study* p.152fn.88–91 for more details.

5. See Mikyo Dorje's *gZhan stong sgron me* p.2.

6. NTC cassette 2.

7. Takasaki's *Study* p.171 refers us in some detail to the *Astasahasrika Prajnaparamita*.

8. See Obermiller p.139 where he refers to the *Dartik* explanations p.48a 4–6.

9. See Kongtrul's RGV comm.19a for reference to "inward looking meditative approach."

10. See *gZhan stong sgron me* p.5.

11. *dar yug*, a ribbon-like piece of silk stuff [Jaschke]; *patta*, [CD]; *patta*, a strip of cloth [MW].

12. See Takasaki's Introduction IV and later comments in this present section.

13. See Cook *Hua Yen Buddhism* p.53; "This is also called Dharmadhatu-Buddha present, not only in beings, but in everything, animate and inanimate."

14. See Chapter 4 "The Shentong View of Absolute Reality" section 4.2 "Inseparable Qualities," 4.3 "Buddha Activity."

15. 197fn,6 - see also Stcher. 2.395fn.5 *upacarat* - metaphorically, and *La Théorie* p.510–11.

16. See *Kun bzang bla ma'i Zhal lung* by Patrul Rimpoche.

17. See his Appendix 1 p.393ff.

18. RGV 1.40, aspiration is linked to Gotra.

19. See Takasaki p.216fn.125 and this present work Chapter 5 "Means of Apprehending Absolute Reality," section 5.2.

20. See Conze's comments on the *Astasahasrikaprajnaparamita* in *The Prajnaparamita Literature* p.14.

21. See Takasaki's comments *Study* p.211fn.96.

22. See Takasaki's *Study* p.216fn.120 *acintyaparinamikicyuti* and SMS 531 cha 266.

23. *anapakarsa* is translated into Tibetan as *brid*. Since there is a word *bri* in Tibetan meaning to diminish, perhaps the spelling *brid* is a mistake.

24. *snon*, to add, impose, *samaropana*, to transfer, impose.

25. Johnston's Sanskrit edition and Tibetan versions, see Takasaki p.219.

26. See *La Théorie* p.143 for Nya dbon's explanation of these verses.

27. See Guenther's *Jewel Ornament of Liberation* p.270fn.18.

28. See *La Théorie* p.290fn. and BSOAS 39 p. 344 for Ruegg's discussion of the two kinds of gotra in these verses of the RGV and RGVV.

29. See his *dBu ma dgongs pa rab gsal* in Hopkin's translation, *Compassion in Tibetan Buddhism*. It is one of the eight difficult points Tsongkapa discusses in his *rTsa shes rab dKa' gnas brgyad pa*.

30. See *The Seven Points of Mind Training* by Atisa.

31. Takasaki's comment p.315fn.14 of his *Study* supports this view.

32. See SKK hum 13ba where Kongtrul refers to Maitreya's Prophecy Wheel—*lung bston 'khor lo*.

33. See *The Torch of Certainty* p.135.

34. See Kongtrul's *Nges don sgron me*, 'Torch of Certainty' p.113fn.

35. See also ZND p.2b.

36. See RC p.344ff on the Absolute Qualities.

37. See *gZhan stong sgron me* p.3.

38. See *Thar rgyan* chap.20.

39. *Study* p.361 and 362fn.65 and 67.

40. Quoted in the *Bodhicaryavatara-panjika* and the *Siksasamuccaya*: see Takasaki's *Study* p.385fn.44 & 46.

Chapter 11

1. *"Unassailable Lion's Roar"* This term also occurs in the *Majjhimanikaya* I, 69–71. It is a common expression in Sutras for a fearless pronouncement of the truth, for example, the *"Lion's Roar"* of Queen Srimala*. See also the image of the Four Fearlessnesses of the Buddha being like a lion's roar [RGV 3.10].

2. Regent (*rgyal tshab*) is literally, King's representative. In the text, it refers to Maitreya standing in for the Buddha. Until he takes birth in this world he will not be "crowned" Buddha. Nevertheless he is already Enlightened and teaching from the Buddha's throne in Tusita. Kongtrul [RGV commentary 6b] mentions that Maitreya has been Buddha already for countless kalpas. He might have meant it in the sense that all beings have been Buddha from beginningless time, in the sense that in the *Vimalakirtinirdesa* [Lamotte's transl. p. 193], Maitreya is reprimanded

for saying he would become Buddha when in fact he and all beings were Buddha from the very beginning. However, in the context of this text, he means Maitreya is a Bodhisattva emanating from an Enlightened Buddha as a tenth level Bodhisattva on the throne in Tusita. Therefore, he calls Maitreya "Lord of the Tenth Level"—the last Bodhisattva Bhumi [RGV commentary 2a].

3. The "three secrets" refers to the Body, Speech, and Mind of a Buddha [RGV 4.81]. In Shentong terms, it refers to the Absolute Qualities freed from their samvrti counterparts.

4. Aryan Assembly—Buddhas, Bodhisattvas, Pratyekas, and Sravaka Arhats, that is, all those who have defeated the grosser klesa, and are beyond the level of ordinary beings (*prthag jana*).

5. "Hundred divine beings" (*lha*)—Lama Thubden assumes it refers to the hundred deities who inhabit Tusita. They are like the revolving stars (*rgyu'i skar*, literally the moving stars). The stars seem to revolve in the sky due to the rotation of the earth, hence their general name (*rgyu'i skar*). As the moon outshines the other stars in the night sky, so Maitreya outshines the assembly in the Tusita heaven.

6. Dagpo (*Dwags po*) lineage—the lineage of Gampopa, who was from Dagpo, in Tibet, and often referred to as Dagpo Rimpoche. He was the chief disciple of Milarepa of the Kagyu lineage. "Great Charioteer" is an epithet for a great teacher who bears many beings to liberation. Gampopa's lineage is called a "golden rosary" because every holder of the lineage is as perfect as the one before, like a rosary, each bead of which is pure gold.

7. One of the highest titles awarded to a Lama is "Omniscient One" (*Kun mkhyen*). Rangjung Dorje, Dolpopa, and Longchenpa were the three great "Omnisciences" of the fourteenth century. " . . . of genuine omniscience"—"omniscience" in the Mahayana is rather a controversial subject (see *Thar rgyan* 168b). In Shentong terms, it means nondual Knowledge of the Absolute Inseparable Qualities: it is not like a clever person knowing everything about everything.

8. "Lord of Sages" Skt. *muni*, Tib. *thub dbang*, literally, to be able to do; hence an accomplished sage who is capable of superhuman feats. Often used as an epithet of the Buddha.

9. Tenpe Nyinche, Eighth Situpa. The Situpas are an important line of incarnate Lamas of the Karma Kagyu school. See Gene Smith's comments about Kongtrul's special connection with the Palpung synthesis; was this Yogacara—Madhyamaka?. Palpung is the seat of the Situpas.

10. "Enjoy the lotus lake of my heart . . ."—a poetic way of offering one's whole heart in devotion to the Guru. Like a lake of lotuses opening in the warmth and light of the sun, one's heart opens through the blessing of the Guru. The idea is that, though the Guru's blessing (like the Tathagatagarbha) is always present, it takes a prayerful gesture on the part of the disciple to stimulate or arouse it into action.

11. *rtog ge pa* means dialecticians. In colloquial Tibetan it is used for people who are so intellectually clever that they can argue black is white. It is often associated with intellectual arrogance and spiritual barrenness—the typical die-hard philosopher.

12. The self-manifesting melodious voice or speech of the Buddha (*sangs rgyas kyi rang snang gi gsung dbyangs*). Self-manifesting means the same as *lhun grub*, that is, spontaneous. (See note 3 above and chapter on "Inseparable Qualities." See also RGV 4.81 where the Buddha's speech is compared to an echo). In Shentong terms, the real Sutra is Absolute Buddhajnana, while the oral and written transmissions of it i.e. (b) and (c) are samvrti manifestations that seem to arise dependent on conditions; however, they never truly arise at all.

13. *ngag gi rnam pa don dam*—Absolute Speech or the Absolute as speech. In Shentong terms, this is the Absolute Essence of speech. (See notes 3 and 12 above).

14. Lati Rinbochay, *Mind in Tibetan Buddism* p.130, *sgra spyi (sabdasamanya)*—the verbal or sound approximation apprehended by a conceptual consciousness. Napper chooses "sound generality," but I prefer "approximation" because its SOED definition is a "result of the process of approaching a correct estimation or conception," which seems to capture the meaning of *samanya* (*spyi*) quite well.

Arthasamanya (don spyi) (see Kongtrul's RGV comm. 26a) is the meaning approximation apprehended by a conceptual consciousness. Stephen Batchelor translates *sabdasamanya* as nominal image and *arthasamanya* as experiential or mental image (see *The Mind and its Functions* by Geshe Rabten p. 20). An example of an experiential image is a young child's conception of an object directly apprehended but not named. The conception occurs merely through the appearance of experiential images to his mind without any image based upon verbal descriptions. Kongtrul (RGV commentary 26a) explains that the RGV makes the Nitartha known in a conceptual way, based on a mental image arising from one's own experience: this contrasts with direct non-conceptual knowledge, which comes through meditation experience and the Lama's special instruction.

15. F. Th. Stcherbatsky, *Central Conception of Buddhism*, p. 43, 78. *zag pa med pa'i chos* (*anasrava dharmas*). *Sasrava*, influenced by ignorance; *anasrava*, influenced by prajna. *Marga*, "Path," is one of the *anasrava* dharmas, for *marga* is the cause or condition for the arising of *nirodha*, the cessation of *duhkha*; see also Nyanatiloka's dictionary p. 20: the four asavas are *kamasava, bhavasava, ditthasava*, and *avijjasava*, (the flow of sensuality, existence, views, and ignorance respectively). *Anasrava* literally means not having outflow, that is, non-defiled. In this context the Mahayana Sutras should be understood as non-defiled dharmas in the sense of being free from sense desire and influenced by prajna. Truly existent (*yongs grub, parinispanna*) refers to the Reality that one focuses upon in order to effect one's liberation. Lama Thubden gives *yang dag bden pa* (perfect Reality) as a synonym for it.

In this context, the spoken and written Dharma is referred to as parinispanna because, by focusing on it, one's veils are given up.

16. Tibetan Lamas frequently recite these lines before giving a Dharma discourse. "Sakya" refers to Sakyamuni—the accomplished one of the Sakya clan. He is also referred to as the Great Muni.

17. The text says "*sDud pa*," which is a condensation of *Theg chen mdo sdud pa*, *Mahayanasutrasamuccaya*.

18. Jambudvipa (Jam bu'i gling in the text). This refers to the southern continent of the ancient Indian cosmological system, which consists of Mt. Meru in the center with four continents around it. The Indians and Tibetans think of themselves as living on the southern continent. However, due to the lack of continuity between this ancient system and the world as we know it, the exact limits of its geographical extent remain unclear. The example given here is alluding to the ancient Indian tradition that rain is controlled by the king of the nagas. Nagas are classed as a kind of animal and they are believed to guard treasure in deep oceans and pools and so on. They have the power to transform their bodies, which are half-serpent and half-human, into serpents (snakes or dragons) or humans.
The Buddha himself is sometimes poetically referred to as the Great Naga. See also *Ma dros pas zhus pa'i mdo*, (*Anavataptanagaraja pariprcchasutra*). See RGV 5.18–19 for similar sentiment.

19. *bstan bcos* (sastra)—A Sastra is a commentary on the Sutras. The etymology for *bstan bcos*, which also applies for Sastra, is *bstan* (*sas* or *sasana*), meaning the doctrine, and *bcos* (*tra*), meaning to protect and restore. This is glossed to mean that the Sastras were written to help disciples find strength and sustenance from the scriptures from which, without the Sastras, they could not benefit.

20. *rigs gsum mgon po*—Manjusri, Avalokitesvara, and Vajrapani who, together with Maitreya, are included in the standard list of the eight chief Bodhisattvas.

21. See RGV [1.157] on the five faults.

22. *'rGyan stug po bkod pa*, *Ghanavyuha* (see *La Théorie* p. 18). Dolpopa [RC 13.5] quotes it as saying *Sugatagarbha* is a synonym for *Alaya*.

23. By "ordinary reasoning" Kontrul presumably means the paramartha *pramana* that is referred to in RGV 1.55 that is commented on by Dolpopa. He calls these four Sutras the Cittamatra Sutras in spite of Dolpopa's objections.

24. *Shes rab gsum*—the three wisdoms (prajna) of listening, reflecting, and meditating. Listening is understood to include studying which is, in fact, an extension of listening to the oral transmission, using the help of a text. Here again we see how the Buddhist tradition adheres strictly to the structure of an oral tradition al-

though backed up by the written word. First one listens, then reflects and meditates (*sgom,* this means "to inwardly digest" but is loosely translated "meditation"). The implication here is that the *sgom* that arises from listening and reflecting is still subtly conceptual. In the end, one's own nature is known simply through relaxing the mind in naked awareness.

25. *rjes su bzung ba* are those who are taken care of. In this context, it refers to beings in the care of the Buddhas and Bodhisattvas.

26. Rongton (*Rong ston shes bya kun gzigs smra ba'i seng ge chen mo*)– 1367–1449–was a disciple of the Redawa (*Red mda' ba*).

27. *Mahakarunanirdesa* belongs to the Tathagatagarbha Sutras (third Dharmacakra). *Saddharmapundarika* belongs to the Prajnaparamita Sutras (second Dharmacakra).

28. Good Kalpa—the present era in which it is said a thousand Buddhas will appear and teach. This contrasts with an empty kalpa in which no Buddha appears.

29. *mngon shes (abhijna)*—special cognition. Generally understood to refer to super-normal powers such as knowing the future, knowing the minds of others and so forth; it includes Enlightenment itself.

30. Haribhadra (750–800) was a disciple of Santaraksita and Vairocana. He was a Yogacara-Svatantrika-Madhyamaka and very important for the spreading of the Prajnaparamita doctrine. He was descended from a long line of Brahmin Saivites. He was born in Taxila, which was under Kashmir at that time. He was an important lineage holder of the Dzogchen Mind Collection (*rDzog chen Sems sde*) tradition. LM 102 gives more details about Haribhadra.

31. Abhaya—probably Abhayakaragupta (*'Jigs med*)—late eleventh century to 1125 [BA 795]. He was a leading later representative of Santaraksita's Yogacara-Svatantrika-Madhyamaka school and of the Madhyamaka Vajrayana synthesis [LM 103]. Ruegg mentions [LM 115] that he wrote on Tathagatagarbha and the one final vehicle. He was a disciple of Naropa and an important transmitter of the *Kalacakra Tantra.*

32. David Seyfort Ruegg, *Prajnaparamita* p. 284: Santipa (Ratnakarasanti or Santipada)—first half of the eleventh century. Shonupal [BA 842] describes how he was defeated by Maitripa in debate. (See *La Théorie* 61 for his link with the *Brhattika.*) He was a harmonizer of the Vijnanavada and Madhyamaka in the manner of the synthesizing movements especially characteristic of later Buddhist thought in India [LM 122].

33. *Sa la'i pho nya mo*—this presumably refers to a *mantra* for increasing intelligence. *Sa la* may refer to the sal tree and *pho nya mo* to some kind of *dakini.*

34. This is alluding to the Asanga legend. It is said that Asanga practised twelve years in strict meditation retreat in order to see Maitreya. Every few years or

so he would leave his retreat in despair because of his failure to see him. He would then see some sign that encouraged him to persevere, such as a man polishing a bar of metal with a silk cloth, in the hopes of wearing it down to the size of a needle. Eventually he saw Maitreya who appeared to him as a mangy dog. When Asanga stooped to lick the maggots out of its sores, Maitreya appeared to him in his divine form and transported him to Tusita.

35. In my version of Kongtrul's commentary this reads "*gcud 'bum sde go dgu*"—according to Tenpa Gyaltsen "*gcud*" is a misprint for "*bcud*" (essence or quintessence). This whole line refers to the story of Vasubandhu, who recited the *Hundred Thousand Verses* [of Prajnaparamita] by heart. According to the legend (obtained here from Lama Thubden) a little bird sat nearby listening to these recitations. When the bird died, it was reborn as the son of a king; while still a small child, he told his father that his Guru was Vasubandhu. The king searched out Vasubandhu but, when he brought his child to him, Vasubandhu did not recognize him as his disciple. The boy then explained how he had been a bird listening from the eaves of the house. Vasubandhu then accepted him; he later became the great scholar Sthiramati (*bLo gros brtan pa*).

36. Dignaga—fifth century A.D. [*La Théorie* 124]. Either he, or Vasubhandu, was the teacher of Arya Vimuktasena, the first Madhyamika to write on gotra.

37. Sthiramati A.D. 510–570 [BA 344 and LM 61]. He was a disciple of Vasubandhu and author of the *Trimsikavijaptibhasya* and *Madhyantavibhagatika*.

38. See Tulku Thondrup Rinpoche, *Hidden Teachings of Tibet*. Terma (*gter ma*)—literally hidden treasure. They are sacred texts or artifacts, which are extracted from hiding places in caves, lakes, buildings, and even the sky or mind; for example, the Prajnaparamita Sutras and the RGV. The hidden treasures of Guru Rimpoche are particularly famous; they are still found by Tibetan Lamas, such Lamas being called *Tertons* (*gter stons*, treasure revealers). The tradition explains that Gurus of an earlier age write teachings for disciples of another—when times and conditions have changed and new teachings are needed. *Tertons* are often suspected of disguising the fact that these works are their own innovations (and therefore inauthentic). However, once a *Terton* has established his reputation as an accomplished yogi his *Terma* is accepted.

39. The earlier promulgation of the Buddhist religion in Tibet came to an end in the reign of Langdarma (*gLang dar ma*, 839–42?) [BA XIX]. He almost succeeded in destroying the Dharma in Tibet, so that soon after his reign a new effort to obtain teaching and texts from India began. This is called the "later promulgation," which gave rise to the new translation schools. Only the Nyingmapas trace their lineages back to the early promulgation and use the old translations. The Sakyas, Kagyus and Gelugpas all belong to the new translation school [BA XIV].

40. *lung*—ritual reading of a text that represents its oral transmission. In theory, a text should not be used until this authorization has been given. However, these days the practice is often allowed to lapse.

41. This whole section and the one following seem to be taken, for the most part from BA 347.

42. Sajjana—(also spelt Sanjana [BA 347] and Satyajnana—[Johnston p.vi])—second half of 11th century [BA 325–6, 328, 347–50]. Sajjana's is the only known Indian commentary on the RGV [La Théorie 35fn 4]. See also G. Tucci Minor Buddhist Texts II Rome 1956 [p.xi; and BA kha f 4b, ca f 37b, cha f 7b and following], Taranatha rGya gar chos 'byung [p.183], P. Cordier Catalogue du fonds Tibetain de la Bibliotheque Nationale III [p.304–429]. Ruegg thinks Sajjana may be identical to the Sajjananda who inspired Ksemendra to write his Bodhisattvavadanakalpalata, (see prologue slokas).

43. Outer and inner tenets is the usual expression for non-Buddhist and Buddhist tenets (grub mtha'). Outer and inner can also be used to contrast ordinary and esoteric teachings, but these are not normally referred to as tenets.

44. Ngog (rNgog), the great translator (Lo chen), 1059–1109. A Kadampa (bka' gdams pa) [BA Book VI and BA 325]. He studied in Kashmir for seventeen years from the age of seventeen under six teachers including Sanjnana [BA 329 and Chattopadhyaya—Atisa in Tibet p.393]. His uncle, also a great translator, Ngog Legpa Sherab (rNgog legs pa'i shes rab), was a personal disciple of Atisa. See Leonard W. J. Kuijp's Contributions to the Development of Tibetan Buddhist Epistemology (Wiesbaden: Steiner, 1983, CDTBE) in his translation of Sakya Chogden's (gSer mdog panchen sakya mchog ldan), Tshad ma'i mdo dang bstan bcos kyi shing rta'i srol rnams ji ltar byung ba'i tshul gtam bya ba nyin mor byed pa'i snang bas dpyod ldan mtha' dang dga' bar byed. Kuijp on [p. 50] of his translation distinguishes the Analytical school (thos bsam pa'i lugs) and the Meditation school (sgom lugs), which were the two well-known approaches transmitted from India concerning the Teachings of Maitreya. Like Kongtrul he considers that of these two, Ngog belonged chiefly to the former. On [p. 43] he refers to La Théorie and concludes that Ngog's interpretation of Tathagatagarbha as negation qua nonexistence (med par dgag pa, prasajyapratisedha) was by and large accepted by Gandenpas (dGa' ldan pa, members of Ganden, one of the chief Gelugpa monasteries) such as Gyaltsab and by the later Gelugpas. Notice that Kuijp uses mengag (med par dgag pa) to refer to a nothing or nonexistence as opposed to being a non-affirming negative statement.

45. Atisa, 982–1054 [LM 110] also known as Dipamkarasrijnana, was a Madhyamika who followed Candrakirti even though he received instruction in Yogacara Madhyamaka from Avadhutipada and in Vijnapti Madhyamaka from Ratnakarasanti [Alaka Chattopadhyaya, Atisa and Tibet; S. C. Das, Life of Atisa]. Atisa Dipankara (Jo bo rje) was the founder of the Kadampa school in Tibet. He went to Sumatra to study with Suvarnadvipa Dharmakirti (not to be confused with Dharmakirti, the seventh century logician and author of the Pramanavarttika). A great teacher of the Indian monastic university of Vikramasila, he was invited to Tibet to restore Buddhism there after the persecutions of Langdarma. Atisa was extremely influential in

shaping the development of how the Mahayana was taught in the Kagyu, Sakya, and in particular the Gelugpa schools. See Nagwang Nyima and Lama Chimpa, in *Atisa and Tibet* by Chattopadhyaya [p. 434]:

His exposition of the Madhyamika view was directly inspired by Maitreyanatha through Nagarjuna.

A curious statement, but indicative of the great importance of both the Maitreya-Asanga and Manjusri-Nagarjuna traditions as the foundation of basic Mahayana practice in Tibet from Atisa's time onwards. Some of his doctrines on mind training (*blo sbyong*) coming from Suvarnadvipa agree mainly with the False Aspectarian (*rNam rdzun pa*) branch of the Yogacara school [*Atisa and Tibet* by Chattopadhyaya, p. 396]. See BA 843 and 844 for account of how Atisa received RGV transmission from Maitripa and translated it. See also Chattopadhyaya [p. 353–356] and BA 455–6 where Milarepa is quoted as saying:

The Kadampas (*bKa' gdams pa*) possess hidden precepts (*gdams ngag*), but they have no secret instructions (*man ngag*).

In this quote, Mila distinguishes between *gdams ngag* and *man ngag*, though both words mean instruction (*upadesa*). See also David Seyfort Ruegg *La Théorie* p. 37. According to Ruegg the tradition that Atisa received the RGV from Maitripa and that he and Nagtso (*Nag tsho*) were the first translators is put in doubt by Panchen Sonam Dragpa (*bSod nams grags pa*, 1478–1554), a Gelugpa scholar. Sonam Dragpa's commentary on the RGV is another not mentioned by Kongtrul; Sonam Dragpa points out that Atisa was not likely to be a disciple of Maitripa. He is no doubt alluding to the account [in Taranatha's *bKa' babs bdun ldan*] of how Atisa expelled Maitripa from Vikramasila. Elsewhere Taranatha says Maitripa was a successor of Atisa (*rGya gar chos 'byung* 84–188). The fact that Maitripa succeeded Atisa, however, does not preclude his transmitting the RGV to him.

46. Nag tsho tshul khrims rgyal ba, the translator Jayasila of Nagtso—the monk sent by the Tibetan king to invite Atisa to Tibet.

47. Sharawa (*Sha ra ba*), 1070–1141. See BA 267 (spelt *Shar ba pa*) and 271. He was the successor of Potowa (*Po to ba*), who made particular use of the five treatises of Maitreya. He explained the RGV in Nagtso's translation. An incomplete translation by Ngog was brought to the class and during the second exposition of the text the students used mostly Ngog's translation. He rebuked them slightly saying, "Unfortunate men! You do not trust the translation made by the master."
But after that on the two last occasions he expounded the text according to the translation by Ngog. He and Langtangpa (*gLang thang pa*) were known as the Great Pillars of the Central Land (*dBu*).

48. Patsab (*sPa tshab lo tsa ba nyi ma grags*, 1055–twelfth century). He went to Kashmir in his youth and studied with Sajjana's two sons and others for twenty-three years [*La Théorie* 59].

49. Marpa Dopa (*Mar do*) [BA 383] went to India, met Naropa and studied with the direct disciples of Naropa and Maitripa. He was a contemporary of Marpa the translator from Lodrak (*lho brag pa*), Milarepa's Guru; therefore, he must have lived in the eleventh century even though Kongtrul calls him "a later writer."

50. Lodro Jungne (*bLo gros 'byung gnas* of *Gro Lung*)—chief disciple of Ngog and a teacher of Chapa (*Phywa pa*) [BA 332].

51. Shangtse Pongpa Choki Lama (*Zhang tshe spong ba*) [BA 326, 328,332]. Shangtse and Drolung (*Gro lung pa*) were two of Ngog's "Four Principal Sons." Shang was Ngog's successor to the chair of Palsangpu (*dPal gSang phu*).

52. Nyang Tenpa (*Nyang bran pa chos kyis shes rab*) [BA 332].

53. Chapa Choseng (Phywa pa chos seng) [BA 186 and 332 give dates as 1109–1169. Kuijp gives ?–1171]. He occupied Ngog's chair and wrote commentaries on all five treatises of Maitreya. As a Svatantrika he wrote many refutations of Candrakirti's works [BA 334]. Chapa was the first Tibetan author to compose an independent work on logic and was the creator of a special Tibetan logical style [Stcherbatsky *Buddhist Logic* 55 and *La Théorie* 302fn.3].

54. Tsang Nagpa Tsontu Senge (*gTsang nag pa brtson 'grus seng ge*)—although a disciple of Chapa he followed Candrakirti [BA 334]. Kuijp [p. 38] mentions that Kongtrul calls Tsangnagpa both a Prasangika-Madhyamaka and a Great Madhyamaka. Although Kuijp thinks there must be some inconsistency in his use of the term Great Madhyamaka, this is not necessarily so because Great Madhyamikas (Shentongpas) accept Prasangika-Madhyamaka.

55. Dan Bagpa Mawe Senge (*Dan bag pa smra ba'i seng ge*, index of BA has *Dan bug pa* but text has *Dan bag pa*). Another disciple of Chapa.

56. Lodro Tsungme (*bLo gros mtshungs med*)—a contemporary of Rangjung Dorje and so forth [BA 524–5 and 532].

57. Drogon Pamo Dru Gyaltsen Zang po (*'Gros mgon phag mo gru rgyal mtshan bzang po*, 1110–70). One of the chief four disciples of Gampopa, who founded one of the Great Four (*che bzhi*) lineages of the Dagpo Kagyu; [G. Tucci *The Religions of Tibet* (London and Henley: Routledge and Kegan Paul, 1980) p. 36]. Eight small lineages arose from him including the famous Drigung (*'Bri khung*) lineage, which made many commentaries on the RGV. It appears that Pamo Dru could have had transmission from both the Ngog and the Tsen [see fn. 60] tradition; Lama Karma Thinley *The History of the Sixteen Karmapas* [p. 24].

58. In other words Kongtrul says that essentially all the above mentioned commentators agreed with Ngog even though they sometimes used terms differently. Whether this is true or not requires further research.

59. Tsen Kawoche (*bTsan Kha bo che*), eleventh century. The *Blue Annals* records that his method was taught to Candradhvaja, who was Pamo Dru's teacher.

Thus, it might have been through Pamo Dru's branch of the Kagyu lineage that Rangjung Dorje and so forth received the transmission from Tsen's lineage. Since Kongtrul gives so much importance to Tsen's tradition, it is relevant to quote from the *Blue Annals* p. 347:

> Though the great *lo tsa ba bLo ldan shes rab* and *bTsan Kha bo che* have heard their exposition from the same Sanjana . . . their methods of exposition of the basic texts show certain differences. . . . At the age of 56 he proceeded to Kashmira.

and p. 348:

> Sanjana entrusted him to the translator Zu (*lo tsa ba gZu dGa' ba'i rdo rje*) who is said to have instructed (*gdams pa*) Tsen (*bTsan kha bo che*). In those days there existed a text-book on the *Uttaratantra* (RGV) commented on by Zu. A translator named Padma seng ge explained it in conformity with the commentary by Tsen . . . Tsen returned to Tibet before Ngog (*rNgog lo tsa ba*). At various places he preached the doctrine of Maitreya to *Kalyanamitras* who were in search of it. . . . There exists also a commentary on the *Uttaratantra*, in which the name of the author is not mentioned, but was (commonly) regarded to be a commentary belonging to the school of Tsen (*kha bo che*), and in which precepts on practice (*man ngag nyams len*) are added to the text of the exposition (i.e. the exposition of the text is made from the standpoint of meditative practice). There also exist several short treatises, such as the *Ye shes kyi bzhag sa* (*Repository of Wisdom*) and others containing precepts of the school of Tsen . . .

The passage continues [DN (Chinese edn.) p.424] in my own translation:

> . . . The great translator and Tsangnagpa held that, though the Tathagatagarbha is paramarthasatya, paramarthasatya is not a direct object of terms and concepts (*sgra dang rtogs pa'i dngos kyi yul ma yin*) nor is it a mere conceived object (*zhen pa'i yul* * *tsam ma yin*). The teacher Chapa said:
> "The non-implicative negation (mengag, nothingness) that is the emptiness of reality had by all existent things (*dngos po*) is paramarthasatya. That is held as an object of terms and concepts.
> Those of Tsen's tradition (*bTsan lugs pa rnams*) say: "Since the Mind's Nature, the Clear Light is *Sugatagarbha*, this is the living cause (*grung po rgyu*[†]) of Buddha."

See also F. Theodore Stcherbatsky *Buddhist Logic* (New York: Dover Publications; 1962) p. 45:

---

* N.B. *zhen yul* (*abhinivesadesa*), literally object of attachment. See Geshe Rabten *Mind and its Functions* p. 56 fn. 18. He translates it as "conceived object."

[†] N.B. *grung po*—a corn seed that is not rotten [CD], hence "living" in this context.

A pure perception only becomes a meaningful source of knowledge when there is a judgment of "this is blue"—Dharmakirti.

See also vol 2 p. 417–418, 193, and 424: *zhen yul ma yin* is explained as what is not known by the judgment that eliminates what it is not (i.e. it is not known in the way that a cow is known for example. A cow is known by the judgment "This is not "not a cow"").
La Théorie [302fn3] adds that, since Chapa also held that the Dharmata exists absolutely (*don dam par grub pa*), his doctrine approaches that of the Jonangpas and Sakya Chogden.

60. Death Dharma practice (*'chi chos*)—this is a technical term for the teaching that one will use as the focus for one's awareness as one dies in order to pass safely from this life without losing one's spiritual direction.

61. Karma Konshon (*Karma dkon gzhon* or *Karma pa dkon gzhon*), a famous scholar and disciple of Rangjung Dorje [BA 518]. He was born in 1333 and defeated in debate by Rinchen Shonu (Rin chen gzhon nu) [BA 721].

62. Karma Tinlaypa (*Karma 'phrin las pa*)—fifteenth century. He was a contemporary of the seventh Karmapa, 1454–1506, who appointed him abbot of Chos Khor lun po, a large monastic college. He was famous for his commentary on the *Doha khor gsum*, and the *Mystic Songs of Saraha*. Pupil of the third Situpa and a teacher of Mikyo Dorje. He was a Shentongpa and held views close to the Jonangpa position. The present Karma Thinley (recognized as the fourth incarnation) lives in Canada and is author of *History of the Sixteen Karmapas of Tibet* 1980.

63. The Go translator Shonupal (*'Gos lo tsa ba gZhon nu dpal*) 1392–1481, author of *Blue Annals*. Abbot of the Karma Nying (*rnying*) monastery. Shonupal comments [BA 349–50]:

Though many had reproached the All-Knowing Jomonangpa* for having erroneously admitted the Tathagatagarbha to represent a material truth (*bden rtag tu khas blangs*), numerous persons in Wu (*dBus*) and Tsang (*gTsang*) who had studied assiduously the *Uttaratantra* appear to have been instructed by him. The *Uttaratantra* and its commentary were first translated by the master Atisa and Nagtso. Then by Ngog, Patsab (*sPa [sic] tshab lo tsa ba*) and the Yarlung translator (Yar klungs lo tsa ba†). The

---

* N.B. Jomonangpa. Jonang is short for Jomonang. Jomo means "nun." Kalu Rimpoche informs me that there is a famous nunnery at Jomonang.
† The Yarlung translator *(Yar klungs lo tsa ba grags pa rgyal mtshan)* was a disciple of Kotragpa (*Ko brag pa*) and Menlungpa (*Man lungs pa*, early thirteenth century). He was an important Tantric Guru (Kalacakra and others) [BA788–91]. Kuijp [p. 42], however, says Yarlung was another name for Tsen Kawoche. This would explain why Kongtrul does not mention him.

Jonang translator (*lo tsa ba*, Dol po pa?) made a translation of the basic text only. It is also stated that Marpa Dopa had translated all the five Treatises of Maitreya (*Mar pa Do pa Chos Kyi dbang phyug* of Ya 'brog).

The Tibetan text [DN 424] and an alternative translation of the first part of this passage are as follows:

> *Kun mkhyen jo mo nang bas de bzhin gshegs pa'i snying po bden rtag tu khas blangs pa nor ro zhes kha zer ba dag yod kyang. rgyud bla ma yi dam du byed pa dbus gtsang na mang du 'dug pa rnams ni khong gi drin las yin pa snang ngo.*

There were those who said the Omniscient Jomonang was wrong to maintain that the Tathagatagarbha was permanent and real (*bden rtag*), but it appears that many living in Central Tibet (*dBu*) and Tsang who made the Uttaratantra their *Yidam** owed this to his kindness.

Kongtrul mentions Shonupal [in his commentary on p. 45], in connection with the explanation of RGV [1.27]—the three commentarial verses on the signs that all beings have Tathagatagarbha. Although Kongtrul's comments make it appear Dolpopa (1292–1361) wrote after Shonupal, from the latter's dates and comments on Dolpopa, it is clear Dolpopa preceded him.

64. See G. Tucci *Tibetan Painted Scrolls* [196–198]. Taranatha—sixteenth century Jonangpa and Kalacakra master; famous for his *History of Indian Buddhism* (*rGya gar chos 'byung*). He was noted for his close contact with Indian and Nepalese pandits. He was the last of the great representatives of the Jonangpas because after his death, the main Jonangpa monasteries were taken over by the Gelugpas. His line of incarnations was transferred to Mongolia.

65. Choki Dondrub (*Chos kyi don grub*)—the eighth Shamarpa. Together with the Situpas, the Shamarpas are key figures in the Karma Kagyu lineage; they are two of the most high ranking Kagyu Tulkus alive today.

66. See Chogyam Trungpa Rimpoche, *Born in Tibet*. Zurmang—an important monastery in Kam (*Khams*, East Tibet) and the seat of the Trungpa Tulkus—the tenth incarnation of his line.

67. The two non-selves—the non-self of the person and the non-self of the dharmas. In Shentong terms, when one truly sees the non-self nature of the person and the dharmas, one sees their true nature, which is not to say one sees nothing (*med par dgag pa*).

---

* N.B. *Yi dam du byed pa* usually refers to practicing with a particular *istadevata* in order to reach spiritual realization. In this instance, it seems to mean they committed themselves to practicing the doctrine of this text, in order to gain realization. Thus, Shonupal is saying that, though others may criticize Dolpopa, there is no doubt his instruction was effective for those who committed themselves to making this text their main practice.

68. *dngos po med pa (Abhava)*—non-existence, absence, lack [MW]. Hence, it could be interpreted both as an absolute negation (*mengag*), that is, a non-affirming negation or non-existence (*rangtong*), or an affirming negation (*mayingag*), that is, something in which there is an absence (Shentong).

69. *dgnos po (bhava)* is often translated as "substance" but it is defined in Khenpo Tsultrim's textbook on valid cognition (*pramana, tshad ma*) as "able to perform a function" (*don byed pa'i nus pa*). See also SKK [a '252ba] where paratantra is said to be *dngos po*, for it is *don byed nus pa*. Khenpo Tsultrim often gives the example of a dream which can function to produce a result, for example, happiness or sadness that affects the dreamer even when he reawakes. So the dream is *dngos po* by this definition [LM 91]. Dharmakirti established causal efficiency (*arthakriya*) as the criterion for existence (*Pramanavarttika, svarthanumana*). Also Santaraksita argues that the non-compounded (*asamkrta*) can not exist because it is not *arthakriyasamarthyam*. However, according to Khenpo Katar this is simply the customary definition when teaching elementary *pramana*; it is not always so defined. He says that in general *dngos po* means to be comprised of the smallest divisible particles and therefore must be included in the eighteen dharmas, the five faculties and so forth. Tenpa Gyaltsen suggests the best translation for *dngos po* is simply "thing," since it is defined as *chos can (dharmin)*, the holder of a characteristic, which means, in fact, there is nothing that cannot be called *dngos po*. Thus, it includes matter, mind, abstract concepts (*ldan min 'dus byas*), non-compounded things (*'dus ma byas pa'i dngos po*) and even emptiness itself. This is in accordance with the Tibetan Chinese Dictionary (1984) which gives *nor rdzas, ca lag, yo byad*, as well as *don byed nus pa*. There is an ambiguity in Kongtrul's quotation here. Nonexistence (*dgnos med*) could mean emptiness in both the rangtong and the Shentong sense. Samvrti things (individuals and dharmas) are nonexistent (*dngos med*) but that non-existence (*dngos med*) is their true nature, which is existent Reality (*dngos yod*) [See SKK hum 34 and Appendix 2].

70. Kongtrul writes:

gang zag dang ni chos rnams kyi. dngos po med 'dir stong pa nyid. de dngos med pa'i dngos yod pa. de nyid de la stong pa nyid.

Presumably he is quoting MAV [1.20]:

Pudgalasyatha dharmmanam abhavahśunyatā 'tra hi tad-abhavasya sadbhavas tasmin sa śunyatā 'para.

This translates as:

gang zag dang ni chos rnams kyi. dngos po med pa'i dngos yod pa. de ni de la stong nyid gzhan.

Thus, Kongtrul's quotation does not agree with either the Tibetan or the Skt. versions of the MAV (see Nagao), which both read "other emptiness" rather than "emptiness itself." (Could it be a misprint?) Dolpopa always quotes the correct version in the RC.

71. Skt. *sattvadhatu*. This is translated simply as *sems can* (*sattva*). However, there is not necessarily a great difference between *sattva* and *sattvadhatu* (beings and the nature or element of beings), just as there is little or no difference between *akasa* and *akasadhatu* (space and the nature or element of space).

72. "The Path of Non-obstruction" refers to the stage after the Path of Seeing (at the first level of a Bodhisattva) from which one can no longer fall back into *samsara*. One has direct (though not complete) realization of Buddhajnana so that one can use this experience as the base for stabilizing the realization. Thus, Buddhajnana is the essence of that path as well as the essential nature of those on that path (i.e. the Bodhisattva).

73. *ldog pas phye*—Khenpo Tsultrim explains this as *ngo bo'i sgo nas dbye ba ma red, ldog pa tha dad pa'i sgo nas dbye ba*, "not divisible in essence, but divisible in terms of different aspects." This accords with the Tibetan Chinese Dictionary (1984), which has *ngo bo gcig la ldog pa tha dad pa'* with *ldog* defined as *phyogs*, or *ngos*. *ldog cha* means aspect; e.g. Khenpo Tsultrim gives the example of a flame, which is one thing having the two aspects (*ldog cha*), heat and light.

74. Kongtrul explains here that the "Vajra" in the seven "Vajra Bases" is Absolute Reality (variously known as Dhatu, Gotra, Tathagatagarbha, Buddhajnana etc.). Beings who have entered the path (i.e. Bodhisattvas of the first *bhumi* onwards), who realize the Element directly, are bases of the Vajra, for they are pure (i.e. unspoiled by nature) though veiled. The Samgha is a base for the Vajra because it is Bodhisattvas on the Path of Seeing, who directly realize the Jnana Element. The Path of high level Bodhisattvas is similarly a base of the Vajra, for their path, the Path of Non-obstruction and so forth, consists of realizing the Vajra Nature more and more clearly.

Thus, the Buddha, Dharma and Samgha, the Base, Path, and Fruit, the Reality of the Path and of Cessation and so forth are all bases of the Vajra.

75. Here Kongtrul is expressing (somewhat unclearly one feels) the sentiments of Dolpopa, that is, that the first Dharmacakra is also teaching the Nitartha, the Buddhajnana which (in Shentong terms) is the real "base" to be purified.

Dolpopa (RC p. 166.6) says that although in general the skandhas are taught to be the base to be purified (*sbyang gzhi*), what is meant is the pure by nature (*rang bzhin dag pa'i*) skandhas, which are Tathagatagarbha.

Thus, in Shentong terms, the non-self of the Hinayanists is about what is not the case, and the Self of the Third Dharmacakra is about what truly Is. The fruit of Hinayana purification is a "pure" mind-stream, which in Shentong terms is samvrti. The fruit of Shentong purification is Paramartha Buddhajnana—an infinitely superior achievement. The Hinayana "inferior base" is purified by the "inferior agent," analytical wisdom, which discerns accurately what is not the case. The inferior fruit is the level of a Sravaka or Pratyeka Buddha Arhat. The Shentong superior or true agent of purification is the Absolute Buddhajnana, which gives rise to the superior or true fruit, complete and perfect Buddhahood.

76. Bhavaviveka—sixth century founder of the Svatantrika, adopting Dignaga's logical methods to prove the Madhyamaka doctrine. His system used independent (*svatantra*) inferences as opposed to *prasangika* type reasoning [LM 58ff].

77. Arya Vimuktasena—contemporary of Sthiramati. He was reputed to be a pupil of Dignaga, Bhavaviveka, and Vasubandhu in the first half of the sixth century. He is considered the parent of the Yogacara-Madhyamaka and the first Madhyamika to write on gotra. According to Ruegg, Arya Vimuktasena and his successor Bhandata Vimuktasena both interpreted the AA as a Svatantrika work [*La Théorie* 124] whereas the Jonangpas interpret it as Great Madhyamaka; they deny that the two Vimuktasenas interpreted it as a Prajnaparamita work of the second Dharmacakra. To add to the confusion Ruegg remarks [397] that Tsongkapa and Ketrub considered them to be Prasangika-Madhyamikas while [on 446fn.4] he records that Tsongkapa regarded both Arya Vimuktasena and Haribhadra as Yogacara-Svatantrika Madhyamikas. This latter view agrees with the account in *Crystal Mirror v* [88], which says that Arya Vimuktasena was the first to synthesize the teachings of the Prajnaparamita Sutras and the AA—this synthesis being the precursor of the Yogacara-Svatantrika-Madhyamaka [LM 87].

78. Candrakirti—600–650 [LM 71]—follower of Buddhapalita and chief exponent of the Prasangika school, refuting the Svatantrika doctrines of Bhavaviveka. According to Candrakirti [LM 413], the natural luminosity of all the dharmas comes from the purity of the Prajnaparamita. For the Gelugpas Candrakirti is far and away the most important Indian commentator on emptiness [see P. Hopkins *Meditation on Emptiness* Ann Arbor, Mich: University Microfilms Inc. 1973]. He is not so popular with Shentongpas [see LM 78 and fn.253 for ref. to Ruegg's own article in JIP 5, 1977, 49–50].

79. Jnanagarbha (*Ye shes snying po*). Ruegg records that Jnanagarbha was reported to be a teacher of Santaraksita (probably first part of eighth century) [LM 68]. In conformity with the Yogacara-Madhyamaka position, he alludes to the doctrines of paratantra and Cittamatra as steps leading to the ultimate understanding of the non-self of the dharmas.
It is worth noting that even though Vimuktasena, Jnanagarbha, and Haribhadra all had Yogacara-Madhyamaka leanings, according to Kongtrul, they accepted the Tathagatagarbha as a non-implicative negation. One assumes therefore they were actually Yogacara-Svatantrika-Madhyamakas.

80. *Nyer btags*, *upacara*—see explanation of RGV 1.27 in Part III of this present work.

81. Here Kongtrul uses the actual Sanskrit word *hrdaya*, transcribed into Tibetan as *hri da ya* (with a reversed i). See also Takasaki *Study* p. 21 *sara*, essence.

82. "base-time" (*gzhi dus*)—see Chapter 6.1 on "Base, Path, and Fruit" in this present work.

83. "support for accomplishing," that is, that which one uses as the focus for one's meditation.

84. See RGV [1.34]. The four accomplishments are aspiration, wisdom, concentration, and compassion.

85. *sbyang bya*—that which is to be cleared away. See *Thar rgyan* [chapter 19] on the spiritual levels. Enlightenment is the relinquishment of veils, impurities, delusion and so forth, and the emergence of wisdom. Each level of the Bodhisattva. Path marks the relinquishment of progressively subtler veils (*sbang bya*).

86. *yongs sbyong drug cu*—the sixty perfect purifications (*visuddhiguna*) (See RGVV 1.2 and Takasaki's *Study* p.150 notes 64, 65 and 88.)

87. See RGV [1.32]. The four obstacles to realizing the Buddhajnana are hostility to the Dharma, excessive desire, faintheartedness, and insufficient compassion.

88. See also Chapter 6 on Tathagatagarbha for *Alaya / alayavijnana* distinction. The traces (*bag chags*) of samsara and nirvana mentioned by Kongtrul belong to the *alayavijnana*. This passage is not clear; maybe Kongtrul is making a correspondence between the *alayavijnana* that obscures the *Alaya* and the adventitious stains. If the transformation of the *alayavijnana* (referred to in Cittamatra texts) is really the same as the giving up of the adventitious stains, then the transformation Jnana is none other than the Jnana experienced in the Base, Path, and Fruit-time.

89. *gnas 'gyur*—tranformation—see Chapter 6, endnote 2, of this present work.

90. *Rigs pa'i tshogs* "Collection of Reasonings." It refers to texts of Nagarjuna's Madhyamaka reasoning.

91. *zhen pa'i yul*—conceived object. See fn.59.

92. Though Kongtrul quotes the line found in the BA slightly differently than Shonupal, it does not change the meaning [DN cha f.10a7]:

> *slob dpon phya pa ni dngos po rnams bden pas stong pa'i med par dgag*
> *pa ni don dam pa'i bden pa yin zhing de sgra rtog gi zhen pa'i yul du*
> *yang bzhed'.*

Kongtrul:

> *slob dpon phya pa ni don dam bden pa ni dngos po rnam bden pas stong*
> *pa'i med dgag de nyid yin cing sgra rtog gi zhen pa'i yul du'ang rung ba*
> *bzhed.*

If Chapa was indeed a Svatantrika this passage must be understood in terms of the two kinds of paramartha found in that tradition.

93. *kun nas nyon mongs pa*, (*upaklesa*)—total klesa. *Kun nas* is a Tibetan translation of the Sanskrit prefix *upa* and does not seem to add much to the general meaning of klesa (Tibetan, *nyon mongs*, trouble). Perhaps it refers to the whole complex of the klesas as opposed to the basic five.

94. This passage is also alluding to RGV 1.154. See Chapter 4 'Inseparable Qualities' in this present work.

95. Rongton (17b.4) explains RGV [1.27]: *"rdzogs sangs sku ni 'phro phyir,"* as *"sems can rnams kyis thob tu rung ba'i phyir."* The RGVV does not explain it in this way, and there seems to be no reason to think either *phro*, to radiate, or Skt. *spharanat*, mean "to be obtainable."

96. *De kho na nyid bcu pa (Tattvadasakatika)*. Presumably this is the text by Advayavajra (another of Maitripa's names [*La Théorie* 37fn5]). It is accompanied by a commentary by Sahajavajra. Although Kongtrul [RGV comm. 15b] mentions an important commentary by Vajrapani, Shonupal comments on this text in connection with Gampopa's Sutra-Mahamudra, [BA 724–725]. I could not find any reference to Mahamudra in it though.

97. *ngo sbrod* refers to the Guru's oral instruction that directly introduces the disciple to the nature of the mind.

98. [BA 724]. Though Gampopa gives a Rangtong account of the Tathagatagarbha doctrine in the opening chapter of the *Thar rgyan* his explanations are more Shentong in later chapters.

99. Kyoba Jigten Sumgi Gonpo (*sKyob pa 'jig rten gsum gyi mgon po*)—a disciple of Pamo Dru (Phag mo gru pa).

100. From this it seems Dolpopa was an incarnation of Kyoba Jigten Sumgi Gonpo.

101. Dolpo Sangye—the Dolpo Buddha—an epithet of Kunchen Jonangpa Dolpopa Sherab Gyaltsen (*Kun mkhyen jo nang pa dol po pa shes rab rgyal mtshan*).

102. Padampa Sangye (*Pha dam pa sang rgyas*) came to Tibet twice; this could refer to the teachings he gave on each occasion. Shiche (*Zhi byed*)—"Pacifying Suffering"—is one of the eight main practice lineages from India called the "Eight Charioteers Practice Lineages." It is famous for the "Cutting" (*gcod*) practice of offering one's body to demons to eat.

103. Maitrigupta (spelt Maitrigubta in the text). Presumably this is Maitripa from whom the Kagyu Mahamudra transmission derives.

104. See the RGV doctrine that the inherent nature of the Buddhagarbha is to move toward Enlightenment, and the inherent nature of the Dharmakaya to act everywhere in samsara (i.e. on all beings) to Enlighten them [RGV 4]. (See Chapter 4.3 on Buddha Activity of this present work.)

105. See Chapter 6.4 on Gotra in this present work.

106. The preceding section is about the Shentong interpretation of Gotra and Tathata and the following section is about the Shentong interpretation of Dharmakaya. Therefore, the reference to the teaching Dharmakaya that follows should be

understood in terms of the Absolute Buddha Activity. (See Chapter 4.3 on Buddha Activity). The teaching Dharmakaya is the self-manifesting voice of the Buddha. In Shentong terms, since everything is in essence nothing other than the Buddha's non-dual Jnana, everything is an expression of Dharma and every being expresses the profound nature of the Absolute and the diverse nature of the samvrti effortlessly all the time. This links with the next section about the Absolute and samvrti Tathata. In general, "Tathata" means true nature, so there is the true nature of the Absolute Clear Light Nature of Mind and the true nature of the samvrti, which is emptiness of self-nature.

107. The three Heart-Essences refer to the Gotra, Tathata, and Dharmakaya. With reference to the Absolute and samvrti aspects see Kongtrul's RGV comm [25b]. Gyaltsab and other commentators also divide each of the Vajra bases and the three "heart-essences" into absolute and samvrti aspects. For Rangtongpas, however, the RGV is about both the absolute and the samvrti gotra, tathata, and Dharmakaya; whereas for Shentongpas (as Kongtrul points out), it is chiefly about the Absolute Gotra, Tathata, and Dharmakaya. As we have seen, normally for Shentongpas, Dharmakaya is not samvrti, but presumably the samvrti Dharmakaya alluded to here is the mind of the Buddha's Nirmanakaya as it appears to beings, that is, as having the ten powers of perfect recollection and so forth.

108. *sems nyid*—Mind Itself. This expression refers to Absolute Mind as opposed to the samvrti mind-stream.

109. Ignorance tendency patterns. See SMS and Chpater 5.2 on Nisprapanca of this present work.

110. See RGV 1.32.

111. See RGV 1.34.

112. *rang chas kyi ngo bo yin pa*—*rang chas*, from one's own side, inherently. Ruegg translates it as "spontaneously present."

113. This is a much quoted example. It means that just as there is no yellow in the conch, but only whiteness, there are no faults or stains in the Clear Light Nature of Mind, but only the Inseparable Qualities.

114. Sakyapa (*Sa skya pa*)—presumably Sa skya Pandita—1182–1251. In his influential work *sDom gsum rab dbye*, he attacks an aberrant interpretation of the Tathagatagarbha doctrine promulgated by a Tibetan school which, according to him, was influenced by the Samkhya. Ruegg [JOAS 82 no.3 320–321]. Many commentators understand him to be criticizing the view of the Jonangpas or maybe Yumo Mikyo Dorje (*Yu mo mi bskyod rdo rje);* Buton [Introduction to *Dzes rgyan* 32] quotes Sakya Pandita as saying that if the Element actually existed it was like the self of the Tirthikas and that Candrakirti according to the *Madhyamakavatara* taught the *Sugatagarbha* to be neyartha.

115. *mtha' bral*—see Chapter 5.2 on Nisprapanca in this present work.

116. Simultaneous occurrence of both-at-once (*zung 'jug*). See Chapter 5.3 on the two Satyas in this present work.

117. Yumo Mikyo Dorje (*Yu mo mi bskyod rdo rje*)—twelfth–thirteenth century. See Chapter 8 in this present work.

118. Maybe there is evidence of this "difference" in the *gSal sgron skor bzhi* or his other works. In the *Ri chos*, he quotes from the Tathagatagarbha Sutras, but adds very little himself to what they say on the four Paramita Qualities.

119. *Mahamudri (Phyag rgya chen mo)*. The Empty-base Dharmakaya is the Absolute *Dakini* with various bodies (*sna tshogs gzugs can*) [RC 42].

120. This is a common method of counting divisions and subdivisions in Indian systems, that is, there are six proper divisions of the qualities: non-compoundedness, spontaneity and self-arisen, and knowledge, love, and power. The first three are one's own realization (Own Welfare); the second three one's power to help others (Other's Welfare). If these two divisions are added to the first six there are eight divisions altogether. The two welfares are the welfare of self and others. One's own welfare is the realization of Enlightenment; the welfare of others is the activity bringing them to Enlightenment.

121. See RGV 1.17 and 18. "Inferiority" here refers to the veils that prevent the Buddhajnana being seen directly. Since the Bodhisattva Samgha does not have these, they are the supreme refuge having the Buddhajnana (even though they still have the ground of ignorance tendency patterns) [see RGVV 1.37 and SMS].

122. Konchog (*dkon mchog*), rare and precious—Tibetan translation of *Ratna* in the phrase *Triratna* (Triple Gem), that is, Buddha, Dharma, and Samgha. The Triple Gem is the goal (*thob bya*) [RGVV 1.26] and the Element, Enlightenment, Qualities, and Activity are the means of attaining it (*thob byed*).

123. In Shentong terms, since each refers to non-dual Jnana, even by each reason alone, the existence of the Tathagatagarbha is established. This contrasts with the Rangtong point of view in which each reason refers to a different condition necessary for a being to reach Buddhahood.

124. This comment by Kongtrul suggests that the ten headings refer to ten doctrines found in the Sutras and the intention of the RGV is to show they all refer to the same thing—the nondual Buddhajnana, which is present in its completeness from the beginning and through all stages of the path.

125. *chos can (dharmin)*, literally, quality-haver, or that which bears the quality (*dharma*) in question. The *chos nyid* (Dharmata), literally dharma-ness, is the true nature of phenomena (dharmas—either rangtong or Shentong depending on context). Here the quality (dharma) in question is the true nature of phenomena (Dharmata). It is always the same true nature (Dharmata) but there are three bearers (*dharmin*) of it—beings, Bodhisattvas, and Buddhas.

126. *rang spyi'i sgo nas*—the common aspect of each of these is the Dharma-dhatu.

127. See RGV [1.49–50]—space in the inferior, mediocre, and superior pot being the same. See also RGV 1.52 and 3.16.

128. RGVV [1.4] *'jig tshogs lta ba (satkayadrsti)*—these are the various views held by non-Buddhists concerning the nature of the self. They believe it is in some way associated with the skandhas. Since the skandhas are subject to destruction, anything associated with them is fleeting, conditioned, subject to suffering, that is, not of the nature of self.

129. See RGVV 1.153 and SMS p. 100.

130. Doubly pure—pure in both senses, that is, unspoilt by nature and unobscured by veils.

131. *rjes thob*—post-attainment, refers to the process of carrying over the meditation experience of practice sessions into daily life.

132. *yan lag* means aspects in the sense of what is rooted in it and stem from it.

133. RGV 2.3. These six points correspond to the examples of:

1. the ocean with the jewels that are the samadhis on the Bodhisattva path (i.e. deliverance),
2. the sun of the two accumulations,
3. the sky of ultimate realization,
4. the treasure to be discovered (i.e. beings),
5. the clouds to be removed (i.e. the klesa),
6. the wind of the Buddha's compassion that removes them.

134. *Bodhicittotpada, sems skyed*—in Tibetan this is sometimes glossed as *byang chub tu sems skyed* or *byang chub kyi sems skyed,* that is, the resolve to Enlightenment or the giving rise to the Enlightened Mind. In general *sems skyed* means to make up one's mind to do something, hence resolve. The *Bodhicittotpada* is the resolve to reach complete and perfect Buddhahood for the sake of all sentient beings. This is in contrast to the resolve of a Sravaka or Pratyeka Buddha who simply aim to remove all the klesa veils and reach the cessation of their own suffering. The actual words of the vow made by the Bodhisattva when he is formulating his resolve vary and one of the most well-known formulations is the vow not to enter nirvana until all other beings have attained it. A simplistic understanding of this, carried to its logical conclusion, conjures up the absurd image of a queue of Bodhisattvas, waiting to usher each other in to nirvana first. This formulation could simply be a device to purify the motivation of the aspirant; however, understood on a deeper level, it could relate to the doctrine such as interpenetration and so forth. Elsewhere *Bodhicittotpada* is taken to mean the gotra of proper adoption or the expanding

gotra; it is understood according to how those terms are defined in any particular system (see Chapter 6 "The Nature of Beings" section 4 "Gotra" in this present work).

135. In Dolpopa's terms, the division between Absolute Reality and the apparently real (samvrti) centers around the special Tathagatagarbha (Shentong) doctrine that the essence of the form-kayas, their qualities and activity is actually the spontaneous, Absolute Qualities of the Dharmakaya or *Svabhavikakaya*. Kongtrul does not bring this out in his analysis, however. For example, the RGVV describes each of the Three Jewels from an Absolute point of view, whereas Kongtrul describes Dharma and Samgha as samvrti. Compare Kongtrul's with Gyaltsab's divisions [*Dartik* p. 5b]:

- Absolute Buddha is Dharmakaya, samvrti Buddha is the form-kayas.
- Absolute Dharma is the truth of cessation and of the path, samvrti is the Buddha word.
- Absolute Samgha is the Mahayana realization and liberation; samvrti is the Mahayana Aryas.
- Absolute Element is the tathata emptiness of self-nature of the mind continuum of beings while stained; samvrti is the power in the mind capable of giving rise to supra-mundane dharmas.
- Absolute Enlightenment is Dharmakaya; samvrti is the form-kayas.
- Absolute qualities are the thirty-two liberation qualities; samvrti are the thirty-two maturation qualities.
- Absolute Activity is the all-accomplishing jnana; samvrti is the collections of teachings.

Notice that whereas Kongtrul refers to the Dharmakaya activity as Absolute, Gyaltsab only mentions the activity of the Jnanakaya, because for him the Dharmakaya is inert emptiness.

136. *tshad ma gsum*—the three *pramana*. [See Hattori, *Dignaga on Perception* 28]. The three means of valid cognition, that is, scriptural validity (*lung gi tshad ma*), perceptual validity (*dbang po or rig pa'i tshad ma*), and logical validity (*rjes dpag tshad ma*).
Khenpo Tsultrim states (*bLo rtags kyi rnam gzhag rig pa'i mun sel*):

There are three valid cognitions (*tshad ma*) that ascertain the characteristic (*mtshan nyid*) in the characterized (*mtshan gzhi*). The characteristic of the cognition (*blo*) that arises is the essence of clarity and awareness. This cognition can be valid or invalid (*tshad ma dang tshad min gyi blo gnyis*). Valid cognition can be Absolute (*don dam*) or conventional (*tha' snyad*). Absolute *pramana* reveals what is not known i.e. non-dwelling Nirvana, Sugata, Madhyamaka etc.. Conventional *pramana* is the non-mistaken knowledge of the senses including mind. Thus the object (*yul*) of Absolute and conventional *pramana* is quite different so that when conventional *pramana* holds sway Absolute *pramana* has to be ignored (*btang snyoms su 'jog dgos*); when Absolute *pramana* is employed to cognize the Absolute, conventional *pramana* is unreliable (*bslu ba'i chos can*) and must be ignored. Conventional *pramana* can be direct (*mngon sum*) or inferential (*rjes dpag*). Direct *pramana* is a non-conceptual (*rtog pa med pa*) non-mistaken awareness (*rig pa*).

Geshe Rabten, in *The Mind and its Functions* (Mt. Pelein Swit: Tharpa Choeling, 1978) [p. 32], names three kinds of inferential *pramana* (translated as "ideal inferences"—*rjes dpag tshad ma*). The first (*dngos stobs kyi rjes dpag*) is arrived at through ordinary reasoning, for example, "sound is impermanent because it is compounded." The second (*grags pa'i rjes dpag*) is arrived at through knowing conventions, for example, "the Rabbit Bearer is a well-known convention for referring to the moon." The third (*yid ches kyi rje dpag*) is arrived at through scriptural authority, for example, "wealth arises from generosity." These three *pramana* establish truth through these three kinds of reason. Thus, this system places scriptural validity under the heading of inferential *pramana*. Other systems put it in a separate category of its own. In Dignaga's system, there are only two basic categories of *pramana*: direct and inferential. All the rest are subdivisions of these two.

137. *rton pa bzhi*—the four things to rely on:

gang zag la mi rten chos la rton. tshig la mi rten don la rton. drang don la mi rten nges don la rton. rnam shes la mi rten ye shes la rton.
Do not rely on the person, rely on the Dharma. Do not rely on the words, rely on the meaning. Do not rely on the neyartha, rely on the Nitartha. Do not rely on vijnana, rely on Jnana.

138. The three faiths are the faith of appreciation (*dang ba'i dad pa*), application (*'dod pa'i dad pa*), and realization (*rtogs pa'i dad pa*). The first is to appreciate or be impressed and attracted to the Buddha and so forth; the second is the wish to apply oneself to the practice of Dharma, and the third is to realize the truth of the Dharma directly for oneself in order that faith actually becomes knowledge at this point [see *Thar rgyan* p.13]. See *Le Trentaine* [86] where the three kinds of faith are given and their importance for removing veils is stressed.

139. *nying dgos*—"nying" can mean the same as *snying po*—pith or heart. Tenpa Gyaltsen says it means "ultimately" in this instance.

140. *bdag gcig gi 'brel ba* means *ngo bo gcig gi 'brel ba* which means an identity relationship and *de byung gi 'brel ba* means causal relationship, that is, the one comes from the other.

Chapter 12

1. See Prof. David Bohm's '*Wholeness and the Implicate Order*' 1980.

2. See Choygam Trungpa 'Shambala. The Sacred Path of the Warrior'.

3. This quotation is from Thar rgyan p. 171 which is p. 261 in Guenther's translation.

Appendix 4

1. SNS II.2 rtog ge thams cad las 'das pa'i mtshan nyid gang yin pa ni don dam pa yin par rig pa bya'o."Know that that which is the characteristic beyond all concepts is paramartha."

2. See Ruegg's article JIP 13 p.315 and for further discussion see the following articles:

M. Broido Bshad thabs; Some Tibetan Methods of Explaining the Tantras. WSZTB (WIEN 1983).

M. Broido Abhipraya and Implication in Tibetan Linguistics JIP 12 1984.

M. Broido Intention and Suggestion in the Abhidharmakosa: Sandhabhasa Revisited. JIP 11 1985.

David Seyfort Ruegg Purport, Implicature and Presupposition; Sanskrit abhipraya and Tibetan dgongs pa/dgongs gzhi as Hermeneutical concepts. JIP 13 1985).

CONVENTIONS USED

The Glossary of Terms overleaf defines common Sanskrit words and a few Tibetan terms which have been used unitalicized throughout the text rather than translating them. These are often technical terms that are defined differently by different Buddhist systems: it is inappropriate to "fix" them into a translation that is not suitable in all contexts. Sometimes the terms are so well known, it is not necessary to translate them—for example, Buddha, Nirvana, Guru. Others are terms that are more conveniently coined in Sanskrit than in English; they are technical expressions the meaning of which must be learnt by the reader. An approximate translation is deemed to be of no more help than the Sanskrit. Once the meaning has been learnt the "new" Sanskrit expression not only acquires its own place in the English language but also adds to its richness. An English translation on the other hand would be awkward and not precise. Generally diacritical marks are not employed in the main text since they are meaningless and disconcerting for the general reader. They are supplied in the index should they be required.

The only terms that have been rendered in Tibetan and not Sanskrit throughout are the key terms rangtong and Shentong, also mengag and mayingag, and gagshi and gagcha. The former two terms belong to the Tibetan commentarial tradition. Even though they could be translated into Sanskrit, it would be misleading, for these terms are not found used in juxtaposition in the Indian tradition (Appendix 2). The latter two pairs of terms are so long in both Sanskrit and English that it is easier to use the Tibetan.

Tibetan names and terms are rendered phonetically and are not transliterated (which would produce unpronounceable consonant clusters), unless they appear alongside their translation. The transliteration of Tibetan names and words rendered phonetically in the text can be found in the index. Also in the index, the definition of terms not found in the glossary are indicated by "def." When "*pa*" or "*ba*" is added to a Tibetan adjective, it denotes a person with that attribute: hence Shentongpa is a follower of the Shentong tradition. "Je" (*rje*) means Lord and is added to certain eminent Lama's names, for example, Gyaltsabje, Ketrubje, Je-Tsongkapa, Je-Milarepa. Unfortunately the phoneticizing of Tibetan has not yet been standardized. A number of conventions are in frequent use. For example the Tibetan sound "*ay*" is usually written with an "*e*" as if it were a French "é" with an acute accent. Thus, Rimpoche (a Lama's title) should by rights either have an acute accent or be written Rimpochay. However, it has become such common practice for Lamas' names to be spelt with an "*e*" without an accent that I have adopted this convention. Sometimes, however, I have deviated from this rule when the tendency would be for a reader to adopt a completely unrecognizable pronunciation, for example, Rimay is better than Rime.

In general, terms such as "reality", "emptiness", "jnana", "qualities", are not capitalized unless they clearly refer to Absolute Existence in the Shentong sense. Thus a Shentongpa adheres to a Shentong doctrine about Absolute Reality being Shentong, which is the Clear Light Nature with Inseparable Qualities. A Rangtongpa adheres to the Rangtong doctrine that ultimate reality is rangtong.

GLOSSARY OF TERMS

Arhat—a general term for an Enlightened person who has destroyed the klesa. It often refers more specifically to a person with the inferior Enlightenment of perfecting only the Hinayana teachings

Arya (Aryan)—a person who has progressed sufficiently on the path so as to be beyond the danger of falling back into samsara

Bodhisattva—a person who practices Mahayana, which means they have taken the Bodhisattva vow to deliver all beings from suffering

Buddha—a completely and perfectly Enlightened being

Cakravartin—Universal Emperor: in Buddhist cosmology, he is the most powerful human being in the whole universe

Dharmadhatu—Dharma Element: the expanse of phenomena

Dharmacakra—the Wheel of the Dharma: a cycle of the Buddha's teachings

Dharmakaya—Dharma Body: the formless aspect of the Buddha

Dharmata—Dharma Nature: the true nature of phenomena

dharma—phenomenon

Dharma—the Buddha's Doctrine (the words, truth, or Reality of it)

Dhatu—Element: often in the sense of an open expanse or the expanse of emptiness and wisdom inseparable

gagcha (Tib.)—the thing that is negated or the existence of which is denied

gagshi (Tib.)—the base or place in which the presence of something is negated

gotra—lineage and the power within the members of a lineage to procreate

Guru—the highest spiritual guide

Hinayana—the Lesser Vehicle: the first, most simple, teachings given in Triyana Buddhism for removing the grossest klesa

jnana—wisdom: the wisdom energy of the Enlightened mind

kalpa—a vast cosmic time period

karma—action (inseparable from its cause and effect)

kaya—body

klesa—mental defilements such as greed, hate, delusion, pride, jealousy, and meanness

Mahayana—the Great Vehicle: the second teachings of Triyana Buddhism concerning the Bodhisattva path

mayingag (Tib.)—(Skt. *paryudasapratisedha*): an affirming negation that implies something is present.

mengag (Tib.)—(Skt. *prasajyapratisedha*): a non-affirming negation that implies nothing is present.

naga—a creature comparable to mermen and dragons who live under the ground or water, guarding treasure. They can appear to humans as snakes or in human form, but are typically portrayed with a human upper body and a serpent-like lower body.

neyartha—introductory teachings that are not entirely accurate when seen from the ultimate point of view

Nirmanakaya—Emanation body: a form of the Buddha that appears to ordinary beings in order to teach them

nirvana—the state of freedom from the suffering of samsara

nisprapanca—freedom from mental creations and the process of mental creation

Nitartha—certain, direct, definite, or final teachings

pandit (or pandita)—a learned teacher

paramarthasatya—Absolute or ultimate reality

Paramita—a transcendental quality of a Bodhisattva or Buddha

paratantra—dependent nature

parikalpita—imaginary nature

parinispanna—truly existent nature

paryudasapratisedha—(see mayingag above)

prajna—wisdom, intelligence, the faculty to discern truth

Prajnaparamita—the perfection of wisdom, the wisdom that understands ultimate emptiness

prapanca—conceptual creations, elaborations

prasajapratisedha—(see mengag above)

Pratyeka Buddha—a certain kind of Arhat who followed a path discovered by himself without a teacher

rangtong (Tib.)—self-emptiness

Shentong (Tib.)—Emptiness-of-other

samadhi—concentrative absorption

Sambhogakaya—Enjoyment Body of the Buddha: a celestial form made of light that appears to Bodhisattvas

Samgha—the Buddhist religious community

samsara—the endless cycle of birth and death caused by ignorance, klesa, and karma

samvrtisatya—apparent reality

Sastra—an explanatory commentary on a Buddhist text

satya—reality or truth

siddha—an accomplished yogin

siddhi—the power accomplished by a yogin

skandha—the elements of the psychophysical continuum of a being. The five skand-
    has include all elements of a personality, that is, body, feelings, percep-
    tions, mental tendencies, and moments of consciousness.
sloka—a Sanskrit verse form
Sravaka—literally a Listener: a disciple of the buddha who is a practitioner of the
    Hinayana as opposed to the Mahayana teachings
sunyata—emptiness
stupa—a symbolic representation of the Dharma containing sacred objects and sub-
    stances such as relics and Dharma texts.
Sutra—a Buddhist text reputed to be the word of the Buddha
Tantra—a Buddhist tradition of yogic practice based on texts called "Tantras" used
    in Vajrayana Buddhism.
Tathata—true nature
Tathagatagarbha—Buddha Nature
tika—a small commentary on a text
Triyana—the Three Vehicles: Hinayana, Mahayana, and Vajrayana. Tibetan Bud-
    dhism is more correctly Triyana Buddhism; it consists of the teachings of
    all three vehicles that originated in India
vajra—diamond or Indra's weapon that can destroy anything and is itself indestruc-
    tible. It is used to symbolize the indestructible nature of Reality.
Vajrayana—the third vehicle of Triyana Buddhism. It is also called "Tantra" and
    "secret mantra." Although many elaborate skillful methods are the
    hallmark of Vajrayana, its essence is Guruyoga and depends on special
    oral instruction
vijnana—ordinary consciousness: the momentary stream of dualistic awareness
yoga—literally "union" but has come to mean meditation
yogin—a practitioner of yoga: someone who gains knowledge and experience of
    ultimate reality through meditation

BIBLIOGRAPHY

Sanskrit Sources

Akṣayamatinirdeśasūtra, Toh. 175 *bKa' 'gyur* (D) Ma 79a–174b, *'Phags pa blo gros mi zad pas bstan pa*.

Aṅgulimālīyasūtra, *bKa' 'gyur* (H), t. ma. Toh. 213 *bKa' 'gyur* (D) Tsha 126a–206b.

Anavataptanāgarājaparipṛcchāsūtra, Toh. 156 *bKa' 'gyur* (D) Pha 206a–253b, *'Phags pa klu'i rgyal po ma dros pas zhus pa*.

Anūnatvapūrṇatvanirdeśaparivarta, Taisho ed. of *Chinese Tripiṭaka* XVI, no. 668 (not in *Tohoku Catalogue*).

Abhidharmakośakārikā by Vasubandhu. Ed. V. V. Gokhale, Journal of the Bombay Branch, Royal Asiatic Society 22 (1946), p. 73–102; 23 (1947), p. 12.

Abhidharmakośabhāṣya by Vasubandhu. *bsTan 'gyur, mDo 'grel (P)*, t. gu.

Abhisamayālaṃkāra attributed to Maitreya. Ed. by G. Tucci (Gaekwad's Oriental Series No. 69).

Avataṃsaka (Buddhāvataṃsaka). *bKa' 'gyur, Phal chen (H)*, t. ka-cha.

Aṣṭadaśasāhasrikāprajñāpāramitā (chapters LV–LXX). Ed. E. Conze Rome, 1962. Ed. by P. L. Dharbhanga, Mithila Institute, 1960.

Gaganagañjaparipṛcchā Toh. 148 bKa' 'gyur (D) Pa 243a–330a, *'Phags pa nam mka' mdzod kyis zhus pa*.

Gaṇḍavyūha. Ed. D. T. Suzuki and H. Idzumi, Tokyo, 1949.

Ghanavyūhasūtra. Tibetan translation in the *bKa' 'gyur, mDo (H)*, t.cha *'phags pa rGyan stug po bkod pa*. Toh. 110 (D) cha 1b–55b.

Jñānālokālaṃkārasūtra, i.e. *Sarvabuddhaviṣayāvatārajñānālokālaṃkārasūtra*, Toh. 100 *bKa' 'gyur* (D) Ga 276a–305a, *'Phags pa sangs rgyas thams cad kyi yul la 'jug pa'i ye shes snang ba'i rgyan*.

Tattvadaśakaṭīkā Toh. 2254 (D) wi 160b–177a, *De kho no nyid bcu pa rgya cher 'grel pa* by Lhan cig skyes pa'i rdo rje, Sahajavajra.

367

Tathāgatagarbhasūtra. Tibetan translation in the *bKa' 'gyur, mDo* (H), t. zha.

Tathāgatamahākaruṇānirdeśasūtra. Tibetan translation in the *bKa' 'gyur, mDo,* (P), t. nu. (The first chapter is entitled in Tibetan *rGyan bkod pa zhes bya ba 'dus pa'i le'u*; the following section contains the *Dhāraṇisvararājasūtra*). Toh. 147 (D) pa 142a–242b, *'Phags pa de bzhin gshegs pa'i snying rje chen po nges par bstan pa.*

Triṃśikakārikā by Vasubandhu. Toh. 4055 *bsTan 'gyur* (D) Shi 1b–3a, *gSum cu pa'i tshig le'ur byas pa.* Ed. S. Levi, *Vijñāptimātratasiddhi,* Paris 1925.

Triṃśikāvijñāptibhāṣya by Sthiramati. Ed. S. Levi with the *Triṃśaka.*

Daśatattva Toh. 2236 (D) wi 112b–113a, *De kho na nyid bcu pa* by gNyis su med pa'i rdo rje.

Dharmadharmatāvibhaṅga attributed to Maitreya. Toh. 4022 *bsTan 'gyur* (D) Phi 46b–49a, *chos dang chos nyid rnam par 'byed pa.* Tibetan translation edited with Vasubandhu's *Vṛtti* by J. Nozaawa, *Studies in Indology and Buddhology* (S. Yamaguchi, Kyoto, 1955), p. 9–49.

Dharmadhātustava by Nāgārjuna. Toh. 1118 *bsTan 'gyur* (D) Ka 63b–67b, *Chos kyi dbyings su bstod pa.*

Dhāraṇīsvararājasūtra. Included in the Tibetan translation of the *Tathāgatamahākaruṇānirdeśasūtra.*

Pratītyasamutpādahṛdayakārikā vol. 7 ascribed to Nāgārjuna. See V. V. Gokhale *Der Sanskrit Text von Nagarjuna's Pratītyasamutpādahṛdaya—kārikā. Studia Indologica Festschrift für Willibald Kirfel,* Bonn 1955 s. 101ff. Toh. 3836, 4553 (D).

Pramāṇavārttika by Dharmakirti. The first chapter with the autocommentary edited by R. Gnoli, Rome, 1960—Chapters II–IV edited by R. Sankṛtyayāna, Patna, 1953. Toh. 4210 *bsTan 'gyur* (D) Ce 94b–151a, *Pramāṇavārttikakārikā, Tshad ma rnam 'grel gyi tshig le'ur byas pa.*

Prasannapadā Madhyamakavṛttiḥ by Candrakirti. Ed. by L. de la Vallee Poussin, *Bibliotheca Buddhica* IV, St. Petersbourg, 1903–1913 (with the [*Mūla*] *Madhyamakakārikā* by Nāgārjuna). Toh. 3860 *bsTan 'gyur* (D) Ha 1b–200a *Mūlamadhyamakavṛttiprasannapadā, dBu ma rtsa 'grel pa tshig gsal ba.*

Bodhisattvacaryāvatāra by Śāntideva. Toh. 3871 *bsTan 'gyur* (D) LA 1b–40a, *Byang chub sems pa'i spyod pa la 'jug pa.* Ed. L. de la Vallee Poussin, *Bibliotheca,* Calcutta, 1901–1914.

Bodhicaryāvatārapañjikā by Prajñākaramati (*Shes rab 'byung gnas blo gros*). Toh. 3872 *bsTan 'gyur* (D) La 41b–288a. Ed. L. de la Vallee Poussin with the *Bodhicaryāvatāra,* Calcutta, 1901–1914.

Mahābherīhārakaparivartasūtra. Tibetan translation in the *bKa' 'gyur, mDo* (H), t. tsa. Toh. 222 (D) Dsa 84b–126b, *'Phags pa rnga bo che chen po'i le'u.*

Madhyamakāvatāra by Candrakirti. Tibetan translation (*dBu ma la 'jug pa*) ed. with autocommentary by L. de la Vallee Poussin, *Bibliotheca Buddhica* IX, St. Petersbourg, 1912. Toh. 3861. *dBu ma la 'jug pa* (D) 'a 201b–219a.

Madhyāntavibhāṅgakārikā attributed to Maitreya. Ed. G. N. Nagao, Tokyo, 1964. Toh. 4021.

Madhyāntavibhāgabhāṣya by Vasubandhu. Ed. with the *mūla* by G. N. Nagao, Tokyo, 1964. Toh. 4027 (D) Bi 1b–27a.

Mahāyānasaṃgraha by Asaṅga. Tibetan translation ed. E. Lamotte, Louvain, 1938–1939. Toh. 4048.

Mahāyānasūtralāṃkāra attributed to Maitreya. Ed. S. Levi, Paris, 1907. (*Mahayana*) *Sūtrālaṃkārabhāṣya* attributed to Vasubandhu. Ed. S. Levi. Paris, 1907 (with the *Mūla*). Ed. S. Bagchi Darbhanga: Mithila Institute 1970. Toh. 4020.

Mahāyānottaratantraśāstra. See *Ratnagotravibhāga.*

(*Mūla*) *Madhyamakakārikā* by Nagarjuna, Ed. L. de la Vallee Poussin, *Bibliotheca Buddhica* IV, St. Petersbourg, 1903–1911. J. W. de Jong. Adyar: The Adya Library and Research Centre 1977. Toh. 3824 *bsTan 'gyur* (D) Tsa 1b–19a, *Prajñā-nāma-mūlamadhyamakakārikā, dBu ma rtsa ba'i tshig le'ur byas pa shes rab.*

Yogācārabhūmi attributed to Asaṅga. Ed. Vidhusekhara Bhattacarya, Calcutta, 1957 (first part only). *bsTan 'gyur, mDo 'grel* (P), t. dzi.

Ratnagotravibhāga-Mahāyānottaratantraśāstra attributed to Maitreya (or Sāramati). Ed. with the *Vyākhyā* attributed to Asaṅga by E. H. Johnston, Patna, 1950 (cf. the edition of Z. Nakamura, Tokyo, 1961, which contains the Johnston's Sanskrit text and the Chinese translation).

Ratnacūḍapariprccha-nāma-mahāyānasūtra, Toh. 91 *bKa' 'gyur* (D) Cha 210–254b. *Taisho Catalogue of the Chinese Tripiṭaka* XIII, no. 397 (11), *Ratnacūḍasūtra.*

Ratnasūtra (or *Ratnadhārikasūtra*), *Taisho Catalogue of the Chinese Tripiṭaka* XIII no. 397 (3). Not in Toh..

Laṅkāvatārasūtra. Ed. B. Nanjo, Kyoto, 1923. Ed. P. L. Vaidya, Darbhanga, Mithila Instit. 1963. Toh. 107 *bKa' 'gyur* (D) Ca 56a–191b, *'Phags pa lang kar gshegs pa.*

Vajracchedikāsūtra. Ed. by M. Miller. Toh. 16 *bKa' 'gyur* (D) Ka 121a–132b, *'Phags pa shes rab kyi pha rol tu phyin pa rdo rje gcod pa.*

Vimalakīrtinirdeśa, Toh. 176 *bKa' 'gyur* (D) 175a–239b, *'Phags pa dri ma med par grags pas bstan pa.* E. Lamotte's translation, *'L'Enseignement de Vimalakīrti,'* Louvain, 1962.

Śrāvakabhūmi (chapter XIII of *Bahubhūmikavastu* of the *Yogācārabhūmi*) attributed to Asaṅga. Tibetan translation in the *bsTan 'gyur, mDo 'grel* (P), t. vi. (Portions of the original Sanskrit text were published by A. Wayman, '*Analysis of the Śrāvakabhūmi Manuscript*,' Berkeley and Los Angeles, 1961).

Śrīmālādevīsiṃhanādasūtra, bKa' 'gyur, dKon brtsegs (H), t. cha: ed. by K. Tsukinowa (with the *Ratnacandraparipṛcchāsūtra*), Kyoto, 1940. Toh. 92 (D) Cha 255a–277b, '*Phags pa lha mo dpal phreng gi seng ge'i sgra*.

Śatasāhasrikāpañcaviṃsatisāhasrikāṣṭadaśasāhasrikaprajñāpāramitā-Bṛhaṭṭīkā (often attributed to Vaśubandhu, but possibly by Daṃṣṭrasena). *bsTan 'gyur mDo 'grel* (P), t. pha (*Yum gsum gnod 'joms*). Toh. 3808 (D) Pha 1b–292b, '*Phags pa she rab kyi pha rol tu phyin pa 'bum pa dang nyi khri lnga stong pa dang khri brgyad stong pa'i rgya cher bshad pa*.

Saddharmapuṇḍarīkasūtra. Ed. U. Wogihara and C. Tsuchida, Tokyo, 1958. Toh. 113.

Sandhinirmocanasūtra, Tibetan translation in the *bKa' 'gyur* edited by E. Lamotte, Louvain and Paris, 1935. Toh. 106 (D) Ca 1b–55b, '*Phags pa dgongs pa nges pa 'grel pa*.

Sarvabuddhaviṣayāvatāra-jñānālokālaṃkārasūtra, bKa' 'gyur, mDo (H), t. ga. Toh. 100 (D) Ga 276a–305a, '*Phags pa sangs rgyas thams cad kyi yul la 'jug pa'i ye shes snang ba'i rgyan*.

Sāgaramatiparipṛcchā, Toh. 152 *bKa' 'gyur* (D) Pha 1b–115b, '*Phags pa blo gros rgya mtsho zhus pa*.

Suvarṇaprabhāsottamasūtrendrarāja, Toh. 556, 557, '*Phags pa gser 'od dam pa mdo sde'i dbang pa'i rgyal po* (D) Pa 151b–273a.

Tibetan Sources

mKhas grub rje (?–1438). *rGyud sde spyi'i rnam par gzhag pa rgyas par brjod*. (Toh. 5167), 12. Transl. by Lessing and Wayman in the '*Fundamentals of Buddhist Tantra*'.

sGam po pa bsod nams rin chen, (Dvags po lha rje) 1079–1153. *Dam chos yid bzhin gyi nor bu thar pa rin po che'i rgyan zhes bya ba theg pa chen po'i lam gyi rim pa bshad pa* (*Lam rim thar rgyan* or *Dvags po thar rgyan*). 126 f. 'Brug yul edition.

'Gos lo tsa ba gZhon nu dpal (1392–1481). *Deb ther sngon po* (composed in 1476–78). Kun bde gling edition. Śatapiṭaka Series vol. 212 New Delhi 1974. Chinese edition 1984 (2 vols.). Abbreviation DN. (See Roerich's translation *The Blue Annals*—BA).

rGyal tshab Dar ma Rin chen (rGyal tshab rje) 1364–1432. *Theg pa chen po rgyud bla ma'i tika* (*rGyud bla'i dar tik*). Composed at dPal gnas snying go chos grva chen po). 230f. (*gSung 'bum*, lHa sa edition, t. ga). Abbreviation RGV *Dartik*.

rGyal tshab byams pa mgon po. *Byams chos sde lnga* Karmapa's Printing Press New Delhi.
Theg pa chen po rgyud bla ma'i bstan bcos. Tohoku catalogue no. 4024. NB.
Theg pa chen po rgyud bla ma'i bstan bcos rnam par bshad pa. Toh. 4025.

Taranatha kun dga' snying po (1575–?). *dPal gyi 'byung gnas dam pa'i chos rin po che 'phags pa'i yul du ji ltar dar ba'i tshul gsal bar ston pa dgos 'dod kun 'byung (rGya gar chos 'byung)* A. Schiefner, St. Petersbourg, 1868 *gZhan stong snying po.*
gZhan stong dbu ma'i rgyan. 12f.

Dol po pa (or Dol bu pa) Shes rab rGyal tshan (1292–1361). *Ri chos nges don rgya mtsho zhes bya ba mthar thug thun mong ma yin pa'i man ngag.* 493f. *rGyud bla ma'i legs bshad nyi ma'i 'od zer.* Commentary on the RGV attributed to Dol po pa. New Delhi. *Kun mkhyen dol po'i gsung 'bum.* pod Ka. Collected Works of Kun-mkhyen Dolpopa Volume 1 Jamyang Khyentse's Monastery, P.O. 136 Baudh Nath Kathmandu, Nepal. 1988.

Bu ston rin chen grub (1290–1364). *De bzhin gshegs pa'i snying po gsal zhing mdzes par byed pa'i rgyan (bDe snying mdzes rgyan).* 39f. (Zhol par khan's lHa sa edition, *gSung 'bum,* t. va). *bDe ba gshegs pa'i bstan pa'i gsal byed chos kyi 'byung gnas gsung rab rin po che'i mdzod* (Bu ston *chos 'byung*). 212f. (*gSung 'bum,* t. ya).

Mi bskyod rdo rje (1507–1554). *dBu ma gzhan stong smra ba'i srol par phye ba'i sgron me. (dBu ma gzhan stong sgron me.)* Printed in Delhi between 1960 and 1980. *dBu ma la 'jug pa'i rnam bshad dpal ldan dus gsum mkhyen pa'i zhal lung dwags brgyud grub pa'i shing rta.* Printed in India by Karmapa.

Mi pham 'jam dpal dgyes pa'i rdo rje (1846–1912). *bDe gshegs snying po'i stong thun chen mo seng ge'i nga* ro 19 f. *Theg pa chen po rgyud bla ma'i bstan bcos kyi mchan 'grel Mi pham zhal lung.* 560 f. Mipham's collected works Vol. 3 Gangtok 1976.

'Jam mgon kong sprul blo gros mtha' yas (1813—1899). *Theg pa chen po rgyud bla ma'i bstan bcos snying po'i don mngon gsum lam gyi bshad srol dang sbyar ba'i rnam par 'grel pa phyir mi ldog pa seng ge'i nga ro.*
Shes bya kun khyab pa'i gzhung lugs nyung ngu'i tshig gis rnam par 'grol ba legs bshad yongs 'du shes bya mtha' yas pa'i rgya mtsho zhes bya.
Nges don sgron me.
Nges don rgya mtsho.
Theg pa'i sgo kun las btus pa gsung rab rin po che'i mdzod bslab pa gsum legs par ston pa'i bstan bcos shes bya khyab. Kongtrul's *Encyclopaedia of Indo-Tibetan Culture'* edited by Prof. Dr. Lokesh Chandra, New Delhi 1970
rNal 'byor bla med pa'i rgyud sde rgya mtsho'i snying po bsdus pa zab mo nang don nyung ngu'i tshig gis rnam par 'grol ba zab don snang byed ces bya ba bzhugs so. Printed by the Sixteenth Karmapa at Rum gtegs chos kyi sgor chen (Rumtek).

rNam par shes pa dang ye shes 'byed pa'i bstan bcos kyi tshig don go gsal du 'grel pa rang byung dgongs pa'i rgyan. Printed by the sixteenth Karmapa.

Tsultrim Gyamtsho (Khenpo) (1934–). *bLo rtags kyi rnam gzhag rig pa'i mun sel*. Varanasi (text book for bKa' brgyud students at the College for Higher Studies).

Tsong kha pa blo bzang grags pa'i dpal (1357–1419). *Yid dang kun gzhi'i dka' ba'i gnas rgya cher 'grel pa legs pa bshad pa'i rgya mtsho*. 57 f. (*gSung 'bum*, t. tsha).
rTsa ba shes rab kyi dka' gnas chen po brgyad kyi bshad pa. *dGe lugs rang gZhung*. Text book for the third year Acarya students at Varanasi Tibetan college of higher education (*Wa' nar bod kyi mtho rim slob grva chen mo'i a'-tsa'rya' la rim gsum pa'i slob tshan khong*). *Legs bshad gser phreng*.

Rang byung rdo rje (1284–1339). *Zab mo nang gi don*. Rumtek. *Phyag chen smon lam* (from *sMon lam lnga*). Rumtek.
sNying po bstan pa.
rNam shes ye shes 'byed pa.

Rong ston (chen po) smra ba'i seng ge shes bya kun rig, sakya rgyal mtshan dpal bzang po (Sar rgyal mo rong pa) (1367–1449).
Theg pa chen po rgyud bla ma'i bstan bcos legs par bshad pa. Reproduced from a rare manuscript from Jakhar Tshang. Gangtok 1979.

kLong chen rab 'byams (1308–1364). *Chos dbyings rin po che'i mdzod* (ga). Ed. Do drup chen Rin po che Gangtok 1964.

Sa skya Paṇḍita Kun dGa' rGyal mtshan (1182–1251). *sDom pa gsum gyi rab dbye ba* (*sDom gsum rab dbye*). 50 f.

gSer mdog pan chen Śakya mchog ldan (1428-1507)
Tshad ma'i mdo dang bstan bcos kyi shing rta'i srol rnam ji ltar byung ba'i tshul gtam bya ba nyin mor byed pa'i snang bas dpyod ldan mtha' dag dga' bar byed pa In the Collected Works of Gser Mdog panchen Śakya mchog ldan Vol. 19 Thimphu 1975.

Western Sources

Bareau, A. *Les Sectes Bouddhiques du Petit Véhicule*. École fr. d'extreme Or., vol 38. Saigon: 1955.

Batchelor, Stephen. *A Guide to the Bodhisattva Way of Life*. Trans. of the Bodhicaryāvatāra by Śāntideva. Dharmasala: Library of Tibetan Works and Archives, 1979.

———— . *Stone Lion, An Introduction to the Buddhism of Korea*. Typed copy, 1984.

Beyer, Stephan. *The Cult of Tārā, Magic and Ritual in Tibet*. Berkeley: University of California Press, 1973.

————— . *The Buddhist Experience; Sources and Interpretations.* Encino: Religious Life of Man Series, 1974.

Broido, M. M. *bShad thabs: Some Tibetan Methods of Explaining the Tantras.* *Wiener Studien zur Tibetologie und Buddhismus*, Kunde Heft 11 Proceedings of the Csoma de Körös Symposium Austria 1981.

————— . *Abhiprāya and Implication in Tibetan Linguistics.* JIP 12: 1984.

————— . *Intention and Suggestion in the Abhidharmakośa: Sandhābhāṣā revisited.* JIP 11: 1985.

————— . *Pad ma dKar po on the Two Satyas.* JIABS vol. 8 no. 2. 1985.

Chang, Garma C. C. *The Buddhist Teaching of Totality: The Philosophy of Hwa Yen Buddhism.* London: Allen and Unwin, 1971.

————— . *A Treasury of Mahāyāna Sūtra. Selections from the Mahāratnakuta Sūtra.* Trans. from the Chinese by Buddhist Association of US, general editor Garma C. C. Chang. IASWR Series: 1983.

Chattopadhyaya, Alaka. *Atīśa and Tibet. Tibetan Sources.* Translation by Lama Chimpa. Calcutta: 1967.

Conze, Edward. *The Prajñāpāramitā Literature.* Indo-Iranian Monographs Vol. VI. s'Gravenhage: Mouton and Co., 1960.

Cook, Francis H. *Hua Yen Buddhism: The Jewel Net of Indra.* Pennsylvania State University Press, 1977.

Dalai Lama, H. H. Tenzin Gyatso. *Kindness, Clarity and Insight.* Trans. and ed. by J. Hopkins, co-ed. by E. Napper. Ithaca NY: Snow Lion Publications, 1984.

Douglas, K., and Bays, G. *Life and Liberation of Padmasambhava* by Yeshe Tso-gyal. Trans. into French by G. C. Toussaint.

Gimello, Robert M., and Gregory Peter N. *Studies in Ch'an and Hua Yen.* Kuroda Institute Studies in E. Asian Buddhism No. 1. Honolulu: University of Hawaii Press, 1983.

Gokhale, Professor V. V. "A Note on the *Ratnagotravibhāga* 1.52—*Bhagavadgita* XIII32. In *Studies in Indology and Buddhology,* presented in honor of Professor S. Yamaguchi. Publisher: Kyoto, 1955.

Guenther, H. V. *Jewel Ornament of Liberation.* London: Rider, Reprint 1970, 1959.

————— . *The Royal Song of Saraha: A Study in the History of Buddhist Thought.* Trans. and annotated by H. V. Guenther. Berkeley and London: Shambhala, 1968.

Hakeda, Yoshito S. *Awakening of Faith*, (Trans. with commentary). Attributed to Aśvaghosha. New York: Columbia University Press, 1967.

Hanson, Judith, Trans. *Torch of Certainty* of *Nges don sgron me* by Kong sprul. Shambhala, Boulder and London: The Clear Light Series, 1977.

Hattori, Masaaki. Review of *La Théorie*. JIP, Vol 2. 1972, p. 53–64.

Hoffman, H. *Religions of Tibet*. Allen and Unwin, 1956.

Holmes, K. *The Changeless Nature*. Kagyu Samye Ling, 1979.

Hopkins, P. *Meditation on Emptiness*. Part 1. Ann Arbor, Michigan: University Microfilms Inc., 1973. (See Sopa & Hopkins.)

Johnston, E. H. ed. *The Ratnagotravibhāga Mahāyānottaratantraśāstra*. With introduction. Patna: Bihar Research Society, 1950.

Karma Thinley Rimpoche. *The History of the Sixteen Karmapas of Tibet*. Boulder, Colo.: Prajna Press, 1980.

Keenan, John P. *Original Purity and the Focus of Early Yogacara* JIABS 1983 No. 1.

Konchok Jikmay Wangpo—See Sopa & Hopkins.

Kuijp, Leonard W. J. van der. *Contributions to the Development of Tibetan Buddhist Epistemology—from the eleventh to the thirteenth century*. Wiesbaden: Steiner (Alt-Neu-Indische Studien 26) 1983.

Lati Rimpochay. *Mind in Tibetan Buddhism*. Trans. by E. Napper. London: Rider, 1980.

Nalanda Translation Committee. *The Rain of Wisdom*. Boulder, Colo.: Shambhala and London, 1980.

Namgyal, Takpo Tashi. *Mahāmudra—The Quintessence of Mind and Meditation*. Trans. and annotated by Lobsang P. Lhalungpa, Shambala. Boston and London: 1986.

Ñanamoli, (Bhikkhu). *The Path of Purification*. Trans. of *Visuddhimagga* by Bhadantacarya Buddhaghosa. Ceylon: 1956.

Ñāṇananda, *Concept and Reality in Early Buddhist Thought*. Kandy, Ceylon: Buddhist Publication Society, 1971.

Nyanatiloka, Mahathera. *Guide through Abhidhamma Pitaka*. Kandy, Ceylon: Buddhist Publications Society, 1971.

Obermiller, E. *The Sublime Science of the Great Vehicle to Salvation being a Manual of Buddhist Monism. The work of Ārya Maitreya with commentary by Āryāsaṅga*. Acta Orientalia vol. IX parts ii, iii and iv., 1971.

Park, Sung Bae. *Buddhist Faith and Sudden Enlightenment.* Suny series in Religious Studies. Albany: State University of New York Press, 1983.

Poussin, de la Vallee. *Vijñāptimātratāsiddhi, La Siddhi de Hiuan-Tsang.* Trans. and annotated. Paris: P. Guethner, 1928–48.

Rabten, Geshe. *The Mind and its Functions: A Textbook of Buddhist Epistemology and Psychology.* Trans. by Stephen Batchelor. Mt. Pelerin, Switzerland: Tharpa Choeling, 1978.

Roerich, G. N. Trans. *The Blue Annals. Deb ther sngon po* by gZhon nu dpal. Delhi: Motilal Banarsidas. Report 1976, 1949 edition. Abbreviation BA.

Ruegg, David Seyfort. *The Jo nang pas: A School of Buddhist Ontologists according to the Grub mtha' sel gyi me long.* JAOS 83, 73–91, 1963.

———. *On the dGe lugs pa Theory of the Tathagatagarbha,* in *"Prajñāpāramitā and Related Systems—Studies in honor of Edward Conze."* Pratidanam. 1968.

———. *Ārya and Bhadanta Vimuktasena on the Gotra: Theory of the Prajñāpāramitā.* WZKSO 12–13, 1968–69, p. 303–317.

———. *The Meanings of the term Gotra and the Textual History of the* RGV. BSOAS vol. 39. 1976.

———. *La Théorie du Tathāgatagarbha et du Gotra.* Paris: École d'Extreme Orient, 1969.

———. *The Dharmadhātustava Études tibetaines dediées à la mémoire de M.Lalou.* Paris: 1971.

———. *The Uses of the Four Positions on the Catuṣkoṭi and the Problem of the Description of Reality in Mahāyāna Buddhism.* JIP 5, 1977, p. 1–71.

———. *The Literature of the Madhyamaka School of Philosophy in India—A History of Indian Literature.* Vol. VII Fasc. 1. Wiesbaden: Harrassowitz, 1981.

———. Translation of *De bzhin gshegs pa'i snying po gsal zhing mdzes par byed pa'i rgyan* by Bu ston.

———. *Purport, Implicature and Presupposition: Sanskrit Abhipraya and Tibetan dGongs pa/dGongs gZhi as Hermeneutical Concepts.* JIP 13, 1985, p. 309–325.

Schuh, D. *Tibetische Handschriften und Blockrucke* Teil 6 Weisbaden, in the series *Verzeignis der Orientalischen Handschriften in Deutschland*: 1976.

Schmithausen, Lambert. *Philosophische Bemerkungen zum Ratnagotravibhāga, Wiener Zeitschrift fur die Kunde Sudasiens,* XV/1971 p. 123ff. Zu D. Seyfort Ruegg.

————. *Zu D. Seyfort Rueggs Buch 'Theorie du Tathagatagarbha et du Gotra'*. WZKSO 16–17, 1972–73, p. 123–160.

————. *Alayavijñāna*; *On the Origin and Early Development of a Central Concept of Yogacāra, Studia Philologica Buddhica* Monograph Series IV. Tokyo, IIBS:1987.

Seng Chao, *Chao lun. The Treatises of Seng chao.* Translated into English with bibliography, introductory notes and appendices by Walter Liebenthal. Hong Kong: Hong Kong University Press, 1968.

Smith, Gene. *Introduction to the Index of Kong sprul's Encyclopaedia of Indo-Tibetan Culture.* Ed. by Professor Dr. Lokesh Chandra. New Delhi: 1970.

————. *Autobiography and Diaries of Situ Panchen.* Ed. Lokesh Chandra, foreword Gene Smith. New Delhi: 1968.

Sopa & Hopkins. *Practice and Theory of Tibetan Buddhism*, translation by Geshe Lhundup Sopa & Jeffrey Hopkins of *Precious Garland of Tenets* by Konchokjikmay Wangpo. Rider and Company, London: 1976.

Stcherbatsky, F. Th. *Buddhist Logic.* Vol. 1 and 2. New York: Dover Publications Inc., 1962.

Takasaki, Jikido. *A Study on the Ratnagotravibhāga Being a Treatise on Tathāgatagarbha Theory of Mahāyāna Buddhism* (contains trans. of RGV and RGVV). Rome: Is.M.E.O. *Serie Orientale Roma* Bd XXXIII, 1966.

————. *The Tathāgatotpattisaṃbhavananirdeśa of the Avataṃsaka and RGV with special reference to the term tathāgata gotrasaṃbhava.* JIBS vol. 7 no. 1. Tokyo: 1958, p. 48–53.

Thondrup Tulku Rinpoche. *Hidden Teachings of Tibet: An Explanation of the Terma Tradition of the Nyingma School of Buddhism.* Ed. Harold Talbott. Wisdom, 1986.

Thrangu Rimpoche. *The Open Door to Emptiness.* Trans. by Sakya Dorje. Ed. Michael Lewis. Nepal: Lhundrub Teng, Boudha, Kathmandu, 1978.

————. *A Commentary on the Uttara Tantra Śastra* by Ken and Katia Holmes. Published by Namo Buddha Publications, 1390 Kalmia Avenue, Boulder, Colo. 80302, USA.

————. *Buddha Nature* translated by Erik Pema Kunsang, 1988.

Trungpa, Chogyam. *Shambhala. The Sacred Path of the Warrior.* Boulder, Colo.: Shambhala, 1984.

Tucci, G. *Tibetan Painted Scrolls.* Roma: 1946.

————. *The Religions of Tibet.* London and Henley: Routledge and Kegan Paul, 1980.

Tsultrim Gyamtso, Khenpo. *Progressive Stages of Meditation on Emptiness.* Translated by Shenpen Zangmo. Longchen Foundation, 30 Beechey Ave., Oxford, England: 1986.

————. *NTS Tutorial 8/85* Series of cassettes explaining SKK on rangtong and Shentong. Available from the Marpa Institute, P.O. Box 4017, Kathmandu, Nepal.

Wayman, A., and Lessing F. D. mKhas grub rje's *Fundamentals of Buddhist Tantra.* The Hague: Mouton, 1968.

Williams, Paul M. *On Rang Rig,* in *Proceedings of Csoma de Körös Symposium.* Published by *Wiener Studien zur Tibetologie und Buddhismuskunde Series,* 1981.

————. *Silence and Truth, Some Aspects of Madhyamaka Philosophy in Tibet. Tibetan Journal* Vol. VII nos. 1/2. (Spring/Summer), 1982, pp. 67–80.

————. *A Note on Some Aspects of Mi bskyod rdo rje's Critique of dGe lugs pa Madhyamaka.* JIP, 1983, p. 125–145.

————. *Mahāyāna Buddhism—The Doctrinal Foundations.* London and New York: Routledge, 1989.

Zangmo, K. Yeshe (Bikkhuni Sik). *An Index to the sDe dGe bKa' 'gyur.* With book titles and volume contents. Cambridge: 1981.

Zimmer, H. *Philosophies of India.* Princeton: Bollingen, 1951.

INDEX

Experience, Direct (*continued*)
36, 38, 60, 87; Buddha as, 48, 55–
56; and faith, 60–63; stability of,
61, 91
—As basis for meditation, 37, 56,
59–69, 91; importance of
Tathāgatagarbha doctrine for,
59; and tantric practice, 77–79,
86–87
—Non-dual, vs. conceptual knowledge/
reason, 4, 25–26, 33, 35, 37, 48,
55–56, 59–64, 264, 280; comple-
mentary approaches in Shentong; 77;
Sūtra basis for, 122; Rangtong view
(Gyaltsab), 322
—Path of (*mgon sum lam byed*, meditation tradition of RGV. *See also*
Meditation School), 150, 158, 264,
277–81, 284–85, 288
External World. *See* Outer objects
Extreme Positions (*anta, koṭi, mtha',
mu*, also translated as 'philosophical
positions'. *See also* False Assertion
and False Denial; *Catuṣkoṭi*; Limit),
6, 71–77, 121, 206–7, 301; and
Rangtong criticism of Shentong, 24–
25, 42, 72; in the RGVV, 207

Fa Hsien, 103
Fa Tsang, 102, 117, *165–66*, 169,
191–2
Faith (*śraddhā, dad pa. See also* Devotion), 1, 21, 25, 50, *57–66;* and
reason, 4, 32, 63–65; causes Buddha
to appear, 53; as the activity of the
Dharmakāya, 54; and *Buddhajñāna*,
57, 59; blind faith (*mig med pa'i
dad pa*), 57; faith and direct experience, 59, 60–63, 119, 122, 124;
Rangtong/Shentong distinction 57–
65; faith and removal of *prapañca*,
73; in *Dharmadhātustava*, 155; the
three kinds, 288, 361n.138
False assertion (*samāropita, sgro 'dogs*
or *sgro btags*) *and* False denial

(*abhyākhyāna, skur 'debs*), 24–25,
42, 73, 158. *See also* Extreme
Positions
Faults, the Five, 130, 234, 266
Fear, 124, 261
Field (*gocara, spyod yul*). *See under*
Object/object-haver
Form (*See also* Appearance; Outer ob-
jects): form empty of form, 27, 35–
36, 84, 87; Absolute Form (*see also
under Kāya*), 36, 39; Empty Form
(tantric term), 139, 159–60
Form *kāyas. See Kāya; Nirmāṇakāya;
Sambhogakāya*
Fruit (*See also* Base: Base, Path and
Fruit; Cause): apparent and Absolute,
92–94; the *Dhatu* as fruit: the four
Transcendental Qualities, 198, 201–
209; the fruit of enlightenment (free-
dom from veils), 235, 239–40

Gaganagañjaparipṛcchā, 110, 128, 170,
214, 227
Gagcha (*dgag bya*, that which is to be
negated) *usually in conjunction with
Gagshi* (*gags gzhi*, base of the negation), **19–21**, 23–24, 25, 30, 364;
empty base or ground (*stong gzhi*),
6, 16, 29, 31, 131, 151
Gagshi. See Gagcha
Gampopa (*sGam po pa*): 152 (Table),
162, 206, 226, *341n.6;* on gotra,
104–8, 178; on *Tathāgatagarbha* and
Dharmakāya (Rangtong and Shentong aspects of the *Thar rGyan*),
110, 178, 293–94, 356n.98; *Sūtra*
and *Tantra Mahāmudrā*, 141, 146,
176–78; Kagyu RGV transmission
lineage and RGV as a source for
Mahāmudrā, 146, 176–77, 277; the
Two Traditions of Madhyamaka, 167
Ganden, 346n.44
Garbha (*snying po. See also* Heart-
essence; *Tathāgatagarbha*): the term,

qualified inseparable, **47**, 83; Rang-
tong/Shentong distinction, 38, 42–
43, 83–85, 290; Dolpopa on, 83–87;
saṃsāra and *nirvāṇa* inseparable,
83–85; two truths inseparable, 83–
85; Appearance/manifestation and
emptiness, 36–37, 84–87, 91, 159–
60; awareness and emptiness, 68,
79, 129; clarity, bliss and emptiness,
68, 79; inseparable qualities of base,
path and fruit, 91–92, 211–13; Base,
path and fruit inseparable, 92; or
not, 94
Instruction (upadeśa, man ngag, gdams
ngag. *See also* Transmission;
Abhiṣeka): special, 12, 32, 91–92,
122–23, 293, 247n.45; and *abhiṣeka*,
37; oral, 56, 59, 65, 343n.24; pointing out (*ngo 'phrod*), 62, 114, 150–
51, 277–78, 356n.97; sems khrid,
62; Shentong and RGV meditation
transmission as special instruction,
142–43, 151, 178, 277–78
Intention. *See* Meaning, Intended
Interpenetration (in Chinese
Tathāgatagarbha tradition), 37, 194–
95, 198, 220, 259, 291–92
Intuition, 4, 55–57,
Iṣṭadevatā (yi dam, meditation deity).
See Yidam
Itaretaraśūnyatā. *See under* Emptinesses

Jambudvīpa, 265, **343n.18**
Jamgon Kongtrul Lodro Thayay. *See*
Kongtrul, Jamgon
Jamyang Kyentse Wangpo ('*Jam dby-
ang mkhyen brtse'i dbang po*), 162
Jamyang Shepa ('*Jam dbyang bzhad
pa*), 332n.15
Jayasila (*Nag tsho lo tsa ba*). *See*
Nagtso Lotsawa
rJes thob. See Meditation: between ses-
sion practice
Jewel Ornament of Liberation. See
Gampopa

Jewels, the Three (*triratna, dkon
mchog gsum*): as divisions of the
'Jewel Lineage' (*Gotra*), in title of
RGV, 109, 181–82; as *Vajra* Bases,
183, 186–192, 281–82, 358n.122;
absolute and *saṃvṛti*, 287
Jigme Lingpa, 163
Jñāna (1) (*ye shes*, Wisdom Mind. In
Shentong tradition used
synonymously with *Buddhajñāna* and
combined with adjectives such as
non-dual, self-aware, self-born,
niṣprapañca, Absolute *Dharmadhātu*,
Tathāgatagarbha, Emptiness, Heart
Essence, etc.. *See also* Awareness;
Clear Light Nature of Mind; Non-
conceptuality; Non-duality; Cognition, Valid: *Dharmatā Pramāṇa*;
etc.): as main subject of this book,
33; difference between Rangtong and
Shentong views, Chapter 2; as Emptiness, Chapter 3; as Absolute Reality, Chapter 4; as means of
apprehension, Chapter 5; as nature of
beings, Chapter 6; as subject matter
of third *Dharmacakra*, Chapter 7; as
discussed in RGV and RGVV, Chapter
10; Kongtrul's analysis, Chapter 11;
summary of all views, Chapter 12;
more details, Appendices 2–5
—Key points: 54–55, 60, 107, 190,
193, 191, **197,** 212
—*Jñāna* when fully manifest: *See*
Qualities, Inseparable; Qualities,
Buddha. *See also* Enlightenment;
Buddha; Visions, the Two; Shentong
View: on *Buddhajñāna*, and Qualities, Buddha; Rangtong View: Ultimate Reality
—*Jñāna* in beings: *See* Shentong;
Shentong View: on Nature of beings;
Rangtong View: the Nature of Be-
ings; Nature of Mind; Clear Light
Nature of Mind; *Gotra*: naturally
present

Rangjung Dorje (*Rang byung rdo rje,*
third Karmapa), 115, 152 (Table),
124, 341n.7; and Shentong view, 2,
136, **173–74**, 178, 182; on manifestation and emptiness inseparable, 84,
88; tantric approach to base, path
and fruit, 91–92; on *gotra,* 105,
224–25, 278; on Great Madhyamaka,
150, 157; on *Mahāmudrā,* 157, 178;
and RGV transmission, 172–174,
263–64, 271–72, 277, 349n.59; on
Tathāgatagarbha, 292–93
Rangjung Yeshe (*rang byung ye shes*).
See Self: self-born *jñāna*
Rangtong (*rang stong,* self-emptiness.
See also following entries, and
Rangtong-Shentong Distinction), 1–
4, 14–15, 35; origin of term, 4, 13,
136–37, 299–302; a mode, not a
base of emptiness, 302
Rangtong Tradition (*See also* Rangtong;
Rangtong View; Rangtong-Shentong
Distinction)
—Outlined, *3,* 4–5, 13, 16–18, **21;**
Rangtongpas, 14, **21,** 64, 115, 140,
et passim; Exclusive Rangtongpas,
13, 16, 18, 37, 92, 129
—Differences among Rangtong tradi-
tions, **175;** Gelugpas compared with
other Prāsaṅgika Madhyamakas, **13–
14,** 16–17, 20–21, 29, 69–71, 72,
97, 175; Candrakīrti, 72, 80–81;
Buton, Redawa and others, with
Rongton and Gyaltsab, 127–29, 175;
Rongton and Ngog, 93, 175; Rongton and Gyaltsab, 40–44, 74, 92–94,
111, 289–90, 317–23
—History: early Tibetan Madhyamaka,
115, *144,* 156–57; Cittamātra and
Svātantrika, 144; Nāgārjuna (MMK),
155; Great Madhyamaka, 159, *167–
68;* Rangtongpas claim Maitreya-
Asaṅga tradition, 168; Gampopa
and *Sūtra Mahāmudrā,* 177–78; Gelugpa school, 4–5, 13, 16–17, 317;

other schools, 5, 17; infuence on
Western scholars, 5, 17, 29–30,
295–98
—View on the RGV (*for view on content, see* Rangtong View): **3,** 16–17,
37–38, 50, 65; on title, 109; RGV
viewed as Rangtong, 127–29, 159,
168, 175; as *nītārtha* of second
Dharmacakra, 127–29, 268; as
neyārtha, 'taught for a purpose',
129; as Cittamātra, 128–29; commentators and their transmission lineages, **172–76**
Rangtong View (*See also* Rangtong-
Shentong Distinction; *and under
some individual entries*) on:
—Emptiness, 4, 30–31, 71–73, 79–80,
322–23, *et passim;* and apparent reality, **20–22,** 26–29, **33–35,** 42, 64,
72, 74–75, 92–94; and extreme positions, 71–73; and the two realities,
83–84
—Ultimate reality, 44, 32, 79; and
Buddhajñāna, 33–35, 43, 50, 68,
321–22; Buddha qualities and compoundedness, 40–46, 50, 245–46;
pure nature/natural purity, 43,
317–323; and the *Dharmakāya,*
42–46, 94, 317–323, 357n.107,
360n.135; Buddha's speech, 258; the
seven *Vajra* Bases, 321–22,
360n.135
—Means of apprehension: faith and
reason, 64–65; *niṣprapañca,* 68–71,
73, 77–79, 97; the two visions, 87–
89; the experience of the Clear Light
Nature, 37, 61, **97,** 190; purification, 40, 92–94, 185; meditation,
64, 68; *tantra,* 37, 77–78
—The nature of beings: base, path and
fruit, 92–94, 322; the element/
Tathāgatagarbha, 40–41, 50, **92–
100,** 317–23, 358n.123; Buddha
activity in beings, 43, 108–109, 198;
gotra, 93, 105–111, 223, 228, 317–

Sthiramati (*Blo gros brtan pa*), 152
(Table), 269, 345nn.35, 37
Stotra (or *stava, stod pa,* praise,), 144,
154–55, 168
Śubhapratibhāsa. See Pure Vision
Substantialist, 149
Suffering, 54–55, 101, 204–5, 210–11
Sugata (father of Sajjana), 270
Sugatagarbha (*bde gshegs snying po,*
another name for *Tathāgatagarbha*),
84, 225, 274, 276, 287, 343n.22,
349n.59
Śūnyatā (*stong pa nyid*). *See* Emptiness
Śūraṃgamasamādhi, 200
Sūtras (*Sūtras referred to are indexed
individually*), 366; and Rangtong/
Shentong distinction, 4, 13–14, 113–
31 *passim;* Kongtrul on the threefold
supreme scripture, 265; relationship
of *Sūtra* and *Tantra, see under Tantra;* sources of Shentong, *see under*
Shentong; sources of RGV, *see under*
RGV; Kongtrul's two-fold division of
third *Dharmacakra sūtras,* 117, 266–
67, 343n.23
Sūtras and *Tantras:* assigned to *Dharmacakras,* 113–31 *passim. See also
under Dharmacakra*
Suvarṇadvīpa, 346–47n.45
Suvarṇaprabhāsa, 267
Suvarṇaprabhāsottamasūtra, 244–45
Suzuki, D. T., 96
Svabhāva (self-nature, *rang bzhin, ngo
bo,* also translated as 'inherent existence', 'essence', 'nature', 'True Nature'. *See also* Emptinesses:
svabhāvaśūnyatā; Prakṛti; Existence:
inherent; Mind, Nature of): as that
which is refuted, **20,** 23–32, **40,**
42–44, 151, 154; as spontaneously
existing nature, **49;** two aspects of
absolute (*Paramārtha*) *svabhāva,
svabhāva* (*rang dngos*) and
parabhāva (*gzhan dngos*), **82–83,**
300–2, and *niḥsvabhāva,* same in

Buddhas and beings, 155; synonym
for *Tathatā,* 196–97; 'Essence' as a
definition: of *Dhātu,* 197, 198–99,
283; of Enlightenment, 235, 236–39,
284; of the *Tathāgatagarbha* teaching
in the RGV, 264–65; 'apparent' and
'absolute' absolute essence, 300;
pure nature/pure-by-nature, *see* Purity
Svabhāva, the Three. *See* Natures, the
Three
Svabhāvaśūnyatā. See under Emptinesses
Svābhāvikakāya, 274–75, 278, 287
Svasaṃvedanasvaprakāśa (*rang rig
rang gsal,* self-aware self-
illuminator): difference between
Cittamātra and Yogācāra Madhyamaka, 61, 305; essence of self-aware
self-illuminator as the *Vajra,* 272
Svātantrika. See Madhyamaka,
Svātantrika
Svayambūjñāna. See Self: Self-born
jñāna
Synonyms, explanation of how different
terms become synonymous at higher
levels in Shentong, **138, 182**

Takasaki, J., on the RGV as a text, 38,
165, 235, 258, 295–97; on the 'original' RGV, 200, 203, 208, 210, 214,
247, 249, 254, 255, 260–61; on the
Tathāgatagarbha and related themes,
87–88, 126, 185, 190, 191, 195,
197–98; on translation of '*garbha*'
and '*ātman*', 99, 100; on the Chinese tradition, 143, 165, 190,
295–97
Tantra (*See also Sūtras* and *Tantras;*
Mantrayāna; Meditation, Vajrayāna;
Shentong Tradition: Tantric Shentong), 366; *Sūtra-Tantra* relationship,
and RGV/*Tathāgatagarbha* teaching as
bridge, 4, 77, 140–41, 145–46, 160,
277; *Tantra-siddha* tradition, 4, 84,
141, 144–45; *Tantra* and Shentong,

Printed in Great Britain
by Amazon